Decolonizing Family Systems, Relationships, and Practices

Centering liberation, justice, and cultural wisdom in the heart of relational work, this book provides a comprehensive and integrative examination of human development and the family life cycle through a decolonized, anti-racist, and intersectional lens.

Written by a diverse collection of practitioners, educators, and scholars, the book challenges the colonial roots of foundational family therapy models and offers bold alternatives that center agency, community, and healing. Chapters discuss essential topics such as family development and stages of the life cycle, relationship norms, gender and sexuality, neurovariance, grief and loss, healing, and more – all while exploring the ways in which systemic inequalities shape the lived experiences of individuals and families from diverse backgrounds. With real-life stories and perspectives, this book provides essential practical guidance and tools to help mental health practitioners navigate and resist systemic barriers in their work and support an ongoing practice that fosters more inclusive, equitable, and responsive therapeutic relationships.

This book offers a new path forward for anyone who wants to practice healing in ways that are culturally affirming, politically conscious, and radically human. It is an essential resource for graduate students and practitioners in mental health programs seeking to develop their skills in working with diverse families.

Jennifer M. Sampson, PhD, LMFT, CST-S, is an educator, systemic clinician, AASECT Certified Sex Therapist and Supervisor, and AAMFT Approved Supervisor.

Fiona E. O'Farrell, PhD, LMFT, CST-S, is the Program Director of the Marriage and Family Therapy program at Pacific Lutheran University, an AASECT Certified Sex Therapist and Supervisor, and an AAMFT Approved Supervisor.

Decolonizing Family Systems, Relationships, and Practices

Intersectional Perspectives

Edited by
Jennifer M. Sampson and Fiona E. O'Farrell

Routledge
Taylor & Francis Group

NEW YORK AND LONDON

Designed cover image: Getty Images

First published 2026
by Routledge
605 Third Avenue, New York, NY 10158

and by Routledge
4 Park Square, Milton Park, Abingdon, Oxon, OX14 4RN

Routledge is an imprint of the Taylor & Francis Group, an informa business

For Product Safety Concerns and Information please contact our EU representative
GPSR@taylorandfrancis.com. Taylor & Francis Verlag GmbH, Kaufingerstraße 24,
80331 München, Germany.

ISBN: 978-1-032-67124-6 (hbk)
ISBN: 978-1-032-67105-5 (pbk)
ISBN: 978-1-032-67908-2 (ebk)

DOI: 10.4324/9781032679082

Typeset in Sabon
by codeMantra

We dedicate this book to our extensive community—our kin (both gifted and chosen), friends, neighbors, peers, colleagues, trainees, and our own providers—those who gather with us, feed us, laugh with us, and hold us when we fall. Thank you for keeping our feet on the ground. To our loved ones, thank you for being the steady rhythms behind the scenes, reminding us what love, safety, and presence can be.

This book is for all the systemic practitioners—especially the trainers, educators, and supervisors—who have committed their lives to the work of transformation. This includes those who carry the weight of the field's legacy with hope for continuous growth, those who raise bold questions instead of providing answers, and those who disrupt the status quo with creativity and conviction. You are the ones who critically explore the frameworks handed down and forge new paths that center on justice, relationality, and liberation.

To the therapists practicing amid systems that bind, restrict, and oppress—your fatigue is valid, and your hard work is deeply felt. Even when the work feels heavy, you continue to show up. You continue to believe that change is not only possible but necessary.

To our students and trainees—past, present, and future—thank you for keeping us honest, curious, and awake. You challenge us to deepen our commitments and stay in alignment with our values. Stay steady. The world is eagerly awaiting your time and attention.

To our mentors and professional elders—thank you for lighting the way. Your courage and care have shaped the contours of our work and our integrity.

Finally, to our clients, who entrust us with their hearts, minds, and souls, thank you for your vulnerability and for wanting more for yourselves and your communities. Thank you for letting us witness your sorrow, your joy, and your becoming. Your stories are those of humanity, bravery, wisdom, and hope. Thank you for dreaming of more, even when the world has told you to settle for less. We are with you every step of the way.

Contents

A Note from the Editors   *ix*
Editors and Contributors   *xi*
List of Acronyms and Abbreviations   *xix*

Introduction: Breaking the Jar: Decolonizing Family Therapy
from the Inside Out   1
JENNIFER M. SAMPSON AND FIONA E. O'FARRELL

PART 1
Unpacking Origins: Decolonizing the Foundations of Family Therapy   **15**
JENNIFER M. SAMPSON AND FIONA E. O'FARRELL

1   Breaking the Colonial Frame: Power, Privilege, and Family Therapy   17
CAYLA MINAIY

2   From Pathology to Liberation: Decolonizing Family Well-Being   31
ZAIN SHAMOON AND JARRYN ROBINSON-ELLIS

3   Beyond the Binary: Decolonizing Gender, Sexuality, and Family Development   47
SAR SURMICK

4   Family Therapy in the Era of AI: Will Technology Advance or Erase
Indigenous and Non-Western Practices?   66
JACEY SAUCEDO COY

PART II
**Decolonizing Life Cycle Narratives: Systemic Intersections in
Family Development**   **85**
JENNIFER M. SAMPSON AND FIONA E. O'FARRELL

5   Goodbye Birds and the Bees: How Systemic Therapists Can Use a
Reproductive Justice Framework to Rethink Family Building   87
JENNIFER M. SAMPSON

6 Rethinking Childhood: Neurovariance, Cultural Strengths, and Decolonialized Development Perspectives   117
   JESSICA LEITH CLAUS

7 Grieving in the Wake of Colonialism: Using Creative Arts to Explore, Process, and Integrate Bio-Psycho-Social-Cultural Perspectives of Loss and Grief Across the Lifespan   131
   DANI BAKER AND ALYSSA GRISKIEWICZ

PART III
Beyond Therapy: Collective Healing, Advocacy, and Alternative Knowledge Systems   **165**
JENNIFER M. SAMPSON AND FIONA E. O'FARRELL

8 Liberating Love: Rewriting the Fairytale and Expanding Relationship Norms   167
   FIONA E. O'FARRELL

9 Agency-Centered Relational Therapy: Decolonizing Healing and Relationship Work   187
   TAI LEE

10 How Family Therapy Knowledge is Made and The World It Makes: Nonprofit Practice, Capitalism, and the Politics of Knowledge   204
   MARCELA POLANCO

   Conclusion: A Vision Beyond The Jar: The Journey Toward Liberation   220
   JENNIFER M. SAMPSON AND FIONA E. O'FARRELL

   Index   233

A Note from the Editors

This book was born out of necessity—a response to how colonial legacies, Eurocentric frameworks, and institutional forces have constrained the field of systemic therapy. It is also the product of our shared experiences as therapists, educators, and individuals navigating systems never built to serve all of us equitably.

While our journeys to this work have followed different paths, they have converged in a shared truth: decolonization, the process of undoing colonization's effects on mental health and therapy, is not optional. It is imperative.

Our backgrounds, identities, and histories have shaped how we arrived at this work.

Jennifer: I come to this work as a systemic, relational therapist, an educator, a leader, and most importantly, a human being shaped by histories, relationships, and responsibilities beyond myself. My ancestry tells the story of colonization—of the Philippines occupied and reshaped by Spanish and American imperial forces, of generations before me navigating the imposed fractures of language, identity, and belonging. My European lineage tells another story, that of the colonizer—a history of power and expansion, of systems built to divide, extract, and control. I hold these truths together, knowing that my existence is a convergence of histories shaped by both oppression and privilege. This complexity does not bring easy answers, but it does bring clarity: I cannot undo the past, but I can work toward a different future.

This work profoundly entwines my roles as a mother, partner, daughter, friend, and sibling. Many of those closest to me do not—or have not—recognized the extent of the challenges we face in a colonized world. I know what it is to love people who do not see the structures that shape our realities. And I know what it means to persist in this work anyway, to hold space for difficult conversations, to plant seeds where I can, and to walk alongside those who are ready to see and to act.

I know firsthand what it means to fight against entrenched systems of oppression. As a former academic and department chair in higher education, I have seen firsthand how institutions built on colonial values resist transformation—even when that transformation is urgently needed. I have witnessed how these systems punish those who challenge them and how they work to silence and suppress voices calling for justice. I have felt the personal and professional cost of standing up for decolonization within structures that were never meant to serve all of us equally. This experience has only strengthened my resolve, and this book is born out of that.

Fiona: My experience of decolonization is complex. I am of Irish, European, and Armenian descent. I hold many identities of privilege. And as a third-generation survivor of the Armenian genocide my positionality is a living example of the minimization and eventual erasure of differences and a success story of dominant cultural assimilation. I did not understand the full extent of my Armenian heritage or my grandfather's refugee status and our family's survival stories until late into adolescence. The absence of that narrative reflects a broader legacy of silence surrounding histories of displacement, survival, and identity. It was in uncovering this history that I first encountered the intersections of gender, power, and survival—learning how young Armenian boys escaped assassination by donning skirts and earrings and presenting as girls. My entry into the study of sexuality and gender seemed far from my family-of-origin's values. I now know that the curiosity to learn more has resided within my family legacy and linked to my own intergenerational narrative of gender practices.

I did not grow up in the United States. I spent my childhood in Dublin, Ireland, where I witnessed firsthand the ongoing impact of colonial rule through the country's efforts to reclaim its language, laws, and culture. Ireland remains my heart's home, the place that most informs my understanding of identity and belonging. At present, I have lived in the United States for more years than the handful of years during my coming of age in Dublin, and yet, I continue to find aspects of US culture—particularly its emphasis on individualism and commodification—confounding. As a white person living in the US, I hold immense privilege—and I see how myself and those with privilege are seduced by the very systems that uphold oppression.

As a systemic therapist, clinical sexologist, and educator, my work has centered on challenging dominant relational frameworks—ones that privilege nuclear families, monogamy, and linear milestones as markers of success—and center multidimensional relational practices. In my work and my personal experiences, I have witnessed how dominant relationship norms erase cultural and relational diversity, reinforcing white supremacy, heteronormativity, and patriarchy in ways that harm those who do not conform.

To us, decolonization is not a theoretical exercise—it is deeply relational. It demands that we interrogate the systems we operate within and how we have internalized them ourselves. It is about naming the harm, resisting erasure, and expanding our collective imagination of what healing can look like.

This book is a product of collaboration, resistance, and refusal—a refusal to accept therapy as it has been handed to us, a refusal to allow our field to continue upholding the very systems that harm the communities we serve. It is a call to action, not just to see the structures that confine us but to break them apart and rebuild something new.

We did not write this book alone. It exists because of the collective labor of brilliant, committed individuals who refuse to accept the status quo. Our contributors come from diverse backgrounds, bringing their experiences, clinical expertise, and critical perspectives to challenge, disrupt, and reimagine family systems and relational therapy.

We hope this book challenges you, inspires you, and reminds you that liberation is not done alone. It is done in relationship, community, and the ongoing pursuit of a world where all families, relationships, and identities are honored in their full complexity.

This book is not just a critique—it is an invitation. We invite you to ask questions. We invite you to imagine. We invite you to act.

Because decolonization is not a destination but a lifelong process of learning, unlearning, and building.

Editors and Contributors

Honoring the Voices That Shape This Work

This book would not exist without its contributors' collective wisdom, courage, and dedication. Each author in this collection brings their professional expertise and their lived experience—their stories, histories, and radical reimagining of what systemic therapy can be. These voices do more than critique the status quo; they actively carve out new pathways for liberation, justice, and healing in our field.

The contributors to this book were not selected simply for their credentials or affiliations but for their commitment to dismantling oppressive systems and reshaping family therapy through a decolonized lens. Some have spent years working at the intersections of mental health and activism, challenging the institutions that attempt to silence marginalized voices. Others have built their practices in resistance to colonial legacies, creating spaces where cultural knowledge and community healing take precedence over Western diagnostic frameworks. All of them—without exception—are engaged in reimagining what therapy can and must become.

We sought authors who were not just scholars or practitioners but also thought disruptors and change makers—those who have stood at the edges of traditional systemic therapy and dared to push beyond it. Many of our contributors have had to fight against institutional barriers, personal and professional risks, and even direct retaliation for challenging the dominant paradigms in mental health. Their inclusion in this book is an act of both recognition and resistance.

At the core of our selection process was an unwavering commitment to diverse representation—not as a box-checking exercise but as a fundamental necessity for decolonizing family therapy. We prioritized voices from historically excluded and systemically marginalized communities, ensuring that this book reflects the experiences of:

- **Indigenous, Black, and Brown practitioners** whose work challenges the colonial legacies embedded in systemic therapy.
- **Queer, trans, and nonbinary voices** who have resisted the pathologization of gender and sexuality in mental health care.
- **Neurodivergent practitioners** whose perspectives push back against the ableism inherent in many therapeutic frameworks and challenge traditional definitions of "normal" cognitive and relational functioning.
- **Practitioners rooted in collectivist and intergenerational healing traditions** that directly counteract Western individualism.

- **Disability advocates** who have firsthand knowledge of how systemic ableism shapes access to care, notions of resilience, and definitions of well-being.
- **Those with lived experience of systemic harm,** including those who have worked within and against institutions to advocate for justice.

At its core, this book is a collaborative effort that would not be possible without the voices of those who have generously shared their work. **To each contributor: We honor your bravery, knowledge, and unwavering commitment to decolonization.** Your words will resonate beyond these pages, shaping the next generation of therapists, educators, and activists who refuse to accept the jar of colonization as the only reality.

This work is only the beginning. As we continue to challenge and reimagine the field of systemic therapy, we extend an open invitation to future contributors. If you are an academic, practitioner, or community healer who believes in the power of writing as resistance, we invite you to share your voice in future editions. The world is shifting, and our work must evolve with it.

The journey of decolonization is not a solitary one—it is a collective effort. We are grateful to every contributor who has helped shape this book into what it is: a powerful call to action, a map for reimagining therapy, and an unwavering commitment to breaking the jar.

Editors

Dr. Jennifer M. Sampson, PhD, LMFT, CST-S (she/her), is a systemic, relational therapist, educator, and social justice advocate with nearly 20 years of experience in systemic therapy, clinical education and supervision, and anti-oppressive therapeutic practice. She founded Lovewell Initiatives, an organization dedicated to decolonizing systemic therapy and advancing justice-centered training for mental health professionals. She is also the owner of a group therapy practice in Tacoma, Washington.

A Licensed Marriage and Family Therapist (LMFT) and an AASECT Certified Sex Therapist and Supervisor (CST-S), Dr. Sampson has spent her career challenging the colonial foundations of mental health practice. She is an Approved Supervisor with the American Association for Marriage and Family Therapy (AAMFT) and a recognized leader in justice-oriented, liberation-based education and supervision. She writes and teaches on the intersection of systemic oppression, reproductive justice, and decolonized approaches to leadership and healing.

Dr. Sampson's personal and professional journey is shaped by her complex, colonized history. As a biracial Filipino American cis woman, she carries the intergenerational impact of Spanish and American colonization in the Philippines alongside the privileges and contradictions of her European ancestry. She has witnessed firsthand how colonial legacies dictate which families, relationships, and identities are legitimized while others are erased, pathologized, or forced into conformity. These legacies are not relics of the past but are deeply embedded in contemporary reproductive policies, mental health frameworks, and systemic barriers to care.

Dr. Sampson is no stranger to institutional resistance. As a former academic and department chair in higher education, she has experienced firsthand the consequences of advocating for decolonization within systems never designed for true liberation. Her work in academia was met with direct systemic pushback, reinforcing the reality that institutions often protect their colonial foundations at the expense of those seeking change. Rather than retreat, she has built alternative spaces for education, mentorship, and systemic change that honor the full complexity of identity, relationality, and justice.

Her leadership is rooted in mentorship and lifting others to their highest abilities and desires. Whether working with students, clinicians, or community members, she believes in fostering environments where people are empowered to challenge oppressive narratives, reclaim their stories, and build new pathways forward.

As a contributor to this collection in her chapter, *"Goodbye Birds and the Bees: How Systemic Therapists Can Use a Reproductive Justice Framework to Rethink Family Building,"* Dr. Sampson brings both critical analysis and practical tools for therapists seeking to move beyond performative inclusion toward actionable, justice-oriented practice. She sees this work not as a solitary endeavor but as part of a collective movement toward dismantling the barriers that confine us and reimagining therapy in ways that truly honor the diverse realities of the families and communities we serve.

Dr. Fiona E. O'Farrell, PhD, LMFT, CSTS (they/them/she/her), is a systemic therapist, clinical sexologist, and educator with over 15 years of experience in relational therapy, sex therapy, and anti-oppressive therapeutic practice. They currently serve as the Program Chair of the Marriage and Family Therapy Program at Pacific Lutheran University in Tacoma, WA, USA. Dr. O'Farrell is an Approved Supervisor with the American Association for Marriage and Family Therapy (AAMFT) and a Certified Sex Educator, Therapist, and Supervisor with the American Association of Sex Educators, Counsellors, and Therapists (AASECT).

Dr. O'Farrell runs a small clinical practice in Seattle, WA, where they offer relational sex therapy and run therapist training retreats. Their clinical and academic work focuses on relational development, consent-based practices, and the integration of intersectional, feminist, and queer perspectives in therapy. They coedited *Decolonizing Family Systems, Relationships, and Practices: Intersectional Perspectives* and have contributed extensively to the discourse on relational diversity and dismantling colonial frameworks in systemic sex therapy.

Dr. O'Farrell writes from the vantage point of a scholar-practitioner, educator, and clinician deeply deconstructing normative assumptions in systemic therapy. Their identity and background shape the ways they understand and critique the field. Raised within and shaped by Western relational ideals, they have witnessed how these frameworks have constrained, erased, and pathologized relational diversity. Their professional and academic journey has been one of both complicity and resistance—trained in models that uphold colonial legacies of relational development while working to disrupt and expand them in their teaching, supervision, and clinical practice. They recognize their position within the academy as a site of privilege and a space for critical intervention. As an educator, they are committed to fostering epistemological plurality in the training of future therapists, challenging students to interrogate the racialized, gendered, and ableist assumptions embedded in dominant therapeutic models.

Their connection to this subject matter is both personal and professional. Over the years, Dr. O'Farrell has worked with countless individuals, couples, and families whose lived experiences defy the rigid relational scripts prescribed by Eurocentric models of development. They have witnessed how dominant frameworks of intimacy and relational success—monogamy, marriage, reproduction, nuclear family structures—fail to account for the complexity and fluidity of human relationships. Their clinical work and scholarship seek to elevate alternative relational possibilities rooted in cultural specificity, interdependence, and collective care.

As a contributor to this collection, Dr. O'Farrell brings a commitment to decentering the Western "fairytale" of relational development that has long shaped the field of systemic therapy. Their chapter, "Liberating Love: Rewriting the Fairytale and Expanding Relationship Norms," critically examines dominant narratives in relational models and provides practical approaches for supporting diverse relationship structures. They explore how these ideals uphold oppressive systems—patriarchy, heteronormativity, white supremacy, and ableism—while offering ways to embrace relational fluidity and cultural specificity in practice. They see this work as part of a broader project of decolonization, one that requires a fundamental reimagining of how we conceptualize relationships, family systems, and human connection.

Contributors

Dani Baker, PhD, LMFT, ATR-BC (she/her/), has over 18 years of experience as a Licensed Marriage and Family Therapist, Board-Certified Art Therapist, Educator, Supervisor, and Collaborator. She is the founder of Creative Works Collaborative, where she offers supportive and inclusive spaces for individuals, families, and groups grieving the loss of a loved one or navigating significant loss events across the lifespan.

Dani also provides consultation and community outreach presentations nationally and internationally focused on Culturally Sensitive, Natural Responses to Loss and Grief via Meaning-Making and Post-Traumatic Growth, helping the Brain Identify, Communicate, and Integrate Affect Imaging with Emotion Regulation in Therapy; and Exploring the Intersection of Attachment, Trauma, Loss, and Posttraumatic Growth in Creative Arts and Family Therapy.

Finally, Dani partners with other relational clinicians and integrative experts in the fields of counseling and therapy, to offer comprehensive Continuing Education through Creative Works Co-Lab Series via Self as the Therapist Retreats and Online Trainings such as IFS and Nature-Based Therapy; Integrated Art Therapy Techniques in Clinical Practice; Canine-Assisted Therapy Interventions in Attachment/Attunement for Healing Complex Trauma; Integrative Somatic and Mindfulness-Based Techniques in Therapeutic Practice; and Self-as-Therapist Collage and Expressive Writing Practice.

Jessica Leith Claus, LMFT, CST (she/her/hers), is a white, cisgender female, licensed Marriage and Family Therapist, AAMFT Approved Supervisor, and AASECT Certified Sex Therapist in WA State. With a strong commitment to examining systemic oppression, she advocates for decolonizing therapeutic practices and is dedicated to integrating this lens into her work. Jessica works with youth, couples, and families in her private practice in Seattle, WA, using evidence-based treatments and humanistic family therapy models. Her therapeutic approach is grounded in a deep awareness of the impact of systemic forces on individuals and communities.

With a long history of working with youth and families in community behavioral health settings, Jessica continues to provide State-sponsored family therapy training to providers using the research-informed family therapy model [STAY Training], which she codeveloped while at the University of Washington. Jessica is also the former Director of Clinical Training for a COAMFTE-accredited Couple & Family Therapy Program and volunteers as an accreditation reviewer with COAMFTE. Her area of research focuses on translational studies examining the cross-cultural implementation of Westernized therapy models in both local and global contexts. Through her work, Jessica strives to promote culturally responsive, decolonized approaches to therapy that empower marginalized voices and challenge oppressive systems.

Dr. Jacey Coy, PsyD, LMFT (he/him), is a licensed Marriage and Family Therapist, researcher, professor, operator, husband, and dad. As a Latino man of Mexican descent and an advocate for systemic thinking in mental health, he believes that relationships are the most important aspect of our lives.

Dr. Coy holds a Doctorate of Psychology in Couple and Family Therapy from Alliant International University and a master's in communication studies from Texas State University. He is also a licensed Marriage and Family Therapist (LMFT) and has extensive clinical experience working in outpatient, inpatient, substance use, nonprofit, and hospital settings. More recently, he has worked in the digital health startup space.

Dr. Coy is an Assistant Teaching Professor in the Psychology Digital Immersion program at Arizona State University. His research interests include ethics, clinical decision making, and the intersection of artificial intelligence and mental health.

Alyssa Griskiewicz, ATR-BC, LMHC (she/her), believes meaningful personal and social change can be trauma-informed, healing-centered, and focused on collective liberation. She embodies her privileged and marginalized identities with humility, activism, and a centered compassion for self and others. She is an educator, art therapist, counselor, supervisor, and consultant in private practice. Alyssa integrates tenets of cultural humility, liberation psychology, somatic engagement, and a sense of playfulness in her diverse roles and global experiences. Her work and learning are based on creative practice and span from coast to coast in the United States and in communities around the globe.

Tai Lee (they/them/theirs) was born in Taiwan and immigrated to the United States at five years of age. Taiwan has a long legacy of being colonized by Western and Asian powers. Tai is of Hokkien and Dutch descent, so their ancestors were colonizers and the colonized at different times. Before becoming a sex therapist, they provided peer and relational support in a community of queer, BIPOC, kinky, multi-partnered, disabled, and neurodivergent members. This space influenced their work on Agency-Centered Relational Therapy, which advocates for restoring agency at all Social-Ecological levels.

Dr. Cayla Minaiy, PhD, LMFT (she/her/hers) is a licensed therapist and the Director of Training and Education at Lovewell Initiatives. She is the eldest daughter of Iranian immigrants, the wife of an immigrant, and a holder of generational trauma. Dr. Minaiy profoundly understands the complexities of identity, belonging, and the unspoken weight of intergenerational wounds. Her lived experience informs her work as a therapist, where she offers a space of deep understanding, cultural responsiveness, and decolonized healing.

With over a decade of clinical experience, Dr. Minaiy specializes in working with individuals navigating the intersections of culture, family expectations, trauma, and self-liberation. She believes that healing is not just about symptom reduction but also about reclaiming power, unlearning harmful narratives, and reconnecting with ancestral wisdom. Through a decolonized framework, she guides clients in exploring their struggles' systemic and histori-cal roots while cocreating pathways toward healing and wholeness.

Dr. Minaiy's journey in the mental health field began in a community agency. It continued on in her role as faculty and associate chair of a COAMFTE-accredited Couple and Family Therapy program in the Pacific Northwest. During her tenure in academia, she mentored and trained numerous aspiring therapists, fostering a deep commitment to the growth and development of future clinicians. This experience also instilled in her a passion for clinical supervision, which she continues to integrate into her current practice.

Central to Dr. Minaiy's therapeutic approach is her dedication to ongoing professional development, mainly through Person of the Therapist (POTT) training. This framework emphasizes self-awareness, introspection, and the therapist's impact on the therapeutic process. In addition, Dr. Minaiy is committed to practicing with a lens of social and cul-tural humility. She recognizes the importance of cultural awareness in therapy and con-tinually strives to deepen her understanding of diverse cultural backgrounds and identities. Dr Minaiy believes the role of supervision is to foster the identity of the therapist, and if therapists are supported, they will, in turn, thrive in their clinical work.

marcela polanco (ella/she) As a racialized person of color and gendered ella/she person, and an immigrant in the United States, I have a deep commitment to diverse decolonial projects thought and felt from Abya Yala, the land I owe my existence to. Colombiana living in California, I am a westernized family therapist, Spanglish speaker, and member of the fam-ily therapy faculty team at San Diego State University, located in unceded Kumeyaay land.

Dr. Jarryn Robinson-Ellis, PhD, LMFT (she/her), is a distinguished Marriage and Family Therapist and Counselor Educator with over 14 years of experience in the field. She earned her master's degree from the University of Louisiana at Monroe and her Ph.D. from the University of Texas at San Antonio.

Currently, Dr. Robinson-Ellis serves as Program Director and core faculty member in the Couple and Family Therapy Program at Antioch University Seattle. In this role, she teaches, mentors, and supervises students in the Master of Arts in Marriage and Family Therapy program, bringing her extensive expertise to courses.

Dr. Robinson-Ellis specializes in trauma, attachment, and relational therapy in her clini-cal practice. She is deeply committed to creating a safe and inclusive therapeutic space for individuals and couples, with a particular focus on women's issues, motherhood, and parenting. Her approach is grounded in systemic and relational perspectives, utilizing evi-dence-based interventions to help clients navigate challenges, build resilience, and foster deeper, more fulfilling relationships.

Beyond her academic and clinical roles, Dr. Robinson-Ellis co-owns Be Rooted Therapy, PLLC, based in Seattle, Washington, where she continues her dedication to supporting diverse populations. Her research interests include exploring the experiences of women of color in academia, racialized trauma, microaggressions, and ethical ambiguity, reflecting her commitment to addressing systemic issues and promoting equity in mental health care.

Dr. Zain Shamoon, PhD, LMFT (he/him), is a South Asian Muslim man who comes from Punjabi people. He has been practicing and teaching in the field of couple and family ther-apy for 16 years. He is dedicated to creating spaces where people can tell their personal stories en route to their own wellness. He believes collective gathering storytelling is a collectivist tradition that ought to be reclaimed. He currently practices therapy online at Northwest Relationships in Tacoma, Washington, and is also the host and founder of the Narratives of Pain storytelling showcase.

He received his Ph.D. in human development and family studies and his Master's in Couple and Family Therapy from Michigan State University. His research focused on domestic violence in South Asian communities and how survivors' personal stories help address service needs.

Sar Surmick, LMFT (she/her), is a systemic LMFT based out of Redmond, WA, USA and a professor at Antioch University. She specializes in Identity, Consensual Non-Monogamy, Consent, and Human Sexuality. Sar is the author of "The Consent Primer," an internationally known Consent educator, an MFT supervisor, and an advocate for nonbinary & Trans individuals. She identifies as a nonbinary Trans Fem in search of meaning, understanding, and authenticity.

Acronyms and Abbreviations

Throughout this book, you will encounter several foundational terms and acronyms central to systemic therapy from a decolonized and intersectional perspective. We've provided definitions and brief explanations of these key concepts below to ensure clarity and promote deeper engagement.

BIPOC

BIPOC stands for Black, Indigenous, and People of Color. This term acknowledges the unique experiences and historical impacts of colonization and systemic oppression on these groups, particularly highlighting the distinct and profound injustices faced by Black and Indigenous communities.

POTT (Person-of-the-Therapist)

Person-of-the-Therapist (POTT) emphasizes the therapist's self-awareness, authenticity, and the conscious use of personal experiences and identity in therapy. Through ongoing reflexivity and self-examination, therapists recognize and responsibly utilize their own cultural, social, and relational positions to foster genuine and transformative therapeutic relationships.

CFT / MFT / Family Systems Therapy / Systemic Therapy

Couple and Family Therapy (CFT), Marriage and Family Therapy (MFT), Family Systems Therapy, and Systemic Therapy are often used interchangeably. They are all terms that represent the practice of systemic therapies that focus on understanding individuals within their relational contexts, viewing issues as arising from interactions within family systems and broader sociocultural contexts rather than from isolated individual pathology.

First-, Second-, and Third-Order Change

- **First-order change** involves superficial adjustments within a family or system that do not significantly alter the fundamental dynamics.
- **Second-order change** transforms a system's deeper patterns, rules, and structures, creating lasting shifts in relationships and interactions.
- **Third-order change** extends beyond immediate relationships to broader systemic, societal, and cultural contexts, advocating for transformative shifts toward equity and justice.

ADDRESSING Model and Expanded ADDRESSING Model

The ADDRESSING model, initially developed by Pamela Hays, is a framework therapists use to recognize and address multiple aspects of identity: Age, Disability, Religion, Ethnicity/Race, Socioeconomic Status, Sexual Orientation, Indigenous Heritage, National Origin, and Gender. The Expanded ADDRESSING Model further incorporates intersectionality, adding nuances to these categories and explicitly addressing power dynamics, systemic oppression, and the importance of social justice advocacy in therapeutic practice.

BPSC

BPSC stands for Biological, Psychological, Social, and Cultural. It's a holistic model therapists use to understand and address the complexities of clients' experiences. By integrating biological, psychological, social, and cultural factors, therapists can more effectively identify systemic influences and support nuanced interventions.

FOO

Family of Origin (FOO) refers specifically to the family in which an individual was raised or grew up. Typically, it encompasses primary caregivers, siblings, and immediate or approximate family members.

COO

Culture of Origin (COO) extends beyond the immediate family to include the broader cultural context (traditions, practices, values, and beliefs) that influences an individual's identity, worldview, and relational patterns. Differentiating these terms helps therapists explore both relational and cultural dimensions of a person's background.

"Self" and "Other"

In systemic and psychological terms, "self" refers to one's internal identity, thoughts, feelings, experiences, perspectives, and sense of autonomy. "Other" denotes individuals or groups distinct or outside from one's "self," emphasizing relational dynamics, differences, and interactions across identities. Acknowledging the relational interplay between "self" and "other" helps therapists navigate identity formation, relational boundaries, and interdependence in therapy.

These terms will ground you in the foundational language used throughout this book, enhancing your understanding and engagement with the transformative possibilities of systemic family therapy from a decolonized perspective.

Introduction

Breaking the Jar: Decolonizing Family Therapy from the Inside Out

Jennifer M. Sampson and Fiona E. O'Farrell

Growing up, at the end of every summer, my dad would take my siblings and me caterpillar hunting in the highway ditches near our family lake home in central Minnesota. We'd capture these little striped worms in empty pickle jars, bring them home, and wait. After a few days, we'd watch them crawl up to the top of the jar, form their chrysalises, and let nature take over. A couple of weeks later, they'd emerge in a different form—transforming into beautiful orange, black, and white butterflies. The metaphor of metamorphosis is one that's often used to describe transformation: shedding old versions of ourselves to embrace something new. It's comforting and poetic. But it's not the metaphor I'm talking about here.

Sometimes, when we searched for the caterpillars, we'd find a chrysalis that had already formed on a leaf in the wild. We'd pluck the plant, chrysalis intact, and place it directly into the jar. We'd take it home, put it on a shelf in our bedroom, and wait. Now, imagine for a moment, what that must have been like for that butterfly in the first few moments after it poked its little head out of its cocoon, stretched its wings, and looked around. Where there was once sunshine and freedom, there are now glass walls. Where it once belonged to an expansive, open world, it is now trapped, confined in a jar, surrounded by artificial light (and in my case, walls covered with boy band posters). I cannot even fathom another possible alternative to the first thoughts in that poor butterfly's mind than, "Where the hell am I, how did I get here, and *how do I get out?*"

This is the metaphor I want to talk about.

For many of us—especially those in the mental health field—there comes a moment when the world as we've known it starts to shift. Maybe it's a conversation that doesn't sit right. Or a story shared by a client that challenges everything we thought we understood. Perhaps it's a class discussion, a training session, or a personal moment of reflection that begins to pull at the seams of the frameworks we've relied on thus far. What once seemed natural and expansive—our understanding of families, development, and relationships—now feels narrower, constrained by assumptions we didn't even know were shaping our work.

This is often how the lens of decolonization first takes shape: with a flicker of discomfort, a realization that what we've been taught—what we've taken for granted as universal truth—may not, in fact, tell the whole story. We start to notice the cracks in the walls, the invisible boundaries that limit how we think about healing, family, and justice. And yet, even as the cracks come into focus, the walls themselves can feel impenetrable. Like the butterfly waking up in the jar, we find ourselves asking the same questions: *Where am I? How did I get here? And how do I get out?*

DOI: 10.4324/9781032679082-1

This book is about answering those questions. It's about helping you, the reader, see the "jar" for what it is—recognizing how systemic oppression, colonial legacies, and inequities have shaped the families, relationships, and systems we navigate every day. It's about understanding how these glass walls were built—through histories of colonialism, racism, patriarchy, and other forces of control—and how they create a false universality. Instead, this book will help you to see that these walls continue to limit the possibilities for individuals and families alike. But it's also about something bigger: reminding you that a vast, beautiful world exists outside the jar. And once we understand what it is, how it was created, and how it functions, we can begin to make a plan to break free.

Whether you're a therapist, a mental health practitioner, or someone invested in supporting families, this book is an inspirational collection of narratives to help you map out the journey beyond the jar. It will challenge you to look beyond the individual stories of your clients or communities and see the systemic forces at play. It will ask you to rethink what *family* means, what healing looks like, and how we can honor the vast diversity of human experience. Most importantly, it will equip you to guide others—and yourself—toward a more expansive, liberated way of being. The butterfly cannot change the fact that it woke up in the jar. But it *can* begin to understand where it is, how it got there, and what it will take to return to the open world where it belongs. And so can we.

The Reader's Problem: Why Our Work Falls Short

Therapists and students entering the field of mental health often begin with a desire to create meaningful change—whether by supporting individuals, fostering family resilience, or addressing larger social issues. Yet, as we learn and grow in our training, it becomes clear that the tools we're given to accomplish these goals often feel incomplete. They rely on frameworks that are narrow in scope, rooted in Western values, and blind to the broader systems that shape clients' experiences.

In 1981, Audre Lorde wrote, "For the master's tools will never dismantle the master's house. They may allow us to temporarily beat him at his own game, but they will never enable us to bring about genuine change." Lorde's essay has been quoted in activist spaces for decades since it was first published, naming the importance of abandoning all structures of oppression in order to successfully create a world where all will flourish. The authors invite you to consider the same for how we consider family development; the tools we have within our scope cannot be the tools for expansion and liberation.

The tools we commonly use as systemic therapists—whether in the form of diagnostic manuals, developmental frameworks, or family therapy models—claim universality when the reality is far more complicated. Current therapeutic practices often reduce human behavior to individual pathology or nuclear family events and overlook the impact of systemic oppression. The most common frameworks our field relies on to understand the human experience fail to account for the lived realities of families outside the white, Western, middle-class, heteronormative ideal. The result is a practice that, at best, feels disconnected from the complexity of our clients' lives and, at worst, perpetuates harm.

Reimagining Therapy Through a Decolonized Lens

Therapy has the power to heal, but it also has the power to harm. Too often, existing models of family therapy and systemic thinking fall short because they are rooted in Eurocentric, colonial frameworks that prioritize Western ideals while marginalizing the lived realities of diverse families. These frameworks uphold rigid definitions of family, ignore the impacts of systemic oppression, and offer little guidance on how to challenge inequities in the systems that shape our clients' lives.

This book offers a way forward.

Introducing the Decolonized Framework

At its heart, this book is about action. It equips therapists not only with the tools to recognize systemic oppression but also with strategies to disrupt it. A decolonized lens is not just a shift in perspective—it is a commitment to actively dismantling systems of harm and rebuilding them in ways that center equity, justice, and liberation.

But what exactly is a decolonized lens?

A Decolonized Lens Defined

Decolonization is a global and interdisciplinary topic, with increasing scholarly attention and contributions from various countries (Mahat et al., 2024). Scholars argue that colonialism's effects extend beyond political independence, permeating all aspects of life, including family dynamics and social systems (Byrne & Alexander, 2023). A decolonized lens critically examines the historical and ongoing impacts of colonialism on families, relationships, and systems (Emery-Whittington, 2024). It challenges power structures that perpetuate oppression and seeks to amplify the voices, knowledge, and practices of communities that have been marginalized. Decolonization is not about rejecting all Western frameworks; it is about interrogating whose experiences and knowledge are excluded, dismantling oppressive systems, and reimagining approaches that honor the diversity and complexity of human experience.

Key principles of a decolonized lens to understanding family systems include:

- *Centering Context*: Families do not exist in isolation. They are shaped by histories of colonialism, systemic inequities, and cultural traditions. A decolonized lens requires therapists to understand and honor these contexts rather than defaulting to universalized, Western-centric models.
- *Valuing Relationality*: In many cultures, relationality and interdependence are central to family life. This approach rejects Western individualism as the sole marker of health and instead celebrates collective caregiving, kinship systems, and community support.
- *Honoring Fluidity and Diversity*: Families are dynamic, adaptive, and varied. A decolonized framework validates all family structures—from queer-chosen families to multi-generational households—and rejects rigid, binary definitions of what a "healthy" family should look like.

By integrating these principles into your work, you will be better equipped to support families navigating the compounded impacts of systemic oppression while affirming their resilience and agency.

Action and Disruption: Moving Beyond Awareness

Awareness of systemic oppression is not enough. While understanding the "jar" that confines us and our clients is a necessary first step, a decolonized approach demands that we take action to dismantle it. This book challenges you to go beyond recognizing inequities and actively disrupt the systems that perpetuate them by:

- *Interrogating Power Structures*: Recognizing how colonialism, racism, patriarchy, and other systems of oppression are embedded in the frameworks we use, the institutions we work within, and the policies we uphold. As therapists, we must examine not just how these systems impact our clients but also how they show up in our own practices.
- *Advocating for Systemic Change*: Therapy cannot be confined to the individual or family level. A justice-oriented approach requires us to engage with the broader systems that shape our clients' lives—whether through policy advocacy, community organizing, or pushing for institutional reforms within the field of mental health.
- *Centering Community-Led Solutions*: True change begins with the communities most impacted by systemic oppression. This book emphasizes the importance of amplifying community voices, integrating cultural knowledge, and respecting Indigenous, non-Western, and historically excluded epistemologies as foundational to therapeutic practice.
- *Practicing Reflexivity*: A decolonized lens also requires ongoing self-reflection. Therapists must critically examine their own positionality, assumptions, and potential complicity in perpetuating harm. Reflexivity is not a one-time exercise—it is a lifelong practice of accountability and growth.

What Makes This Book Different

While there is no shortage of books critiquing systemic inequities in therapy, few provide both a robust theoretical foundation and actionable strategies for change. This book bridges that gap. It offers:

- *Theory Meets Action*: You will find explanations of how colonial legacies shape family systems, paired with practical tools for disrupting these legacies in your work. Each chapter includes concrete strategies, reflective exercises, and case studies to help you put theory into practice.
- *Lived Experiences and Case Studies*: This book centers the stories of real families and communities navigating systemic oppression. These examples illuminate the resilience and ingenuity of diverse groups of people while offering insights into how therapists can better support communities that are different from their own.
- *A Pathway for Transformation*: Rather than presenting decolonization as an abstract concept, this book provides a roadmap for integrating justice-oriented practices into your work—whether you are a student, an early-career therapist, or a seasoned practitioner.

This book challenges you to see yourself not just as a therapist but as a potential disruptor of systemic oppression. By adopting a decolonized lens, you are committing to more than just improved practice—you are committing to justice. This means rethinking the frameworks you use, questioning the assumptions you hold, and taking action to challenge inequities within and beyond the therapy room.

We understand that this process can feel daunting. It requires humility, courage, and a willingness to unlearn. But it also offers immense potential—for you as a practitioner, for the clients you serve, and for the field of systemic therapy as a whole. This book is here to guide you through that process, equipping you with the tools, insights, and inspiration needed to create meaningful change.

Ultimately, this book is both an invitation and a call to action. It invites you to critically examine the "jar" that confines both you and your clients, understand how it was built, and imagine a world beyond it. And it challenges you to take action—to disrupt oppressive systems, amplify marginalized voices, and co-create spaces where families can thrive in their full complexity and humanity.

The work of decolonization is not easy, nor is it linear. It requires constant reflection, accountability, and a commitment to justice. But it is also profoundly rewarding. By embracing this framework, you are not only transforming your practice—you are joining a movement to create a more equitable, inclusive, and liberated future for all families.

This book is a guide. The journey is yours to take.

What You'll Learn

In this book, you'll find tools, strategies, and real-world examples that will empower you to integrate a decolonized, anti-racist, and intersectional lens into your work as a mental health professional. By unpacking the colonial legacies embedded in traditional family-systems theories and therapeutic frameworks, this book equips you to critically examine your practice and reimagine how therapy can truly support the diverse families you serve. Some of the avenues for reimagining practice include:

1. Tools for Decolonizing Family Therapy

    a. Critique and deconstruct harmful assumptions embedded in traditional models like the Family Life Cycle.
    b. Center cultural contexts, relationality, and fluidity in your understanding of families.
    c. Use a decolonized lens to identify and address systemic inequities in your practice.

2. Strategies for Integrating Intersectionality and Justice-Oriented Practices

    a. How to center marginalized voices and amplify the knowledge and resilience of diverse communities.
    b. Practical approaches for integrating culturally rooted healing practices, such as collaborating with traditional healers or embracing community-led initiatives.
    c. Strategies for advocating for structural change and justice within and beyond the therapy room.

3. Case Studies to Bridge Theory and Practice

    a. Highlight the experiences of families and individuals navigating systemic barriers, cultural stigmas, and relational challenges.
    b. Showcase how decolonized approaches can be applied in diverse contexts, from reproductive justice to intergenerational healing.
    c. Provide practical guidance for addressing unique client needs while honoring their cultural, historical, and relational contexts.

4. Advocacy, Cultural Humility, and Reflexivity

    a. Engage in ongoing reflexivity to ensure that your practice remains attuned to the needs of diverse families.

b. Build cultural humility by centering community knowledge and rejecting the "expert" mentality.

c. Use your role as a therapist to advocate for systemic changes that promote equity and justice.

By the end of this book, you'll have the tools to support an ongoing practice to help navigate and resist the systemic barriers you and your clients face. More than that, you'll embrace pathways to challenge the oppressive systems shaping the mental health field and contribute to a more equitable, liberated future for all families.

Let this book inspire you to be part of the change.

What This Book Is—And What It Isn't

This book is both a critique and a call to action. This book is a collection of reimagined narratives by clinicians in the field who are sharing their approach to decolonization. Through a series of essays, case studies, and reflections, it explores how systemic therapists, reproductive health professionals, and family-systems thinkers can contribute to the decolonization of their fields. Each chapter offers a unique perspective on dismantling oppressive frameworks and amplifying marginalized voices.

This book is not an exhaustive history of colonialism or a comprehensive manual for family therapy. If you're looking for a step-by-step guide that neatly fits into existing therapeutic frameworks, you won't find that here. Instead, this book is an invitation to rethink, unlearn, and reimagine. What you will find in these pages is a challenge to our current stories about family development and how they fail to account for the richness, fluidity, and resilience of diverse family systems.

This book is not about discarding everything Western but about critically examining whose experiences and knowledge are valued and whose are erased or invisible. Existing models of development are not inherently flawed, but their attempt at universality often comes at the expense of diverse ways of knowing, being, and relating. This book invites the reader to interrogate these imbalances and offer a more expansive approach to understanding families and relationships.

We don't claim to have all the answers. Decolonization is not something to achieve—it's an ongoing process—one that requires humility, reflection, and a willingness to sit with discomfort. More importantly, this book is a call to reimagine. When we "reimagine families," we explore the vast possibilities that emerge when we break free from rigid, normative definitions of family and embrace the diversity of human relationality.

This is not just theoretical—it is deeply practical. So, if you are ready to question the frameworks you have inherited—or perhaps just beginning to learn, then engage in this book with the context and curiosity you lend to your current and future clients.

Writing as Resistance

This book is far from an academic critique or a theoretical exercise—it is an act of resistance. It stands in direct opposition to the forces seeking to erase the histories, lived experiences, and systemic realities that shape our work as mental health professionals. It refuses to let therapy be stripped of its capacity to challenge oppression.

The current political climate is waging a campaign of erasure—erasing language about racism from education, erasing protections for marginalized communities, and erasing histories that challenge the dominant narrative. When therapy is forced into neutrality, it becomes complicit in harm. Avoiding conversations about racism, gender oppression, and systemic inequities does not make these realities disappear—it only makes it easier for them to thrive unchecked. When clinicians are discouraged from practicing anti-oppressive work, entire communities lose access to care that affirms their lived experiences. The removal of DEI initiatives and justice-oriented training means that the next generation of therapists may never be exposed to the knowledge and tools they need to serve diverse populations. When therapy is reduced to individualistic solutions, it reinforces the very systems that cause the issues in the first place. Clients are told to "cope" with oppression rather than being supported in challenging the structures that uphold it.

This book supports client growth and development beyond simply coping.

Resistance is not just about naming what is wrong but building what is needed. This book aims to inspire therapists and students with examples of knowledge, strategies, and frameworks necessary to practice in alignment with justice and liberation. Decolonization is not an abstract concept or a destination we will arrive at—it is a daily practice. It is a commitment to interrogating how we have been conditioned to see the world and actively unlearning the frameworks that uphold injustice.

This book is not the work of one voice or one perspective—it is the collective labor of authors, therapists, and scholars who challenge the status quo in their field. Their contributions form a tapestry of resistance, offering multiple entry points into the work of decolonization. Some chapters directly challenge dominant frameworks, critiquing the Eurocentrism embedded in traditional models of family development. Others offer counternarratives, centering the voices of communities that have long been excluded from mental health discourse. Still others focus on practical application—readers walk away with ideas for implementing justice-oriented approaches in their work. This is the power of collective resistance. No single person has all the answers, but together, we can dismantle oppressive systems and build something new.

A Commitment to Liberation

Ultimately, this book is an invitation—a call to action for therapists, students, and mental health professionals to engage in the lifelong practice of decolonization. The tools provided here are not meant to be passively absorbed; they are meant to be used. The need for a new framework is clear. This book is about helping you, the reader, see the "jar" that confines both you and your clients—recognizing how colonial legacies shape the practice of therapy. But it is also about showing you that the jar can be broken.

By embracing a decolonized perspective, therapists can begin to reimagine what healing looks like. They can honor the diversity of human experiences, amplify the voices of marginalized communities, and build practices that affirm the dignity and humanity of all families. The work is not easy, but it is necessary. And it begins with asking hard questions: Whose knowledge is missing from our models? Whose experiences are erased in our frameworks? And how can we do better?

Disclosures

Case Examples and Confidentiality

This book includes case examples and clinical scenarios to illustrate and contextualize key concepts, strategies, and interventions. These examples are inspired by real therapeutic encounters and often represent an amalgamation of multiple client experiences to enhance clarity, protect confidentiality, and respect client privacy. All names, identifying details, and specific circumstances have been significantly altered to safeguard client identities. Any resemblance to actual persons, living or deceased, or specific situations is entirely coincidental and unintended.

Honoring Contributor's Writing Style

We have intentionally honored each contributor's unique voice, writing style, and organizational preferences. Contributors were encouraged to express their ideas authentically, even if that meant departing from conventional grammatical norms or stylistic guidelines. This approach is a decolonizing practice, affirming the value of diverse epistemologies, cultural expressions, and writing styles. By embracing this intentional diversity, we aim to disrupt traditional academic norms and celebrate the richness of each author's lived experience and knowledge.

The Use of Artificial Intelligence (AI)

Throughout the development of this book, the editors utilized AI as a collaborative tool to support the writing and editing process. AI-assisted drafting allowed us to accurately cite sources, organize complex frameworks, and enhance clarity while maintaining the integrity of our voices and perspectives. However, the substance of these pages, arguments, and insights remain entirely original to the editors and contributors. In the spirit of decolonized practice, we recognize that technology—when used critically and intentionally—can serve as a means of accessibility, efficiency, and collective knowledge sharing rather than replacing human expertise. By leveraging AI as a tool rather than an authority, we remain committed to centering lived experience, community wisdom, and the liberatory goals of this work.

What's Our Why? And What's At Stake?

At the heart of this text is the reality that therapy and mental health care do not exist in a vacuum. It is deeply embedded in systems shaped by colonial legacies, Eurocentric frameworks, and rigid definitions of family. These systems dictate who receives care, how care is provided, and what forms of healing are considered legitimate. They define "healthy families" as nuclear, independent, and heteronormative, ignoring the rich diversity of family structures around the world. Some examples include: (a) Indigenous kinship systems rooted in communal caregiving and intergenerational support are often dismissed as "enmeshed" or "codependent" by Western frameworks; (b) Black families impacted by systemic racism such as tropes that perpetuate stereotypes like the "absent father" narratives, while ignoring the ways structural inequities, such as mass incarceration, can shape family dynamics; or how (c) Chosen families and nontraditional relationships within the Queer community are often sidelined, with practitioners failing to recognize their legitimacy or their strengths.

These examples are not just theoretical—they represent the lived realities of clients navigating systems designed to exclude them. When therapists fail to acknowledge and address these systemic forces, they risk reinforcing the inequities their clients struggle against.

The stakes are high for therapists and students in training. Failure to engage with systemic inequities doesn't just harm clients—it limits our growth and effectiveness as practitioners. When we rely on outdated, one-size-fits-all models, we miss opportunities to connect with the richness and diversity of human experience. We inadvertently replicate colonial harms by framing clients' struggles as individual or even nuclear family problems rather than symptoms of systemic oppression.

This lack of a critical lens also contributes to therapist burnout. Many therapists find themselves feeling disillusioned, stuck in systems that prioritize productivity over people and pathologize clients without addressing the root causes of their challenges. Without a broader framework to understand the intersecting forces shaping our clients' lives, it's easy to feel overwhelmed and ineffective.

The Limitations of Existing Models

Carter and McGoldrick's (1980; 2005) Family Life Cycle theory emerged as a way to understand the predictable stages families undergo over time. When it was first introduced, the Family Life Cycle theory was considered a significant contribution to the field because it emphasized the interdependence of family members and the relational shifts that occur over time. This was a departure from earlier models that focused primarily on individual development, as it underscored the ways in which family members impact one another through life transitions. At its core, the theory embraced a systemic perspective, acknowledging that families are not static but rather evolving entities in which changes in one part of the system reverberate throughout the entire structure. The systemic nature of this model aligned well with the growing recognition of family therapy as a distinct field, offering a framework for understanding how life transitions shape familial relationships. This theory does not stand alone as an example of a well-intended model to support clinicians in understanding normative processes of development; Erikson, Piaget, Bronfrenbrenner, Bowlby & Ainsworth, Maslow, and many more have all attempted to find a universal approach to how we develop over our lifetime (Pelaez et al., 2008).

Yet, these models reflect the same colonial assumptions that shaped Western reproductive policies: a linear progression toward independence, biological parenthood as normative, and rigid, gendered roles within heterosexual unions. The following limitations illustrate the need for a broader, more inclusive perspective:

- *Marriage as a Milestone*: The Family Life Cycle treats heterosexual marriage as a central transition point, sidelining nontraditional unions, chosen families, and queer relationships.
- *Biological Parenthood as Normative*: Families are seen as incomplete without biological children, disregarding childfree families, adoptive families, and alternative parenting structures.

- *Linear Progression and Individualism*: The model idealizes a trajectory where children grow up, move out, and form their own nuclear families. This pathologizes intergenerational and interdependent family systems, which are central to many non-Western cultures.
- *Static Gender Roles*: Traditional family-therapy models often replicate patriarchal assumptions, framing men as providers and women as caregivers.

For the purpose of this book, we will focus primarily on the Family Life Cycle theory, which has roots in systemic family therapy.

At the time of its development, the Family Life Cycle theory was also considered to meet the prevailing professional standards for cultural competency. It acknowledged that family structures change over time and that transitions between life stages can be complex. The model's emphasis on relational patterns across generations provided a helpful tool for clinicians seeking to understand the ways in which past experiences influence present dynamics. However, despite its systemic strengths, the theory was developed within a predominantly white, middle-class, Western context. As a result, its assumptions about family life were deeply embedded in Eurocentric norms that did not fully account for the diversity of family structures and relational experiences across different cultures.

A closer examination of the Family Life Cycle theory through a decolonizing lens reveals several key limitations. One of the primary concerns is its reliance on a linear and nuclear family–based model, which assumes that families follow a predictable trajectory consisting of marriage, child-rearing, and eventual retirement. This perspective marginalizes extended kin networks, chosen families, and caregiving structures that exist outside the Western nuclear framework. Many non-Western cultures, including Indigenous, Black, Latinx, and Asian communities, emphasize multigenerational living arrangements and collectivist caregiving, where responsibilities are distributed across extended family members rather than confined to a single household unit. The assumption that a family progresses in a linear fashion through clearly defined stages fails to capture the fluid and adaptive nature of many non-Western and marginalized family systems.

The Impact on Families and Communities

For the families we serve, these limitations are frustrating and potentially harmful. Pathologizing nontraditional families erases their resilience, delegitimizes their ways of being, and compounds the challenges they already face in navigating oppressive systems (Ravulo et al., 2024). This harm is especially acute for marginalized communities who are already bearing the brunt of systemic inequities. For example: (a) Black mothers face disproportionately high rates of maternal mortality, rooted in racism within the health care system (Taylor, 2020); (b) Indigenous families continue to experience the intergenerational trauma of forced child removal and cultural erasure (Walls, 2023); or (c) immigrant families navigate policies that prioritize economic contributions over familial bonds, often at the expense of their mental health and well-being (Ramos-Sanchez & Llamas, 2024). When therapy fails to acknowledge these realities, it becomes complicit in their perpetuation. Therapists risk becoming part of the problem rather than part of the solution.

The Dismantling of Culturally Responsive Care

The consequences of these systemic rollbacks don't just affect therapists—they have devastating effects on the clients and communities we serve. When policies are designed to erase discussions of oppression, marginalize already vulnerable populations, and limit access to culturally responsive care, the mental health field is not just failing to meet its ethical obligations—it is actively perpetuating the cycles and systems of oppression.

For many marginalized communities, therapy has never been fully accessible or affirming. However, in recent years, significant progress has been made toward integrating culturally responsive, anti-racist, and decolonized approaches into mental health care. That progress has advanced significantly enough that it is threatening the very systems it was meant to undermine. When those who benefit the most from colonial legacy feel a cultural shift, the most expected reaction is to increase oppressive tactics in an attempt to return to the status quo. The progression of culturally responsive care has and will continue to be effective despite the efforts to attack and dismantle equitable care. When systems of care that acknowledge the impact of generational trauma, systemic racism, and colonial violence are dismantled, Black, Indigenous, and other communities of color face increased barriers disproportionately (Hwang & Kong, 2024). The erasure of these frameworks means that their experiences are once again being reduced to individual pathology rather than understood in the context of historical and systemic oppression. When gender-affirming care is criminalized, trans youth are denied basic rights, and LGBTQ+ families are erased from conversations about relational health and family systems (Pietrosanti, 2024). When immigrant and refugee families are left unsupported as policies become more restrictive, separation from loved ones becomes more common, and the emotional toll of displacement is dismissed as a personal struggle rather than a systemic issue (Sandhya, 2024).

The consequences are undeniable. Our work as therapists is to stay steady in the seeds of progress we have planted without a decolonized, justice-oriented approach. Therapy risks backing the very systems of oppression that contribute to distress, trauma, and intergenerational harm. Some key considerations include:

- *The Medicalization and Pathologization of Oppression*: When therapy ignores the impact of oppression, it risks placing blame on individuals rather than the systems harming them.
- *Increased Barriers to Access*: Therapy has always been shaped by economic and political forces, determining who gets care, what kind of care they receive, and how that care is structured.
- *The Silencing of Clients and Clinicians Alike*: Perhaps the most insidious consequence of this political climate is its chilling effect on the voices of both clients and therapists. Many state laws attempting to restrict reproductive and gender-affirming care have implicated the clinician.

If therapists do not actively resist these forces, the field will regress into an era where mental health care is either labeled as "wellness" and reserved for the privileged, or it is medicalized and pathologized, and therapy becomes a tool of assimilation for marginalized communities rather than liberation.

This is what's at stake.

At this point, we hope the primary objective for you, the reader, is clear. This book is a collection of voices hoping to inspire you to move beyond surface-level inclusion to actively interrogate how power, privilege, and oppression shape family-systems therapy. It asks you to engage in the difficult but necessary work of examining yourself, disrupting dominant narratives, centering community wisdom, and transforming your practice into one that fosters liberation rather than conformity.

Before we begin the work of dismantling colonial frameworks, we must first understand the structures that uphold them. The chapters embedded in Part I of this book will lay the essential groundwork by unraveling the colonial histories embedded in family systems therapy. It explores how Eurocentric models have defined "healthy" relationships, erased cultural and relational diversity, and sustained harm systems under the guise of neutrality. The chapters in Part II will bring critical inquiry to the traditional ideals surrounding specific experiences of development and expand clinical considerations to the reader. Finally, the chapters in Part III of the book will inspire application frameworks from the micro- to the macro-systems of our clients and our field. By exposing these hidden influences, we create space for reimagining therapeutic practice—one that centers relational fluidity, interdependence, and cultural specificity.

Let's begin.

References

Byrne, A., & Tanesini, A. (2015). Instilling new habits: addressing implicit bias in healthcare professionals. *Advances in Health Sciences Education, 20*(5), 1255–62. https://doi.org/10.1007/S10459-015-9600-6

Byrne, D.C., & Alexander, J. O. (2023). Special section editorial. *Image & Text*, (37), 1–9. https://doi.org/10.17159/2617-3255/2023/n37a28

Candib, L. M. (1989). Point and counterpoint: Family life cycle theory: A feminist critique. *Family Systems Medicine, 7*(4), 473–87.

Carter, E. A., & McGoldrick, M. (Eds.). (1980). *The family life cycle: A framework for family therapy.* Gardner Press.

Carter, B., Garcia Preto, N., & McGoldrick, M. (2005). *The expanding family life cycle: Individual, family and the social perspectives.* Allyn and Bacon.

Emery-Whittington, I. G. (2024). Undoing coloniality. In T. Brown et al. (Eds.), *Human occupation* (pp. 191–208). Routledge. https://doi.org/10.4324/9781003504610-13

Hwang, W., & Kong, Y. (2024). Addressing systemic racism in mental health care. *Review of General Psychology, 28*(4), 315–25. https://doi.org/10.1177/10892680241289349

Lorde, A. (1981). *The master's tools will never dismantle the master's house.* In Moraga, C. & Anzaldua, G. (Eds.), *Kitchen table* (pp. 94–101). Women of Color Press.

Mahat, D., Karki, T. B., Neupane, D., Shrestha, D. P., & Shrestha, S. K. (2024). Decolonization in focus: A bibliometric analysis of scientific articles from 2010 to 2023. *Nepal Journal of Multidisciplinary Research, 7*(1), 1–21. https://doi.org/10.3126/njmr.v7i1.65142

Murry, V. M., Nyanamba, J. M., Hanebutt, R., Debreaux, M., Gastineau, K. A. B., Goodwin, A., & Narisetti, L. (2023). Critical examination of resilience and resistance in African American families: Adaptive capacities to navigate toxic oppressive upstream waters. *Development and Psychopathology, (35)*5, 1–19. https://doi.org/10.1017/s0954579423001037

Naseh, M., Zeng, Y., Ahn, E., Cohen, F., & Rfat, M. (2024). Mental health implications of family separation as the result of migration policies in the United States: A systematic review. *Social Science and Medicine, 352.* https://doi.org/10.1016/j.socscimed.2024.116995

Pelaez, M., Gewirtz, J. L., & Wong, S. E. (2008). A critique of stage theories of human development. *Comprehensive handbook of social work and social welfare* (pp. 503–18). John Wiley & Sons.

Pietrosanti, P. (2024). The lavander scare: Discrimination and inequality towards the lgbtqia+ community in the past and present. *U.S. Sexuality and Gender Studies Journal, 2*(1), 35–45. https://doi.org/10.33422/sgsj.v2i1.657

Ramos-Sánchez, L., & Llamas, J. D. (2024). Immigration policy and Latinx/é children from mixed-status families: Mental health consequences and recommendations for mental health providers. *Children (Basel), 11*(11), Article 1357. https://doi.org/10.3390/children11111357

Ravulo, J., Hollier, J., Waqa, M., Vulavou, I., & Dina, E. (2024). Queer resilience: Reviving Indigenous-Pacific perspectives and practices. *eTropic: Electronic Journal of Studies in the Tropics, 23*(2), 213–34. https://doi.org/10.25120/etropic.23.2.2024.4071

Sandhya, S. (2024). *Displaced*. Oxford University Press. https://doi.org/10.1093/oso/9780197579886.001.0001

Taylor, J. K. (2020). Structural racism and maternal health among Black women. *The Journal of Law, Medicine & Ethics, 48*(3), 506–17.

Walls, M. (2023). The Perpetual Influence of Historical Trauma: A Broad Look at Indigenous Families and Communities in Areas Now Called the United States and Canada. *International Migration Review, 59*(2), 651–67. https://doi.org/10.1177/01979183231218973

Unpacking Origins

Decolonizing the Foundations of Family Therapy

Jennifer M. Sampson and Fiona E. O'Farrell

Exploring our Origins

Every profession has its origin story. The field of family therapy, for all its aspirations toward relational healing, was born from a distinctly Western, colonial, and heteronormative worldview—one that has dictated what it means to be a "healthy" family, a "well-adjusted" child, a "functional" relationship. Theories of human development and family systems have long been presented as objective truths, as though they emerged from universal human experience rather than the cultural, political, and economic forces that shaped them.

But theories are not neutral. They are stories written and rewritten by those in power. In the case of family therapy, these stories have often served to erase, pathologize, and discipline families that do not fit into their rigid, Eurocentric ideals. The nuclear family, the linear life cycle, and the gender binary are not simply descriptive models but prescriptive mandates, enforcing conformity while dismissing the complexity of human relationships across cultures, histories, and resistance movements.

This section asks us to return to the foundation—to take apart the frame before we build something new. What assumptions have we inherited about family, identity, and well-being? What knowledge has been erased, invalidated, or ignored in professionalizing family therapy? Most importantly, how do we move forward in ways that do not simply diversify these models but fundamentally transform them?

In "Breaking the Colonial Frame," we begin by interrogating the dominant life-cycle models that have shaped family therapy, exposing the ways they exclude immigrant families, queer and trans relationships, and non-Western ways of being. This chapter provides alternative frameworks—rooted in intersectionality, decolonial theory, and cultural responsiveness—allowing therapists to work more effectively with their communities.

In "From Pathology to Liberation," we shift the conversation from individual well-being to systemic oppression, examining how race, immigration, and institutionalized inequities shape family experiences. This chapter challenges therapists to move beyond hyperindividualistic models of care and embrace collective healing approaches that honor the wisdom and resilience of marginalized communities.

In "Beyond the Binary," we take on one of colonialism's most deeply embedded legacies: the policing of gender and sexuality. By deconstructing heteronormative, cis-normative, and monogamous ideals, this chapter opens space for a radically inclusive vision of identity work in therapy—one that prioritizes authenticity, relational diversity, and the liberation of self-expression.

DOI: 10.4324/9781032679082-2

Finally, in "Family Therapy in the Era of AI," we explore a rapidly emerging force in the field—artificial intelligence. While AI has the potential to increase accessibility and innovation in therapy, it also carries the risk of reinforcing the same colonial logic that has historically shaped mental health care. This chapter challenges therapists to engage critically with technology, advocating for AI that supports liberation rather than deepening existing systems of control.

Decolonizing family therapy does not start with technique. It begins with reckoning—a willingness to unlearn, sit in discomfort, and name how our field has been complicit in harm. Only by breaking the colonial frame can we begin to imagine what comes next.

Chapter 1

Breaking the Colonial Frame

Power, Privilege, and Family Therapy

Cayla Minaiy

Where are you from?

The question "Where are you from?" always gets me. I never know what people are really asking. Are they asking where I was born or where my heritage is from? As an Iranian American woman, I often feel like I am on the outside. I have "interesting" food, "exotic" traditions, and a "different" look. There's always a comparison of my culture with white culture, and how my culture stands out—not in an honorable way, but just different. Curious with caution. Growing up, my parents firmly knew where they were from, but because neighbors, classmates, teachers, and those surrounding me could not place where I was from, it somehow made it difficult for me to place myself. Once I married an immigrant, this displacement only grew. I found and still find myself belonging and not belonging to pieces of both Iranian and American culture. I don't think I am alone in this, as many children— more specifically, daughters of immigrants—feel this way.

But this experience, my experience and that of the millions of immigrants and children of immigrants' experience is not often captured in traditional frameworks of psychology. Traditional frameworks often base their assumptions on white, heterosexual, middle-class families, failing to capture the experiences of other families. This highlights the broader need for a decolonized perspective in understanding family and human development. Traditional frameworks, such as the Human Development and the Family Life Cycle, do not base their assumptions on the complexities of diverse cultural backgrounds. These models, rooted in Western ideologies, do not represent the realities of many individuals and families today.

My personal and professional journey to Couple and Family Therapy (CFT) is deeply rooted in my cultural background and the immigrant experience that informed my upbringing and shaped my worldview. The Iranian diaspora, coupled with my commitment to feminist and anti-racist approaches, underscores the importance of challenging traditional perspectives in family and human development. It is essential to envision a decolonized lens of many Westernized principles and teachings.

The Human Development and Family Life Cycle Model

The Human Development and Family Life Cycle model (Carter & McGoldrick,1980) is a model often considered standard in the field and has long dominated our understanding of power dynamics and growth throughout different life stages. The Human Life Cycle refers to the process of growth and change that occurs throughout the human lifespan, from

DOI: 10.4324/9781032679082-3

conception to death. It encompasses physical, cognitive, emotional, and social development. The framework is divided into the following stages:

1. **Prenatal Development:** This stage begins at conception and ends with birth. It involves rapid physical growth and the formation of organs and bodily systems.
2. **Infancy:** The infancy stage spans from birth to around 2 years old. It is characterized by significant physical growth, development of motor skills, and the beginning of language acquisition.
3. **Early Childhood:** This stage typically ranges from ages 2 to 6 years old. Children continue to refine motor skills, develop more complex language abilities, and begin to engage in symbolic play. Social skills and emotional regulation also develop during this period.
4. **Middle Childhood:** Middle childhood covers approximately ages 6 to 12 years old. Physical growth slows down, but there is continued development in cognitive abilities, social skills, and the refinement of motor skills. Formal education begins and friendships become more important.
5. **Adolescence:** Adolescence spans from approximately ages 12 to 18 years old. It is marked by rapid physical changes associated with puberty, as well as significant cognitive and emotional development. Adolescents strive for independence, establish personal identity, and form more mature relationships.
6. **Early Adulthood:** Early adulthood generally ranges from ages 18 to 40 years old. It is characterized by completing education, starting a career, establishing intimate relationships, and possibly starting a family. This stage focuses on achieving personal goals and identity formation.
7. **Middle Adulthood:** Middle adulthood spans from approximately ages 40 to 65 years old. Physical changes continue but at a slower rate. Career consolidation, contributing to society, and maintaining relationships become central concerns. This stage often involves reflection on accomplishments and future goals.
8. **Late Adulthood:** Late adulthood begins around age 65 and continues until death. This stage is characterized by further physical changes, such as a decline in sensory abilities and physical strength. Older adults may face challenges such as retirement, adjusting to changing roles, and dealing with loss. However, many older adults also experience a sense of fulfillment and wisdom gained from life experiences.

Throughout these stages, individuals experience varying degrees of change and growth across physical, cognitive, emotional, and social domains. The model provides a snapshot of what dynamics could look like as we move through each stage. However, the model does not capture the experience of many families. The stages reflected in the Human Development and Family Life Cycle model could not fit for many families, contributing to those feeling left out, "abnormal," and "behind" in life. Immigrant families, already navigating power imbalances in their new environments, may encounter further challenges when engaging with models that do not resonate with their experiences. There is strong pressure to assimilate to Western thought and traditions to belong and avoid discrimination. This pressure to conform to the model could lead individuals to believe they should abandon their cultural roots entirely, contributing to isolation and loss of identity.

A Decolonized Model of Human Development: A Shift in Perspective

The Human Development and Family Life Cycle model, a widely accepted model in the field of human development, has historically dominated our understanding of family dynamics. The model, as traditionally conceived, has been critiqued for its Eurocentric, classist, and heteronormative biases (Arnett, 2008; Nsamenang, 2006). Rather than adapting this framework to include cultural variations, a decolonized approach reimagines human development as dynamic, relational, and shaped by historical, ecological, and communal contexts. This alternative perspective prioritizes diverse ways of knowing, being, and growing beyond Western psychological theories. To grasp the complexity of human experiences, it is crucial to (a) acknowledge and address the power dynamics within the model and (b) expand our theoretical frameworks.

Acknowledging and Addressing Power Dynamics

Traditional models of human development, such as the Human Development and Life Cycle model, offer valuable insights into growth and change across the lifespan. However, these models often fail to account for the power structures that shape individuals' experiences, particularly for marginalized communities. This section outlines key power imbalances that require greater attention in systemic work. Table 1.1 summarizes *seven key power imbalances* that traditional human-development frameworks tend to overlook.

As Table 1.2 illustrates, traditional human-development models require expansion to incorporate systemic and structural inequities that influence developmental trajectories.

Table 1.1 Power Imbalances in Human Development Models

Power Dynamic	Description	Impact
Cultural Bias and Hegemony	Western-centric models assume universal applicability.	Marginalization of non-Western cultural perspectives and developmental milestones.
Gender Inequality	Developmental models often ignore the impact of patriarchy and gendered expectations.	Gendered barriers to autonomy, education, and economic opportunities.
Socioeconomic Barriers	Frameworks frequently assume access to stable economic conditions.	Economic disparities affect healthcare, education, and access to developmental resources.
Racial & Ethnic Oppression	Systemic racism shapes life trajectories but is rarely considered.	Discrimination impacts mental health, social mobility, and identity development.
Colonial Legacies	Many communities continue to experience intergenerational trauma from colonization.	Cultural loss, language suppression, and forced assimilation shape identity formation.
Power in Family Systems	Traditional models assume a nuclear family structure, ignoring diverse family systems.	Immigrant families and collectivist cultures experience unique developmental challenges.
LGBTQ+ Exclusion	Heteronormativity dominates developmental frameworks.	The erasure of LGBTQ+ experiences, including identity formation and discrimination.

Table 1.2 Decolonized Perspectives on Human Development

Principle	Key Insights
Development as Nonlinear and Relational	Growth is cyclical and shaped by relational bonds, intergenerational knowledge, and storytelling (Smith, 1999).
Collective and Interdependent Identity Formation	Identity is relational and shaped by cultural continuity, resistance, and historical memory rather than individual self-actualization (Nsamenang, 2006; Rogoff, 2003).
Expansion of Family and Kinship Systems	Family structures extend beyond the nuclear model to include chosen families, community caregiving, and intergenerational support (Collins, 2000).
Healing, Resistance, and Resilience as Developmental Markers	Growth is defined by cultural preservation, healing from intergenerational trauma, and acts of resistance, such as language revitalization and land reclamation (Mohanty, 1988).
Ecological and Spiritual Growth	Development is deeply connected to land, sustainability, and spiritual well-being rather than economic milestones (Smith, 1999).

A decolonized model of human development recognizes multiple, coexisting pathways to well-being rooted in interdependence, cultural continuity, and collective care. This framework rejects the rigid, linear progression of life stages in favor of an adaptable, fluid understanding of growth that aligns with various cultural worldviews and lived realities. By embracing these decolonized perspectives, therapists can create a more inclusive and supportive environment for all families, honoring their unique narratives and cultural identities.

Development as Nonlinear and Relational

Traditional Western psychological models conceptualize development as a stepwise progression based on cognitive and economic milestones. However, in many Indigenous and non-Western traditions, growth is a cyclical, relational process—deeply embedded in storytelling, intergenerational exchange, and ancestral wisdom (Smith, 1999). This perspective shifts the focus from individual accomplishment to collective well-being, emphasizing how cultural transmission and relational bonds shape human development. Clinical application includes:

1. Assess development within a relational and cultural context rather than solely through Western psychological frameworks.
2. Use narrative approaches that encourage storytelling, ancestral knowledge, and collective meaning making.
3. Ask questions that support expansive and collective experiences: *How does intergenerational wisdom shape this client's sense of self and development?*

Identity as Collective and Interdependent

Western developmental psychology often emphasizes individual autonomy and self-actualization as central to identity formation (Rogoff, 2003). However, in many cultural traditions, identity is relational—shaped by family, language, historical resistance, and collective memory (Nsamenang, 2006). Instead of viewing identity as a singular, self-contained construct, a decolonized approach acknowledges personhood as deeply embedded within social, cultural, and historical systems. Clinical application approaches:

- Shift from individualistic identity frameworks to collective identity formation in therapy.
- Explore how cultural history, family ties, and communal narratives shape a client's self-concept.
- Instead of asking individually focused assessment questions such as *Who are you?* ask, *How do your relationships, traditions, and histories shape your identity?*

Expanding Family and Kinship Systems

Traditional psychological models often center the nuclear family as the primary unit of development. However, many cultures rely on extended kinship networks, communal caregiving, and chosen families to support child-rearing and resilience (Collins, 2000). These kinship systems provide crucial emotional, financial, and cultural support sources, particularly in migration, displacement, and systemic oppression. Clinical approaches include:

- Validate and affirm nontraditional family structures in therapy.
- Ask relationally oriented questions: *Who are the people you rely on for support? How do they function as family in your life?*
- Challenge Western-centric definitions of family that may not reflect a client's lived experience.

Healing, Resistance, and Resilience as Markers of Growth

In many decolonized frameworks, healing from historical trauma is a core component of development. Rather than defining success through career stability or traditional family structures, a decolonized model recognizes cultural preservation, language revitalization, and social activism as central well-being indicators (Mohanty, 1988). Clinical application includes:

- Recognize activism, cultural preservation, and community resilience as forms of psychological healing.
- Incorporate trauma-informed approaches that acknowledge historical and intergenerational wounds.
- Ask about legacy and healing traditions embedded in the client's relational structures: *What healing traditions and cultural practices have sustained you and your family across generations?*

Integrating Ecological and Spiritual Development

Many Indigenous and global cultures view human development as deeply interconnected with nature, sustainability, and spirituality. In contrast to Western models prioritizing industrial productivity and economic progress, a decolonized perspective centers on ecological balance, land-based knowledge, and spiritual well-being as fundamental growth aspects (Smith, 1999). Clinical application can be experienced by:

- Encouraging land-based healing practices and nature-connection therapies that align with the client's intergenerational and culture of origin practices.

- Recognize spiritual resilience as an integral part of psychological well-being and an area for exploration and discovery.
- Ask: *How does your relationship with land, spirituality, and cultural traditions shape your sense of self?*

By embracing decolonized perspectives, therapists can create more inclusive, culturally attuned, and justice-oriented practices that honor clients' lived experiences, communal narratives, and healing traditions. Moving beyond Western psychological frameworks, this approach calls for relational, collective, and resistance-based models of development that center well-being as an interconnected, holistic process.

Expanding on Theoretical Frameworks

The Human Development and Family Life Cycle model can be adjusted to be more broadly applicable by interweaving alternative theoretical frameworks that address its limitations. The ADDRESSING model (Hays, 2008) offers a comprehensive lens for understanding family dynamics by considering multiple intersecting identities, including Age, Developmental disabilities, Disability acquired later in life, Religion, Ethnicity, Socioeconomic status, Sexual orientation, Indigenous heritage, National origin, and Gender. Traditional models often fail to account for these dimensions, leading to an oversimplified and exclusionary understanding of family development. By incorporating the ADDRESSING framework, we can better capture the diverse experiences and structural barriers that shape family trajectories, particularly in immigrant communities.

Queer theory (Butler, 1990) further enhances this discussion by challenging binary constructs of identity and relationships, emphasizing fluidity, diversity, and the social construction of norms. The Human Development and Family Life Cycle model assumes a standardized path through life stages, often privileging heteronormative and nuclear family structures. However, queer perspectives reveal that identity and relational structures are far more dynamic, necessitating a framework that recognizes non-traditional pathways. This perspective is particularly relevant for immigrant families, who often redefine family roles and relationships in response to cultural shifts and systemic pressures.

The Person of the Therapist model (Aponte & Kissil, 2016) underscores the importance of reflexivity in professional practice, prompting therapists and researchers to examine their biases. Developmental theories, often rooted in Eurocentric assumptions, can marginalize non-Western and immigrant family experiences. By fostering self-awareness and cultural humility, professionals can adopt a more inclusive and decolonized approach, ensuring that the diverse realities of families are accurately represented rather than assessed against a rigid, predetermined standard.

Research from migration studies, cultural psychology, and critical race theory further highlights the inadequacies of traditional developmental models in capturing immigrant experiences. Portes and Rumbaut (2014) describe assimilation as a nonuniversal process where different immigrant groups experience varying degrees of integration based on race, class, and policy contexts. Berry's (1997) acculturation framework challenges the linear trajectory assumed in dominant Western models, illustrating how immigrant families navigate the tension between cultural maintenance and adaptation. Rather than a straightforward progression, their development is often cyclical or fragmented, marked by challenges such as acculturation stress, language barriers, and economic hardships.

Critical race theory (Crenshaw, 1991) critiques dominant frameworks by exposing how structural inequities shape immigrant experiences. Discriminatory policies and racialized economic opportunities create systemic barriers that impact developmental trajectories. The assumption that all families follow a universal life course overlooks the compounded disadvantages faced by marginalized communities.

For many immigrant families, the Human Development and Family Life Cycle model falls short in capturing their lived experiences. This model presumes a linear progression from childhood through old age, marked by specific milestones. However, the reality for immigrant families often diverges dramatically due to challenges such as acculturation, language barriers, and the preservation of cultural heritage. These factors can lead to a nonlinear trajectory, where traditional milestones like marriage and family formation may be delayed or redefined, and new milestones, such as maintaining transnational connections, emerge.

Take, for example, my family's journey from Iran to the United States in the late 1970s. Both of my parents arrived with aspirations of pursuing higher education and achieving the "American dream." However, the outbreak of revolution in Iran severed their ties with family back home, thrusting them into a struggle to make ends meet while pursuing their degrees in a foreign language. They faced prejudice in their daily lives, economic hardship working at a diner, and constant worry for the safety of loved ones abroad. Their experience starkly contrasts with the typical trajectory outlined in the Human Life Cycle model, where peers were focused on academic and social milestones unencumbered by such challenges.

Immigration, particularly when undertaken alone as an adolescent or young adult, disrupts the Western notion of launching into adulthood at eighteen. It involves leaving behind familiarity, language, and support systems to pursue a better life, often amid great emotional upheaval. Upon graduating from college, while their peers were celebrating milestones and planning futures, my parents continued to navigate adversity, facing limitations in career advancement and delayed family planning due to economic constraints and ongoing cultural adjustments.

This narrative underscores the inadequacy of traditional models in capturing the complexities of immigrant experiences. Despite its historical dominance, the Human Development and Family Life Cycle model fails to account for these diverse realities and can inadvertently marginalize those who do not fit its prescribed path. Immigrant families often contend with navigating new legal and social systems with limited resources, perpetuating challenges across generations

The impact of these experiences extends beyond the initial generation, influencing attitudes and behaviors passed down to children and grandchildren. Raised in an environment shaped by a scarcity mindset and cultural duality, I learned early on the precariousness of stability and the imperative to navigate multiple identities simultaneously.

While pervasive, the Human Development and Family Life Cycle model does not reflect the resilience and adaptability inherent in immigrant experiences. Immigrants are frequently measured against this model, potentially diminishing their self-esteem and sense of achievement when they diverge from its expectations. Adopting a decolonized perspective is imperative as it acknowledges the diversity of family structures and developmental trajectories that exist beyond Eurocentric frameworks.

By integrating frameworks like the ADDRESSING model, which encompasses a wide array of intersecting identities (Hays, 2008), Queer theory, which challenges normative constructs of identity and relationships (Butler, 1990), and the Person of the Therapist model, which encourages reflexivity and awareness of biases (Aponte & Kissil, 2016), we can better understand and validate the experiences of immigrant families. These frameworks provide a more nuanced lens to explore and appreciate the rich tapestry of immigrant experiences, advocating for inclusive and respectful approaches to studying and supporting families across diverse cultural and societal contexts.

Intersections of Identity

When you are a child of immigrants, every step is filled with fulfilling dreams they did not have. Those dreams are deeply aligned with the Human Development and Family Life Cycle model, including being married and having children by a certain age. However, given Iranian culture, expectations and pressures do not apply the same way for all genders. In my experience, boys are free, but girls must abide by the culture perfectly and represent the entire family.

Consider the case of Nika, an Iranian American girl who grew up in a household where her brother, Ali, had the freedom to pursue his interests and make his own choices. Ali was encouraged to explore his passions and was not pressured to adhere strictly to cultural expectations. In contrast, Nika was constantly reminded of her role as the family's cultural ambassador. She was expected to excel academically, maintain her modesty, and prepare for a future that included marriage and children. This double standard significantly strained Nika, who felt torn between her desire to fit into American society and her obligation to uphold her family's Iranian values.

Often, first-generation children receive the message that they need to be American to survive socially and economically but fully devoted to Iranian culture to be accepted by family, despite clashes with American culture. In high school and college, perfect grades and education are often highly stressed, but as soon as you finish college, the message will become that you are now "behind" and need to get married right away.

Take the hypothetical scenario of Sarina, a high-achieving Iranian American student who excelled in high school and was accepted into a prestigious university. Throughout her academic journey, she faced immense pressure to perform perfectly to secure a successful future. However, upon graduation, her family shifted their expectations, emphasizing the urgency of finding a suitable partner and getting married. This sudden change in priorities left Sarina feeling conflicted and overwhelmed as she struggled to balance her professional aspirations with her family's cultural expectations.

Attending college is pivotal in the Human Development and Family Life Cycle model. Still, when you are an immigrant or the child of an immigrant, this path can look very different. The Western ideology emphasizes a launching period, where eighteen-year-olds move out and start independent adult life. However, this ideology is not practiced in many cultures, especially when a daughter or female is about to attend college. Many cultures stress that women are to leave home when they are married, and not to attend college.

This leaves many women sticking to colleges close to the family home rather than exploring options. For instance, imagine Mona, another daughter of Iranian immigrants, who dreams of attending a university across the country to pursue a degree in a specialized field. Her parents, however, insist that she stay close to home to maintain family ties and ensure her safety. This restriction limits Mona's educational opportunities and perpetuates the idea that her primary role is to remain within the family until marriage. In addition, when you are a daughter of an immigrant family, this can create big clashes of ideology and what it means to be an adult. In the Westernized ideology, someone staying at home during college years is "behind" and did not follow the path correctly, whereas leaving home could be seen as disrespectful and selfish, especially if you are female, in many other cultures.

The intersection of cultural identity, immigration status, gender, and race within families requires a nuanced understanding. Applying a decolonized lens involves recognizing how these intersections influence family dynamics, emphasizing the need to move beyond one-size-fits-all approaches.

Consider the experience of Meena, a South Asian American woman whose family strongly emphasizes cultural preservation. Meena's decision to pursue a career in a field traditionally dominated by men is met with resistance from her family, who believe she should focus on more "appropriate" roles for women within their cultural context. This clash of expectations highlights the complexities immigrant women face as they navigate multiple identities and strive to honor both their heritage and personal ambitions.

The immigrant experience is not uniform; it encompasses many stories shaped by unique combinations of identities. Acknowledging and respecting these intersections is fundamental in crafting therapeutic interventions that resonate with the lived experiences of immigrant families.

Connecting to Clinical Practice

In therapeutic practice, a decolonized perspective challenges the therapist to move beyond rigid models and embrace flexibility. Even therapists trained in systems theory and family dynamics have biases and may not realize how the Human Development and Family Life Cycle model informs their view of the world. Knowing that the model may not capture the essence of the immigrant family experience, clinicians are encouraged to take the time to be curious about individual and family experiences of immigration and co-create narratives with families that honor their unique developmental trajectories.

Step-by-Step Guidance and Tips for Therapists: Beyond the Current View of Development

Traditional Human Development and Life Cycle models assume a linear, universal progression through life stages, often centered on Western, middle-class norms. These models can pathologize or marginalize families whose experiences do not fit these rigid structures. Instead of merely making therapy "more inclusive," a decolonized approach actively disrupts these assumptions by recognizing multiple, nonlinear developmental pathways rooted in cultural, historical, and systemic contexts.

Cultivate Self-Awareness and Reflect on Biases

If we move beyond a linear framework, therapy can adapt by:

• Recognizing that developmental milestones are not universal but are shaped by culture, migration histories, and systemic barriers.
• Questioning the notion that autonomy and individuation are the "goals" of development, instead embracing interdependence as equally valid.

Strategies Include:

- **Critical Self-Assessment:** Regularly interrogate how your cultural background and training influence your views on "normal" life stages. Ask: *"How do I unconsciously impose Western developmental norms onto my clients?"*
- **Education Beyond Competency:** Move past "cultural competency" toward a lifelong practice of cultural humility. Engage in ongoing learning about how systems of oppression shape developmental pathways.

In practice, actively embracing relationship interdependence, cultural specificity, and cultural humility is essential to supporting clients' diverse lived experiences. Therapists can begin this with a critical inquiry into their own cultural ideals and experience influences their view of development.

Center the Family's Experience Rather than the Therapist's Expertise

If we reject the therapist as the primary expert on family development, therapy can adapt by:

- Positioning the family as the authority on their own developmental trajectories rather than imposing standardized life cycle models.
- Shifting from "fixing" developmental deviations to understanding them as adaptive responses to historical and systemic realities.

Strategies include:

- **Narrative Inquiry:** Use open-ended questions that allow families to define their growth. For example: *"What does thriving look like in your family?"* rather than *"How has your family adjusted to American expectations?"*
- **Reframing Challenges as Resistance:** Instead of seeing intergenerational conflict as dysfunction, recognize it as an ongoing negotiation of cultural survival and adaptation.

In practice, working with a family experiencing tensions between traditional cultural values and their children's aspirations explores how both perspectives are acts of resilience. Encourage storytelling that honors generational wisdom while validating change as a form of cultural continuity.

Disrupt Eurocentric Developmental Models: Adapt Therapeutic Techniques

If we acknowledge that dominant models erase non-Western family structures, therapy can adapt by:

- Challenging assumptions that nuclear families are the "ideal" developmental unit.
- Recognizing transnational, extended, and chosen families as equally valid structures of support and growth.

Strategies Include:

- **Decolonized Genograms:** Adapt genograms to include extended family, transnational kin, and nonbiological community ties.

- **Nonpathologizing Lenses:** Reframe "enmeshment" or "over-involvement" as expressions of collectivist values rather than dysfunction.

In practice, working with a multigenerational household, use an adapted genogram to map out family dynamics beyond the immediate nuclear unit. This helps visualize how power, caregiving, and decision making operate within their unique cultural framework rather than forcing a Westernized interpretation.

Address Structural Barriers Instead of Individualizing Problems

If we shift the focus from individual pathology to systemic oppression, therapy can adapt by:

- Recognizing how racism, xenophobia, and economic barriers shape developmental trajectories.
- Addressing survival strategies (such as code-switching or family separation) as systemic responses rather than maladaptive behaviors.

Strategies Include:

- **Structural Analysis in Therapy:** Instead of asking, "How can this family better adapt?" ask: *"What systemic barriers are shaping their experiences?"*
- **Advocacy as Intervention:** Connect clients with community resources, legal advocacy, and policy initiatives that support immigrant and marginalized families.

In practice, working with a family experiencing stress due to anti-immigrant policies validates their fears as accurate rather than overreactions. Support them in navigating legal and social resources while acknowledging that the burden should not fall solely on them to adapt.

Co-Create New Cultural Narratives with Families

If we reject the idea that assimilation is the ultimate goal, therapy can adapt by:

- Encouraging families to define their cultural identities rather than conform to dominant norms.
- Recognizing identity formation as an ongoing, relational process rather than a fixed developmental milestone.

Strategies Include:

- **Empowerment through Storytelling:** Help clients author new cultural narratives that honor their heritage and evolving identities.
- **Validation over Normalization:** Validate the discomfort of being "in-between" cultures rather than pressuring clients to resolve their identities neatly.

In practice, when working with clients struggling with feelings of displacement, I invite them to explore and integrate multiple cultural influences without forcing a binary choice. I guide them in crafting a dynamic, flexible, and self-defined cultural identity.

Moving Forward: A Commitment to Decolonized Practice

A decolonized therapeutic approach does not merely "include" diverse experiences—it fundamentally challenges the Eurocentric assumptions embedded in traditional development models. By embracing nonlinear growth, centering client expertise, and addressing systemic barriers, therapists can create space for families to thrive on their terms. True transformation in therapy comes from an active commitment to disrupting dominant narratives and co-constructing new, liberatory possibilities for healing.

Like many cultures, the Iranian culture's emphasis on collective identity and familial interconnectedness challenges individualistic frameworks embedded in traditional models. The Human Development and Family Life Cycle model assumes that most milestones are achieved through individual decision making and accomplishment. However, this can look very different for collectivistic and immigrant families. When making college decisions, immigrant families may have to weigh their finances more heavily than other families, and the pressure to attend a prestigious college to represent their family and culture may be pretty high. Therefore, attending college is not just about the person planning to study but about how this will affect the entire family and culture. This can also apply to marriage. Some cultures still practice arranged marriages. These arrangements may benefit the family, such as ensuring the person is financially stable and has a reputable job. Additionally, the marriage may be arranged to help preserve family culture and traditions or to ensure the continuation of the family lineage.

Integrating Non-Western Philosophies and Practices in Therapeutic Practice

Emphasizing Collective Identity and Familial Interconnectedness

In many Eastern philosophies, such as Confucianism, the family unit is central to social and personal life. The individual's well-being is intrinsically linked to the well-being of the family and community. Therapists can incorporate family systems therapy, recognizing the family as an interconnected unit rather than focusing solely on the individual. This approach involves inviting family members into sessions and exploring how family dynamics influence individual behaviors and decisions. In practice, working with a relational unit where multiple generations live together, the therapist facilitates discussions about how decisions regarding education and career paths affect each family member. By acknowledging the interconnectedness of their choices, the therapist helps the family find a collective path forward.

Considering Financial and Cultural Pressures

Many African and Asian cultures emphasize the importance of contributing to the family's financial stability and upholding the family's honor through educational and professional achievements. Therapists can help clients explore how financial and cultural pressures impact their decisions. This might involve creating a decision-making framework that includes the family's economic situation and cultural values. In practice, working with first-generation college students, the therapist can discuss the financial and cultural implications of attending a distant university versus a local one. Together, they explore scholarships, financial aid options, and the potential impact on family dynamics.

Recognizing the Role of Arranged Marriages and Cultural Traditions

In cultures where arranged marriages are practiced, the emphasis is on family unity, social stability, and cultural preservation. Therapists can approach arranged marriages with cultural sensitivity, understanding the family's motivations and values. This involves facilitating open conversations about expectations, desires, and cultural practices. In practice, working with a relational unit, the therapist acknowledges the parents' desire to arrange a marriage for their daughter based on cultural traditions. The therapist helps the daughter express her feelings and desires while guiding the family toward a mutually respectful understanding.

Weaving in Cultural Wisdom

Non-Western Philosophy: Indigenous and holistic healing practices often emphasize balance, harmony, and connection with nature and community. Therapists can integrate mindfulness, meditation, and communal activities that align with the client's cultural background. This holistic approach honors the wisdom embedded in diverse creative practices.

In practice, the therapist inquires about and incorporates mindfulness and meditation practices rooted in the client's heritage. These practices help family members manage stress, improve communication, and foster a sense of peace and interconnectedness.

Developing a Holistic and Inclusive Approach

The Ayurvedic tradition from India emphasizes balance in physical, mental, and spiritual health, considering the individual's relationship with their environment. Therapists can adopt a holistic approach that considers physical health, mental well-being, and spiritual practices. This might include dietary recommendations, exercise, and spiritual activities that align with the client's cultural values. In practice, the therapist explores principles of balance and well-being. They discuss dietary habits, daily routines, and spiritual practices that can support the family's overall health and harmony.

Therapists can enrich their understanding of family dynamics by weaving in cultural wisdom and embracing non-Western philosophies. This approach encourages a more holistic and inclusive sense of human development, honoring the wisdom embedded in diverse cultural practices. Therapists who integrate these perspectives can offer more meaningful and culturally responsive interventions, ultimately supporting the well-being of immigrant families.

Conclusion: Envisioning Equitable Futures

Challenging the status quo in the Human Development and Family Life Cycle model requires a decolonized perspective acknowledging these theories and their limitations. By embracing and accepting diverse stories, recognizing the intersections of identity, and integrating cultural wisdom, we pave the way for more inclusive, equitable, and responsive therapeutic practices.

As we envision equitable futures, we must advocate for a shift in our conceptualizations of family development. A decolonized approach invites us to honor the resilience of immigrant families and embrace the richness of their unique journeys. In doing so, we contribute to a culturally responsive, socially just mental health therapy landscape that affirms the diverse ways families navigate the complexities of human development.

References

Aponte, H. J., & Kissil, K. (Eds.). (2016). *The person of the therapist training model: Mastering the use of self.* Routledge. https://doi.org/10.4324/9781315719030

Arnett, J. J. (2008). The neglected 95%: Why American psychology needs to become less American. *American Psychologist, 63(7),* 602–14. https://doi.org/10.1037/0003-066X.63.7.602

Berry, J. W. (1997). Immigration, Acculturation, and Adaptation. *Applied Psychology, 46(1),* 5–34. https://doi.org/10.1111/j.1464-0597.1997.tb01087.x

Butler, J. (1990). *Gender trouble: Feminism and the subversion of identity.* Routledge.

Carter, E. A., & McGoldrick, M. (Eds.). (1980). *The family life cycle: A framework for family therapy.* Gardner Press.

Collins, P. H. (2000). *Black feminist thought: Knowledge, consciousness, and the politics of empowerment.* Routledge.

Crenshaw, K. (1991). Mapping the margins: Intersectionality, identity politics, and violence against women of color. *Stanford Law Review, 43(6),* 1241–99. https://doi.org/10.2307/1229039

Hays, P. A. (2008). *Addressing cultural complexities in practice: Assessment, diagnosis, and therapy* (2nd ed.). American Psychological Association.

Mohanty, C. T. (1988). Under western eyes: Feminist scholarship and colonial discourses. *Feminist Review, 30,* 61–88. https://doi.org/10.1057/fr.1988

Nsamenang, A. B. (2006). Cultures in early childhood care and education. *UNESCO Policy Brief on Early Childhood, 38,* 1–4.

Portes, A., & Rumbaut, R. G. (2014). *Immigrant America: A portrait* (4th ed.). University of California Press.

Rogoff, B. (2003). *The cultural nature of human development.* Oxford University Press.

Schwartz, S. J., Unger, J. B., Zamboanga, B. L., & Szapocznik, J. (2010). Rethinking the concept of acculturation: Implications for theory and research. *American Psychologist, 65(4),* 237–51. https://doi.org/10.1037/a0019330

Smith, L. T. (1999). *Decolonizing methodologies: Research and Indigenous peoples.* Zed Books.

Chapter 2

From Pathology to Liberation

Decolonizing Family Well-Being

Zain Shamoon and Jarryn Robinson-Ellis

Introduction

This chapter will review the importance of core family needs for communities that have been historically (and are currently) oppressed, using a framework of sociocultural attunement (Knudson-Martin et al., 2020) to address various intersectional family factors. Systemic oppression impacts families in a multitude of ways, including barriers in accessing daily life resources, abusive treatment by various institutions, and a host of disparities with regard to mental health resources.

As such, we (Dr. Zain Shamoon and Dr. Jarryn Robinson-Ellis) will address how family therapists can make space to discuss and act upon the needs of families whose lived experiences exist beyond reductive impositions about what success and development look like. Specific focus will be given to matters of power, as well as racial, religious, and immigrant factors. In our view, true systemic thought must include attention to these factors to adequately address diverse family life cycle needs.

To counter hyper-individualistic notions popularized in Western psychological frameworks, we will discuss *collective needs* for the families discussed throughout this chapter. We also invite readers to consider the information in this chapter as central to our understanding of human development overall, rather than a niche "special topic" that needlessly exoticizes the families in question. We invite readers to interrupt this unhelpful status quo and join us in valuing these families at a fundamental level instead.

Person-of-the-Author

To begin this chapter, each author will share their personal investment in sociocultural attunement and decolonized therapy when working with families. We have both observed systemic barriers to wellness that impact families, both in the lives of clients we work with and in our own lived experiences.

Dr. Zain Shamoon

My (Dr. Shamoon) teen years were spent in an area of post-9/11 xenophobia, with daily encounters of fellow Americans who conflated various countries and peoples to maintain their operative discrimination. I experienced this firsthand on several occasions as a youth, but I decided during my college years to sublimate these experiences into a call to action. In

DOI: 10.4324/9781032679082-4

other words, I found fulfillment and meaning in advocating for groups who are demonized, pathologized, and misunderstood. And even if this ignorance persisted in a wider world, I remember thinking how I would not accept that health providers could maintain these same inhumane stances, especially those who claim to serve the needs of "all people." As such, I spent my graduate years focused on the specific needs of South Asian and Muslim communities (and the intersections between them) to demonstrate proud conviction for my people and their family needs.

My father was a social service provider, and he taught me that nothing is more important than treating other human beings with dignity. I have learned time and time again, through my own experiences and in witnessing the stories of others (as a clinician, in community work, and amongst friends), that American society does not readily provide that dignity. To fight this, we need socioculturally attuned family therapists who understand that impasses to wellness are not simply held in an individual or their family but in society at large.

I do not know how to be a provider without being an advocate, and I am proud of this. I do not see that as a niche professional lane but as a celebratory calling. Colonizers and colonized minds, beware that a renaissance is happening, and it will not be led by white men. It will be led by communities of the global majority and the local knowledges of historically oppressed peoples whose wisdoms have been either pathologized or conveniently appropriated by Western society (including by therapists). I am excited for a new season of professional life where our cultures are celebrated by and for the people who are from them. I am excited to be in a community with the family therapists who will join me in this movement.

Dr. Robinson-Ellis

Growing up a Black girl in America is a complex and nuanced experience. I was raised in a household that ensured we were educated (myself and my siblings) on the history of triumph and oppression for generations of Black people before us. As I began to explore the world more deeply in my teenage years, I saw how various aspects of my identity impacted my experiences in unique ways. Being a girl meant facing sexism, and being Black meant confronting racism, but being both simultaneously created a distinct reality that couldn't be fully captured by discussing either alone. I realized that the struggles and triumphs of Black women like me were often sidelined in broader conversations about race and gender. This realization ignited a passion in me for advocating for an integration of intersectionality in all discussions about justice and equality. This ultimately led me to pursue a profession that I felt intentionally advocated for the consideration of nuance and facilitated the development of skills that honored identities and context when considering the manifestations of distress.

I began to seek out stories and voices that resonated with my own, those that understood the nuanced reality of navigating life as a Black woman. I found solace in the writings of scholars like Kimberlé Crenshaw, who articulated the need to consider the intersections of various identities when addressing social justice. This framework empowered me, helping me to articulate my own experiences and those of others in my community. I started to see the world differently, recognizing that true justice and equality could only be achieved when all aspects of a person's identity are acknowledged and valued. Through my dissertation, I was able to highlight a research agenda that encapsulated that passion. I want to create spaces where the voices of those who experience multiple forms of marginalization are not just heard but centered. I believe in a future where young Black girls like me can grow up seeing themselves reflected in the narratives of justice, where their unique experiences are recognized and celebrated. It is through this lens of intersectionality that I seek to contribute to a world that is more equitable and inclusive, not just for some but for all.

Decolonizing Spaces of Service

To effectively serve diverse family needs, adequate attention must be given to how oppression and misuse of power have hurt so many families. These misuses of power include colonizing ideas about families of the global majority that frame them as pathological or less evolved than Western "norms." As such, we charge that wellness can only exist for families at various intersections if *liberation* from dehumanization is part of the way we approach our therapeutic work. In her writings about love and justice in the book *All About Love: New Visions*, bell hooks explains that "Cultures of domination rely on the cultivation of fear as a way to ensure obedience" (hooks, 2018, p. 93). She also writes, "When greedy consumption is the order of the day, dehumanization becomes acceptable. Then, treating people like objects is not only acceptable but is required behavior" (p. 115). When unjust societal infrastructures are meant to serve the few instead of the many, and many communities are painted by mass media (and by many Western psychological textbooks) as fundamentally pathological, then resistance to these norms is necessary to foster more health for families at large.

Moreover, it would be naive to believe that these forces of domination and oppression have not permeated the world of psychotherapy, as well as couple and family therapy. For those who claim to "serve diverse populations," it is essential to address how our systems of care fundamentally block care from migrant families, refugee communities, racial minorities, and religious minorities. Not only do our infrastructures block care, but these very systems also reinforce harm and trauma upon those communities. To decolonize spaces of services and address family needs equitably, there must be a paradigm shift in how we teach about public wellness.

As such, we ought to train the providers who occupy those spaces to think differently from status quo impositions about "normal family needs." In other words, spaces of service cannot be decolonized until the minds of providers are also decolonized. For example, Champine et al. (2022) suggest the following strategies to counteract structural racism in the ways we consider public wellness:

- Circulate course materials about public wellness that reflect an anti-racist mission focused on health equity.
- Intersectionality should be a fundamental consideration in all our work.
- Students in the field should be encouraged to engage in critical self-reflexivity.

In our teaching in a COAMFTE-accredited Couple and Family Therapy (CFT) graduate program, both of us utilize the Person of the Therapist (POTT) framework for therapist reflexivity, where students are required to consider the personal themes that come up for them when conducting therapy (Aponte et al., 2009). We believe that training programs like these can go a long way in helping providers attend to intersectional matters in the therapy room and that this will help them become less reactive to their prejudicial issues, which are steeped in colonized socialization or white supremacy.

Another way to transform spaces of services into becoming more equitable and just is to consider the larger contexts that impact family and individual wellness. This contradicts assumptions that symptoms *live inside* people or that people are prone to certain patholo-gies due to their cultures or identities. One way to counter these assumptions is to adopt a *human ecological* framework in addressing family needs (Bronfenbrenner, 1986). In doing so, assessments for individual and family needs during therapy can consider how ecologi-cal matters such as laws, policies, racism, and disparities in access to services impact men-tal health. Family therapists can spend quality time with those they serve discussing these matters, validating the challenges that these ecological conditions present, and codesigning pathways of care that have to do with removing access barriers in people's lives. One exam-ple of this could be to collaboratively complete a cultural genogram (Hardy & Laszloffy, 1995) alongside a conversation about honored intergenerational and cultural traditions that have been preserved, even as these families have experienced systemic challenges along the way. Doing an activity like this is counter to the hyper-pathological and hyper-diagnostic systems that form alliances based on *presenting problems*. Instead, the focus would be on honoring each family's *cultural being* in a fundamental way (rather than as a niche subject or afterthought). Decolonizing spaces of services means adopting an ongoing commitment to context sensitivity instead of pathology in these ways.

Pause and Envision

We introduced the cultural genogram here and how it can be used to decolonize spaces of service. To clarify the application of this exercise, it would be beneficial to provide an exam-ple of how this intervention can be introduced and implemented. Below is a brief look into a family therapy session where the therapist introduces and navigates a cultural genogram with a current family client.

Therapist: I'd love for us to explore something called a cultural genogram. This tool helps us visually map out family relationships, traditions, values, and essential cul-tural influences that have shaped your family over time. It allows us to see patterns, strengths, and challenges that may influence your experiences today. Would you all be open to cocreating this?

(Family agrees.)

Therapist: We'll start by sketching out a basic family tree. We'll also add elements that help us understand your cultural background. This could include things like migra-tion stories, religious or spiritual beliefs, languages spoken, traditions passed down, or even messages you received about emotions, success, or relationships.

(Therapist begins drawing the structure.)

Therapist: For example, let's say your family has a strong tradition of passing down fam-ily recipes—maybe that's been passed down for generations. Or maybe there were messages about community and the influence of considering our impact on those around us. These cultural pieces help us see how family values have shaped each of you.

(Therapist asks guiding questions while adding details to the genogram.)

- What traditions or rituals do your family have that feel important to you?
- Were there any major migrations or moves in your family history?
- How did your family talk about emotions when you were growing up?
- Are there any religious beliefs that have influenced how your family operates?

(As the genogram develops, the therapist reflects back, and family members deepen the richness of their shared experiences.)

Therapist: This genogram helps us honor the strengths and resilience within your family while also noticing areas where different values may cause tension. Ideally, this gives us a way to talk about how these cultural pieces shape your family dynamics and how we can use this awareness to strengthen your relationships moving forward.

Ideally, this example provides insight into how a therapist can incorporate a cultural genogram into their practice, expanding foundational couple and family therapy interventions to deepen their understanding of culture's influence on the family system. As we continue to deconstruct information in this chapter, think about ways to reimagine the cultural genogram in clinical work.

Another way to work towards the decolonization of family therapy is to address health disparities that impact mental health, placing the responsibility of change on harmful infrastructures instead of the people who have to survive them. Dannis et al. (2023) discuss the health damage upon children following the Flint, Michigan, water crisis. In reviewing how the community had been exposed to unsafe drinking water for a prolonged period, their research showed how already existing health disparities can amplify pediatric-health challenges. Said another way, the damaging effects of environmental disasters (in this case, *human-made* water pollution) upon children and their families are emulsified when there are barriers to health services anyway. Without discussing the health inequities that are embedded in these challenges, family therapists would be at risk of implying that mental health distress is something to solve rather than to validate as a natural human response to inequality and lack of structural protection by lawmakers and governing leaders. Naming the social forces that harm families is called *externalizing the problem* in Narrative therapy (White & Epston, 1990), a form of treatment that requires clinicians to apply systems thinking beyond family patterns alone. In other words, people are not distressed because they have not self cared enough. People are distressed because their conditions are distressing, and shared acknowledgment of this with one's therapist can foster relief and reduce internalizations of shame/guilt.

Another essential way therapists and clinical educators can work toward decolonization is to challenge corruption in our institutions and workplaces. In our view, this means challenging leaders in the field who misuse their power, including chancellors of universities, government officials, and even popular therapists in the field who ignore health disparities or use pathological language to discuss members of society depending on their identities. They may include challenging leaders' language about peaceful gatherings or protests when those institutions frame them as "disrespectful" or "hateful." These misuses of language are often used to obfuscate facts and penalize people when they call for the humanization of diverse populations. There are many examples that abound in the current global landscape regarding these institutional harms, including many racist and xenophobic proclamations of people of color or those who support a liberated Congo, Sudan, Palestine, and so forth.

This resistance to pathological frameworks also applies to disenfranchised groups, which we will address in this chapter. As will be discussed, working with migrant and refugee groups who are dealing with the pressures of acculturation requires cultural humility and an honoring of their traditions on the part of the therapist. In this way, the clinical goal is not simply to help families "adapt" to social norms or to force them to reshape their identities. Instead, it is to honor their heritages as part of our therapeutic alliance with these families.

Decolonization challenges not only the pathologizing narratives imposed upon marginalized communities but also the hyper-individualistic lens through which wellness is often framed in Western mental health paradigms. Suppose we are to address the impact of structural inequities on families meaningfully. In that case, we must also embrace the power of collective healing, recognizing that wellness is deeply rooted in relationships, communities, and cultural traditions. This shift calls for a move away from isolating, deficit-based models of care toward frameworks that honor interdependence as a fundamental human strength.

Collective Gathering as a Form of Resistance

We would like to draw attention to instances of communal and family gatherings as a fundamental form of liberation from hyper-individualism embedded in Western mental health frameworks. These hyper-individualistic norms may take the form of over-explanatory individual pathology, insurances that cover individual care more readily than family or couple sessions, and a host of other examples that prioritize the individual over the collective unit. As a counter to this, family systems perspectives call providers to consider the value of bringing more than one person into the therapy room. Rich examples are apparent in popular family therapy frameworks, such as in *family therapy using the Satir process* (Loeshen, 2020), Framo's *family-of-origin* therapy (Framo, 1976), or in the structural family therapy work of Salvador Minuchin (Minuchin & Fishman, 1981).

To truly decolonize therapy, the collectivism embedded within many of the world's cultures, including the intersectional cultures of both present authors, must be celebrated as a core strength. When mental health providers observe collective gatherings and cultural celebrations as mental health resources, then group therapy, family therapy, and other mental health gatherings in the community can be seen as viable spaces for healing. While privacy and individual spaces are essential, this can be conflated with the isolation that keeps people from the networks of care we should be tapping into. Too often, we have encountered notions in our work that the collective unit is "traditional," "archaic," or a threat to individual wellness. Another common judgment about strong relationships is the fear of "codependence," a framework that does not make room for exploring healthy *interdependence*. This thin framework only serves to justify the pathology of collectivist cultures and to remove people from collective talents and resources. As bell hooks states, "Rarely, if ever, are any of us healed in isolation. Healing is an act of communion" (hooks, 2018, p. 215).

We charge family therapists to adopt this as a core sensibility, addressing not only the family unit as an essential unit of wellness but also the neighborhoods, communities, and kinship systems surrounding them. Doing so would allow us to focus on the following proposed action items:

- Build greater neighborhood bonds through communal events and direct clients to these spaces.
- Minimize community threats, such as counteracting over-policing and reducing costs for basic family needs.
- Advocating for family-based legislation (such as proper leave time for the entire parental unit after children are born into the family).
- Support affinity groups in their identity intersections as a refuge and mental wellness source.
- Help those who peacefully gather in upholding their convictions, such as when clients share with us that they have protested something in a peaceful manner or that they attended a communal event that uplifted their mental health.

Considering these types of action items becomes more possible when family therapists consider the power of the collective unit.

For therapists to leverage collective family strengths, counteracting Western fears of "enmeshment," questions can be asked to extract *knowledge* about the collective unit. For example, a therapist could ask any of the following questions:

1. What is the story of your family, and what is the desired family story going forward?
2. In what ways does supporting each other support individual growth at the same time?
3. What have you all done together recently or in the past that you value highly?
4. How can families have boundaries while experiencing a tight bond at the same time?

Asking questions like this indicates to clients that the therapist observes *self* and *other* as unifying, instead of oppositional, forces. Beyond this, therapists can also ask questions such as:

1. What are the ways in which you can continue to find community and belonging in your lives?
2. What values from your family lineage do you want to carry forward from your family lineage, and how?
3. In what ways are you already living out your desired family legacy?
4. How do you honor your people?
5. What type of community experiences do you need to support your family goals?

These questions represent the family therapist axiom that *one's client is the relationship instead of simply each individual*. More therapists need to demonstrate this conviction in how they speak to clients from collectivist backgrounds. These conversations can also be paired with discussions about cultural organizations and community connections that are part of the client's overall goals for wellness.

Isomorphism and Sociocultural Attunement

We refer to *isomorphism* as a concept of reciprocal and ongoing influence between multiple layers of any system, be it a family system, couple system, or therapeutic system. Todd

(1989) argues that *isomorphism* is a central component of the therapeutic relationship, an essential common factor of positive therapeutic change (Sprenkle & Blow, 2004). Instructors from our couple and family therapy department have written about the utility of this concept, discussing "The Isomorphism of POTT" (Pennant & Shamoon, p. 186) as a parallel process between instructors and students, where highly reflexive students inspire the professors' introspection and vice versa.

It is essential to address how this parallel process can also be applied to sociocultural attunement in family therapy (Knudson-Martin et al., 2020), where attuned therapists inspire cultural reflexivity from their clients and vice versa. Personal accounts from friends and colleagues have included testimonials that therapy is not always a culturally sensitive space. In our estimation, the exception is when therapists set the stage for culturally attuned care, demonstrating their willingness to listen and broach a host of cultural topics impacting clients' lives. The more inspired the clinician is to do this work, the more the isomorphic exchange will allow the client to bring out relevant cultural topics.

This must include attention to matters of power and oppression in society that impact mental health for families. When family therapists signal that they *will* tend to these matters, such as in their website biographies or in their introductions to clients in the first session, this can let clients know that the therapy sessions can also include cultural broaching. Signaling this about the system of care has the potential to inspire more openness from the client. Similarly, if one is aware that their therapist cares about matters of power out in the world, such as when having extensive anti-racist training or writing articles about *third-order* change, in this case, one can invite clients to open up about how oppression has impacted their mental health. There is no shortage of this in our current world, where clients may be spending time *doom-scrolling* on social media or observing a live genocide on their phones. When therapists demonstrate that their therapeutic care will not shy away from these matters, the parallel process allows for a richer exchange, tending to multiple factors that impact family, couple, and individual wellness. This contrasts any therapeutic approach that deems itself *apolitical* or devoid of care about the outside world and its power structures. We contend that therapists cannot be truly systemic if they do not attend to the isomorphic parallel between society and families or between therapists' and clients' willingness to "go there."

Power and oppression shape our understanding of intersectionality and the complexity of converging identities. In the next section, we will examine how intersectionality deepens our comprehension of complex lived experiences and their impact on transitions through the family life cycle. Additionally, we will explore what decolonization looks like when approached through an intersectional lens.

Intersectionality and Family Life Cycle Needs

Rooted in the work of Black feminists (i.e., Kimberle Crenshaw), Indigenous scholars, and postcolonial theorists, intersectionality theory challenges the notion that identity categories can be understood in isolation (Hankivsky et al., 2014). Instead, it posits that these categories are inextricably linked and mutually constitutive, shaping an individual's access to power, privilege, and marginalization (Gopaldas, 2013). For Couple and Family therapists (CFTs), intersectionality parallels the systemic lens from which the discipline is rooted. Systems theory tells us that people are better understood from the complex network of identities and environmental connections that they exist in.

In the context of couple and family therapy, intersectionality allows educators, students, and practitioners to engage clients and communities from a framework that honors the converging context of their lived experiences. This will enable CFTs to align with the systemic perspectives of the more socially attuned modalities of the field to offer holistic support and treatment to clients. Within the family life cycle context, intersectionality becomes particularly pertinent as it sheds light on the nuanced ways these identities shape familial roles, relationships, and transitions. Families do not experience life stages—such as marriage, parenting, and aging—in isolation but are deeply affected by the intersecting social categories that members embody (Van Hook & Glick, 2020).

Moreover, intersectionality reveals the differential impacts of societal structures and policies on family experiences. Immigrant families, for instance, often face unique challenges related to cultural assimilation, legal status, and economic stability that intersect with their familial roles and responsibilities. By incorporating an intersectional perspective, clinicians and educators can better understand and address the complexities of family dynamics, ensuring more inclusive and effective therapeutic interventions. By adopting an intersectional lens, family therapists can gain a deeper understanding of the complex dynamics that influence family dynamics, relationships, and overall well-being (Figueroa et al., 2021). This approach encourages clinicians to move beyond simplistic, single-factor analyses and instead consider the intricate web of social, cultural, and historical factors contributing to an individual's or family's experiences (Gopaldas, 2013).

Expanding Beyond Oppressive Conceptualizations of Human Development—A Liberated Life Cycle Approach

If we accept that layers of social systems impact each other, such as described by Bronfenbrenner's (1986) human ecological model, then intersectionalities produced therein should be a common understanding for systemic thinkers. However, we have both met practitioners who claim to care about systems, though the analysis stops at the family unit. In other words, systems thinking seems to be only applied by way of people's comfort, excusing them from broaching topics that make them uncomfortable or topics that may require their own reflexivity and/or accountability.

If we accept that systems thinking *must* go beyond the family unit, then expanding our view of the family life cycle is inevitable. An expanded view of family life would consider all the social forces that impact families, including laws, acculturation stresses, health disparities, and so on. One way to expand our understanding of human development is to consider development as nonlinear. For example, consider collectivist family homes or collectivist kinship systems, where "launching" from the home is not a set milestone as it would be for a hyper-individualist framework. Consider the trope that one who "has not left the nest" has failed to begin their adult life. This rigid life cycle paradigm fundamentally pathologizes all cultures where members of kinship systems live close by or live together.

Under a Western and hyper-individualistic framework, these intergenerational bonds would be described as *enmeshed* without further assessment required. Therapists who claim to be systemic but do not take into account the resourcefulness of such kinship systems would be in danger of reinforcing this unhelpful pathologizing. Instead of deciding for families whether they are *meeting their* milestones or not based on archaic and colonizing ideas of what family life *should look like,* therapists can cocreate nonlinear family timelines with clients during sessions, validating and celebrating their divergence from Western norms.

We find it essential to acknowledge that, as a Western society shaped by Western ideals, we often reduce collectivism to a perceived loss of individual agency. However, true decolonization of our understanding of collectivism requires recognizing that agency and connectedness are not mutually exclusive—they can and must coexist. Our sense of self is formed through autonomy and relational interconnectedness, and embracing this duality allows for a more holistic and liberated perspective on collective well-being.

Another way an expanded family life cycle framework could be achieved in therapy is through collective storytelling. Family members can be invited to celebrate their cultural traditions in the *here-and-now* moments of therapy. Recently, a prospective client came to me, (Dr. Zain Shamoon), for a consultation. She reported to me that her current therapist's views required her to hide cultural and religious aspects of her identity for fear of the therapist viewing her as a "woman who is not free." When therapists choose a liberated pathway that not only counteracts such prejudice but invites clients to tell layered stories about their cultural backgrounds instead (which may include simultaneous reflections about traumas, challenges, successes, and celebrations), a liberated life cycle model can come alive in our therapy sessions.

Acculturation and Family Life Cycle Development—Race and Ethnicity

Race and Ethnicity are significant tenets to consider when exploring the decolonization of wellness in this country. In a National Institutes of Health article by Thomas G. McGuire and Jeanne Miranda (2008), they explore statistical and research-based evidence to support the assumption that a significant disparity exists between BIPOC people and their white counterparts when studying mental health care. Scholarly literature continues to substantiate that accessibility, willingness to procure, and quality of care all inform the use of mental health resources to deal with several mental health disorders and wellness-related issues. Research shows that racial minorities often experience higher rates of chronic diseases, mental health disparities, and premature mortality (Williams & Mohammed, 2013). This can be attributed to a complex interplay of factors, including discrimination, bias in health care settings, and the stress of navigating a society where racism is pervasive. Addressing these disparities requires acknowledging and dismantling structural racism while promoting equitable access to resources that support the well-being of all racial groups.

The traditional notion of the "nuclear family" has been challenged by the emergence of a wide range of alternative family forms, such as single-parent families, stepfamilies, cohabiting couples, older-parent families, adoptive families, same-sex families, and multiracial families (Powell et al., 2018). These diverse family structures reflect the changing social, cultural, and political landscape, and therapists need to approach them without the lens of pathology or judgment. A crucial aspect of depathologizing different family structures is acknowledging these families' resilience and adaptability.

The dynamics of multiethnic, immigrant, and transnational families are complex as they must navigate the integration of members living in host societies and those dispersed across multiple home societies (Trask, 2013). Acculturation, the process of cultural and psychological change that occurs when individuals from different cultural backgrounds come into contact, can significantly impact family relationships and structures (Bhui et al., 2012). Existing research has found that as minority ethnic groups in the United States face the economic, social, and psychological challenges of the dominant culture, it often results in changes to family roles and dynamics. These changes in family structure can highlight areas of concern within the system while also introducing new challenges within the family based on the newness of the cultural norms they are attempting to integrate (Van Hood & Glick, 2020).

As such, family therapists are uniquely positioned to affirm the cultural and intersectional ways families *are* instead of imposing oppressive demands about who they ought to be. Doing so can look like adopting concepts from narrative therapy (White & Epston, 1990), where acculturation demands can be effectively externalized rather than blaming family members for "failure" to adjust. In doing so, it will be important to affirm that the stress from dissonances between societal demands and the family's lived experiences are real. In this way, affirming both the challenges of an oppressive society and affirming the client's cultural constellation can be done simultaneously. To achieve this, therapists can ask questions, like:

1. What are the barriers you are facing in preserving your values? What resources do you need to navigate this? (Rather than asking what they need to conform or fit in.)
2. What are the ways you can continue to celebrate values that are important to you? (Rather than asking clients what they need to adjust towards Western values.)

As previously stated, this open-ended exploration includes *rich story descriptions* (White & Epston, 1990) by way of inviting family members to share their acculturation journeys, adjustments *they* would like to make to navigate their circumstances, and their ancestors' life cycle stories and triumphs. In true narrative therapy form, these conversations can represent story plots that exist outside of imposed norms and pressures; these plots are referred to as unique outcomes (and historical, unique outcomes) in narrative therapy (White & Epston, 1990).

The following three sections will highlight key systemic considerations in family therapy, focusing on refugee and immigrant families and the role of religion in shaping therapeutic approaches.

Spotlighting Family Needs: Refugee Families

Specific attention should also be paid to the unique needs of refugee families. These families are forced to flee their countries due to oppressive factors and are managing many life cycle shifts at once, including those that are unexpected and traumatic.

In their community-based participatory research (CBPR), Rosenberg et al. (2022) provide the example of Afghani refugee families, where parents in these families described acculturation stress and having to adjust to a new country's systems, among other factors, in arriving in the United States. If family therapists were to miss these contextually sensitive themes, such as having newfound relief from the trauma of prolonged wars in Afghanistan (Rosenberg et al., 2022), changing family needs and parenting roles may not be supported adequately. In other words, mental health professionals need to examine evolving communication needs between parents and children rather than assume that family roles are static in the way that they were before the family arrived in the United States. In addition, family therapists can validate refugee acculturation stress in sessions directly and pair this with opportunities for parents and children to broach Afghani cultural topics. This can help with the integration process of families adjusting to a new country without imposing the pressure of leaving their culture behind.

Bürgin et al. (2022) take a multi-level approach to understanding the needs of children who have endured the conditions of war. This includes supporting not only the children through trauma-informed and strengths-based care but also ensuring resources and support for their parents. Their multilevel approach also calls for professionals to consider advocacy and "political action" when considering the needs of these children. This fits with our call for socioculturally attuned and trained family therapists to understand their professional roles beyond the therapy room and to mend the systemic conditions that impact families in the first place. Bürgin et al. (2022) note that "collective engagement" is necessary to reduce negative impacts on children who have endured war, and this, of course, includes refugee children. We encourage readers of this chapter to consider their commitments to healing that go beyond therapy sessions and into third-order change opportunities.

Despite specific risks for a range of mental health challenges, including social adversity and discrimination, refugee families rarely encounter empirically backed services that reflect their lived conditions or family needs (Weine, 2011). As such, Weine suggests that a socioculturally attuned and ecological approach is necessary to develop more contextually sensitive support. Among other factors, contextually sensitive variables may include feasibility, whether the refugee families accept the interventions offered, cultural fit, and the extent to which interventions are effective in real-life situations for these families (Weine, 2011). Weine also discusses the importance of community collaborations and resilience-based approaches to preventative intervention design. This fits our charge that respecting family needs at the intersections must be systemic. As it stands, far too many mental health services are produced without utilizing the wisdom of these communities, leaving refugee families neglected.

The importance of culturally sensitive and family-centered care for refugees was also demonstrated in the research of Eruyar et al. (2018), where a cross-sectional study was conducted with 263 Syrian refugee child-parent dyads in Turkey. In observing the link between war trauma and post-traumatic stress in children, this research demonstrated the importance of parental mental health in promoting wellness among children. As such, family therapists trained in the reciprocal process of parent and child mental health wellness are well-suited to help these families. Additionally, this study demonstrated the importance of cultural fit in research and produced questionnaires in bilingual formats, such as the Arabic and Turkish ones used in Eruyar et al.'s research. These researchers agree with our charge for a human ecological approach in serving diverse populations, such as Syrian refugee families. They state, and we agree, that "child development cannot be fully understood without considering the child's relationship with their micro- (parents, teachers, and peers) and macro-environment (community, culture, and religion)" (Eruyar et al., 2018, p. 407).

Spotlighting Family Needs: Immigrant Families

The unique contexts of immigrant families should also be addressed from a place of sociocultural attunement. Young et al. (2024) review the unique needs of unaccompanied immigrant children who arrive in the United States from the Mexican border. They discuss that these children often experience long waiting periods, during which they may not have proper medical evaluation, food, or shelter. Furthermore, Young et al. point out that when they do receive care from professionals, this may be from untrained and unqualified personnel who do not work from a place of contextual or cultural sensitivity. The damage of this is compounded by the extended amounts of time these children will spend in holding areas, where they are at risk for a variety of harms upon release. Given the grave nature of these children's conditions, we will review specific recommendations from Young et al. (2024). Although these suggestions are meant for federal funding institutions, we believe these action items are well-suited for the role of socioculturally attuned family therapists. These suggestions are:

1. Providers who take care of immigrant children should have proper training, onboarding, and recertification expectations.
2. The unique needs of immigrant health should be centered in the care provided.
3. Professionals should be educated in trauma-focused care.
4. Interpreters and bilingual providers are essential.
5. Discharge from services should be thoughtful as to prevent children from the risks of harm (such as the potential of ongoing abuse, poor mental health, social marginalization, and a high risk of being trafficked or exploited).

Concerning the latter suggestion, Young et al. encourage focusing on providing these children with a social worker (this can also be a family therapist) for at least twelve months post-discharge so that proper connections to services can be made. This may include advocating for mental health support, full-time schooling, and connections to nonprofits that focus centrally on immigrant needs. In this way, socioculturally attuned therapists can understand their service roles in ways that go beyond the therapy room. For instance, Young et al. suggest that immigrant children's needs can be more adequately met when community healthcare providers are trained in culturally sensitive ways that respond to their contextual needs. Family therapists trained in systems theory or socio-culturally attuned therapy methods are well-suited to provide these trainings.

Family therapists also ought to be networked to appropriate advocacy services and public programs that support immigrant families so that proper referrals to these services can be made without consequences to the children or families in question. Kapadia (2024) discusses the combined nature of various threats to children who are taken away from their families if their parents are criminally charged for crossing the border "without permission" or for "operational" reasons. In addition to the layered trauma incurred by these children, Kapadia points out that they are subject to poor sanitary conditions and lack food options when held by our government.

Family therapists who are trained in systemic viewing can find alignment with Kapadia's call to consider practices, policies, and xenophobic frameworks that negatively impact these children and their families. One way to combat this is to provide affirming family therapy, which is culturally centered and focused on the well-being of immigrant children directly. Another way of demonstrating attunement to immigrant family needs is to be in constant connection with public programs and services that do not have punitive or harmful infrastructures. This is because, as Kapadia points out, immigrant families may refuse to participate in public programs out of fear that this may impede their ability to obtain US citizenship. Receiving care without punitive measures or punishment is essential, especially as these families are already under heavy duress. Family therapists are well suited to use their systemic thinking to seek out state, local, and community organizations that provide adequate and culturally sensitive care without significant consequences. In our view, socioculturally attuned therapists should connect immigrant families and their children to these services and consider this as part of true systemic therapeutic care.

Spotlighting Family Needs: Religion

More attention should also be paid to the needs of families across religious groups, with a specific focus on how religiosity and spirituality impact mental health. In a qualitative study interviewing social service providers, Weng (2017) found important themes of support for "nondominant" racial and religious groups. Weng points out that these groups are at increased risk for discrimination due to their racial or religious identities or both. Weng notes that their study's purpose is to counteract societal harms that are inflicted upon religious and racial minority groups, which social service providers are uniquely suited to support. However, suppose these providers' attitudes and beliefs are not interrogated. In that case, clients from specific religious backgrounds are at risk for experiencing compounding instances of discrimination or alienation in therapy itself. Qualitative themes identified in this research included (a) marginalization of small-sized religious and racial groups, (b) the importance of religious organizations in mental health wellness, and (c) the importance of intersectional understandings for race and religion in mental health services. This fits with our call for intersectional viewing when considering family-level needs in mental health.

Weng (2017) highlights a theme in the research study that found that "social service providers believe social service organizations can partner with religious organizations to better meet the needs of the clients" (p. 159). Here again, sociocultural attunement and true systemic care extend beyond the therapy room, such as was noted for immigrant and refugee families. Instead of considering religious and nonreligious support entities as separate and with unrelated functions, Weng suggests that these variables can be used in concert. As such, family therapists would do well to gather information about local mosques, churches, and so forth. Reciprocally, it would behoove family therapists, including those who may not be religious themselves but claim to serve diverse populations, to let local religious organizations know about their therapy services. We also want to highlight that Weng (2017) calls for the visibility of religious and racial minorities to enhance the likelihood of mental health services for these groups.

Conclusion

This chapter has underscored the necessity of sociocultural attunement in understanding and addressing the lived realities of historically oppressed communities in an effort to actualize a decolonized lens of systemic intervention. Western therapeutic frameworks often pathologize nondominant family structures, overlooking the broader ecological influences that shape family dynamics. This chapter aims to affirm that true systemic care must center the voices, traditions, and resilience of the families it seeks to serve. Liberation is not an unattainable aspiration—it is an active and resolute commitment that must be reflected in therapeutic practice, education, and advocacy. We call on family therapists and allied professionals to critically examine your own socialization and dissect oppressive narratives. In doing this, we began actualizing an approach to well-being rooted in justice, dignity, and collective care.

References

Aponte, H. J., Powell, F. D., Brooks, S., Watson, M. F., Litzke, C., Lawless, J., & Johnson, E. (2009). Training the person of the therapist in an academic setting. *Journal of Marital and Family Therapy*, *35*(4), 381–94. https://doi.org/10.1111/j.1752-0606.2009.00123.x

Bronfenbrenner, U. (1986). Ecology of the family as a context for human development: Research perspectives. *Developmental Psychology, 22*(6), 723–42. https://doi.org/10.1037/0012-1649.22.6.723

Bürgin, D., Anagnostopoulos, D., Board and Policy Division of ESCAP, Vitiello, B., Sukale, T., Schmid, M., & Fegert, J. M. (2022). Impact of war and forced displacement on children's mental health-multilevel, needs-oriented, and trauma-informed approaches. *European Child & Adolescent Psychiatry, 31*(6), 845–53. https://doi.org/10.1007/s00787-022-01974-z

Champine, R. B., McCullough, W. R., & El Reda, D. K. (2022). Critical race theory for public health students to recognize and eliminate structural racism. *American Journal of Public Health, 112*(6), 850–52. https://doi.org/10.2105/AJPH.2022.306846

Dannis, J., Jenuwine, S., Jones, N., LaChance, J., & Hanna-Attisha, M. (2023). Child mental health status in Flint, Michigan: A worsening health inequity, 2018–2022. *American Journal of Public Health, 113*(12), 1318–21. https://doi.org/10.2105/AJPH.2023.307406

Eruyar, S., Maltby, J., & Vostanis, P. (2018). Mental health problems of Syrian refugee children: the role of parental factors. *European Child & Adolescent Psychiatry, 27*(4), 401–09. https://doi.org/10.1007/s00787-017-1101-0

Figueroa, C A., Luo, T C., Aguilera, A., & Lyles, C R. (2021). The need for feminist intersectionality in digital health. *Lancet Digital Health, 3*(8), e526–33. https://doi.org/10.1016/s2589-7500(21)00118-7

Framo J. L. (1976). Family of origin as a therapeutic resource for adults in marital and family therapy: You can and should go home again. *Family Process, 15*(2), 193–210. https://doi.org/10.1111/j.1545-5300.1976.00193.x

Gopaldas, A. (2013). Intersectionality 101. *Journal of Public Policy & Marketing, 32*(1_suppl), 90–94. https://doi.org/10.1509/jppm.12.044

Hankivsky, O., Grace, D., Hunting, G., Giesbrecht, M., Fridkin, A., Rudrum, S., Ferlatte, O., & Clark, N. (2014). An intersectionality-based policy analysis framework: critical reflections on a methodology for advancing equity. *International Journal for Equity in Health, 13*(1). https://doi.org/10.1186/s12939-014-0119-x

Hardy, K. V., & Laszloffy, T. A. (1995). The cultural genogram: Key to training culturally competent family therapists. *Journal of Marital and Family Therapy, 21*(3), 227–37. https://doi.org/10.1111/j.1752-0606.1995.tb00158.x

hooks, b. (2018). *All About Love: New Visions*. HarperCollins.

Kapadia F. (2024). Protecting immigrant children: A public health of consequence, March 2024. *American Journal of Public Health, 114*(3), 267–69. https://doi.org/10.2105/AJPH.2023.307569

Knudson-Martin, C., McDowell, T., & Bermudez, J. M. (2020). Sociocultural attunement in systemic family therapy. In K. S. Wampler, R. B. Miller, & R. B. Seedall (Eds.), *The handbook of systemic family therapy: The profession of systemic family therapy* (pp. 619–37). Wiley Blackwell. https://doi.org/10.1002/9781119790181.ch27

Loeschen, S. (2020). Family therapy using the Satir process. *Social Work. Experience & Methods/ Socialinis Darbas: Patirtis ir Metodai, 26*(2). https://doi.org/10.7220/2029-5820.26.2.3

McGuire, T. G., & Miranda, J. (2008). New evidence regarding racial and ethnic disparities in mental health: policy implications. *Health affairs (Project Hope), 27*(2), 393–403. https://doi.org/10.1377/hlthaff.27.2.393

Minuchin, S., & Fishman, H. C. (1981). *Family therapy techniques*. Harvard University Press. https://doi.org/10.2307/j.ctvjnrtsx

Pennant, A., & Shamoon, Z. (2022). Reflections on implementing the POTT program in a master's clinical program. *Australian and New Zealand Journal of Family Therapy, 43*(2), 182–96. https://doi.org/10.1002/anzf.1492

Rosenberg, J., Leung, J. K., Harris, K., Abdullah, A., Rohbar, A., Brown, C., & Rosenthal, M. S. (2022). Recently-arrived Afghan refugee parents' perspectives about parenting, education and pediatric medical and mental health care services. *Journal of Immigrant and Minority Health, 24*(2), 481–88. https://doi.org/10.1007/s10903-021-01206-7

Sprenkle, D. H., & Blow, A. J. (2004). Common factors and our sacred models. *Journal of Marital and Family Therapy, 30*, 113–29. https://doi.org/10.1111/j.1752-0606.2004.tb01228.x

Todd, T. (1989). *Becoming isomorphic: A model for family therapy.* (Publication No. 6444404) [Doctoral dissertation, Iowa State University] Iowa State University digital repository. https://doi.org/10.31274/rtd-180813-10262

Van Hook, J., & Glick, J. E. (2020). Spanning borders, cultures, and generations: A decade of research on immigrant families. *Journal of marriage and the family, 82*(1), 224–43. https://doi.org/10.1111/jomf.12621

White, M., & Epston, D. (1990). *Narrative means to therapeutic ends.* W. W. Norton.

Weine S. M. (2011). Developing preventive mental health interventions for refugee families in resettlement. *Family Process, 50*(3), 410–30. https://doi.org/10.1111/j.1545-5300.2011.01366.x

Weng, S. S. (2017). Race and religion in social services. *Race and Social Problems, 9*(2), 150–62. https://doi.org/10.1007/s12552-017-9194-0

Young, J., Binford, W., Bochenek, M. G., & Greenbaum, J. (2024). Health risks of unaccompanied immigrant children in federal custody and in US communities. *American Journal of Public Health, 114*(3), 340–46. https://doi.org/10.2105/AJPH.2023.307570

Chapter 3

Beyond the Binary
Decolonizing Gender, Sexuality, and Family Development

Sar Surmick

Introduction

When we begin to explore sex, gender, sexuality, relationships, and families, there is always the question "Am I enough?"—Good enough? Right enough? Normal enough? These thoughts can haunt us so much that we stop looking to avoid the doubt and pain. We avoid the question "Who am I?" out of fear; fear is influenced by a system that doesn't want a true answer.

Working to decolonize how therapy views these topics touches on our most intimate identities. It's easy to be daunted by the conversation. We're working with multiple interconnected identities, highly influenced and impacted by culture, that can feel taboo to talk or even think about. It's a lot. And it's an important part of how we move away from "tradition" toward creating more inclusive spaces for clients to explore and express their authenticity.

Together, we will explore how to embrace "Who am I?" as part of decolonization. We will journey together with multiple clients amidst their struggles. We will come to a fundamental truth: working against colonized pressures and mandates starts with awareness and ends with authenticity. For in being our truer selves, whoever they are, we begin to move toward freedom and throw off the legacies of the past.

Person-of-the-Author

My name is Sar, a name I chose over a decade ago in my search for a truer self. I grew up Joseph, Joe, or Joey; names were given to me in love but were rooted in a false assumption. I was not a boy, and yet everyone saw me that way. My identity as a child and young adult was tied to my genitalia and social expectations. As I journeyed and discovered more of myself, I couldn't keep the old name. I needed something more, and Sar became that for me.

I am a white psychology professor and therapist pushing beyond middle age. I live in Washington state on ancestral lands taken from the Coast Salish people. I live a middle-class lifestyle, manage an invisible disability or two, work too much, and I am not normal. In terms of this chapter, there are some other things you should know about me:

- Sex: Intersex by choice (AMAB—Assigned Male at Birth)
- Gender: Nonbinary Trans Fem
- Sexual & Romantic Orientations: Pansexual & Panromantic
- Sexuality: Complicated (As of this writing, I'm still in transition and figuring that out.)

DOI: 10.4324/9781032679082-5

- Relationship Orientation: Polyamorous (As of this writing, I have two wonderful partners and a metamore I owe my life to.)
- Spirituality: Agnostic
- COO (Culture of Origin): I grew up in a very white, conservative Catholic suburban enclave in northern Ohio. This included Catholic grade and high schools.
- FOO (Family of Origin): Two parents (still married), one twin sister, a dog, a progression of cats, upper middle class, conservative politics, and a strong work ethic.

I've moved (literally and figuratively) quite a distance from my beginnings. I share this journey of authenticity as an example so you understand who's writing this. To survive, I had to move away from the highly traditional concepts of who I was expected to be. It's not that I want you to follow my journey; it's mine, and I worked hard for it.

Decolonization in this area means creating more inclusive and authentic spaces for clients to explore and express their authenticity. To do that, you must first follow your own journey and understand the cultural biases that drive your understanding of identity. In doing so, you can first show up differently for yourself and then do the same with your clients.

It's About Understanding

To understand the work of decolonizing our identity, we start with three fundamental existential questions. Take a moment to consider your answers to the following:

1. Who was I?—What factors shaped and influenced me? What have I honored and kept from my previous self? What unwanted pieces do I still carry? What might I carry but can't yet see?
2. Who am I now?—Who have I become? What shapes my current thinking and behavior? What do I understand about myself? What am I missing? Who do I want to be?
3. Who are you?—How do I understand others? What biases/assumptions shape my interactions and perceptions? How does this understanding tie into who I am and who I was?

Journal about your initial thoughts. See where your thinking is now. Remember, there are no wrong answers here. It's just you. I often see a drive in my students to be a "professional therapist." For a long time, I tried to counter this directly. I would say things like, "Just be yourself," or "Be the therapist you want to be." It's not so simple. You can't "be yourself" until you understand what's in your way.

Reclaiming Authenticity: Exploring Identity

The reflective exercise in Table 3.1 invites you to deconstruct many imposed expectations, examine their origins, and reclaim a version of aspects of self that better align with your values, identity, and presence. By engaging in this process, you'll move toward a practice prioritizing authenticity over rigid, exclusionary ideals.

Expanding the Practice

While this exercise is for you as a therapist, you can also use it with your clients to facilitate a deeper exploration of their identities and challenge their internalized narratives. Find

Table 3.1 Exercise—Reclaiming Authenticity

Prompt

---

1. List the first 10 things that come to mind when you think of a "good" or "professional" therapist. As you answer, reflect on how your cultural background and personal experiences have shaped your understanding. (If you're not a therapist, you can substitute any other professional identity.)
2. Now, ask yourself:
   a. Which of the above aligns with what you think a therapist "should" be?
   b. Which of the above aligns with standards of productivity, control, authority, emotional distance, separation, or other white supremacist concepts?
   c. Which of the above aligns with capitalism, white supremacy, or acting as a gatekeeper?
   d. Which of the above aligns with capitalism, white supremacy, or acting as a gatekeeper?
   e. Which of the above encourages professionalism over presence? Other over self? Imposition over collaboration?
   f. Which of the above feels forced onto you?
   g. Which of the above are based on unattainable standards?
   h. Which of the above goes against who you are?
   If any of your answers were used in 2 above, cross them out. List any remaining:
3. Now create a list of traits of a "real," "present," or "authentic" therapist. Consider things that bring your truer self into the therapy room.
4. Consider who this person (above) is and how you can become them more often. Question the traits that prevent you from showing up as yourself and consider leaving them behind. You get to define who you will be both as a therapist and in the world. Free write your ideas.

---

where your clients struggle to be true to themselves, adapt the questions to those places, and have the client go through them. This can be done as homework or during a session. Below are examples of how you might explore identities such as gender, sexuality, or parenting.

- **Gender:** "List the first ten things that come to mind when you think of a 'good' or 'proper' woman/man/nonbinary person."
- **Sexuality:** "List the first ten things that come to mind when you think of a 'good' or 'experienced' lover."
- **Parenting:** "List the first ten things that come to mind when you think of a 'good' or 'loving' parent."

You can use this with any identity to get people looking at who they are and the messages they've internalized. Continue the exercise to help the client (or yourself) move into a greater awareness and authenticity space. This type of understanding exercise is important because...

We Cannot Explore in Others What We Have Not Explored in Ourselves

This truism comes from the works of Harry Aponte (2022), Irving Yalom (2017), cognitive processing psychology (Sternberg & Sternberg, 2016), and personal observation. When some part of the self is left unexamined, we naturally shy away from talking about it. After all, it was left unexamined for a reason. Our subconscious automatically avoids the topic in others because we don't want to look at it in ourselves.

When sitting with a client, you might unconsciously avoid asking questions or even shut down topics the client brings up. You might change the subject when the conversation turns toward something like gender identity or sexuality. Or, knowing it's important to cover these, you might only engage on a surface level, avoiding deeper and potentially more painful examination. Don't panic. You don't need to fully explore or heal your wounds around sex, sexuality, or sexual identity. It's more about the journey than the destination. You need only move toward understanding or healing. Please open the door to exploration in yourself so you can open it for others. It doesn't require success (whatever that would mean anyway), only an open mind and a willing heart.

Unlearning and Reclaiming

Let's do some basic exploration exercises to examine our expanded part of the ADDRESS-ING model (Hays, 2016). While thinking about the questions in the following tables, consider what has led you to these understandings. Like the last exercise, question whether you're expressing your authentic beliefs or regurgitating internalized biases and assumptions. Take your time and return to something if your initial answer doesn't feel right.

Sex

Remember that:

1. Sex is not just biology. It is a biopsychosocial construct (Woods, 2019). We can't escape the meanings, practices, and reinforcements constructed by our culture, but we do get to choose how we process and understand those meanings.

Table 3.2 Exercise—Reflection on Biological Sex

Prompt
What is my biological/physical sex? How do I know? How do I define it? What does it mean to be this? If I could change something about my sex, what would it be?

2. Sex is not a binary choice between male and female and is about more than your genitals. There are many options, and you can define it for yourself and others.
3. In working with sex, we must look beyond the narrow binary cultural definitions and meanings given to us by a predominantly white, Western, colonial, medical, and puritanical lens. It's time we explore a broader palette and recognize the inherent complexity.

Gender

Remember that:

1. Gender is about how we see ourselves. It's an internal state, and while influenced by the biopsychosocial constructs of sex, it is not defined by them.

2. Gender is also not a binary choice. There are hundreds of combinations and options.
3. Colonized beliefs tell us sex equals gender and that biology defines identity. This is not true. Millions of people do not follow that rule. As therapists and as individuals, we must explore gender from a much wider lens, with an open mind and an affirming curiosity.

Table 3.3 Exercise—Reflection on Gender

Prompt
What is my gender (the way you self-identify within the larger context of your sex)? How do I know? How do I define it? What does it mean to be this? How does it feel when others don't recognize my gender?

Sexual and Romantic Orientation

Remember that:

1. Who we love or lust for comes from a complicated mix of feelings, desires, and expectations. Some are ours. Many come from our COO and FOO.
2. While we tend to put desire into distinct categories, the truth is messier and more complex than any one orientation. Lust and love are built on complex and idiosyncratic biopsychosocial contexts. Queer theory (Butler, 1999; Foucault, 1978; Rubin, 2011; Sedgwick, 2008) provides a valuable lens for understanding this fluidity and complexity.
3. Colonized beliefs would tell us lust and love are synonymous. They're not. They would tell us to bend desire toward procreative, monogamist, and cis-hetero biases to better control our sexual behavior. Don't bend. Love whomever you love. Lust for whomever you desire. Be the romantic and sexual being you are.

Table 3.4 Exercise—Reflection on Sexual and Romantic Orientation

Prompt
Who am I sexually attracted to? What are the traits of people I want to date, marry, live with, etc.? What do I hide about this part of my identity? What, if anything, keeps me from being with people I desire?

Sexuality

Remember that:

1. Sexuality is about expressing desire, pleasure, and emotion around the act of sex.
2. It's okay if you've never considered these questions before. The colonization of the act of sex (a book unto itself) is the proscription against talking or even thinking about it. The dominant narrative is that you "just know" or "feel" your way into sexual behavior.

   Note: While this book is a good start to the conversation, consider seeking out other books, videos, educators, and classes geared toward sex positivity and authentic sexual expression. Also, talk to people you trust about sex and sexuality. We learn a lot through interpersonal expression.

3. In working with sexuality (our own or a client's), we must look beyond both the puritanical legacy we've inherited and the prurient sex-focused media used to promote capitalism. Instead, follow intimacy and vulnerability to get at what is truer and more real. Act in a sexual way that aligns with who you are, not what you've been told to do (or not do).

Table 3.5 Exercise—Reflection on Sexuality

Prompt
How do I define my sexuality (the expression of my sexual identities)?
How much of that definition is about what I should or should not be doing? Which parts?
How do I experience my best pleasure?
How do I experience or show my desires?
How do I show this part of my identity to others?

Relationships

Remember that:

1. Relationships are a combination of identity, desire, and opportunity.
2. Part of the colonization of relationships and marriage (another book unto itself) is the proscription against considering anything outside of what is dictated by culture or church. Anything else is labeled as "wrong," "cheating," "immoral," or "sinful" and pushed firmly into "don't do that."
3. In doing relational work (on our own or as therapists), we must look beyond the dominant cultural narratives/scripts to what is true and right for us.

Table 3.6 Exercise—Reflection on Relationships

Prompt
What is my current relationship style (the way you currently practice relationships, if any)?
Does it match my relationship orientation (how you are geared to be or feel is most right for you to be in a relationship)?
Who are my ideal partners?
Do I feel pressured in this part of my identity? How and by whom?

Family

Remember that:

1. Family is complex and another example of a biopsychosocial construct. For some, it is joy and comfort. For others, it's a burden and strife. For still others, it's trauma.
2. Part of the colonization of family is a Westernized hereditary, procreative, and hetero lens. Originally constructed to help landed nobility manage inheritance, the view

has spread to all corners of society and would have us ignore anyone outside of blood relations.

3. We can begin to expand our definition as we deconstruct what family means and the structures that go with it. Look to other ways, cultures, subcultures, and concepts. Read and talk to people about how they're pushing back against the Western, narrow view of family. In doing so, find ways to open more avenues for connection, love, support, growth, and joy.

Table 3.7 Exercise—Reflection on Family

Prompt
What family did I grow up with and learn from?
What does my family look like now?
Do I make a distinction between biological/blood family and chosen family? If so, what?
Do I feel pressured to behave in a certain way toward family? How and by whom?

The exercises in Tables 3.2–3.7 only give a small taste of what identity work looks like. It's about exploring:

- How do I understand myself, my wants, feelings, desires, connections, and so forth?
- How do I understand and deconstruct the historical pressures that influenced my learning and understanding through my FOO and COO?
- Understanding I have been influenced toward a colonized stance, how do I take a more open, curious, and authentic look at who I am, who I could be, and who I want to be?

After exploring these parts of your identity, sit with it for a time. Try out new understandings, thoughts, and ideas. Let the pieces you grew up with solidify or change to fit the person you are now. And give yourself time to resettle into a new configuration, a new self.

Then, when you're more comfortable exploring yourself, take these same exercises and use them with your clients. They can be given as homework or done as part of a session. Explore what colonized narratives have forced on them versus their own authentic identities.

It's important to note these identities don't exist alone. They are reinforced by larger social and political systems, some of which are covered in other chapters. Sex, gender, sexuality, family, and many other identities are highly impacted by how we grow up and the "rules" and concepts we inherit from both our FOO and COO. It's common for social constructs like white supremacy, capitalism, classism, and moral supremacy (to name a few) to significantly impact how we see ourselves.

As you explore, focus on questioning colonized beliefs and exploring identity as a way to embrace a truer self. This doesn't mean throwing out everything you've learned or grown up with; much of that can feel right and useful. The important practice is to examine and explore who you were, who you are, and who you want to be to define what is true.

Then, by being more authentic, you can connect more fully to others and start to change your psychotherapy practice.

Moving the Needle

The field of psychotherapy has a lot to answer for. Most of our foundational theories are steeped in a colonized mindset: white focused, cis, hetero, monogamous, and so forth. Even more contemporary theories are still built on this foundation. Often, they are still taught in the same way. It's harmful to us as therapists and to our clients. Our profession has long pushed clients toward integration into "normal" society while ignoring the intersectional impacts of racism, patriarchy, monogenism, religious persecution, and other oppressions.

For years, the work was, "If you can fit in, you will be happy... or at least be considered sane." Think of this as a colonization of the mind and as a mirror of the colonizing mindset that says, "If I have more power, I can force people to be who I want them to be." This thinking has led to psychological atrocities; some examples include the forced internalization of racism, medicating women for "hysteria" and "dissatisfaction," forced pregnancy, and conversion therapies.

While the profession works to rid itself of the worst of these abusive practices, we still lean toward models steeped in dominant cultural narratives (Combs & Freedman, 1996). Many modern theories, like Solution-Focused Brief Therapy (SFBT) and Cognitive Behavioral Therapy (CBT), remain geared toward returning the client to the capitalistic and industrial concept of productivity. It shows up in our diagnostic models, therapeutic treatment expectations, and even in the ways we treat interns and new therapists: expecting them to treat as many clients as possible in as short a time as possible for little to no pay.

So, what do we do about it? While other chapters tackle other concepts, I want to look specifically at the intersections of sex, gender, orientation, sexuality, and relationships. Here are some things you can do to move the professional needle away from colonized practices and toward being more open and integrated.

Ditch the Binary

Too much work around sexual identities revolves around binary concepts. This reductive thinking is common in colonized discourse. Things are either A or B, right or wrong, good or bad, healthy or unhealthy, privileged or oppressed. People are either male or female, masculine or feminine, gay or straight, pure or slutty, married or single, having sex or celibate, and so on. Framing binary issues allows for greater control and forces people to choose and then defines a "wrong" choice.

Consider Dave's story. Dave's parents sent him to therapy for "depression and moping." During our conversations, Dave revealed that he really wanted to date but couldn't figure out who or how. There was a girl in the choir he liked, but also a guy on his hockey team he couldn't stop fantasizing about. Not only was he unsure how to ask someone out (something we worked on with communication role-play and narrative therapy (Tilsen, 2021), but choosing between them caused huge anxiety.

Questions for the clinician:

- *Where would you start?*
- *What's important?*
- *What would you ask or say to Dave to move away from the binary choice?*

At the time, I somewhat blithely asked, "Why not both?" He later told me it was as if I had asked, "Why not date a fish?" His brain couldn't even imagine the idea. He had only known a monogamistic, straight, or gay framework, which we spent a month or so deconstructing. A little while later, after coming out to his family as bi- (or maybe pan) sexual, his parents pulled him out of therapy. His movement away from the narrow, binary choice was too much. They were still invested in a colonized paradigm.

In the case of Dave, we see how deconstructing binary thinking opened new possibilities for understanding and accepting his sexuality. By challenging the constraints of monogamous, straight, or gay frameworks, therapists can help clients explore a spectrum of identities. They don't need to fit into predefined categories. They (and you) can explore themselves in a more inclusive and affirming way.

Consider how you can ask clients about their identities in nonbinary ways. For instance, instead of asking if a client identifies as male or female, ask them to describe their gender experience in their own words. Instead of asking a client if they are kinky, a yes or no question asks them how they prefer to engage in sex. Open-ended questions are a normal part of therapy; however, when it comes to sex, gender, sexuality, and so forth, people tend to revert to the binary, and for understandable reasons.

Binary choices both create and are created from anxiety. When externally enforced, they encourage compliance and do it well (if history is any judge). As therapists, we aren't in the business of encouraging compliance or anxiety. Instead, we create spaces where gender, sexuality, family, or any topic regarding identity are normal and expected parts of the conversation. We hold space for these complex conversations through clear structure and boundaries, therapeutic authority, compassion, affirming curiosity, and by bringing them up as a normal part of therapy.

Here are some examples for helping clients to process binary thinking out of their lives:

- Embrace Systemic Complexity: While there is temptation to simplify things, resist it. Accept the complexity of your client's life (and your own). Watch for the patterns in that complexity instead of trying to boil it down to a binary yes/no choice. Find complex expressions and understanding.
- Embrace Intersectionality (Collins, 2019; Crenshaw, 1991): No person is one thing. We are many things at the same time, and those parts all influence each other. In essence, we are a system of many parts, working together in the complex dance that makes us... us. Allow people to be all of themselves, ask about them, and watch for the patterns of interaction, be they adaptive, neutral, or maladaptive.
- Seek the Third Option: When presented with a binary choice, ask yourself, "What would a third option be?" It may feel odd at first, but with practice, it becomes easy, even second nature. Once you can get to a third option, it's much easier to find a fourth, fifth, or more.
- Consider these:
  - Yes or No... Maybe? Yes, but with boundaries. No, but maybe later. I choose not to answer.
  - Good or Bad... Neutral. Uncertain. Both. Define good.
  - On or Off... 45%. Tops on, bottoms off. Dim. Bright. Neither. Both.
  - Girl or Boy... Child. Little Pterodactyl. Ask them. Not sure today. Yes.

And so forth. Practice. It gets easier.

- Embrace the Use of Spectrums: Spectrums define the space between two points, multiple points on a graph, or even points in three-dimensional space. Percentage scales are one of the most common. Instead of asking, "Do you feel good about what happened?" ask a scaling question instead, "How good do you feel about what happened?" Instead of asking, "Are you a boy or a girl?" ask instead, "Where do you see yourself on the gender spectrum?"
- True, Truer, Truest: This handy concept out of epistemology defeats right/wrong and truth/lie binaries. It allows something can be true, but there may be something truer beneath it, and there may be something even more true under that. It allows us to talk about deeper and more complex issues or realizations without invalidating the original thought or feeling.
- Yes And: This concept out of improv theater defeats yes/no and either/or thinking. It says, "Yes, that is right, and this is also right." "Yes, you can be gay and asexual at the same time." Use it in relationships to allow both people to have their truth without invalidating each other. While some truths may not be compatible, they are still true.
- Use Open Ended Questions: Get rid of binary questions altogether. Instead of asking if they're monogamous or not, ask instead, "How do you practice relationships?" Don't prompt clients to give you specific information about their identities, simply ask how they identify. This can be tricky as we've been trained to check boxes instead of looking for authenticity.

Practice Open Awareness

While this is a staple of all therapists, it can be more difficult than you think. We are conditioned to listen for certain things. Part of this is training. Part is based on our experiences, contexts, and biases, also known as schema—a pattern of learning, linking perceptions, ideas, and actions to make sense of the world (Derry, 1996). While it makes thinking quicker, it also makes it easier to be aware of things we already know and understand.

In therapy, this presents a challenge. Your clients are impacted and influenced by forces, issues, contexts, and/or experiences you've never had. They have lives, feelings, hopes, and dreams you may not understand. They live with pain, oppressions, fears, and memories you may not want.

Consider James and Carmilla. Married for 12 years, they had one nonbinary child (age 10), the usual issues of people in their late 30s, and came to therapy to work on "sexual difficulties." In session, Carmilla tended to poke at James about his manliness, virility, and housework. James tended to shrink back, make excuses, and question why Carmilla stayed.

With the clients in obvious conflict and unable to regulate, I asked to see them separately. Once alone, Carmilla related that she found James dressed in her clothes and underwear one night. She was afraid James was secretly gay, terrified he was going to leave her and worried about his behavior impacting their kid. After a lot of reassurance, James told a story of self-hate, being fed up with his high-stress job, and cross-dressing since he was 14 years old. Dressing up in women's clothes had been satisfying (and sexy) for a long time, but as he got older, it wasn't enough. Moreover, as his child got older, James found himself jealous of their easy gender exploration and expression and found himself wanting to be more of a mom than a dad.

Where would you start in paraphrasing these two stories? Is there anything you shy away from? How would you define the real conflict? What would you do to address that?

Collectively, we worked on relationship stabilization, distress tolerance, and reassurance skills. Individually, we worked on differentiation and identity. After six months, they were able to openly share their fears, hopes, and identities. Carmilla wanted more decision-making power in the relationship, which James was happy to give over. James wanted more of a role in raising their child, which she was thrilled about. James also wanted to explore the transition to being a woman. Carmilla already suspected it, and while she wasn't sure, she was at least willing to talk about it.

Let's imagine seeing that couple from a traditional colonized position of a monogamist, patriarchal, cis-sexist, perspective. Imagine if you'd never encountered cross-dressing, nonbinary children, transness, and so on. Decolonization means we can't (or shouldn't) force this couple into predetermined molds of coupledom, sex, gender, or anything else. It's about finding out who they are and helping them come together to explore what's next.

Here are some ways to stay more open to your client's experience:

- Understand your Own Biases: Watch for places you find yourself thinking, "That's just how it is," or "It's not like that." Watch for things you know to be True. And watch for places where dominant cultural narratives speak louder than your own voice. Examine them, talk about them, determine if the bias is something you want to carry and if not, work to deconstruct it.
- Explore your Client's Reality: Their reality, lives, beliefs, contexts, among other things, are different from yours. Risk stepping outside your own worldview. You don't have to embrace their reality, but you do need to understand what it means to them. This is especially important when working with couples and moresomes, as their multiple realities often create conflict.
- Acknowledge your Client's Reality: Once you see and understand your client's reality, acknowledge it. Validate the client's feelings using affirmations like, "That makes sense," "I can see that," "I get that," and so on.
- Use Systemic Awareness and Perspective Differentials: View the client's system from their perspective, your perspective, and the perspectives of others in the system. Each will have a different way of looking at what's going on. By embracing the complexity, you can find other ways of approaching issues and conflicts.
- Approach from a Place of Not Knowing: Use the Beginner's Mind (Shunryu, 1970). Avoid assuming you understand your clients and what they're going through. They are experts on their lives. They know best what's happening inside them: physically, mentally, emotionally, spiritually, and so forth. Your outside perspective is useful, and why they came to you, but it can't define them. Only they can do that.
- Be Curious in an Affirming Way: Hold a strong desire to understand and learn about your clients. At the same time, be curious. Avoid looking only for what you already understand. Be curious about everything, and when you find something new, confusing, or even discomforting, embrace it to open new avenues for treatment and support.
- Use Your Therapy Skills in an Open Way: Practice paraphrasing, reflective listening, and open-ended questions to fully understand your client's perspective. For example, instead of assuming their experiences, ask, "Can you tell me more about how you experience your gender?"

Embrace Change

Change is part of therapy. We help clients through problems and maladaptive patterns. We support changing behavior and beliefs. And yet, just as they do, we get stuck in behavior and thought patterns. Embracing change is about moving out of homeostasis (the tendency of a system, either internal or external, to stay relatively stable). Even when something feels bad, if it's familiar, we tend to stick with it. To support our client's change, we must be willing to move out of homeostasis ourselves and deal with the disruption, feelings, and effort that comes with it.

Use the skills you've learned here to regularly reflect on who you are now. If someone else isn't asking, ask yourself. Explore your beliefs/biases and ask if they're still valid for you. It's likely to feel uncomfortable at first. Keep it up; it gets easier with practice.

Consider Lucy. Lucy hated life. She worked three jobs: programmer, streamer, and cam girl, all from a tiny studio apartment. She rarely went out, had food delivered, and often went weeks without talking face-to-face with another person. She was lonely, supremely anxious, and approaching agoraphobia. Lucy wanted something to change, yet she'd been living the same way for over four years. She had an excuse for why every intervention couldn't work and a deflection for every question.

What would you do with this client? How would you change things? What might you say to encourage a different direction?

Lucy and I worked together for almost a year before I realized I was the problem. I'd run every concept or theory I knew, and several I tried out of desperation. I felt stuck and almost quit. She wanted change. I wanted change. Yet her maladaptive system was so entrenched: nothing behavioral could make a dent.

So, I stopped trying to change the isolation and turned to identity. Lucy didn't like who she was, but when I asked about her cam-girl persona, she became animated and engaged. We'd both been avoiding the subject (my own biases and her fear of my reaction). Engaging in sexual play was the only time she felt like herself. We talked about her fear of rejection, from me and everyone else, and that led us to old traumas and attachment wounds.

I resisted shutting down the conversation despite feeling uncomfortable. She had every right to be herself, and yet my bias kept seeing her sexuality as wrong and harmful. I worked on it outside of the session, and as I moved out of homeostasis, so did she. She could be honest, and I could stay present and encouraging. She began to embrace the playful and sexual part of her identity more in her streaming and outside life. She began to live instead of hiding.

Would you help a client embrace their sexualized self, or would you see it as the problem? Would you let go of your own bias to join with the part that needed connection? Would you shy away from the sexual aspect out of fear? Would you be able to change what you "knew" in favor of what was needed? It was a hard lesson for me.

Looking at this case study, you can see how being stuck in old and colonized ways of thinking got in the way. Neither of us wanted to change, even when we both understood change was exactly what was needed. Our internalized assumptions encouraged stasis, sameness, and conformity. By embracing change, we automatically step toward decolonizing our thinking and practices.

Here are some ways to do that for yourself (and to help your clients):

- Do Something New: Embracing change is a skill. It's easier when you're not doing the same old thing. Practice trying new things. Start a new hobby. Practice a different type of therapy. Try new foods.

- Let Go of Perfection: Change is messy. When we do something new, we often do it poorly and are prone to mistakes at first. Accept being bad. Accept being new. It's only in trying and failing that we learn.
- Learn to See "Stuck": Repetition is often comforting, and that's okay for adaptive patterns. Repetition of maladaptive patterns is uncomfortable, anxiety producing, and leads to other problems. As such, we tend to ignore them. Practice first with yourself. Where are you stuck? What do you do repeatedly that you dislike? What do you wish would change that hasn't? Once you can see stuck in yourself, it becomes easier to see in others.
- Practice being Uncomfortable: Comfort feels good and easy. Unfortunately, change rarely comes from comfort. While we want to avoid being overwhelmed, it's okay to be uncomfortable. So long as it's a choice, discomfort is more than bearable and an opportunity for growth. Working through discomfort gets easier with practice.
- Engage with Others: One of the best ways to learn new ideas, perspectives, behaviors, and so forth is to enter into someone else's perspective. Talk with people and be open to who they are (instead of focusing on yourself). Read new books and articles, watch new media, listen to different music, etc. When you're open to new concepts, you will find change.
- Practice: When something isn't working, do something else. It's easy to get stuck in maladaptive patterns of thought, feeling, and/or behavior. Stepping outside of your normal patterns gets easier with practice. Practice doesn't need to work; it only needs to be different.

Move Beyond the White Picket Fence

Recognize the fallacy of the "white picket fence": where dad goes to work and mom stays home with 2.5 kids; where men make all the decisions, and women are happy doing thousands of hours of unpaid emotional, mental, and physical labor; where sex is free and available when the man wants it (within a committed marriage of course); where people follow the path laid out for them at birth. This concept is, and has been, ridiculous. And yet it holds a huge influence in our lives, laws, media, and therapy.

Our view of relationships and family structures has been built and refined by a colonized culture, one that conquers and takes. It holds onto a view of the family built on white, hetero, cis, religious, individualistic, and capitalistic needs. It's a concept where "men" and "women" work in defined roles, where children are products of specifically defined unions, and where people are expected to behave based on legacy concepts decades or centuries old.

The world has moved on from 1950s America, slavery, colonial expansion, Victorian England. Modern existence is radically different even from what our parents knew growing up. And yet, our dominant cultural narratives still push "traditional family values," sexual shame, religion-based spirituality, and productivity. It continues to hold to white supremacy, purity culture, patriarchy, heterosexism, cissexism, and monogamy. This toxic soup was fed to most of us as children.

Such patterns are sticky. They're everywhere in our culture, media, relationships, and interactions. As therapists, we must move past them and support our clients in doing the same. Not only do they hold back our personal lives, but they become roadblocks to working with clients who inhabit a complex and messy world. We must consider and understand the wide and wonderful variety of human relationships and families.

Consider Jeanne, Fadima, Amina, and Eric. This foursome came into therapy complaining nothing was getting done around the house. The four had moved in together 16 months previously and while things had worked at the beginning, they slowly devolved. Each had numerous complaints about how the others did things and lengthy explanations for why they couldn't get things done.

Jeanne (trans man), Fadima (cis woman), and Amina (nonbinary Fem) were a triad. Eric (cis man) was legally married to Fadima, but they hadn't been romantically involved in years. Eric was also best friend and occasional lover with Jeanne. Fadima and Jeanne were immigrants from Cameroon, and Fadima relied on her marital status for citizenship. Amina had partial custody of two children from a previous marriage. Eric had three other "casual" partners outside the home. Their relationship was complex.

Where would you start? If you're not familiar with working with triads and other polyamorous relationships, what do you think about this system? What biases, concerns, or conceptualizations might get in your way?

This case was interesting. After we spent time exploring the ins and outs of their relationships and daily lives, we found that romantic and sexual relationships were working well. While there were outside pressures, stresses, and a particular issue with Jeanne's family, they had good skills for working through the normal emotional and scheduling issues that came up. What they couldn't manage was who would take out the trash, who would wash the dishes, who would clean out the gutters, who would mow the lawn, and who would do the laundry. Where would you, as the therapist, go next? Chore charts? Other behavioral interventions?

I asked about childhood. Jeanne and Eric grew up in very traditional and religious families. Neither's mom worked outside the home. Fadima escaped crushing poverty by coming to the United States and spent years without legal citizenship. Amina was the child of multiple divorces, ending up with seven parents, three of whom she refuses to speak to. Each had very different concepts of what doing housework was and who "should" do it. They either clung to or vehemently rejected their birth family's ways. Needing change, we did a three-hour session at their home, physically reviewing each task and talking about who "should" be doing what. We looked at what each of them were doing or not doing. Only then could we create a system that prevented trauma reactions, stonewalling, and resentment.

Imagine trying to fit this family into a traditional "white picket fence" conceptualization. Perhaps you found yourself wondering who was in charge. Who made the most money? Which couple was the "real" couple? Normal things to wonder when you're caught up in that colonized view of family. Yet when you step away, you find a kaleidoscope of relational and familial ways of being.

In this case, we can see how deconstructing cultural norms, biases, and expectations opened up new possibilities and directions. By first accepting their family structure and then digging deeper into how their family system was functioning (and not functioning), we were able to create change. This is true for polyamorous relationships, communal living arrangements, people living alone, travelers, blended families, and even for more traditional relationships. Accept first, explore what's going on, and then challenge the maladaptive structures.

Here are some perspectives to do that more:

- Look at Reality, not Fallacy: Cultural myths hold onto power by asserting, often loudly, the myth is reality. Once enough people believe it, they shape and/or pretend their lives into the myth, thus making it a reality. However, life doesn't fit into expectations easily. Look at the relationships and family structures around you. Look outside your friends, social class, race, religion at the many variations people use to live (or try to live) a fulfilling life.

- Look at other Cultures: Humans tend to group with people like us, but that's not the story of the world, it's only the story of people like us. Read, study, ask about how people in other countries, racial groups, and subcultures structure families. Learn what works and apply it.
- Explore your Own Family: FOO (family of origin) work is essential to understanding how we understand family. You have to engage with your upbringing emotionally as well as intellectually. Understanding how you grew up and what relationship and family means in that context will help you see your biases and assumptions. Once you understand, you can decide what it means to you now.
- Move Beyond Traditional or Western Organizational Structures: Humans are exceptional at finding ways to live together. Each relationship or family is going to find ways that work, though not all will be healthy. Explore the variations and different ways people find to love, live, and coexist.
- Move Beyond Traditional Power Structures: Patriarchy and misogyny are alive and well. While we've made a lot of progress toward equity, we aren't there. Explore your own and your clients' understanding of who has, and who should have, power in relationships. Move beyond traditional hierarchical power structures toward more equitable ones.
- Be Curious: An open and affirming curiosity goes a long way. If you avoid assuming what relationship your clients walk in with, you can more easily enter into a therapeutic alliance with them and learn who they authentically are.

Adapt Existing Theory

Much of the existing psychological theory is based on colonized teachings and assumptions about sex, gender, orientation, sexuality, and relationships. These theories have a lot of interesting and valuable concepts. Still, without adaptation, these can harm clients who don't fit the white, cis, hetero, monogamous, etc. mold they were designed around. As a therapist, you have every right to examine, explore, and adapt existing theories to suit your needs and those of your clients.

Some ways to do that:

- Be Critical: Engage critical thinking as you learn about or reexplore theory. Ask yourself: *What cultural narratives and colonized concepts are built into this? Who was it designed for? Who was it designed by?* Avoid accepting something just because it was written by a "leader" in the field or because "We've always used it that way."
- Learn More: It's hard to adapt to something you don't understand well. Take the time to explore theories and ideas before you start to experiment.
- Use What Works for You: Examine theory for helpful and useful things. Examine what works within your practice of therapy. Pull concepts, ideas, interventions, and other materials that fit who you are as a therapist, and search for shiny ideas you might need later. Ignore what you don't need or what would be harmful to your clients.

- Use What Works for Clients: A theory can be amazing, brilliant, revolutionary, and if it doesn't work for your client, it's worthless in that session. No theory is going to work for 100% of clients. As more diverse people come to therapy, many theories start to break down. Pick and choose what's useful for a given client in each session.
- Try New Things: Mix and match theories. Try them in different configurations, timings, expressions, and so on. Experiment, realizing many experiments fail. Be willing to pivot when something doesn't work. Where experimentation causes a rift in the therapeutic alliance, make sure to repair it before moving on.
- Create New Theory: If you can't find something workable, make something new. Once you've worked it, and it seems to be going well, share it. Every theory started with someone saying, "There's something missing here." As you explore and create theory outside colonized structures and/or for new identities, be the person who fills in the missing piece.

Do the Work

Thinking and examining these concepts is a great place to start. And then, we put thought into practice.

Consider the following for yourself and your clients:

- Expect Struggle and Resistance: This work is not easy. It often brings up anxiety, fear, avoidance, confusion, anger, sadness, and a host of "I don't wanna" feelings. Old patterns are sticky. Expecting change will take time, work, and perseverance. Some things that help:
- Compassion, both for the self and others.
- Talking about it with trusted confidants (including a therapist).
- Journaling or creative expression to help process feelings and thoughts.
- Allowing the time needed to change and taking breaks when needed.
- Focusing on why you (or they) want to change. Define the goal so you can come back to it.
- Manage Pushback: In the same way we struggle internally to do this work, it's common to experience external pushback. We exist within systems—family, peer groups, work, social, etc. Those systems are just as caught in the frameworks discussed above, and influence or force is often applied to prevent change. Some ways to manage this:
- Find others doing the same work who can support and shield against the pushback.
- Limit exposure to systems working against authentic change.
- Talk, read, journal, create, and find means to help process the feelings/thoughts that come up.
- Get strategic. It's hard to fight against a larger system. Find ways to conserve your mental, emotional, physical, spiritual, and logistical energy for when they will be most useful.
- Focus Agency: Agency is your (or your client's) ability to create change. For yourself, focus on your authenticity and what's right for you. When working with a client, focus on their choices and authenticity. While it's tempting to overlay our own understanding and beliefs onto a client, they have to come to their own understanding in their own time. We can't do the work for them; they must do it themselves.

- Make Mistakes: You will make mistakes in your own work and your work with clients. You will achieve understanding, only to realize later that your understanding was flawed. This is a normal, and useful, part of the process. When you find yourself having made a mistake, consider what happened, figure out how to do better, and, where needed, engage in repair with those impacted.
- Embrace "Truer": There are things that are true (that we "know" and are "right" or "correct"). Don't stop there. Explore the depth and breadth of concepts and ideas. Search for deeper and more true ideas, beliefs, thoughts, and feelings. With clients, support them in finding what is "truer" and more authentic for them. Dig into the systemic issues and influences behind the behaviors, thoughts, and feelings they're dealing with.

Our profession doesn't change on its own. The needle doesn't move unless we move it. We don't prevent harm by wishing harm doesn't happen. It takes all of us doing the work to move out of past legacies and into something new. It takes you moving away from traditional/colonized perspectives: white supremacist, patriarchal, cis-focused, monogamist, and so forth, and embracing new concepts, perspectives, and change. We learn, examine, process, practice, make mistakes, and change. As more of us change, therapy changes with us. At first, it's just us. Then, we do it for our clients. But with time and influence, we reach out into the greater work and push the needle away from what was to what can be.

Authenticity is the Goal

Colonized views push a narrow concept of identity geared toward maintaining a system that benefits certain people over others. It creates a concept of "normal" that limits what is good and power worthy into very specific labels. If you're not "normal," you don't get power. It's an oppressive system built over hundreds of years to benefit those willing to harm and exploit people who don't look or act like they do. "It's okay to harm someone different than me" has a long and bloody legacy. Sometimes, the difference is obvious. Sometimes it's arbitrary.

Consider and revisit your answers to our earlier exploration exercises and questions:

- *What is your biological/physical sex?*
- *What is your gender?*
- *Who do you love? Who do you desire?*
- *How do you express yourself sexually?*
- *What do your relationships look like?*
- *How is your family put together?*

More than the answers, think about how you know the answers. How do you understand the questions? Are there questions missing? What have you learned here to change how you consider answering or asking? Do you fit inside that narrow, colonized view of who you're supposed to be? Who gets to define who you're supposed to be? And, what is the potential harm to you if you're not?

Inevitably, we come to the question: "Am I normal?" and "Are you normal?"

Well, I'm not normal. You're probably not, either. And that's all good.

"Normal" is a lie sold to keep us stuck in a system of control. No one is man or woman enough. No one lives their gender enough. No love or lust is "just right." No sexuality is normal or healthy enough. No relationship is perfect enough. No family is strong, healthy, or traditional enough.

If none of us are "normal" enough, then does "normal" even have meaning? I would argue... no.

While it comes with challenges and risks, I reject "normal" for myself and my clients. I'm willing to look outside what I was taught is "right" and "good" to what is right and good for me (and my clients). I'm willing to risk being myself and risk being happy in a world that would harm me for that happiness. I do this because if I spend my time trying to "fix" myself into being a better man, whiter, straighter, and so forth, I won't spend any time asking what's wrong with a system that would harm me or you for being who we are.

Conclusion

Embracing a decolonized approach to sex, gender, sexuality, and relationships as a therapist has its hurdles. It starts with understanding ourselves so we might better understand our clients. It requires moving beyond binary thinking, developing ongoing awareness, recognizing internalized bias, a commitment to personal growth, and a willingness to challenge traditional frameworks. By doing this work, we create more inclusive spaces for clients to explore and express their authenticity.

It starts with you. Be your authentic self as best you can. In doing so, allow your clients to explore who they are without the barriers culture establishes. Model what authenticity looks like. Provide a space to be truer by being more comfortable with your own truths. And in doing so, restart the cycle. One ripple is a small thing. A hundred ripples become a wave. A thousand are a tsunami. As you change your perspective, you help others to change theirs, and so they will go on to help more beyond themselves.

Together, we move against a world that represses the self and into one that honors authenticity for its uniqueness, brilliance, and joy. Together, we challenge a colonized system and say, "I am enough; you are enough." Together, we embrace freedom and throw off the legacy of the past for ourselves, our clients, and the future. Together, we embrace complexity and authentic identity and come to understand who we were, who we are, and who we can be.

References

Aponte, H. J. (2022). The soul of therapy: The therapist's use of self in the therapeutic relationship. *Contemporary Family Therapy: An International Journal, 44*(2), 136–43. https://doi.org/10.1007/s10591-021-09614-5

Aponte, H. (2015). *The person of the therapist training model.* Routledge. https://doi.org/10.4324/9781315719030

Butler, J. (1999). *Gender trouble.* Routledge. https://doi.org/10.4324/9780203902752

Combs, G., & Freedman, J. (1996). *Narrative therapy: The social construction of preferred realities.* W. W. Norton & Company.

Collins, P. H. (2019). *Intersectionality as critical social theory.* Duke University Press. https://doi.org/10.2307/j.ctv11hpkdj

Crenshaw, K. (1991). Mapping the margins: Intersectionality, identity politics, and violence against women of color. *Stanford Law Review, 43*(6), 1241–99. https://doi.org/10.2307/1229039

Derry, S. J. (1996). Cognitive schema theory in the constructivist debate. *Educational Psychologist,* *31*(3–4), 163–74. https://doi.org/10.1207/s15326985ep3103&4_2

Foucault, M. (1978). *The history of sexuality.* Pantheon Books.

Hays, P. A. (2016). The new reality: Diversity and complexity. In P. A. Hays, *Addressing cultural complexities in practice: Assessment, diagnosis, and therapy* (3rd ed., pp. 3–18) http://dx.doi.org/10.1037/14801-001

Jouriles, N., & Whisman, M. A. (Eds.), *APA handbook of contemporary family psychology: Foundations, methods, and contemporary issues across the lifespan* (pp. 75–92). American Psychological Association.

Rubin, G. (2011). *Deviations.* Duke University Press.

Sedgwick, E. K. (2008) *Epistemology of the closet.* University of California Press

Sternberg, R., & Sternberg, K. (2016). *Cognitive psychology 7th edition.* Wadsworth Publishing.

Suzuki, S. (1970). *Zen mind, beginner's mind.* Shambhala.

Tilsen, J. (2021). *Queering your therapy practice.* Routledge

Woods, S. B. (2019). Biopsychosocial theories. In B. H. Fiese, M. Celano, K. Deater-Deckard, E., & Yalom, I. (2017), *The gift of therapy: An open letter to a new generation of therapists and their patients.* Harper Perennial.

Chapter 4

Family Therapy in the Era of AI

Will Technology Advance or Erase Indigenous and Non-Western Practices?

Jacey Saucedo Coy

Author Note: Jacey Coy is an Assistant Teaching Professor in the School of Social and Behavioral Sciences at Arizona State University, which has a collaborative partnership with OpenAI. As a former employee, he also holds stock in the company Spring Health.

Introduction

Whether or not we are consciously aware of it, we have become increasingly dependent on artificial intelligence (AI) in our daily lives. The technology behind even simple tasks like figuring out our commute to work, asking a question on your smartphone, or using automated grammar-checking tools all utilize AI algorithms to make decisions on our behalf. While these examples are clearly helpful in making tasks easier, they also require a lot of trust in the companies and technology behind these decision-making processes, and many of us freely offer it without considering the potential harm. In the coming years, AI technologies are considered to be one of the most transformative technological advances of our time, and with the rise of applications within mental health, AI has the potential to fundamentally change the way family therapy (and the mental health field more broadly) works.

At the same time, AI technologies have also been criticized as having the potential to become tools of colonialism. In fact, many prominent AI models have been found to actively perpetuate dominant ideologies and have the potential to eradicate or devalue the cultural knowledge of indigenous and non-Western communities, deepening social inequalities. Despite mental health professionals being slow to utilize artificial intelligence tools (Zhang et al., 2023), AI-driven technologies are already being deployed into clinical documentation platforms (Lee et al., 2023; Thakkar et al., 2024), as well as therapy-session analytics software (Nguyen & Pepping, 2023). Given the current speed of development, AI may soon play a significant role in the clinical work that MFTs do, whether we are consciously aware of it or not.

Given the transformative potential of AI to reshape our clinical work, it is essential that family therapists critically analyze its impact from a decolonization lens. This is particularly important for the field of family therapy as we have led the way in the development, advancement, and promotion of therapeutic practices that help families experience healing from the effects of colonialism. If AI has the potential to reinforce these harms, family therapists run the risk of inadvertently perpetuating the same problematic forms of oppression that we seek to dismantle.

This chapter explores how family therapists can navigate the increasing integration of artificial intelligence into clinical tools. I recognize that the term "Artificial intelligence"

DOI: 10.4324/9781032679082-6

(AI) has come to mean many different things. For the purpose of this book chapter, I use the term "AI" in a broad sense to refer to the development of technology that is capable of replicating or outperforming the cognitive abilities of humans. It is also important to note that any publication about technology is already outdated as soon as it is published, and with the recent advancements in AI, the speed of change is even faster. In lieu of this, I will not be focusing on any particular AI platform or technology; instead, I will focus on the potential of the technology as a whole and the processes of AI development. By focusing on the process rather than the content, I will attempt to generate a more in-depth discussion about AI technology and its role in family therapy.

I will first discuss the obstacles preventing the widespread adoption of decolonizing practices in therapy while also considering how AI might be able to assist with these efforts. I will then examine the potential harm that can happen when AI technologies reinforce oppressive dominant narratives and prioritize Western knowledge at the expense of indigenous and non-Western communities. Family therapists have the opportunity to offer a unique systemic perspective in influencing AI development and deployment by examining how it can be utilized to either dismantle or perpetuate existing power structures. The chapter closes by addressing the need for family therapists to be actively involved in developing, critiquing, and adopting AI tools in mental health care. I propose specific ways for family therapists to use their systemic expertise in guiding the ethical development, deployment, and use of AI in mental health care.

My Own Experience with The Intersection of AI and Mental Health

I was first introduced to AI in mental health care in 2019 when I left my work in community behavioral health for an opportunity to join the operations team at a mental health tech start-up called Spring Health. I had extensive experience in both clinical and operational roles in mental health care, and I was excited to be involved in the merging of mental health with tech. Spring Health offered a modernized take on employee assisted programs (EAPs) by providing mental health services that were powered by an AI-driven assessment tool developed by cofounder Adam Chekroud, a leader in computational psychiatry (Chekroud et al., 2016; 2021). The software used multiple clinical data points in the form of an online assessment that would determine the optimal treatment for a person based on their mental health symptoms. Instead of clients filling out different assessments for depression, anxiety, substance use, eating disorders, and so on, the tool's algorithms used multiple evidence-based scales to assess for multiple disorders at the same time. This was the first time that I was exposed to the concept of precision mental health: the hope that one day we might be able to utilize technology to help people avoid cycling through different treatments and providers and get them the right care that they need the first time.

This concept of precision mental health was personal to me. My father, a first-generation Mexican American man, was drafted to serve in the Vietnam War. When he returned from the war, he started experiencing severe symptoms of trauma from his time in the military. He initially tried to seek help from his primary care physician, but his symptoms were quickly dismissed, so he suffered in silence for decades until his symptoms became so intense that he had to be hospitalized for suicidal ideation. Even after he was finally able to receive a proper diagnosis of post-traumatic stress disorder (PTSD), he continued to face significant barriers to receiving proper care. In fact, it took multiple hospitalizations for us to finally get him stabilized with the correct medication regimen and a consistent team of appropriate providers. So, the promise of precision mental health has always resonated with me, and the idea of being able to leverage technology to connect families with the right care from the beginning is huge.

Current Challenges in Decolonizing Therapeutic Practices

Though family therapy has long understood the need for decolonized therapeutic practices—approaches that actively recognize power imbalances, acknowledge the larger sociopolitical contexts surrounding clients, and support clients in using their own resources to overcome struggles—widespread adoption continues to be met with challenges. In spite of these obstacles, meaningful progress has been made in the field of family therapy through the growing literature on the intersection of power and privilege and the emergence of culturally responsive frameworks that recognize family systems within their cultural contexts. However, in order to understand these issues in context, we must first align with what has been done within the field to advance this important work.

Colonialism, though it has taken on many different forms, has never been solely about controlling territories or claiming physical land, as often depicted by some historical examples. Instead, ultimately, it has always been about power and control. Described as a "hierarchal establishment of power that benefits the dominant group's ideologies and practices over the cultural voices, beliefs, and practices of others" (McDowell & Hernández, 2010, as cited in Bermúdez et al., 2016), it is a system that is designed to create and enforce inequality. We know that the effects of colonialism are particularly harmful because the impact is not isolated to a specific event or a time period but rather continues to maintain oppressive influence over marginalized populations for generations. Specifically, rather than framing colonialism as a historical event, Bermúdez et al. (2016) use the term "coloniality" to refer to the ways in which the effects of colonialism allow dominant power structures to continuously oppress marginalized communities with devastating consequences. These power structures still exist today, though colonizing practices have evolved to continue to reinforce them. Moving from overt to covert forms of marginalization, institutions of oppression perpetuate the discriminatory narratives of colonialism on marginalized groups (Hutcheon & Lashewicz, 2020; Walsdorf et al., 2020). For example, the cycle of oppression continues to occur in children of color being disproportionately diagnosed with behavioral disorders, which becomes a contributing factor to the overrepresentation of people of color in mental health institutions and prisons (Fernando, 2014; Harp & Bunting, 2020; Jordan, 2021).

While there is plenty of evidence showing how oppression, discrimination, and social inequality harm one's mental health (Fernando, 2017; Unger, 2011; Waldegrave, 2009; Williams & Mohammed, 2009), we also know that these experiences have intergenerational effects on families and communities due to the continued imbalance of power, privilege, resources, and wealth (Uttal, 2009). Ideally, this is where systemic family therapists can be particularly helpful: by addressing the effects of systemic intergenerational trauma as a result of sociopolitical systems of discrimination and oppression. Family therapy, rooted in systems theory, has a long history of recognizing the social and political systems that impact the lives of our clients (Auerswald, 1971; Falicov, 1995; Hair & et al., 1996; Imber-Black, 1991; MacKinnon & Miller, 1987; McGoldrick & Hardy, 2008; Waldegrave, 2009), and much work has been done to provide prescriptive ideas about how to translate this research into clinical practice. A few examples include:

- Falicov et al. (2021) illustrated the ways clinicians can promote client-centered collaboration in their sessions, which is particularly important when working with clients from disadvantaged socioeconomic backgrounds.
- D'Arrigo-Patrick et al. (2017) found that therapists often share a social constructionist perspective and tend to incorporate activism into their work, but their strategies differ based on their own perceptions of ethics and level of comfort. Some therapists directly challenge power structures, while others focus on collaboration.
- McDowell et al. (2019) demonstrated how family therapists can take the systemic concepts of first-order and second-order thinking further to what they call third-order thinking, which includes social justice considerations.
- Holyoak et al. (2021) argue that advocacy by family therapists cannot only happen at the macro level but also must look at ways to create social change on a micro level by supporting individual clients' needs through action.
- Weiling et al. (2020) showed how interdisciplinary projects, including systemic therapists, can positively impact immigrant communities. Their work demonstrates what happens when systemic ideas are translated into action for social justice and transformative change.
- Afuape (2020) revealed an approach for group therapy focused on understanding trauma through a systemic lens of oppression, which can help teens connect their experiences to larger social issues while empowering them to take action and make positive changes.

Still, despite all of the efforts to guide, discuss, and theorize ways to dismantle power imbalances in therapy, clinicians still struggle with translating this rhetoric into action (Watson et al., 2020). This is because, in order to put decolonizing practices into action, therapists must first take on the active role of engaging with marginalized knowledge. Specifically, they must first examine how structural racism operates in their own lives, create and utilize supportive spaces, and actively seek and value marginalized perspectives that have been traditionally ignored or suppressed in the mental health field (Chin et al., 2022). Also, many family therapists are often unsure how to address these issues with their clients (Knudson-Martin et al., 2019), which points to a continued issue with training and supervision. If therapists do address these issues in session, they rarely connect families to opportunities for social change, which may unintentionally uphold harmful power structures similar to colonialism (Vecchio & Lockard, 2004).

No matter how well-meaning, therapists often unintentionally perpetuate dominant ideologies by imposing these cultural norms on minoritized individuals and families (Rober & Seltzer, 2010). In fact, some argue that therapy itself can reinforce oppressive power imbalances by assuming the client is flawed and the therapist is the savior who needs to fix them (Hoffman, 1992). Also, many therapeutic models were created by and perpetuate dominant power structures that are causing distress for families in the first place. Specifically, many traditional therapy models often overlook the impact of societal and systemic inequalities on clients—an oversight that can cause significant harm to clients (Vecchio & Lockard, 2004). For example, Cognitive Behavioral Therapy (CBT), which has been lauded as the "gold standard" of evidence-based practices in mental health care (David et al., 2018), has generated concerns surrounding clinicians' ability to use it effectively with marginalized groups (Ahuvia & Schleider, 2023; Levinson et al., 2023; Moore & Brodt; 2023). Even the diagnostic tools that we use (e.g., the Diagnostic and Statistical Manual of Mental Disorders) risk pathologizing behaviors that are considered normal in marginalized communities (Porter, 2014) and were built on concepts of health and illness based on Western standards (Marsella & Yamada, 2000). Furthermore, family therapy graduate students believe that diversity courses are essential to their clinical preparation and feel social justice discussions should be integrated throughout their training curriculum, yet most programs only offer a single diversity course (Yzaguirre et al., 2022).

While we can continue to work on the known limitations behind therapist training, theoretical models, and diagnostic tools, significant adoption of decolonizing practices will continue to struggle as long as the field remains embedded in Western power structures that marginalize indigenous and non-Western knowledge systems. These structures not only dictate what therapeutic knowledge receives consideration, validation, and adoption, but they also shape how clinicians conceptualize mental health itself. But in light of all of the recent advancements in AI, are there opportunities to use the technology to help therapists dismantle the effects of colonialism within their own lives and practices? Could AI systems be used to identify colonial patterns in therapeutic language, recommend indigenous frameworks for healing, and provide access to previously marginalized knowledge that therapists might not encounter in traditional training? Is it possible that this technology could be used as a tool for reflection, highlighting biases that remain invisible to clinicians who may be immersed in dominant Western paradigms?

Therapists will need to maintain autonomy over their clinical decision-making and critical engagement regardless of any technological tools that are utilized. But by making visible these often invisible colonial influences, is there an opportunity for AI to help therapists recognize when they are reproducing harmful patterns and offer alternative perspectives that honor indigenous traditions of understanding health and healing? The promise of AI in this work is not that the technology would (or could) replace the therapist's decolonization work but in creating tools that support therapists in their journey of self-reflection and cultural humility. For example, imagine being able to utilize AI in the following ways:

- Equipping family therapists with a more holistic view of our clients' intersectional identities by utilizing more data points (e.g., race, sexual orientation, gender, socioeconomic status, etc.).
- Supporting family therapists to become better at actively identifying power imbalances in couple and family relationships.
- Assisting family therapists with recognizing, acknowledging, and addressing larger sociopolitical contexts within the lives of our clients.
- Providing family therapists with an increased awareness of examples of our own biases and privileges to avoid imposing them on clients.

While these ideas might sound far-fetched, AI has already expanded into spaces previously thought impossible, including mental health care. In fact, AI technologies are already being used to predict and screen for mental health symptoms, as well as provide basic mental health support. The question is not whether AI will transform mental health care (it already is) but whether that transformation will perpetuate inequities or help us dismantle them. Family therapists have an ethical responsibility to become active participants in shaping the development of these tools toward inclusion and accessibility rather than tools of further oppression.

The (Potential) Future of AI in Mental Health

Recently, a lot of attention has been placed on specific consumer-facing generative AI chatbots, such as OpenAI's ChatGPT, Anthropic's Claude, and Google's Gemini. These systems are built on large language models (LLMs), and the advancements made, particularly in this realm of AI technology, have been expanding rapidly in handling language-based tasks such as writing like a human, translating between languages, quickly summarizing large amounts of data, while even understanding context (Brown et al., 2020). These advancements have led some researchers to believe in the potential for AI chatbots to one day make mental health care more accessible. For example, though the stigma associated with seeking help for mental health care continues to be a barrier for people (Coombs et al., 2021), access could be increased if people are able to get support discretely through an AI-powered platform (Essien & Asamoah, 2020). Plus, given the fact that so many people have access to the internet via their personal devices, the idea of increasing access to mental health services through AI technology is more of a realistic possibility. As Ettman et al. (2023) imagine one way of AI increasing access to care:

> One could imagine a world where AI serves as the "front line" for mental health, providing a clearinghouse of resources and available services for individuals seeking help. In addition, targeted interventions delivered digitally can help reduce the population burden of mental illness, particularly in hard-to-reach populations and contexts, for example, through stepped care approaches that aim to help populations with the highest risk following natural disasters. (p. 2)

Improving access is important as the number of people needing mental health support is outpacing the availability of therapists, especially in low-income countries. Global estimates show a major shortage of mental health workers worsening over time (Essien & Asamoah, 2020; Gureje & Lasebikan, 2006). For family therapists, the shortage is even more bleak, with estimates showing current shortages of marriage and family therapists continuing to become more substantial by 2036 (National Center for Health Workforce Analysis, 2023). With physical and mental health disparities continuing to be a serious problem for communities of color and low-income families (Hodgkinson et al., 2017), AI holds the potential to provide a basic level of support to more people. While not a replacement for human therapists, offering supplemental support to patients or better tooling for clinicians could be a massive win for the field.

Apart from making mental health services more accessible to people, AI also offers the potential to provide clients anonymous support in the face of stigma, assistance with navigating resources, individualized and contextualized answers to mental health–related questions, and immediate ongoing support whenever clients need it (Denecke & Gabarron, 2021; Laranjo et al., 2018; Miner et al., 2016; Miner et al., 2019; Sallam, 2023). Research already suggests that chatbots can mimic how therapists conduct mental health assessments (Denecke & Gabarron, 2021; Vaidyam et al., 2019), they have been found to be more effective at engaging people in talk therapy in certain situations (Fiske et al., 2019), and have become highly accurate at predicting suicide (Walsh et al., 2017).

Case conceptualization can be a difficult task for systemic therapists working with families and couples (Pinsof, 1994). With multiple people in the therapy session, therapists have to analyze and synthesize multiple data points all at once. This includes intersectional aspects of multiple people's identities, perspectives, and varying experiences interacting with structures of discrimination. One of AI's strengths is its ability to quickly analyze vast amounts of data, which has researchers hopeful that this could offer more comprehensive and individualized decision-making tools for providers, including insights into which treatments and interventions are most likely to work for specific individuals (Chekroud et al., 2021). For example, utilizing AI to help therapists quickly synthesize multiple data points regarding their clients' intersectional identities in terms of race, sexual orientation, gender, ability, and so forth could become critical. Also, gaining an understanding of how these data points connect could also help therapists avoid only focusing on particular aspects of identity or aspects of identity in isolation.

While instances of explicit bias in health care settings have become less common in the United States, unconscious biases still persist. In particular, biases against marginalized populations, including women, people of color, and LGBTQ+ individuals can affect the quality of care providers deliver (FitzGerald & Hurst, 2017), their diagnostic and treatment decisions (Zener, 2019), and patient adherence to treatment (Hall et al., 2015). For example, we know that autism is commonly underdiagnosed in women, which could be because autism is seen as less typical in women; thus, doctors might miss the signs in women (Zener, 2019). But it could also be due to the current way that we diagnose mental health disorders, which relies on observable symptoms, which humans can only assess to a certain point and are prone to biases (FitzGerald & Hurst, 2017). And despite current efforts to reduce bias in health care, so far, it has not worked (Vela et al., 2022). AI's ability to analyze more subtle patterns and synthesize more contextual factors might offer more accurate diagnoses than humans, which could eliminate today's diagnostic biases (Garb, 2021; Zener, 2019).

AI's Potential to Perpetuate Harm

But AI is not without biases of its own. Algorithms that fuel AI technology have been known to be discriminatory, biased, and even dangerous (Hooker, 2021; Miller, 2020; Hundt et al., 2022). If colonialism is a system that is designed to create and enforce inequality, then by this definition, colonialism also has no limits on what, when, or how it can establish and enforce inequality (Bermúdez et al., 2016). The concern that AI could be developed and deployed in order to perpetuate inequalities within our society has legitimacy. After all, mental health has a long history of being one of the most effective ways of establishing a system of power and control. For example, colonial settlers in the United States used psychological pathology (e.g., delusional, lazy, unintelligent descriptions) as a way to justify their actions against Indigenous and enslaved African peoples (Jordan, 2021). Thus, it is healthy to remain skeptical when it comes to proponents of AI being particularly interested in disrupting the mental health field, especially in the name of "helping."

Also, as AI continues to be developed with little regard for ethical considerations and a lack of regulatory oversight, the likelihood is high that we will continue to see algorithmic biases, ignoring of Indigenous and non-Western knowledge, and a continued lack of transparency and accountability (Benjamin, 2019; Chen et al., 2021; Noble, 2018). If family therapists are to embrace AI tools, how can we be certain that the technology is not perpetuating oppressive harm to our clients? The current answer is that we cannot be certain.

But in order to understand why these issues exist in AI, it is important to first have a general understanding of how these technologies work.

AI systems are powered by computational algorithms, which, for simplicity's sake, you can think of as a set of instructions that allow it to make decisions based on predictions. The algorithms use large amounts of data in order to establish and recognize patterns or make predictions. For example, algorithms in social media use data about how you use the platform to learn your preferences and then tailor what to show you. Even simple web searches in a search engine utilize complex algorithms to make decisions about which results to show you and which to hide. In theory, algorithms are intended to make the overall product experience better by being more personalized to the user and, thus, more helpful.

However, in order for these algorithms to be helpful, they must first be trained, which is where data biases and algorithmic discrimination most commonly occur. In the same way that a toddler learns through receiving corrective feedback, AI's algorithms must also receive feedback through training in order for them to learn, adapt, and ultimately improve over time as they become exposed to more data. Because a significant amount of data is often sourced from the internet and used to train large AI models, many of the data sets themself are inherently discriminatory, biased, and harmful (Hooker, 2021; Miller, 2020; Hundt et al., 2022). In fact, when AI is trained with large amounts of data that naturally reflects the values, beliefs, and ideas of dominant, majority groups, AI reflects that world back to us, including racist, sexist, and homophobic narratives. Using data that contains biased or nonrepresentative data of minoritized populations, AI algorithms can perpetuate and amplify existing oppressive views.

In the book "Algorithms of Oppression," Safiya Umoja Noble (2018) recounts her experience of searching the internet for the keywords "black girls" when sexist, racist, and pornographic suggestions were delivered as the top results. More recently, LLMs have been found to confidently repeat false, racist conspiracy theories (Ryan-Mosley, 2023), have political biases (Motoki et al., 2023), and make racist judgments on the basis of users' dialect (Hofmann et al., 2024). All of this evidence concludes that these models are becoming more covert in their racism as the models get larger. Examples of algorithmic discrimination will continue to make headlines as the issue is not with any one company but rather with the technology itself, as it reflects dominant ideas that are rooted in racism, sexism, and homophobia. While it is impossible to know the intentions of the companies responsible for creating these algorithms, we do know that AI can be designed to amplify harmful ideologies.

When AI models are trained on data that often prioritizes Western knowledge, they may not recognize or value non-Western knowledge, context, and healing practices. Thinking about applications within mental health care, this could potentially lead AI models to perpetuate stereotypes, offer inappropriate treatment recommendations, or even guide clinicians to misdiagnose their clients. This could easily happen if an AI model is trained on data that is biased toward and overrepresents Western diagnostic criteria and is unable to pick up on cultural nuances when it comes to clients' mental health symptoms. For example, AI models could mistakenly pathologize specific symptoms that are completely normal within the client's cultural context but considered pathological within Western medicine. AI models that have been trained on biased data might also disregard culturally appropriate healing practices. Disregarding these perspectives is problematic as this can potentially lead to the eradication of cultural knowledge and practices that are essential for the health and happiness of many communities.

Without addressing these issues, there are serious concerns that AI development will continue to occur in a direction that mirrors the exploitative nature of colonialism. AI researcher Abeba Birhane (2020) describes what we are currently seeing in AI development as "digital colonialism" - where Western-based tech companies, driven by profits, wield immense global power. As with traditional colonialism, digital colonialism is also focused on "the desire to dominate, monitor, and influence social, political, and cultural discourse through the control of core communication and infrastructure mediums" (Birhane, 2020, para. 1). One of the most obvious examples of this can be seen in the exploitation of workers engaging in data labeling work that fuels AI training. Data labeling involves humans manually adding labels to raw data, which can then be used to train AI platforms. These labeling tasks can be anything from tagging images with contextual variables, proofreading text, or flagging X-rated content. All of the algorithm models that power AI technology rely on massive amounts of this type of data in order to be trained, function, and (most importantly) improve. Venezuela is a notable country where this type of work has become particularly popular, but workers living in many low-income countries in the Global South have been exploited for their cheap data labeling labor (Birhane, 2020). "Ghost work" is a term coined by Gray and Suri (2022) that refers to the often overworked and underpaid invisible human workforce behind data-labeling tasks. Many workers complete these tasks for pennies, do not get health benefits or sick time, and can be fired at any time for any reason. The growing need for this kind of data (and the cheap labor that creates it) has been fueled by tech giants wanting to capture market share and generate profits as quickly as possible. AI companies are thus incentivized to prioritize building bigger AI models as quickly as possible without considering the safety and potential harm of these technologies. As it stands today, development is happening so quickly that it's difficult to anticipate the full extent of the ethical challenges with the current and future state of AI technology, especially when applied to mental health care.

This problem is not surprising given that, thus far, little regulatory or legislative oversight has been implemented on AI development. Although most AI companies have their own internal ethics divisions that conduct research and advise on product development, historically speaking, this has not been very effective. As a case example, Dr. Timnit Gebru, a prominent AI ethics researcher, was hired by Google to combat the risk of racism and bias in their AI products. However, when Dr. Gebru coauthored a paper highlighting racial biases found in products made by Google (and other tech companies), she was asked to withdraw her paper or resign. And then when Dr. Gebru refused to withdraw the paper from publication, she was asked to resign.

In the paper (Bender et al., 2021), Dr. Gebru and team argued that the sheer speed of AI development was problematic, and they warned that it would lead to biased outputs and unintended consequences. We know that the researchers were correct about their warnings, as we have seen extensive literature written about the various ways that AI technologies are littered with biases, stereotypes, and discrimination (Birhane et al., 2021; Buolamwini & Gebru, 2018; Raji & Buolamwini, 2019). These are not only theoretical in nature, but there is a growing wealth of examples of AI applications having harmful consequences in the real world. For example, AI was utilized to detect skin cancer but only accurately on patients with light-colored skin (Wen et al., 2021), AI-generated images are already being used within the global health community even though the images often perpetuate stereotypes and power imbalances (Alenichev et al., 2023), and an AI facial-recognition crime-prediction tool incorrectly identified several Black men, leading to their arrests (Johnson, 2022).

It is also no secret that the tech industry has historically lagged significantly in its hiring of women and people of color, but the problem is even more prevalent within the AI sector. Specifically, there is a particularly low representation of black, Indigenous, and other people of color working in AI (Howard, 2021). As AI technology continues to impact our lives, ensuring that the teams who are working on the development of this technology encompass diverse perspectives is essential to preventing and overcoming bias. Otherwise, building AI without diverse input means the technology risks reflecting the limitations of its creators rather than the needs of a diverse society. The only way to build truly impactful and unbiased AI is through diverse teams shaping the algorithms and by utilizing inclusive datasets from the very beginning.

The Need for Systemic Perspectives in AI: Where Are The Family Therapists In Mental Health Tech?

While my experience working at a mental health tech company helped me see the potential value of AI technology in mental health care, it also underscored the urgency for family therapists to become more influential in the development of these technologies. Maynard Holliday, Assistant Secretary of Defense for Critical Technologies, said: "If you're not at the table, you're on the menu" (as cited in Johnson, K., 2022). At the time, I was one of the few employees who had a clinical background, and I kept wondering why there were so few clinicians involved in this important work. More specifically, I kept wondering, where are the family therapists? Yet, despite the prevalence and continued expansion of AI, the field of family therapy has been largely silent on this topic.

This might be because specific use cases for AI in clinical work have yet to materialize substantially at scale. Still, many are championing the promise of AI tools for both clients and therapists, and these aspirations range from clients being able to utilize chatbots to supplement their therapy sessions (Fiske et al., 2019) to therapists using AI-powered documentation tools to increase their productivity (Thakkar et al., 2024). Aspects of the technology have already been deployed in some large electronic health record (EHR) platforms (Lee et al., 2023). Soon, the chances are high that AI will have an expanding role in our clinical work. Many see the goal of the eventual integration of AI in mental health care as a way to make therapy more accessible, individualized, and effective for various populations.

However, there are also a number of critics who have drawn attention to this era in technology by warning about the parallels between AI development and colonialism. In fact, these technologies have proven to be some of the most effective ways to spread misinformation, limit exposure to certain information, and reinforce oppressive ideologies (Benjamin, 2019; Chen et al., 2023; Noble, 2018). As interest grows for AI-driven tools to be developed for widespread adoption, with some specifically for therapists, the risks are high as these tools have the power to dismantle or reinforce oppressive ideologies.

More troubling, while a growing body of literature has been discussing the implications of AI development for therapists (Cho et al., 2023; Craig et al., 2018; Dino et al., 2019; Fitzpatrick et al., 2017; Grodniewicz & Hohol, 2023; Howard et al., 2017; Khawaja & Bélisle-Pipon, 2023; Liu et al., 2023; Opel et al., 2023; Sedlakova & Trachsel, 2023; Sin, 2024), family therapy has been largely absent in this conversation. This is unfortunate as family therapists have the unique opportunity to critique and influence AI development by analyzing its abilities through a systemic lens. In fact, any discussion about AI in mental health care should always include systemic family therapists because we are a unique segment of the clinical provider population who are inherently considering the larger socio-political contexts. If we are not actively involved in influencing the development of this technology, we run the risk of allowing AI tools to amplify and perpetuate the harmful effects of colonialism, potentially even in our clinical work, and we might miss opportunities for it to make therapy more accessible, individualized, and effective, as long as we are aware of its limitations.

The future impact of AI on the field of family therapy or the mental health field in general remains unknown. While some have wondered if it could replace human health care providers altogether (Goldhahn et al., 2018; Mainous, 2022), many have warned that the technology will not be as disruptive for a long time, if ever, as it hits its own limitations (Dave et al., 2023; Dergaa et al., 2024; Verghese et al., 2018; Woodnutt et al., 2024; Younis et al., 2024), Still, the growing number of applications of AI technology in aspects of our profession and its continued influence on our lives is irrefutable. For family therapists to be uninvolved in the development and application of AI would be a missed opportunity as, without careful consideration, these tools have proven to have the ability to perpetuate colonialist actions instead of dismantling them.

For this reason, any discussion about how to utilize AI-driven tools in mental health care must include systemic family therapists. We are a unique segment of the clinical-provider population who are inherently considering the larger sociopolitical context of how AI tools might amplify existing inequalities. If we are not actively involved in the development of this technology, we run the risk of allowing it to perpetuate the harmful effects of colonialism, potentially even in our clinical work, and we might miss opportunities for it to help foster equity.

I am not advocating for family therapists to leave the profession in order to become software engineers or data scientists. Instead, I am calling for family therapists to become influential advocates in AI development. The first way to do this is through seeking out educational opportunities and training on ethical AI development in order to become influential advocates. Many organizations have started to offer webinars and courses on foundational knowledge about AI. Universities have also started to offer educational programs specifically in AI. Arizona State University was the first university to have a collaboration with OpenAI and now offers a degree program in AI. However, current options for therapists to learn more about specific applications of AI in mental health are admittedly limited. Therefore, we need more training specifically on responsible AI development for mental health. It is also critical that therapists have access to continuing education that is focused on the ethical issues surrounding the use of AI in clinical settings.

Secondly, family therapists can become influential advocates by lending our systemic perspective in shaping the ethical development of AI. Joining interdisciplinary AI ethics boards can ensure our voices are heard regarding the potential impact and biases of these technologies and ensure that AI-driven tools in mental health are considering the sociopolitical context. Also, joining professional organizations can be useful through networking with others who are already working on AI in mental health. For example, The Partnership on AI is an interdisciplinary organization that is focused on responsible AI development by including diverse voices and perspectives. Being able to offer your expertise in systemic family therapy to engage public policymakers, engineers, data scientists, product designers, and so forth can be helpful in guiding ethical AI development.

Third, family therapists can become influential advocates in AI development by publishing interdisciplinary research on a wide range of issues related to the ethical development of

AI in family therapy. At the time of publication, research on AI in mental health was sparse and virtually nonexistent in family therapy journals. For a technology that could potentially change how we practice, we need to produce impactful research on how AI technologies impact our clinical work and the lives of our clients. Research in our field from family therapy experts is essential to prevent AI from perpetuating the very oppressions we seek to dismantle and help families heal from.

Finally, family therapists can also engage with communities that are focused on the intersection of technology and mental health. Therapists in Tech, for instance, is a network of therapists that advocates for the inclusion of diverse clinical voices in digital mental health. Their community continues to grow through a dedicated workspace in the messaging app Slack. Additionally, diverse representation is crucial for responsible AI development, and groups like Black in AI, Queer in AI, and Indigenous in AI are all examples of communities fostering inclusion within the AI field and advocating for AI to consider the needs of various populations. While not explicitly focused on mental health, their work and research can significantly impact how AI impacts mental health care.

Conclusion

Although there are many unknowns about the future of AI technology, these systems must be designed and implemented as tools to dismantle, not perpetuate, the effects of colonialism. This is especially critical for AI tools that will be used within clinical work. AI holds much potential to either dismantle or replicate existing power structures, but family therapists have a unique opportunity to shape the development and deployment of AI technologies in mental health care. By leveraging our understanding of family systems, power, and oppression, we can help ensure that AI benefits everyone while working toward advancing the adoption of decolonialist therapeutic practices. I call on family therapists to leverage their systemic expertise to influence AI development, particularly regarding applications within mental health care.

As I mentioned before, my focus in this chapter is intentionally broad in order to offer a more holistic discussion on the topic. The example ideas above might not ever become a reality, or there might be better use cases that eventually come into existence. I remain cautious about being too optimistic, fatalistic, or prescriptive when it comes to the future of AI. As it currently stands, we have yet to realize the full potential, limitations, and impact (positive and negative) of the technology on our field and in the world. So, though we must remain cautious, it is important for us to also remain curious.

References

Afuape, T. (2020). Radical systemic intervention that goes to the root: Working alongside inner-city school children, linking trauma with oppression and consciousness with action. *Journal of Family Therapy, 42*(3), 425–52. https://doi.org/10.1111/1467-6427.12304

Ahuvia, I. L., & Schleider, J. L. (2023). Potential harms from emphasizing individual factors over structural factors in cognitive behavioral therapy with stigmatized groups. *The Behavior Therapist, 46*(7), 248–54. https://doi.org/10.31234/osf.io/n65fj

Alenichev, A., Kingori, P., & Grietens, K. P. (2023). Reflections before the storm: The AI reproduction of biased imagery in global health visuals. *The Lancet Global Health, 11*, E1496–E1498. https://doi.org/10.1016/S2214-109X(23)00329-7

Auerswald, E. H. (1971). Families, change, and the ecological perspective. *Family Process, 10*(3), 263–80. https://doi.org/10.1111/j.1545-5300.1971.00263.x

Bender, E.M., Gebru, T., McMillan-Major, A., & Shmitchell, S. (2021). On the dangers of stochastic parrots: Can language models be too big? *Proceedings of the 2021 ACM Conference on Fairness, Accountability, and Transparency, Association for Computing Machinery, New York, NY*, 610–23. https://doi.org/10.1145/3442188.3445922

Benjamin, R. (2019). *Race after technology: Abolitionist tools for the new Jim Code.* Polity.

Bermúdez, J.M., Muruthi, B.A. & Jordan, L.S. (2016). Decolonizing research methods for family science: Creating space at the center. *Journal of Family Theory & Review, 8*, 192–206. https://doi.org/10.1111/jftr.12139

Birhane, A. (2020). Algorithmic colonization of Africa. *SCRIPTed, 17*(2), 389 http://dx.doi.org/10.2966/scrip.170220.389

Birhane, A., Kalluri, P., Card, D., Agnew, W., Dotan, R., & Bao, M. (2021). The values encoded in machine learning research. *Proceedings of the 2022 ACM Conference on Fairness, Accountability, and Transparency, New York, NY*, 173–84. https://doi.org/10.1145/3531146.3533083

Brown, T. B., Mann, B., Ryder, N., Subbiah, M., Kaplan, J., Dhariwal, P., Neelakantan, A., Shyam, P., Sastry, G., Askell, A., Agarwal, S., Herbert-Voss, A., Krueger, G., Henighan, T., Child, R., Ramesh, A., Ziegler, D. M., Wu, J., Winter, C.,... Amodei, D. (2020). *Language models are few-shot learners* [Conference presentation]. Conference on Neural Information Processing Systems, Vancouver, Canada. https://doi.org/10.48550/arXiv.2005.14165

Buolamwini, J., & Gebru, T. (2018). Gender shades: Intersectional accuracy disparities in commercial gender classification. *Proceedings of Machine Learning Research, Conference on Fairness, Accountability, and Transparency, 81*, 77–91. https://proceedings.mlr.press/v81/buolamwini18a.html

Chekroud, A. M., Bondar, J., Delgadillo, J., Doherty, G., Wasil, A., Fokkema, M., Cohen, Z., Belgrave, D., DeRubeis, R., Iniesta, R., Dwyer, D., & Choi, K. (2021). The promise of machine learning in predicting treatment outcomes in psychiatry. *World Psychiatry, 20*(2), 154–70. https://doi.org/10.1002/wps.20882

Chekroud, A. M., Zotti, R. J., Shehzad, Z., Gueorguieva, R., Johnson, M. K., Trivedi, M. H., Cannon, T. D., Krystal, J. H., & Corlett, P. R. (2016). Cross-trial prediction of treatment outcome in depression: A machine learning approach. *The Lancet Psychiatry, 3*(3), 243–50. https://doi.org/10.1016/S2215-0366(15)00471-X

Chen, R. J., Wang, J. J., Williamson, D. F. K., Chen, T. Y., Lipkova, J., Lu, M. Y., Sahai, S., & Mahmood, F. (2023). Algorithmic fairness in artificial intelligence for medicine and healthcare *Nature Biomedical Engineering, 7*(6), 719–42. https://doi.org/10.1038/s41551-023-01056-8

Chin, J., Hughes, G., & Miller, A. (2022). Examining our own relationships to racism as the foundation of decolonising systemic practices: "No time like the present." *Journal of Family Therapy, 44*(1), 76–90. https://doi.org/10.1111/1467-6427.12384

Cho, Y. M., Rai, S., Ungar, L., Sedoc, J., & Guntuku, S. C. (2023). An integrative survey on mental health conversational agents to bridge computer science and medical perspectives. *Proceedings of the Conference on Empirical Methods in Natural Language Processing*, 11346–69. https://doi.org/10.18653/v1/2023.emnlp-main.698

Coombs, N., Meriwether, W., Caringi, J., & Newcomer, S. (2021). Barriers to healthcare access among U.S. adults with mental health challenges: A population-based study. *SSM Population Health, 15*, Article 100847. https://doi.org/10.1016/j.ssmph.2021.100847

Craig, T. K., Rus-Calafell, M., Ward, T., Leff, J. P., Huckvale, M., Howarth, E., Emsley, R., & Garety, P. A. (2018). AVATAR therapy for auditory verbal hallucinations in people with psychosis: A single-blind, randomised controlled trial. *The Lancet Psychiatry, 5*(1), 31–40. https://doi.org/10.1016/S2215-0366(17)30427-3

D'Arrigo-Patrick, J., Hoff, C., Knudson-Martin, C., & Tuttle, A. (2017). Navigating Critical Theory and Postmodernism: Social justice and therapist power in family therapy. *Family Process, 56*(3), 574–88. https://doi.org/10.1111/famp.12236

Dave, T., Athaluri, S.A., & Singh, S. (2023). ChatGPT in medicine: An overview of its applications, advantages, limitations, future prospects, and ethical considerations. *Frontiers in Artificial Intelligence, 6,* Article 1169595. https://doi.org/10.3389/frai.2023.1169595

David, D., Cristea, I., & Hofmann, S. G. (2018). Why Cognitive Behavioral Therapy is the current gold standard of psychotherapy. *Frontiers in Psychiatry, 9,* Article 4. https://doi.org/10.3389/fpsyt.2018.00004

Denecke, K., & Gabarron, E. (2021). How artificial intelligence for healthcare look like in the future? *Studies in Health Technology and Informatics, 281,* 860–64. https://doi.org/10.3233/SHTI210301

Dergaa, I., Fekih-Romdhane, F., Hallit, S., Loch, A.A., Glenn, J.M., Fessi, M.S., Ben Aissa, M., Souissi, N., Guelmami, N., Swed, S., El Omri, A., Bragazzi, N.L., & Ben Saad, H. (2024). ChatGPT is not ready yet for use in providing mental health assessment and interventions. *Frontiers in Psychiatry, 14.* https://doi.org/10.3389/fpsyt.2023.1277756

Dino, F., Zandie, R., Abdollahi, H., Schoeder, S., & Mahoor, M.H. (2019). Delivering Cognitive Behavioral Therapy using a conversational social robot. *IEEE/RSJ International Conference on Intelligent Robots and Systems (IROS), Macau, China,* 2089–95. https://doi.org/10.1109/IROS40897.2019.8968576

Essien, B., & Asamoah, M. K. (2020). Reviewing the common barriers to the mental healthcare delivery in Africa. *Journal of Religion and Health, 59*(5), 2531–55. https://doi.org/10.1007/s10943-020-01059-8

Ettman, C., & Galea, S. (2023). The potential influence of AI on population mental health. *JMIR Mental Health, 10,* Article e49936. https://doi.org/10.2196/49936

Falicov, C. J. (1995). Training to think culturally: A multidimensional comparative framework. *Family Process, 34*(4), 373–88. https://doi.org/10.1111/j.1545-5300.1995.00373.x

Falicov, C., Nakash, O., & Alegría, M. (2021). Centering the voice of the client: On becoming a collaborative practitioner with low-income individuals and families. *Family Process, 60*(2), 670–87. https://doi.org/10.1111/famp.12558

Fernando, S. (2014). *Mental health worldwide.* Palgrave Macmillan. https://doi.org/10.1057/9781137329608_6

Fernando, S. (2017). *Institutional racism in psychiatry and clinical psychology: Race matters in mental health.* Palgrave Macmillan. https://doi.org/10.1007/978-3-319-62728-1

Fiske, A., Henningsen, P., & Buyx, A. (2019). Your robot therapist will see you now: Ethical implications of embodied artificial intelligence in psychiatry, psychology, and psychotherapy. *Journal of Medical Internet Research, 21*(5), Article e13216. https://doi.org/10.2196/13216

FitzGerald, C., & Hurst, S. (2017). Implicit bias in healthcare professionals: A systematic review. *BMC Medical Ethics, 18*(1), Article 19. https://doi.org/10.1186/s12910-017-0179-8

Fitzpatrick, K. K., Darcy, A., & Vierhile, M. (2017). Delivering Cognitive Behavior Therapy to young adults with symptoms of depression and anxiety using a fully automated conversational agent (Woebot): A randomized controlled trial. *JMIR Mental Health, 4*(2), Article e19. https://doi.org/10.2196/mental.7785

Garb H. N. (2021). Race bias and gender bias in the diagnosis of psychological disorders. *Clinical Psychology Review, 90,* Article 102087. https://doi.org/10.1016/j.cpr.2021.102087

Goldhahn, J., Rampton, V., & Spinas, G. A. (2018). Could artificial intelligence make doctors obsolete? *BMJ: British Medical Journal, 363,* Article k4563. https://doi.org/10.1136/bmj.k4563

Gray, M.L. & Suri, S. (2019). *Ghost work: How to stop Silicon Valley from building a new global underclass.* Harper Business.

Grodniewicz, J. P., & Hohol, M. (2023). Waiting for a digital therapist: Three challenges on the path to psychotherapy delivered by artificial intelligence. *Frontiers in Psychiatry, 14,* Article 1190084. https://doi.org/10.3389/fpsyt.2023.1190084

Gureje, O., & Lasebikan, V. O. (2006). Use of mental health services in a developing country: Results from the Nigerian survey of mental health and well-being. *Social Psychiatry and Psychiatric Epidemiology, 41*(1), 44–49. https://doi.org/10.1007/s00127-005-0001-7

Hair, H., Fine, M., & Ryan, B. (1996). Expanding the context of family therapy. *American Journal of Family Therapy, 24*(4), 291–304. https://doi.org/10.1080/01926189608251042

Hall, W. J., Chapman, M. V., Lee, K. M., Merino, Y. M., Thomas, T. W., Payne, B. K., Eng, E., Day, S. H., & Coyne-Beasley, T. (2015). Implicit racial/ethnic bias among health care professionals and its influence on health care outcomes: A systematic review. *American Journal of Public Health, 105*(12), e60–e76. https://doi.org/10.2105/AJPH.2015.302903

Harp, K.L. & Bunting, A.M. (2020) The racialized nature of child welfare policies and the social control of black bodies. *Social Politics: International Studies in Gender, State & Society, 27*(2), 258–81. https://doi.org/10.1093/sp/jxz039

Hodgkinson, S., Godoy, L., Beers, L. S., & Lewin, A. (2017). Improving mental health access for low-income children and families in the primary care setting. *Pediatrics, 139*(1), Article e20151175. https://doi.org/10.1542/peds.2015-1175

Hoffman, L. (1992). A reflexive stance for family therapy. In S. McNamee & K. J. Gergen (Eds.), *Therapy as social construction* (pp. 7–24). Sage Publications.

Hofmann, V., Kalluri, P. R., Jurafsky, D., & King, S. (2024). Dialect prejudice predicts AI decisions about people's character, employability, and criminality. ArXiv. https://doi.org/10.48550/arXiv.2403.00742

Holyoak, D., McPhee, D., Hall, G., & Fife, S. (2021). Microlevel advocacy: A common process in couple and family therapy. *Family process, 60*(2), 654–69. https://doi.org/10.1111/famp.12620

Hooker, S. (2021). Moving beyond "algorithmic bias is a data problem". *Patterns, 2*(4), Article 100241. https://doi.org/10.1016/j.patter.2021.100241

Howard, A. (2021, August 24). Real talk: Intersectionality and AI. *MIT Sloan Management Review.* https://sloanreview.mit.edu/article/real-talk-intersectionality-and-ai/

Howard A., Zhang C., & Horvitz E. (2017). Addressing bias in machine learning algorithms: A pilot study on emotion recognition for intelligent systems. *IEEE Workshop on Advanced Robotics and its Social Impacts (ARSO), Austin, TX*, 1–7. https://doi.org/10.1109/ARSO.2017.8025197

Hundt, A., Agnew, W., Zeng, V., Kacianka, S., & Gombolay, M. (2022). Robots enact malignant stereotypes. *ACM Conference on Fairness, Accountability, and Transparency (FAccT '22), Seoul, Republic of Korea*, 743–56. https://doi.org/10.1145/3531146.3533138

Hutcheon, E. J., & Lashewicz, B. (2020). Tracing and troubling continuities between ableism and colonialism in Canada. *Disability & Society, 35*(5), 695–714. https://doi.org/10.1080/09687599.2019.1647145

Imber-Black, E. (1991). A family-larger-system perspective. *Family Systems Medicine, 9*(4), 371–95. https://doi.org/10.1037/h0089322

Johnson, K. (2022, March 7). How wrongful arrests based on AI derailed 3 men's lives. *Wired.* https://www.wired.com/story/wrongful-arrests-ai-derailed-3-mens-lives

Johnson, K. (2022, August 18). *How to stop robots from becoming racist. Wired.* https://www.wired.com/story/how-to-stop-robots-becoming-racist/

Jordan, L.S. (2021) Unsettling colonial mentalities in family therapy: Entering negotiated spaces. *Journal of Family Therapy, 44*(1), 171–85. https://doi.org/10.1111/1467-6427.12374

Khawaja, Z., & Bélisle-Pipon, J. C. (2023). Your robot therapist is not your therapist: understanding the role of AI-powered mental health chatbots. *Frontiers in Digital Health, 5*, Article 1278186. https://doi.org/10.3389/fdgth.2023.1278186

Laranjo, L., Dunn, A. G., Tong, H. L., Kocaballi, A. B., Chen, J., Bashir, R., Surian, D., Gallego, B., Magrabi, F., Lau, A. Y. S., & Coiera, E. (2018). Conversational agents in healthcare: a systematic review. *Journal of the American Medical Informatics Association: JAMIA, 25*(9), 1248–58. https://doi.org/10.1093/jamia/ocy072

Lee, R. Y., Kross, E. K., Torrence, J., Li, K. S., Sibley, J., Cohen, T., Lober, W. B., Engelberg, R. A., & Curtis, R. (2023). Assessment of natural language processing of electronic health records to measure goals-of-care discussions as a clinical trial outcome. *JAMA Network Open, 6*(3), Article e231204. https://doi.org/10.1001/jamanetworkopen.2023.1204

Levinson, C. A., Fitterman-Harris, H. F., Patterson, S., Harrop, E., Turner, C., May, M., Steinberg, D., Muhlheim, L., Millner, R., Trujillo-ChiVacuan, E., Averyt, J., Peebles, R., Rosenbluth, S., & Becker, C. B. (2023). The unintentional harms of weight management treatment: Time for a change. *the Behavior Therapist, 46,* 271–82. https://doi.org/10.17605/OSF.IO/SU6ZK

Liu, S., Wright, A. P., Patterson, B. L., Wanderer, J. P., Turer, R. W., Nelson, S. D., McCoy, A. B., Sittig, D. F., & Wright, A. (2023). Assessing the value of ChatGPT for clinical decision support optimization. *MedRxiv.* https://doi.org/10.1101/2023.02.21.23286254

MacKinnon, L. K., & Miller, D. (1987). The new epistemology and the Milan approach: Feminist and sociopolitical considerations. *Journal of Marital and Family Therapy, 13*(2), 139–55. https://doi.org/10.1111/j.1752-0606.1987.tb00692.x

Mainous, A. G. (2022). Will technology and artificial intelligence make the primary care doctor obsolete? Remember the Luddites. *Frontiers in Medicine, 9,* Article 878281. https://doi.org/10.3389/fmed.2022.878281

Marsella, A. J., & Yamada, A. M. (2000). Culture and mental health: An introduction and overview of foundations, concepts, and issues. In I. Cuéllar & F. A. Paniagua (Eds.), *Handbook of multicultural mental health* (pp. 3–24). Academic Press. https://doi.org/10.1016/B978-012199370-2/50002-X

McDowell, T., Knudson-Martin, C., & Bermudez, J. M. (2019). Third-order thinking in family therapy: Addressing social justice across family therapy practice. *Family Process, 58*(1), 9–22. https://doi.org/10.1111/famp.12383

McGoldrick, M., & Hardy, K. Y. (2008). Introduction: Re-visioning family therapy from a multicultural perspective. In M. McGoldrick & K. V. Hardy (Eds.), *Re-visioning family therapy: Race, culture, and gender in clinical practice* (2nd ed., pp. 3–24). The Guilford Press.

Miller, K. (2020). A matter of perspective: Discrimination, bias, and inequality in AI. In M. Jackson & M. Shelly (Eds.), *Legal Regulations, Implications, and Issues Surrounding Digital Data* (pp. 182–202). IGI Global Scientific Publishing. https://doi.org/10.4018/978-1-7998-3130-3.ch010

Miner, A. S., Milstein, A., Schueller, S., Hegde, R., Mangurian, C., & Linos, E. (2016). Smartphone-based conversational agents and responses to questions about mental health, interpersonal violence, and physical health. *JAMA Internal Medicine, 176*(5), 619–25. https://doi.org/10.1001/jamainternmed.2016.0400

Miner, A. S., Shah, N., Bullock, K. D., Arnow, B. A., Bailenson, J., & Hancock, J. (2019). Key considerations for incorporating conversational AI in psychotherapy. *Frontiers in Psychiatry, 10,* Article 441761. https://doi.org/10.3389/fpsyt.2019.00746

Moore, T., & Brodt, M. (2023). When healers have harmed: Towards culturally responsive CBT with ME/CFS patients. *the Behavior Therapist, 46*(8), 347–54.

Motoki, F., Pinho Neto, V. & Rodrigues, V. (2024). More human than human: Measuring ChatGPT political bias. *Public Choice, 198,* 3–23. https://doi.org/10.1007/s11127-023-01097-2

National Center for Health Workforce Analysis. (2023). Behavioral health workforce, 2023. *Health Resources and Services Administration.* https://bhw.hrsa.gov/sites/default/files/bureau-health-workforce/Behavioral-Health-Workforce-Brief-2023.pdf

Noble, S. U. (2018). *Algorithms of oppression: How search engines reinforce racism.* New York University Press.

Opel, D. J., Kious, B. M., & Cohen, I. G. (2023). AI as a mental health therapist for adolescents. *JAMA Pediatrics, 177*(12), 1253–54. https://doi.org/10.1001/jamapediatrics.2023.4215

Pinsof, W. M. (1994). An integrative systems perspective on the therapeutic alliance: Theoretical, clinical, and research implications. In A. O. Horvath & L. S. Greenberg (Eds.), *The working alliance: Theory, research, and practice* (pp. 173–95). John Wiley & Sons.

Porter, D. (2014). Colonization by/in psychiatry: From over-medicalization to democratization. *Journal of Ethics in Mental Health, 9,* 1–7.

Raji, I.D., & Buolamwini, J. (2019). Actionable auditing: Investigating the impact of publicly naming biased performance results of commercial AI products. *Proceedings of the 2019 AAAI/ACM*

Conference on AI, Ethics, and Society, Honolulu, HI, 429–35. https://dl.acm.org/doi/10.1145/3306618.3314244

Rober, P., & Seltzer, M. (2010). Avoiding colonizer positions in the therapy room: Some ideas about the challenges of dealing with the dialectic of misery and resources in families. *Family Process, 49*(1), 123–37. https://doi.org/10.1111/j.1545-5300.2010.01312.x

Ryan-Mosley, T. (2023). How generative AI is boosting the spread of disinformation and propaganda, *MIT Technology Review, 4.* https://www.technologyreview.com/2023/10/04/1080801/generative-ai-boosting-disinformation-and-propaganda-freedom-house/

Sallam, M. (2023). ChatGPT utility in healthcare education, research, and practice: Systematic review on the promising perspectives and valid concerns. *Healthcare (Basel, Switzerland), 11*(6), 887. https://doi.org/10.3390/healthcare11060887

Sedlakova, J., & Trachsel, M. (2023). Conversational artificial intelligence in psychotherapy: A new therapeutic tool or agent? *The American Journal of Bioethics, 23*(5), 4–13. https://doi.org/10.1080/15265161.2022.2048739

Sin, J. (2024). An AI chatbot for talking therapy referrals. *Nature Medicine, 30*(2), 350–51. https://doi.org/10.1038/s41591-023-02773-y

Thakkar, A., Gupta, A., & De Sousa, A. (2024). Artificial intelligence in positive mental health: A narrative review. *Frontiers in Digital Health, 6,* Article 1280235. https://doi.org/10.3389/fdgth.2024.1280235

Unger, J. B. (2011). Cultural identity and public health. In S. J. Schwartz, K. Luyckx, & V. L. Vignoles (Eds.), *Handbook of identity theory and research* (pp. 811–25). Springer Science and Business Media. https://doi.org/10.1007/978-1-4419-7988-9_34

Uttal, L. (2009). (Re)visioning family ties to communities and contexts. In S. A. Lloyd, A. L. Few (Eds.) *(Re)visioning family ties to communities and contexts* (pp. 134–46). SAGE Publications, Inc., https://doi.org/10.4135/9781412982801

Vaidyam, A. N., Wisniewski, H., Halamka, J. D., Kashavan, M. S., & Torous, J. B. (2019). Chatbots and conversational agents in mental health: A review of the psychiatric landscape. *Canadian Journal of Psychiatry, 64*(7), 456–64. https://doi.org/10.1177/0706743719828977

Vecchio, K. D. D., & Lockard, J. (2004). Resistance to colonialism as the heart of family therapy practice. *Journal of Feminist Family Therapy, 16*(2), 43–66. https://doi.org/10.1300/J086v16n02_03

Vela, M. B., Erondu, A. I., Smith, N. A., Peek, M. E., Woodruff, J. N., & Chin, M. H. (2022). Eliminating explicit and implicit biases in health care: Evidence and research needs. *Annual Review of Public Health, 43,* 477–501. https://doi.org/10.1146/annurev-publhealth-052620-103528

Verghese, A., Shah, N.H., Harrington, R.A. (2018). What this computer needs is a physician: Humanism and artificial intelligence. *JAMA, 319*(1), 19–20. https://doi.org/10.1001/jama.2017.19198

Waldegrave, C. (2009). Cultural, gender, and socioeconomic contexts in therapeutic and social policy work. *Family Process, 48*(1), 85–101. https://doi.org/10.1111/j.1545-5300.2009.01269.x

Walsdorf, A. A., Jordan, L. S., McGeorge, C. R., & Caughy, M. O. (2020). White supremacy and the web of family science: Implications of the missing spider. *Journal of Family Theory & Review, 12*(1), 64–79. https://doi.org/10.1111/jftr.12364

Walsh, C. G., Ribeiro, J. D., & Franklin, J. C. (2017). Predicting risk of suicide attempts over time through machine learning. *Clinical Psychological Science, 5*(3), 457–69. https://doi.org/10.1177/2167702617691560

Watson, M. F., Turner, W. L., & Hines, P. M. (2020). Black lives matter: We are in the same storm but we are not in the same boat. *Family Process, 59*(4), 1362–73. https://doi.org/10.1111/famp.12613

Wen, D., Khan, S. M., Xu, A. J., Ibrahim, H., Smith, L. C., Caballero, J., Zepeda, L., de Blas Pérez, C., Denniston, A. K., Liu, X., & Matin, R. N. (2021). Characteristics of publicly available skin cancer image datasets: A systematic review. *The Lancet Digital Health.* https://doi.org/10.1016/s2589-7500(21)00252-1

Wieling, E., Trejo, A. N., Patterson, J. E., Weingarten, K., Falicov, C., Hernández, A. V., Heffron, L. C., Faulkner, M., & Parra-Cardona, J. R. (2020). Standing and responding in solidarity with disenfranchised immigrant families in the United States: An ongoing call for action. *Journal of Marital and Family Therapy, 46*(4), 561–76. https://doi.org/10.1111/jmft.12460

Williams, D. R., & Mohammed, S. A. (2009). Discrimination and racial disparities in health: evidence and needed research. *Journal of Behavioral Medicine, 32*(1), 20–47. https://doi.org/10.1007/s10865-008-9185-0

Woodnutt, S., Allen, C., Snowden, J., Flynn, M., Hall, S., Libberton, P., & Purvis, F. (2024). Could artificial intelligence write mental health nursing care plans? *Journal of Psychiatric and Mental Health Nursing, 31*(1), 79–86. https://doi.org/10.1111/jpm.12965

Younis, H. A., Eisa, T. A. E., Nasser, M., Sahib, T.M., Noor, A. A., Alyasiri, O. M., Salisu, S., Hayder, I. M., & Younis, H. A. (2024). A systematic review and meta-analysis of artificial intelligence tools in medicine and healthcare: Applications, considerations, limitations, motivation and challenges. *Diagnostics, 14*, 109. https://doi.org/10.3390/diagnostics14010109

Yzaguirre, M. M., PettyJohn, M. E., Tseng, C. F., Asiimwe, R., Fang, M., & Blow, A. J. (2022). Marriage and family therapy masters students' diversity course experiences. *Journal of Feminist Family Therapy, 34*(1–2), 15–37. https://doi.org/10.1080/08952833.2022.2052534

Zener, D. (2019). Journey to diagnosis for women with autism. *Advances in Autism, 5*(1), 2–13. https://doi.org/10.1108/AIA-10-2018-0041

Zhang, M., Scandiffio, J., Younus, S., Jeyakumar, T., Karsan, I., Charow, R., Salhia, M., & Wiljer, D. (2023). The adoption of AI in mental health care—perspectives from mental health professionals: Qualitative descriptive study. *JMIR Formative Research, 7*, e47847. https://doi.org/10.2196/47847

Decolonizing Life Cycle Narratives

Systemic Intersections in Family Development

Jennifer M. Sampson and Fiona E. O'Farrell

Family and human development have long been treated as a linear, universal process—a neatly staged progression of birth, childhood, adolescence, partnership, parenthood, and old age. Western psychological models have mapped out these transitions as though they unfold in a vacuum, unaffected by history, power, or the violence of exclusion. In reality, family building, childhood, love, and loss are deeply embedded in social systems, shaped by forces far beyond individual will or biological inevitability. This section asks: *What does it mean to truly decolonize our understanding of family life cycles?*

Decolonization in systemic therapy demands more than adding cultural footnotes to existing theories—it requires dismantling the colonial logics that have long dictated how family is defined and whose families are valued, whose grief is recognized, whose neurodevelopment is considered "normal," and whose reproductive choices are supported or denied. Family building, for example, is not just a matter of individual readiness; it is a site of control and resistance, a landscape where patriarchy, capitalism, and white supremacy have dictated who gets to have children, how those children should be raised, and whose bodies are pathologized along the way. Likewise, childhood development has been narrated through a Eurocentric lens that prioritizes autonomy over interdependence, cognition over relational wisdom, and compliance over creativity—often to the detriment of neurodivergent children and non-Western family structures. Even grief, a profoundly human experience, has been flattened into Western stages and medicalized trajectories, dismissing the communal, ritualistic, and generational ways that loss is held in many cultures.

The chapters in this section invite us to challenge these assumptions, offering frameworks that center justice, cultural knowledge, and liberation in our understanding of family development. In "Goodbye Birds and the Bees," we examine family building through the lens of reproductive justice, disrupting the notion that reproductive decisions exist outside of systems of oppression and control. In "Rethinking Childhood," we deconstruct ableist, Western models of child development, advocating for a neurodiversity-affirming, culturally responsive paradigm that prioritizes relational strengths over pathology. Finally, in "Grieving in the Wake of Colonialism," we reconsider the meaning of loss through a decolonial, bio-psycho-social-cultural lens, exploring how grief is shaped by oppression, migration, and historical trauma and how healing often lies in community rather than clinical detachment.

DOI: 10.4324/9781032679082-7

Decolonizing family development and systemic therapy means recognizing that family life cycles are not neutral—they are politicized, negotiated, and deeply entangled with history. It means rejecting deficit-based perspectives in favor of radical imagination. It means understanding that development, in its most authentic form, is not a straight line but a constellation of possibilities shaped by community, resistance, and reclamation.

Let's continue.

Chapter 5

Goodbye Birds and the Bees

How Systemic Therapists Can Use a Reproductive Justice Framework to Rethink Family Building

Jennifer M. Sampson

Author's Note: As a systemic therapist, educator, and advocate, my journey in this field has been deeply rooted in resistance—resistance to these legacies of control and dehumanization and resistance to the colonial systems that still dictate who has the right to exist, to create, and to care.

I come to this work from a place of both privilege and complicity. My professional training, academic roles, and clinical practice have unfolded within the institutions shaped by colonial frameworks. In those spaces, I have seen firsthand how harm is perpetuated—harm that disproportionately silences, excludes, and disenfranchises. Simultaneously, I have worked to challenge these systems by amplifying the voices and practices of those historically silenced and sidelined.

My personal journey adds layers of complexity and urgency to this work. I am a mother who has relied on Western fertility medicine to build my family, a process both deeply meaningful and tangled in the very systems I seek to critique. I am a woman whose ancestry reflects both settler and colonized lineages–an identity that holds both privilege and pain in its folds. These experiences profoundly shaped my understanding of how reproductive health was weaponized to uphold colonial hierarchies and reinforce systemic inequities. However, they have also fueled my conviction that reclaiming reproductive sovereignty—rebuilding systems of care that honor autonomy, relationality, and cultural wisdom—is both an act of resistance and a necessary step toward healing.

Introduction

The story of reproductive justice is inseparable from the history of colonization. The control of land and resources has always been entangled with the control of bodies, particularly those deemed expendable or threatening by colonial powers. As systemic therapists, we must ask how these colonial legacies shaped the ways we understand family, reproduction, and care in our field.

This chapter argues that systemic family therapy must be decolonized through a reproductive justice lens. Western family therapy models—particularly those rooted in nuclear family ideals, linear developmental frameworks, and Eurocentric notions of autonomy—often fail to recognize the structural forces shaping clients' reproductive and family-building experiences. They position challenges such as infertility, adoption struggles, and parenting obstacles as individual or relational issues rather than as deeply political and systemic concerns.

DOI: 10.4324/9781032679082-8

The central intervention of this chapter is a shift in clinical practice, moving beyond inclusion and cultural responsiveness toward actively dismantling the colonial structures that shape reproductive experiences. Reproductive Justice provides a framework for this shift:

- Expanding how we conceptualize families beyond Western nuclear norms.
- Centering autonomy, relational interdependence, and collective care.
- Addressing intergenerational reproductive oppression and trauma.
- Integrating systemic advocacy into therapeutic work.

By using reproductive justice as both a conceptual framework and a clinical practice, we can transform family therapy into a space of healing, resistance, and liberation.

The Stories Behind Reproductive Justice

When we first met, Lisa sat across from me, her hands clenched tightly in her lap. A successful, single professional in her early forties, Lisa had recently decided to pursue parenthood as a single mother by choice. However, her excitement about starting a family was dampened by repeated instances of implicit bias at her fertility clinic. "They don't say it outright," she explained, "but I feel it—the judgment when I talk about wanting to do this on my own. The assumption that I'll need financial help, or worse, that I'm making a selfish choice." The exhaustion in her voice was palpable. She was not just navigating the emotional complexity of fertility treatments; she was also confronting systemic barriers that made her feel small, as though her dream of parenthood needed to be justified by people who did not understand her life.

In another session, Jesse and Caleb, a married same-sex couple, grappled with what felt like insurmountable roadblocks in their adoption process. "We're jumping through every hoop," Caleb said, his frustration evident. "But it feels like the hoops are designed for us to fail." Jesse nodded in agreement, sharing how they had been asked invasive questions about their relationship and ability to provide a "normal" home. "What does that even mean?" Jesse asked, his voice tinged with both hurt and anger. Their dream of becoming parents had turned into a bureaucratic battle, one where the rules seemed intentionally stacked against them.

Then there was Maria, a Latina mother of two who had recently discovered she was unexpectedly pregnant. When she first came to therapy, she contemplated her options. "My family will never forgive me if I even think about abortion," she told me. However, Maria also spoke about her fears of bringing another child into a household already stretched thin, of navigating a health care system that made her feel invisible, and of how this decision would shape her future. "I don't want to be judged no matter what I decide," she said quietly. "But it feels like I'll lose no matter what I choose."

These are just a few of the many stories that unfold in the therapy room: stories of individuals and families navigating deeply personal and complex decisions about reproduction, parenting, and family building. Yet, as therapists, how often do we stop to consider how the systems these clients are navigating—fertility clinics, adoption agencies, and health care providers—are embedded in a larger framework of colonialism, patriarchy, capitalism, and white supremacy? How often do we question the assumptions we bring into the room shaped by Western ideals of family, autonomy, and progress?

Too often, the field of family therapy frames these challenges as isolated, personal struggles—choices made within a vacuum and divorced from the systems that shape them. Lisa's exhaustion is often reduced by the stress of fertility treatments. Yet, this framing ignores how medical systems have historically devalued single motherhood, labeling certain women's reproduction as "less than." Jesse and Caleb's adoption struggles are labeled bureaucratic hurdles without examining how heteronormativity continues to define who is seen as "fit" to parent. Maria's ambivalence is reduced to individual indecision rather than situated in the intersecting pressures of cultural expectations, economic inequity, and systemic reproductive oppression.

This lens—one that isolates clients' challenges from the systems shaping them— causes profound disservice to the individuals and families we aim to serve. It reinforces a Western colonized perspective that pathologizes to clients while failing to interrogate the structures that create harm. By ignoring the broader forces of oppression, clients feel as though their pain is personal rather than systemic.

These stories reveal that family building is never just about personal choices. Decisions about whether to have children, how to have children, or how to parent are deeply shaped by systems of power: colonialism, patriarchy, racism, ableism, and capitalism. These forces dictate whose families are supported and whose are devalued, whose reproduction is celebrated and whose is constrained, and whose parenting choices are respected versus scrutinized.

Reproductive justice offers a framework for understanding these struggles as manifestations of systemic oppression rather than as individual shortcomings or isolated challenges. It expands our perspective as systemic therapists, pushing us to examine how the legacy of colonialism has shaped the ways we think about family, parenting, and reproductive autonomy. It asks us to go beyond cultural responsiveness and inclusion to dismantle structures that perpetuate harm

Lisa's experience at the fertility clinic cannot be separated from a broader societal narrative that devalues single mothers, particularly women of color. Jesse and Caleb's frustration with the adoption process is tied to a long history of policies that privilege heterosexual, white, and upper-class families. Maria's ambivalence about her pregnancy reflects not only personal and cultural tensions but also the structural inequities of health care access and reproductive freedom.

As family systems practitioners, we are uniquely positioned to address these intersections. But doing so requires a shift in how we approach our work. It requires moving beyond the individual and relational focus of traditional family therapy to examine the systemic forces shaping clients' lives. It requires adopting a reproductive justice lens—one that centers autonomy, equity, and liberation in how we understand and support families.

By beginning this chapter with these stories, we aim to highlight the gap between the Western models of family development and the lived realities of clients navigating systemic oppression. These narratives set the stage for the central argument of this chapter: that family systems therapy must adopt a decolonized framework grounded in reproductive justice to truly serve the families we work with. This means:

- Critiquing Western developmental models that privilege linear, heteronormative, and Eurocentric definitions of family.
- Centering the voices, experiences, and wisdom of marginalized communities into our understanding of family and reproduction.

- Reimagining family systems not as isolated units but as deeply relational and shaped by sociopolitical and historical forces.

Through this lens, the stories of Lisa, Jesse, Caleb, and Maria are no longer just anecdotes of personal struggle. They become powerful illustrations of the need to expand how we think about families, reproduction, and justice in the therapy room. They remind us that the work of family systems therapy is not just about healing individuals; it is about dismantling the systems that harm them.

Reproductive justice (Ross & Solinger, 2017) is more than a framework; it is a movement grounded in human rights, collective liberation, and the radical reimagining of what it means to have true autonomy over one's body, family, and future. Coined in 1994 by Black women activists, including Loretta Ross, reproductive justice emerged as a response to the narrow focus of the mainstream reproductive rights movement, which largely centered white, middle-class women's access to abortion while ignoring the structural inequities that shape reproductive experiences for marginalized communities.

At its core, reproductive justice is the belief that all individuals have the right to:

- Have children.
- Not have children.
- Parent their children in safe and supportive environments.
- Control their reproductive and family-building decisions free from coercion, violence, or systemic oppression (Ross & Solinger, 2017).

Reproductive justice is not just about inclusion; it is also about liberation. While frameworks of equity and inclusion have their place in our work, they alone cannot dismantle systems that commodify and control reproductive health. These systems are not designed to be fixed with a seat at the table; they demand an entirely new table built on sovereignty and self-determination. That means honoring the right of individuals and communities to govern their own bodies, relationships, and family systems without interference.

For me, viewing reproductive justice through a decolonial lens transforms it into something much deeper than policy change or access to care. It becomes a radical act of healing and restoration, an intentional pathway to undo the damage caused by colonization. It is about more than reclaiming autonomy— it is about rebuilding systems of care rooted in ancestral wisdom, relationality, and the inherent value of all lives. This is the work that gives me hope. It's the work I believe we're called to do as systems therapists.

In this chapter, I want to explore what it means to truly embrace a decolonial perspective on reproductive justice in our work as systems therapists—not just in theory but in practice. I will share global examples of people and communities already doing this work, challenging systems that perpetuate inequality, and reclaiming knowledge that has been stolen, erased, or dismissed. Their stories show us what is possible: family building and reproductive care that exist outside colonial frameworks. My hope is that, together, we can imagine a vision of justice that does not stop at equity but moves boldly and unapologetically toward transformation. Because true justice isn't incremental—it's liberating.

Reproductive Justice and Family Systems Therapy: A Transformational Lens

Traditional family therapy often operates within Western, heteronormative, and nuclear family centric paradigms, positioning challenges in family building as personal or relational

Table 5.1 Comparing Traditional Family Therapy and Reproductive Justice Frameworks

Traditional Family Therapy Assumptions	Reproductive Justice Expansion
Family development follows a linear, nuclear model (coupling → childbirth → parenting → launching children).	Family structures are diverse, nonlinear, and shaped by sociopolitical realities (e.g., chosen families, multigenerational homes, communal parenting).
Infertility, adoption barriers, and parenting struggles are primarily psychological and relational challenges.	Reproductive experiences are deeply political and are shaped by systemic inequities in race, gender, class, and ability.
Family therapy addresses intrafamilial conflicts and individual coping strategies.	Family therapy must address structural barriers (e.g., health care inequities, reproductive oppression, economic constraints).
Parenthood is an individual choice, with equal access to reproductive health care assumed.	Parenthood is structurally constrained by systemic forces that dictate whose reproduction is valued, supported, or suppressed.
Therapy provides a space for individual healing and relational support.	Therapy is also a site for resistance, advocacy, and dismantling reproductive injustice.

struggles. A reproductive justice lens expands this view by contextualizing reproductive and family challenges within broader systems of power and oppression.

Table 5.1 illustrates how reproductive justice transforms core assumptions in family therapy, shifting from an individualistic, pathology-focused model to one that acknowledges systemic barriers, collective care, and reproductive autonomy.

Reproductive justice challenges systemic therapists to move beyond individualizing family struggles and instead recognize how reproductive experiences are shaped by larger forces of oppression and resistance. By acknowledging these systems, we can better support clients in navigating barriers to family building, while centering on relational and cultural strengths.

While traditional family therapy often remains focused on interpersonal dynamics, a reproductive justice approach pushes us to examine the broader sociopolitical forces that shape family life. The following sections explore how these systemic realities intersect with family therapy, and how therapists can integrate reproductive justice into their work.

Systemic Context for Family Functioning

Family systems are directly affected by the larger sociopolitical systems in which they exist. Reproductive justice highlights how systems of oppression—such as colonialism, racism, patriarchy, ableism, and capitalism—shape family structures, dynamics, and relationships. For example:

- Systemic poverty limits access to reproductive health care, childcare, and family-supportive resources, creating barriers to thriving (Bidmead et al., 2024; Roll, 2014; Atree, 2005).
- Intergenerational trauma, such as the forced sterilization of Black, Indigenous (Stote, 2022), or disabled individuals (Schoen, 2009), leaves lasting legacies on family systems, impacting how families perceive reproduction, parenthood, and autonomy (Griffin, 2022).

Rather than pathologizing families as "dysfunctional," reproductive justice calls on therapists to address the structural forces that create harm.

Challenging Normative Assumptions in Family Systems Theory

Mainstream family systems theories often reflect Western nuclear family ideals, prioritizing linear life cycle stages, independence, and biological reproduction as markers of family success. Reproductive justice challenges these assumptions by centering non-traditional family structures, collective parenting, and chosen families.

Queer families, multigenerational households, and communal parenting systems demonstrate that healthy family systems are not defined by Western heteronormative ideals but by relationality, care, and community.

Parenting in a safe and supportive environment is not just an individual challenge but a systemic one. Families facing structural barriers have long relied on intergenerational knowledge, community networks, and collective advocacy to resist reproductive oppression and to build thriving family systems.

Relational Autonomy and Family Building

Reproductive justice broadens the concept of autonomy to include the relational dynamics within family systems. Decisions about family building—whether to have children, not have children, or raise children within nontraditional structures—are often deeply relational and shaped by collective cultural, social, and systemic forces. For example:

- An immigrant family navigating restrictive adoption policies may experience relational strain as they attempt to parent within systems designed to devalue their existence.
- A transgender individual seeking to build a family may face unique relational challenges due to systemic discrimination in health care or legal systems. These challenges are not "individual" but collective, requiring family systems to navigate and respond to broader injustices.

Healing Through Justice

Reproductive justice provides a framework for family systems therapy that is not solely focused on healing interpersonal dynamics but also addressing the systemic wounds families carry. Many families experience generational pain stemming from reproductive oppression, whether through histories of forced separations, family erasure, or economic policies that devalue marginalized communities' ability to parent. A reproductive justice framework encourages therapists to support families by reclaiming agency, honoring cultural strengths, and building relational resilience in the face of systemic harm.

A Broader Lens for Family Systems Work

Reproductive justice pushes systemic therapists to think expansively about the families they work with, not just as relational systems defined by their internal dynamics but as entities shaped by broader systems of oppression and possibility. It challenges us to:

- Re-imagine what it means for a family to "thrive" beyond rigid developmental models.
- Expand our understanding of family well-being to include cultural, relational, and systemic justice.
- Address not just individual "problems" but also the structural forces perpetuating harm and inequity.

In this way, reproductive justice moves beyond being a standalone framework and becomes a transformative lens for family systems work. It helps us center the lived realities of families navigating oppression while building practices that empower them to reclaim autonomy, relational strength, and justice in their family-building journeys.

Introduction to Decolonization in Reproductive Justice

At its heart, reproductive justice is about ensuring that every person has the power and resources to make meaningful decisions about how they build their families. However, achieving this vision requires us to go deeper than simply expanding access to or promoting inclusion. It demands that we confront the foundational systems that have dictated who gets to decide who is denied that right. To achieve this, we must adopt a decolonized lens.

In this context, decolonization is not just a theoretical exercise. It is dismantling—a tearing down of oppressive structures and narratives crafted by colonial powers to control bodies, families, and communities. It is important to understand the ways in which these colonial legacies remain embedded in contemporary reproductive policies and practices. It is a call to rebuild systems in ways that honor sovereignty and self-determination, centering Indigenous, non-Western, and historically marginalized knowledge.

However, this process is not about tweaking existing frameworks or extending a more "inclusive" version of the status quo. It is about fundamentally reimagining the systems and values that define reproductive health. This means asking hard questions: Who benefits from the current systems? Whose bodies, choices, and families have been controlled or erased? What would it take to build a world where reproductive autonomy is not a privilege but a birthright?

Colonial Legacies in Reproductive Health

Reproductive injustice does not arise in a vacuum. It is the product of an intricate web of power—colonialism, capitalism, white supremacy, patriarchy, ableism, and heteronormativity— which regulates bodies and determines whose lives are valued, whose choices are constrained, and whose families are supported or dismantled. For those who work in the space of reproductive justice, it is not enough to focus on individual stories of struggle (as important as they are). We must also confront systems that perpetuate these inequities, generation by generation.

Colonialism has laid the groundwork for these dynamics. It was not just about land and resources but also about controlling populations (McCormick, 2022). Colonial powers dehumanized Indigenous communities, enslaved peoples, and communities of color, using their reproductive capacity as a tool for dominance (Andre, 2023). Enslaved Black women were coerced into childbearing to fuel the economic engine of slavery (Aisha, 2024), while Indigenous women were forcibly sterilized to suppress their populations and erase their cultures (Stote, 2022).

These practices did not disappear with the end of formal colonial rule. They have adapted and embedded themselves in modern health care systems, policies, and cultural norms. Consider the United States' eugenics movement, which, under the guise of "public health," forcibly sterilized an estimated 70,000 people—disproportionately Black, Indigenous, Latinx, and poor individuals—between the 1930s and the 1970s (Stern, 2016). This was not a fluke. It was a policy rooted in racialized notions of whose lives were valuable and whose were disposable.

Globally, colonial powers imposed Western medical practices that sidelined Indigenous reproductive health knowledge. For example, in Canada, the forced sterilization of Indigenous women persisted into the late twentieth century, and even today reports the surface of coercive practices aimed at limiting Indigenous populations (Stote, 2022). Across Africa, Western biomedical models have replaced traditional reproductive practices and stripped communities of their autonomy and expertise (Lienjeh et al., 2024). The echoes of these policies persist in contemporary health care systems, where Western medical models often dominate, dismissing Indigenous and community-based practices as irrelevant or "unscientific" (Mothoagae, 2022). These systems, rooted in colonial control, continue to undermine the sovereignty of marginalized communities over their own bodies and family-building choices.

Colonial economies rely on the devaluation of poor and working-class lives, a logic that persists in modern capitalist structures. Today, economic barriers such as lack of insurance (Neugebauer, 2024), inadequate wages (VandeVusse et al., 2023), and restrictive policies such as the Hyde Amendment (Hutnik et al., 2022) limit access to reproductive health care for low-income families. In 1976, it restricted federal funding for abortion services and disproportionately impacted low-income women and women of color (Hutnik, et al., 2022). Policies that deny access to abortion and contraception to those who rely on public assistance perpetuate economic oppression. These barriers are not accidental; they are deliberate attempts to limit the autonomy of marginalized populations while prioritizing profit over care.

Colonial systems have also framed disabled bodies as "unproductive" and unfit for reproduction (Cleall, 2022). This logic persists in modern health care systems that deny disabled individuals reproductive autonomy, either through forced sterilization or assumptions about their parenting capacity (Pacheco et al., 2024). The continued practice of sterilizing disabled individuals without their informed consent reflects the enduring colonial belief that certain lives are less valuable or "unfit" for reproduction (Mercedes et al., 2021).

Capitalist systems continue to commodify health care by placing profits on people. Those with financial resources have access to world-class reproductive care, while low-income families are left to navigate a patchwork system where their choices are scrutinized and policed (Ferreira et al., 2023). Similarly, systemic racism means that Black women in the United States face maternal mortality rates that are not just a crisis (Sanders et al., 2024); they are a reflection of a health care system steeped in white supremacy (Yearby et al., 2022).

And while patriarchy may frame reproductive health as "women's issues," its impact stretches far beyond that. Strict gender norms limit access to care for men and transgender, non-binary, and gender-diverse individuals (Hong et al., 2024). For example, Trans men and nonbinary individuals seeking fertility preservation or family-building resources are often denied affirming care by providers who view their reproductive goals through a pathologizing lens, framing their family-building and reproductive desires as "unnatural" (Zisman, 2024). These denials echo colonial efforts to impose binary gender norms on diverse cultures, erasing the diversity of human experiences (O'Sullivan, 2021). These norms stifle reproductive autonomy for everyone, dictating whose choices are recognized and whose bodies are deemed legitimate.

Decolonizing reproductive justice requires more than simply acknowledging history. It is necessary to address the structures that allow these injustices to persist. It involves actively valuing and amplifying Indigenous and non-Western knowledge systems, challenging the dominance of Western medical frameworks, and advocating policies that affirm the reproductive autonomy of all people. This is the work of repair, reclamation, and, ultimately, justice.

Cultural Resistance and Reproductive Justice in Action

While reproductive oppression has caused profound harm, marginalized communities have long resisted and reimagined family building outside colonial constraints. The following examples highlight how communities have challenged Western nuclear family norms and asserted their reproductive sovereignty:

- Indigenous Kinship Networks—many Indigenous cultures practice extended kinship care, where child-rearing is a communal responsibility rather than solely an individual parental duty. This directly challenges the Western nuclear family model, emphasizing interdependence over independence.
- Black Feminist Reproductive Justice Advocacy—the creation of grassroots organizations such as SisterSong and the National Black Midwives Alliance has actively worked to reclaim reproductive autonomy by restoring community-led birthing practices and advocating birth justice.
- Queer and Trans Chosen Families—LGBTQ+ communities have long practiced chosen family structures in response to systemic exclusion and legal barriers to family recognition. These models illustrate how reproductive justice affirms family-building beyond biological reproduction.
- Disability Justice and Reproductive Rights—activists like Mia Mingus and organizations such as the Disability Rights & Education Defense Fund (DREDF) have fought against ableist medical practices that assume disabled individuals are incapable of parenting. This work affirms that parenting should be accessible to all, regardless of their abilities.

These acts of resistance demonstrate that reproductive justice is not just about combating oppression; it is about affirming and expanding possibilities for all families.

Centering Marginalized Voices

If we are serious about dismantling systems of oppression, we must center the experiences and expertise of those most impacted by reproductive injustice. Marginalized communities—Black and Indigenous people, people of color, disabled individuals, queer, and trans folks—are not just victims of these systems. They are also architects of resistance, holders of wisdom, and leaders envisioning a more just world.

Centering these voices is not about tokenism or performative inclusion. It is about fundamentally shifting power, recognizing that the people most affected by reproductive injustice are the ones best positioned to lead the fight for reproductive justice. Their stories illuminate the nuances of how these systems operate and reveal gaps in our current frameworks. They challenge us to move beyond simplistic, one-size-fits-all solutions and embrace approaches that honor complexity and context.

For example, Indigenous reproductive justice advocates have highlighted the importance of restoring midwifery and traditional birthing practices in their communities (Sarmiento et al., 2022). These practices are not just about health care; they are about sovereignty and reclaiming the right to bring life into the world in ways that honor cultural traditions and resist colonial control. Similarly, Black feminists have reframed reproductive justice as encompassing not only the right to parent or not parent but also the right to raise children in safe, supportive communities (Price, 2010). These are expansive, radical visions that go beyond access to services to address the broader systems that shape reproductive lives.

Reproductive Justice as a Challenge to the Family Life Cycle

Understanding the intersection of coloniality and reproductive oppression allows therapists to move beyond surface-level interventions. It challenges us to see therapy as a space where systems of oppression can be named, confronted, and dismantled and where clients' resilience and agency can be amplified. In this section, we explore how these principles translate into real-world practice by applying a reproductive justice framework to systemic therapy.

Decolonization is often misunderstood as the act of simply inviting previously excluded voices into a room, sprinkling in representation without disrupting the structures that have long perpetuated harm. While inclusion is undeniably important, a decolonized approach to reproductive justice demands that we dismantle existing frameworks entirely and build something new—something rooted in sovereignty.

A reproductive justice framework invites us to rethink the concept of family. Western family therapy models often idealize the nuclear family, emphasizing independence, autonomy, and linear life stages. However, for many clients, this model is not only irrelevant, but also harmful. It erases the richness of relational, interdependent, and non-traditional family systems, privileging a narrow vision of what the family should be.

Many Indigenous and non-Western traditions understand family as inherently relational and interdependent, extending beyond immediate households to include extended kin, community members, ancestors, and the land itself. These frameworks prioritize connections over independence and collaboration over hierarchies. They remind us that family is not a static structure but a living network of relationships.

As systemic therapists, we can learn from these traditions by asking:

- What does family building look like for this client in their cultural and social contexts?
- How do their relationships with their community, culture, and environment shape their understanding of family?
- How can we support these connections, rather than imposing a narrow vision of what families "should" be?

For instance, an Indigenous client may draw strength from the role of aunties, uncles, and grandparents in raising children. A queer client may find belonging to a chosen family after being rejected by their family of origin. In both cases, centering relationality allows us to honor the diverse ways clients experience and create family rather than forcing them into rigid Western molds.

This shift in perspective requires us to reevaluate the dominant frameworks used in family therapy, including one of the most widely referenced models, McGoldrick's Family Life Cycle. Although useful in certain contexts, its rigid developmental stages fail to capture the nonlinear, interdependent, and culturally diverse realities of family building.

McGoldrick's Family Life Cycle Model Critiqued

Building on this critique of traditional family structures, we now examine McGoldrick's family life cycle model (McGoldrick & Shibusawa, 2012), a widely accepted framework in systemic therapy. The family life cycle model, often considered a cornerstone of family systems thinking, outlines predictable stages of family development, such as coupling, childbirth, launching children, and retirement. Although this framework has been a useful heuristic for understanding family transitions, it is steeped in the Eurocentric, heteronormative, and class-bound assumptions of its origins. These assumptions often render the model misaligned or incompatible with the lived realities of diverse cultural practices, systemic inequities, and justice-oriented approaches to family life.

The family life-cycle model has long been used in family therapy to understand life transitions, offering a roadmap for how families evolve over time. However, when examined through a reproductive justice lens, it becomes clear that its original framework reflects a Western, heteronormative, and nuclear family–centric worldview. While useful in some contexts, its rigid developmental stages fail to account for the nonlinear, interdependent, and culturally diverse ways families grow and change. A justice-oriented approach expands this model—rather than discarding it—by incorporating relational, communal, and systemic realities.

To move beyond the limitations of the Family Life Cycle model, we must adopt a justice-oriented, relational framework that aligns with decolonization and reproductive justice principles. This framework envisions family building not as a linear progression of milestones, but as an evolving, contextually rooted process that celebrates diversity, equity, and relationality. Key considerations include:

- *Relationality as the Core:* Replace linear stages with an understanding of family development as a relational process. Growth is measured by connections and contributions to the collective and not by individual markers of independence or progress.
- *Diversity of Family Forms:* Validate all family structures, including chosen families, communal parenting systems, queer and polyamorous relationships, and child-free lives. Honor how families define themselves.
- *Contextual Sensitivity:* Recognize that family building is shaped by systemic oppression, economic inequality, and cultural context. Reject one-size-fits-all frameworks in favor of approaches that reflect the lived realities of marginalized communities.
- *Intergenerational Reciprocity:* Center mutual caregiving and interdependence as sources of strength rather than pathologizing them as deviations from independence. Acknowledge the value of shared responsibility across generations.
- *Cultural Wisdom:* Incorporate Indigenous and non-Western principles, such as collective parenting, centrality of elderhood, and kinship-based care, into our understanding of family life. These practices challenge the dominance of Western individualism and offer holistic, justice-oriented alternatives.

Reproductive justice expands our conceptualization of family growth rather than rejecting family development models outright. Instead of imposing rigid life stages that reinforce nuclear family norms, therapists recognize that family building is fluid, relational, and shaped by systemic forces. By adapting our therapeutic frameworks to honor these realities, we create space for families to thrive on their own terms. This shift challenges systemic

Table 5.2 Revising the Family Life Cycle Model Through a Reproductive Justice Lens Adapted (from McGoldrick et al., 2011a)

Traditional Family Life Cycle Stage	Critique (What's Missing?)	Revised Through Reproductive Justice
Leaving Home	Frames independence as the goal; assumes economic stability.	Recognizes interdependence as a strength and includes economic and systemic barriers.
Coupling	Assumes heterosexual monogamy as the norm.	Includes chosen families, polyamorous relationships, and queer partnerships.
Parenting Young Children	Focuses on biological reproduction.	Centers adoption, kinship care, surrogacy, communal parenting.
Launching Children	Pathologizes adult children remaining in family homes.	Recognizes economic realities and cultural models of extended family living.
Retirement and Aging	Assumes unidirectional care (children care for aging parents).	Frames aging as relational and reciprocal, honoring elderhood as valuable.

therapists to move beyond static developmental markers and instead asks: How do we cocreate healing spaces that affirm the diverse realities of the families we serve? How do we honor interdependence as a source of strength rather than a sign of dysfunction? These are the questions that a justice-oriented family therapy must center.

Reproductive Justice as a Framework for Therapy

Applying a decolonized perspective to reproductive justice and therapy work is not a one-time shift but an ongoing commitment to reflection, transformation, and action. For therapists, this means the following:

- Challenging oppressive systems, moving beyond the therapy room to advocate for systemic change—supporting policy reforms, amplifying community-led initiatives, or challenging inequitable health care practices.
- Honoring the knowledge of marginalized communities and reframing expertise to include the lived experiences and cultural wisdom of clients. Acknowledging that healing often resides outside traditional Western paradigms.
- Reimagining metrics of success; shifting from an individualistic, deficit-based view of progress to one that celebrates relationality, cultural strength, and systemic accountability.

By reclaiming authority over knowledge and disrupting binaries that limit our understanding of health and justice, we open the door to applying these principles in practice. For systemic therapists, this means integrating reproductive justice into our work—not as an abstract concept but as a framework that reshapes how we engage with clients and their families.

Reproductive justice offers a transformative framework for systemic therapy. This invites us to move beyond a narrow understanding of family building as an individual or private matter. Instead, it asks us to consider how broader systems—colonialism, racism, sexism, ableism, and classism—shape clients' reproductive experiences. It challenges us to see that decisions about parenting, family building, and reproductive health are never made in isolation, but are deeply influenced by historical legacies and contemporary systems of power.

For therapists, this means moving away from assumptions about what family building should look like and cultivating a practice that centers on clients' lived realities and cultural strengths. This means asking questions, such as:

- How have systemic barriers impacted the client's choices and opportunities for family building?
- What cultural and relational frameworks shape their understanding of family?
- How can I support their agency while also addressing the systemic challenges they face?

In practice, this might look like affirming nontraditional family structures, such as chosen families within LGBTQ+ communities or multigenerational households in immigrant families. A therapist working with an LGBTQ+ couple navigating adoption could do more than validate their frustrations. By actively providing resources, advocating for affirming legal support, and helping the couple connect with queer parenting networks, the therapist can help the couple reclaim agency and envision family building as an act of resistance.

Interrogating Practitioner Positionality

A decolonized approach to therapy begins with radical reflexivity, an ongoing, intentional process of interrogating how one's identities, training, and assumptions shape their practice. Practitioners must examine their social location and critically question how their work may perpetuate colonial or oppressive practices inadvertently. Reflexivity is not a one-time exercise but a lifelong commitment to growth and accountability. Questions to guide this self-inquiry include the following:

- How has my training been shaped by colonial Eurocentric frameworks?
- What assumptions do I bring into the therapeutic space?
- How can I decenter my perspective and prioritize the knowledge, values, and experiences of my clients?

For instance, a therapist trained in Western models might reflect on how their emphasis on individual autonomy conflicts with the client's cultural value of collective family input. By recognizing this bias, therapists can adapt their approach to honor the client's values rather than imposing their own framework. Reflexivity not only enhances therapeutic alliance but also fosters a more just and culturally attuned practice.

Centering Collective Knowledge and Community

Reproductive justice demands that we look beyond individual experiences and recognize the broader relational, cultural, and systemic contexts shaping family building and reproductive decision-making. A decolonized family systems approach naturally aligns with this vision by challenging the primacy of Western individualism, which often prioritizes personal autonomy over relational interdependence. Instead, it centers on collective knowledge, cultural traditions, and the role of the community in supporting reproductive justice and family well-being.

At its core, Reproductive Justice is about ensuring the right to parent in safe, supportive environments. This right is deeply connected to collective knowledge and community. When families are denied access to cultural resources, communal support, or intergenerational wisdom, they are often left vulnerable to systemic inequities. For systemic therapists, this means recognizing and amplifying the vital contributions of extended families, chosen families, and communal networks as integral to the therapeutic process, not as secondary or optional, but as central to fostering justice and equity in family building.

For example, in many Indigenous and non-Western cultures, family decision-making is a collective process that often includes the wisdom and guidance of elders, extended kin, or community members. These relational dynamics provide families with resilience and strength to navigate systemic barriers, particularly in contexts where reproductive oppression has fractured access to cultural and communal resources. Therapists working with families from these cultural contexts must move beyond nuclear family–centric assumptions and embrace and integrate these collective dynamics into their work.

Practitioners can use the reproductive justice lens to guide this shift by asking:

- Who within this family or community holds wisdom and guidance for decision making?
- How can the guidance of elders, cultural leaders, or matriarchs inform decisions regarding family building or reproductive health?
- What relational or cultural networks offer this family support and strength?
- Are there extended kin, chosen family members, or community organizations that can provide resources or advocacy?
- How can I include these voices and systems in the therapeutic process without imposing Western models of care?
- How can therapy serve as a bridge, rather than a barrier, to integrate collective knowledge and practice?

Examples in Practice

Indigenous Families and Elders' Guidance

Consider an Indigenous family navigating reproductive health challenges in a health care system that often erases or dismisses cultural practices. A therapist practicing through a reproductive justice lens might honor the role of elders in providing cultural and spiritual guidance, actively creating space for these perspectives in family discussions about parenting, fertility, or decision-making. In doing so, the therapist validates the family's cultural strengths while resisting the systemic marginalization of Indigenous practices.

Chosen Families in LGBTQ+ Communities

For queer clients building a chosen family, the therapist might affirm their relationships with friends and community members as equally valid and valuable forms of family support. This affirmation directly addresses reproductive emphasis on the right to parent and form families in environments that are free from discrimination or judgment. By helping the client navigate barriers, such as legal challenges or societal stigma, the therapist reinforces the importance of chosen families as sources of strength and stability.

Centering collective knowledge and community not only validates clients' lived realities but also directly addresses the systemic barriers that reproductive justice seeks to dismantle. For example:

- Many clients face challenges rooted in the devaluation of their cultural or communal practices by Western medical and legal systems. By embracing these practices within therapy, practitioners can help clients reclaim their agency and advocate for their inclusion.
- Clients navigating reproductive health decisions often find strength in collective or intergenerational wisdom, which provides context and guidance outside the narrow individualistic frameworks of Western care. By honoring these sources of knowledge, therapists can help clients to reconnect with cultural practices that affirm their agency and autonomy.
- In addressing the systemic forces that undermine safe and supportive parenting environments, such as economic marginalization, housing instability, and health care inequities, therapists can draw on community-based strategies emphasized by reproductive justice, such as mutual aid networks or grassroots advocacy.

Therapists move beyond validating their individual struggles by centering collective knowledge and community within a reproductive justice framework. Instead, they actively contribute to dismantling systemic inequities while empowering clients to draw strength from their cultural and relational resources. This approach transforms therapy into a space where justice, community, and healing intersect.

Challenging the Therapeutic Status Quo

Therapists and other practitioners often operate within systems that perpetuate inequities, whether through rigid medical protocols, limited access to culturally responsive care, or devaluation of non-Western healing practices. Decolonizing therapy requires challenging these norms and advocating for systemic change. This means questioning institutional practices, resisting policies that prioritize profit over care, and creating space for alternative, culturally rooted modalities. For example, systemic therapists can advocate for reforms by:

- Expanding health care access for marginalized communities.
- Securing funding and resources to support culturally specific reproductive health practices.
- Challenging discriminatory policies, such as restrictive abortion laws and exclusionary adoption regulations.

Stepping beyond the therapy room to engage in structural advocacy allows practitioners to address the root causes of challenges faced by their clients. This aligns with the broader goal of fostering systemic equity and justice.

Systemic therapists are positioned uniquely to address the emotional and psychological dimensions of reproductive justice. While therapy often focuses on individual experiences, a justice-oriented lens invites practitioners to broaden their perspectives, acknowledging the interplay between personal struggles and systemic oppression. This approach involves:

- Supporting clients in processing the emotional impacts of systemic oppression, including reproductive trauma, historical erasure, or the stress of navigating inequitable health care systems.

- Addressing intergenerational trauma tied to reproductive control, such as forced sterilization, coerced adoption, or family separation.
- Promoting resilience by validating clients' experiences and fostering connections to cultural and community resources that affirm their agency and autonomy.

Therapists must move beyond merely validating their feelings to actively engage with systems that shape their clients' struggles. Reproductive justice challenges practitioners in expanding the boundaries of therapy, transforming it from a space of individual healing to collective empowerment.

Systemic therapy, with its foundation in relational dynamics, is inherently compatible with decolonized approaches. By broadening systems thinking to include colonial histories and structures, therapists can better understand and address the interconnected forces that shape their clients' lives. This perspective prompts therapists to consider the following:

- How historical legacies, such as colonialism, racism, and patriarchy, continue to influence family dynamics and reproductive decision-making.
- The ways current policies, health care inequities, and cultural narratives perpetuate harm.
- How these systemic forces manifest relationally, shaping not only individuals but also entire family systems over generations.

Adopting this lens allows therapists to situate client struggles within broader historical and socio-political contexts. For instance, rather than framing infertility as solely a personal challenge, therapists can help clients explore how systemic barriers, such as limited access to fertility treatment, societal expectations, and racial disparities in health care, intersect with their experiences. This expanded understanding empowers clients to see their struggles in a larger framework of injustice and resilience rather than internalizing blame.

Tools and Techniques for Reproductive Justice in Decolonized Practice

Reproductive justice is not just a perspective; it is a call to action that reimagines how systemic therapists approach their work. To truly align with reproductive justice principles, therapists must move beyond traditional frameworks that center Western norms and instead adopt practices that honor cultural knowledge, challenge systemic oppression, and empower clients in their reproductive and family-building journeys. These approaches center on relationality, collaboration, and systemic advocacy, ensuring that therapy becomes a space of transformation—not just for individuals but also for the broader systems that shape their lives. Therapists become active partners in advancing reproductive justice by prioritizing client agency, cultural knowledge, and resistance to systemic oppression.

Decolonial Narrative Therapy

Narrative therapy aligns naturally with reproductive justice principles, as it allows clients to reclaim their stories and agency while challenging the dominant narratives imposed by colonial, patriarchal, and systemic forces. It allows clients to reframe their experiences in ways that align with their values and cultural contexts, helping them resist stigmatizing and pathologizing frameworks.

Reproductive Justice in Practice: A client who has faced stigma in seeking abortion care might work with a therapist to challenge internalized shame and reframe their experience as an act of agency and self-determination. Through this process, the client can reconnect with their values and define their story in their own terms, reclaiming power in the face of systemic oppression.

Culturally Rooted Healing Practices

Reproductive justice recognizes the importance of cultural traditions, ancestral wisdom, and community-rooted practices in healing. Decolonized therapy honors this by incorporating culturally specific healing practices, often in collaboration with community leaders, traditional healers, or cultural knowledge keepers. This approach not only aligns with Reproductive justice but also actively resists the erasure of non-Western modalities of care.

Reproductive Justice in Practice: A therapist working with an Indigenous client may collaborate with a traditional healer to integrate ceremonial practices into the client's reproductive health journey. This approach respects the client's cultural heritage, aligns with their values, and offers a holistic therapeutic process grounded in cultural resonance.

Advocacy Beyond the Therapy Room

Reproductive justice is a fundamental movement in the context of systemic change. It challenges therapists to step beyond individual sessions and engage in active advocacy that addresses the structural barriers faced by clients. Advocacy is not separate from therapy; it is an essential extension rooted in the reproductive justice principle of collective empowerment.

Partnering with Local Organizations

Therapists can collaborate with reproductive justice organizations to support community-led efforts to expand access to equitable care, particularly in underserved communities. This might include participating in workshops, offering professional consultations, or amplifying initiatives that address barriers to reproductive health care.

Reproductive Justice in Practice: A therapist could partner with grassroots organizations to amplify efforts to provide culturally competent doula services or midwifery care. These partnerships not only benefit clients but also foster systemic change by supporting the community's ability to advocate for itself.

Pushing for Systemic Reforms

Therapists can engage in systemic advocacy by supporting policy changes that address structural inequities, such as restrictive abortion laws, health care discrimination, or a lack of funding for marginalized communities.

Reproductive Justice in Practice: A therapist might join reproductive justice coalitions or professional advocacy groups to push for legislative reforms, such as protecting access to abortion care or ensuring inclusive adoption policies for LGBTQ+ families. These efforts align with Reproductive Justice's focus on dismantling systemic barriers to reproductive autonomy.

Educating Peers and Institutions

Therapists can advocate for systemic accountability within their own fields by educating colleagues and institutions on reproductive justice principles and decolonial approaches. This includes workshops, training, and contributing to policy changes within professional organizations.

Reproductive Justice in Practice: A therapist could create a training module for colleagues to integrate reproductive justice into clinical practice, emphasizing how systemic inequities intersect with clients' reproductive health and family-building experiences.

Centering Community Engagement and Collaboration

Therapists can foster deeper connections by directly engaging with the communities they serve, standing in solidarity with their struggles, and building reciprocal partnerships. Fostering trust and humility in working with communities means stepping out of the expert's role and learning from the lived experiences and expertise of clients and their communities. This might involve attending community events, participating in cultural ceremonies, or collaborating with grassroots organizations. For example, a therapist might partner with a local reproductive justice organization to better understand the unique challenges faced by the community and amplify their efforts through shared advocacy work.

Supporting community-led reproductive justice initiatives honors the principles of community sovereignty. Practitioners can provide resources, amplify marginalized voices, and contribute their expertise to align with community priorities. For example, a therapist participating in a campaign led by reproductive justice advocates to improve access to culturally competent reproductive health care for LGBTQ+ communities.

Reframing the 'Problem' Through a Reproductive Justice Lens

Western therapeutic models often frame reproductive and family challenges as "problems" to be diagnosed and fixed, relying on an individualistic and pathologizing framework. For example, clients navigating infertility or single parenthood are often labeled "dysfunctional" or "overwhelmed," with the focus placed solely on their emotional responses or coping strategies. This approach obscures systemic barriers, inequities, and cultural contexts, reinforcing harmful narratives of deficiency and blame.

The reproductive justice lens reframes these challenges by situating them within larger systems of oppression. Instead of locating "problems" within individuals or families, this perspective emphasizes how colonialism, racism, patriarchy, ableism, and classism shape reproductive experiences. It also centers the resilience and agency of clients in resisting systemic harm.

Reproductive Justice in Practice

Addressing Infertility

A Black couple facing barriers to fertility treatment might feel dismissed by medical professionals who assume their struggles are "normal" or inevitable. An reproductive justice–informed therapist would validate their anger and isolation as responses to systemic racism, helping them advocate for culturally competent care while celebrating their resilience in navigating these challenges.

Supporting Single Parents

A single parent navigating reproductive health care and childcare might be labeled as "struggling" in a Western framework. An reproductive justice lens would instead highlight how structural barriers, such as a lack of paid family leave and affordable childcare, create these challenges. The therapist could then focus on supporting the client's strengths, connecting them with resources, and resisting narratives that stigmatized their family structure.

By moving away from pathologizing frameworks, therapists using a reproductive justice lens empower clients to see their struggles as reflections of systemic injustice, rather than personal failure. This approach affirms client agency, while positioning therapy as a tool for systemic accountability and change.

Storytelling as a Tool for Liberation

Stories bridge the gap between personal experiences and systemic forces, making them essential tools for advancing reproductive justice. For systemic therapists, storytelling is not just a method for connecting with clients but also a way to reveal how systems of oppression intersect with individual and family lives. By centering stories, therapists can humanize complex issues, foster empowerment, and drive systemic change.

Humanizing the Systems at Play

By encouraging clients to tell their stories, therapists can help them uncover the connections between their lived experiences and broader systemic forces. Storytelling creates space for clients to name their struggles, honor their resilience, and challenge harmful narratives imposed by systems of power.

Reproductive Justice in Practice: A client might explore how systemic racism impacted their experience with fertility treatment, reframing the narrative to honor their strength in navigating these barriers. The process not only supports individual healing, but also builds awareness of systemic inequities.

Advocacy Through Storytelling

Therapists can use storytelling as a tool for advocacy, sharing de-identified narratives (with permission) to educate peers, challenge systemic oppression, or amplify marginalized voices.

Reproductive Justice in Practice: A therapist might present a case study on intergenerational trauma stemming from forced sterilization to highlight the need for culturally responsive reproductive health care policies. By sharing these stories, therapists can advocate for systemic reforms that align with reproductive justice principles.

Why This Work Matters

Integrating tools and techniques aligned with reproductive justice ensures that therapy becomes a space in which clients' agency, cultural strengths, and resilience are affirmed. By addressing systemic inequities and challenging harmful narratives, therapists create opportunities for healing, empowerment, and liberation, not just for individuals but for the communities they serve.

Bridging the Gap: Supporting Clients Within and Beyond Western Medical Systems

Practical Guidance for Navigating Western Medical Systems

While systemic therapists are called to critique and dismantle oppressive systems, we must also recognize the reality that many clients must navigate these systems to access reproductive health care. This duality—holding a critique while engaging with inequitable systems—is one of the complexities of decolonized practice. Therapists play a critical role in bridging this gap by providing clients with the tools, advocacy, and emotional support they need to navigate these systems while holding space for their frustrations and hopes for change.

This section explores how systemic therapists can address this duality. It highlights strategies for empowering clients to advocate for themselves, navigate cultural mismatches, and integrate their values into reproductive health care experiences. It also underscores the need for therapists to honor the emotional and relational aspects of these journeys, creating space for clients to process the dissonance that often arises between their personal values and systemic realities.

Acknowledge the Realities

While the work of reproductive justice calls for systemic change, we must acknowledge the current realities many individuals and families face. Navigating Western medical systems—though fraught with inequities and rooted in colonial frameworks—is, for many, a necessary step toward accessing reproductive health care. This duality requires systemic therapists to hold both critique and compassion, supporting clients in navigating these systems while advocating for transformation.

As systemic therapists and advocates for reproductive justice, we must acknowledge this duality. We can critique the structural injustices within Western medicine while also supporting clients through their deeply personal and vulnerable reproductive journeys. This is not a contradiction but rather a recognition of the complexity of real-life choices.

Helping Clients Advocate for Themselves

Clients may feel disempowered when navigating complex, highly medicalized systems. One role of systemic therapists is to equip themselves with tools for self-advocacy. Therapists can empower clients in specific ways:

1. Prepare Clients with Knowledge and Encourage Them to Ask Questions—Knowledge is power. Help clients build a foundational understanding of the treatments or interventions they may encounter. This could include:
   a. The IVF process, common medications, and associated side effects.
   b. Alternatives to hyper-medicalized interventions, such as minimal stimulation IVF or natural cycle monitoring.

c. Ethical and personal implications of decisions such as embryo freezing, selective reduction, or egg/sperm donation.

Therapists do not need to have all the medical answers but can connect clients to trustworthy resources (e.g., websites, books, or culturally competent practitioners). They can then equip clients with the language to challenge paternalistic practices that are often embedded in Western medicine. Provide prompts to help them assert their agency, such as:

d. *What are the alternatives to this treatment?*
e. *How does this align with evidence-based practice?*
f. *What are the potential risks and benefits, and what would you recommend in my situation?*
g. *Are there cultural or holistic practices that can be integrated with this care?*

Teach clients that it is not only acceptable, but also necessary to ask these questions and seek clarity. Providers should be collaborators in care, and not unquestioned authorities.

2. Connect Clients to Culturally Attuned Providers—Clients navigating Western systems benefit from culturally responsive providers and organizations that prioritize inclusivity. Some strategies include the following.

   a. Directory Searches: Provide access to resources such as the National Black Midwives Alliance, directories of LGBTQ+-friendly providers, or networks of Indigenous health practitioners.
   b. Doula Support: Encourage clients to seek doula support, which can bridge the gap between Western medical systems and their own cultural or emotional needs.
   c. Peer Communities: Point clients toward community-based reproductive justice organizations that provide advocacy and support.

3. Affirm Clients' Right to Change Providers—Clients may feel trapped by health care providers who fail to respect their cultural values, choices, or identities. Therapists can help normalize the idea that clients can seek secondary opinions, change doctors, or even leave practices that fail to meet their needs. Advocating for oneself in this way can be daunting, but it is an act of self-respect and empowerment.

Holding Space for Clients' Emotional Journeys

Western medical systems often fail to account for the emotional, spiritual, and relational dimensions of reproductive journeys, leaving many clients feeling dehumanized. Systemic therapists are uniquely positioned to provide space for clients to process and integrate these experiences, particularly when clients experience dissonance between their values and the medical interventions they pursue.

1. Naming the Disconnection—Many clients express grief or unease when their fertility journey feels overly clinical and detached from their cultural or spiritual practices. Therapists can help clients name these feelings without shame or judgment. For example:

   a. It sounds like this process doesn't feel connected to the values you hold about family or reproduction.
   b. What do you wish was different?

  c. Can we explore ways to bring your culture, values, or spiritual practices into this journey?

2. Ritualizing the Journey—Encourage clients to integrate rituals, ceremonies, or personal practices into their reproductive journeys, even if they are engaging in highly medicalized treatments. For example:

  a. A client may light a candle or recite a prayer before each injection.
  b. Another might create a personal altar to honor ancestors as a source of strength and resilience.
  c. Some may turn to movement, art, or storytelling as ways to process the emotional weight of their journeys.

These practices remind clients that their reproductive journey is not just a medical event but also a deeply personal and sacred process.

3. Normalizing Ambivalence—Clients may struggle with ambivalence or guilt, particularly if they pursue treatments that conflict with broader critiques of Western systems. For instance:

  a. A client might feel uneasy about using donor eggs due to concerns about commodification but still proceed due to a deep desire for a child.
  b. Another might feel conflicted about accessing care in a system that has harmed their community but recognizes that they have no viable alternatives.

Therapists can affirm that holding such ambivalence is natural and valid. Reproductive justice is not about prescribing what is "right" but about ensuring individuals have the freedom to make the best decisions for themselves within the systems available to them.

Balance the Duality of Critique and Engagement

The tension between critiquing and engaging with Western medical systems is an ongoing challenge for both clients and therapists. A decolonized lens does not require rejecting all aspects of these systems but rather equips clients with tools to navigate them with intention, agency, and critical awareness.

1. Support Clients Without Judgment—Therapists must meet clients where they are, whether they are deeply skeptical of Western systems, fully engaged with them, or somewhere in between. The goal is not to impose a moral framework but to empower clients to define what justice and autonomy look like for themselves.
2. Empower Clients to Resist Systemic Harm—Therapists can help clients identify where and how they can push back against systemic harm, even while engaging with these systems. This may be encouraging clients to speak up about implicit bias or racism they encounter during appointments or supporting clients to advocate for alternative approaches that align better with their values. Therapists may help clients connect with, organize, or participate in reproductive justice movements.

Systemic therapists can help clients navigate Western medical systems with agency and intention by integrating cultural wisdom, practical advocacy, and emotional support. This approach acknowledges the complex realities of reproductive journeys and offers both critique and compassion. Clients deserve care that honors their cultural values while equipping them to engage with systems in ways that feel empowering and just.

Case Examples: Applying Reproductive Justice in Therapy

Building on the tools and techniques discussed earlier, this section provides case examples demonstrating how systemic therapists can integrate a reproductive justice framework into their work. These narratives highlight the practical application of decolonized, justice-oriented approaches to therapy.

The following case examples illustrate how therapists can integrate reproductive justice into their clinical practice. They highlight the key aspects of justice-oriented systemic therapy: navigating systemic barriers, affirming nontraditional family structures, addressing intergenerational trauma, and confronting reproductive oppression. By weaving reproductive justice principles into practice, therapists can support clients in reclaiming their agency, navigating inequities, and fostering resilience in the face of systemic challenges.

Navigating Systemic Barriers

Tamara and Marcus

A Black couple seeking fertility treatment enters therapy, feeling exhausted and discouraged. Tamara shares how her concerns about fibroids were dismissed by her doctor, who minimized her symptoms as "normal for Black women." Marcus describes being treated with suspicion at the clinic and frequently questioned about finances in ways that their white peers had not experienced. As the only Black patients in the waiting room, they often feel isolated and unwelcome.

The Therapist's Role

A reproductive justice–informed therapist validates their feelings of anger and exhaustion, reframing these emotions as natural responses to systemic racism rather than personal inadequacy. The therapist encourages them to share specific incidents of mistreatment and helps them process the emotional toll of their experiences. Together, they strategize ways to advocate for themselves, including preparing questions for medical providers and exploring clinics with a reputation for cultural sensitivity.

The therapist also connects Tamara and Marcus to community support groups for Black families navigating infertility, offering a space where their experiences are understood and affirmed. Additionally, the therapist acknowledges the impact of systemic racism on emotional and relational dynamics, helping them identify ways to lean on one another as they navigate these challenges. By centering their lived experiences and affirming their resilience, the therapist empowers Tamara and Marcus to advocate for their needs with confidence and clarity.

Affirming Nontraditional Families

Jesse

A trans man expresses his fears about starting a family with his partner. He is anxious about societal stigma, legal discrimination in adoption or surrogacy, and scrutiny of his gender identity as a future parent. "What if they think I'm unfit to raise a child just because I'm trans?" Jesse asks.

The Therapist's Role

Using a reproductive justice lens, the therapist affirms Jesse's family-building vision and validates his concerns as legitimate responses to systemic oppression rather than internal weaknesses. They explore Jesse's fears in-depth, normalizing his apprehension while reframing his desire to parent as a source of strength. The therapist helps Jesse identify LGBTQ+ affirmative resources, such as legal support for adoption, surrogacy, and fertility clinics with inclusive practices.

The therapist also works with Jesse to create an emotional plan for navigating potential discrimination, including role-playing responses to invasive questions or judgmental comments. To empower Jesse further, the therapist encouraged him to connect with queer parenting networks, where he could share experiences and gain support from others who have faced similar challenges. By addressing the structural barriers while affirming Jesse's identity and capacity as a future parent, the therapist helps Jesse move forward with confidence and pride in his family-building journey.

Addressing Intergenerational Trauma

Lila

A Native American woman shares the story of her grandmother being forcibly removed from her family and placed in a residential school. This legacy left a deep imprint on Lila's family, creating cycles of disconnection and fear around expressing love. As Lila considers whether or not to have children, she worries about unintentionally passing down this inherited pain.

The Therapist's Role

The therapist validates Lila's experiences and acknowledges the profound impact of colonial violence on her family's dynamics. They explore the ways in which historical trauma manifests in Lila's relationships and her fears about parenting, helping her identify the patterns she wants to break. Together, they reclaim cultural traditions as sources of strength and healing, such as storytelling, rituals, and language preservation.

The therapist collaborated with Lila to develop parenting approaches that honored her cultural values while fostering emotional connection and resilience. For example, they might explore ways to integrate ceremonies that celebrate family milestones or create opportunities to share intergenerational wisdom with the elders in their community. The therapist helped Lila envision a parenting journey rooted in pride, belonging, and healing by grounding the therapeutic process in cultural reclamation and resilience.

Parenting with a Disability

Maya

A 34-year-old woman with cerebral palsy comes to therapy to address feelings of isolation as she prepares for the birth of her first child. She described her encounters with medical providers who questioned her ability to parent because of her disability. One doctor even suggested sterilization during her prenatal appointment, assuming that her pregnancy was unintentional.

The Therapist's Role

The therapist validates Maya's anger and fear, framing them as responses to systemic ableism rather than personal shortcomings. They help Maya process the harm caused by these experiences and explore ways to assert her rights as a parent. The therapist equips Maya with tools for self-advocacy, such as preparing questions for medical providers and rehearsing assertive communication strategies to address bias.

Additionally, the therapist connects Maya with disability rights organizations and peer networks for disabled parents, helping her build a support system that reinforces her confidence and autonomy. Together, they explore ways for Maya to prepare for parenthood in alignment with her values, such as by integrating assistive technologies or adapting caregiving practices. By affirming Maya's strengths and providing practical tools, the therapist helped her navigate the path to parenthood with pride and empowerment.

Fighting for Queer Family Legitimacy

Jules and Erin

A married lesbian couple seeks therapy after a long and taxing adoption process. They described facing repeated delays, intrusive questioning about their relationship, and outright bias from agencies. "Every time we think we are close, another roadblock pops up," Jules laments. Compounding their stress is judgment from extended family members, who question why they don't pursue "traditional" methods like surrogacy.

The Therapist's Role

The therapist creates a safe space for Jules and Erin to process frustration and grief while affirming their family-building choices. They work to reframe adoption as a powerful form of family creation, helping the couple see their resilience in navigating systemic homophobia. The therapist provides emotional support while also helping Jules and Erin identify adoption agencies with LGBTQ+ affirming policies and legal resources that align with their needs.

To address the stress caused by family judgment, the therapist helps Jules and Erin to develop communication strategies for setting boundaries and responding to criticism. The therapist also encouraged the couple to connect with queer parenting groups, where they could share their experiences and gain validation from others who had walked a similar path. By combining emotional support with practical advocacy, the therapist empowers Jules and Erin to continue their journey with renewed confidence and pride in their future family.

Why These Stories Matter

These case studies demonstrate that reproductive justice is not just a theoretical framework; it is also a practice of validation, empowerment, and systemic accountability. Each story reveals how systemic oppression manifests in deeply personal ways and how therapists can bridge the gap between individual healing and structural change. By centering lived experiences and addressing systemic inequities, systemic therapists create space for clients to reclaim agency and foster connection, resilience, and justice.

Reflection Questions for Therapists

The following questions invite therapists to reflect on how their beliefs, biases, and practices align with the principles of reproductive justice. By examining past cases or envisioning future approaches, therapists can deepen their understanding of how systemic oppression and family building intersect. These prompts encourage not only personal reflection, but also center advocacy and action, ensuring that therapeutic spaces honor the lived experiences of clients while pushing for systemic transformation.

- Personal Reflection: *How do your own beliefs about family building and reproductive justice shape your work with clients? Where might implicit bias appear?*
- Case Reflection: *Think of a current or past client whose reproductive experience intersected with systemic oppression. How might the reproductive justice lens influence your approach?*
- Advocacy: *How can you use your role as a therapist to advocate for systemic change in reproductive health and family-building systems?*
- Storytelling in Practice: *How can you create space for clients to share their stories in ways that honor their experiences and foster empowerment?*

Conclusion: A Path Toward Reproductive Justice and Decolonized Family Systems

Reproductive justice is not merely a lens for analysis; it is a transformative call to action—one that demands that we reimagine how we engage with family systems, health, and healing. This chapter explored how systemic therapists, advocates, and practitioners can integrate decolonial principles into their work, challenging oppressive frameworks while cocreating spaces of empowerment and liberation with their clients. By critiquing colonial legacies, reclaiming cultural knowledge, and amplifying marginalized voices, we move beyond theory into meaningful actions.

As we move forward, the path toward reproductive justice and decolonized family systems requires both reflection and commitment. To ground this work, here are three actionable steps that practitioners can take to build more equitable, inclusive, and justice-centered practices—not just in principle but in everyday therapeutic work.

Expand Beyond Cultural Competence: Adopt a Systemic Justice Approach in Family Therapy

Many therapists have been trained to apply cultural competence frameworks in their work, yet cultural competence alone is insufficient when addressing deeply embedded systemic barriers. Moving toward a systemic justice approach requires shifting from viewing culture as an individual characteristic to understanding how systemic inequities shape family experiences. This means positioning family challenges not as personal deficits but as relational responses to structural oppression. The following guidelines can support the therapist in moving from a cultural competency to a culturally integrated approach:

- Reframe client concerns as systemic challenges, not individual pathology.
- Use power-conscious language when conceptualizing family struggles. For example, instead of considering "dysfunctional family patterns," explore "relational responses to systemic oppression."
- Validate nontraditional family systems such as chosen families, communal caregiving, and extended kinship networks in all case formulations, treatment plans, and clinical documentation.
- Ask: *How do systemic barriers shape my clients' reproductive and family-building experiences?*
- Actively adjust your process. For example, during intake, incorporate explicit questions about systemic barriers (e.g., reproductive access, legal challenges, immigration policies, financial constraints) and explore how they shape clients' family experiences.
- In practice, expand your definition of kinship and family structures. Instead of *"Tell me about your family of origin,"* ask, *"Who are the people you consider family? How do they support you?"*

From Neutrality to Active Engagement: Centering Justice in Clinical Work

Traditional therapy models often emphasize neutrality, encouraging therapists to remain objective observers rather than active participants in justice work. However, neutrality can reinforce systemic harm by failing to acknowledge the oppressive forces shaping clients' experiences. To truly integrate reproductive justice into therapy, practitioners must recognize that all therapeutic work exists within systems of power—and actively engage in addressing these dynamics. The following guidelines can support the therapist in considering their positionality and systems of power:

- Acknowledge the therapist's role as an active participant in systems of power.
- Provide psychoeducation on reproductive justice issues when relevant (e.g., discussing racialized disparities in maternal health outcomes and supporting LGBTQ+ clients in navigating family-building barriers).
- Refer clients to justice-oriented resources that address their needs (e.g., abortion funds, trans-affirming health care, reproductive health doulas, and housing support).
- Ask: *How do I incorporate systemic justice into clinical work without assuming that all clients share the same political views?*
- Actively adjust your process by engaging clients in sharing their reflections and stories rather than assuming a singular justice perspective.
- In practice, if a client is struggling with fertility and expresses shame or guilt, expand the frame beyond personal responsibility by asking: *"What messages have you received about who is 'deserving' of parenthood? How do those messages shape your experience?"*

Build Justice-Oriented Consultation and Supervision Spaces

Justice-informed therapy does not end at the individual client level; it must also be woven into the fabric of professional consultation and supervision. Many therapists and supervisors were trained in systems that implicitly uphold neutrality, Eurocentrism, and traditional hierarchies of expertise. Shifting toward a liberation-based approach in consultation requires rethinking how knowledge is shared, how power is distributed, and how systemic justice is integrated into professional spaces. The following guidelines can support the therapist in expanding their practice beyond client sessions:

- Challenge colleagues and supervisees to examine their assumptions about family structures and reproductive decision-making critically.
- Create spaces for therapists to unpack their positionality—how their own identities, privileges, and lived experiences shape their clinical work.
- Incorporate liberation-based supervision practices that center on relationality and systemic consciousness in case conceptualization.
- Ask: *How do I create a professional culture where justice-informed practice is the norm, not the exception?*
- Actively adjust your process by forming peer consultation groups that apply reproductive justice principles to clinical dilemmas and ethical decision-making.
- In practice, during group supervision or consultation, ask: *"How might systemic barriers shape this client's distress? What are we missing when we focus only on individual coping strategies?"*

A Collective Call to Liberation

The work of reproductive justice and decolonization is relational at its core. It requires us to show up for one another with humility, empathy, and an unwavering commitment to equity. As systemic therapists, advocates, and allies, our role is not to impose solutions but to walk alongside clients and communities, as they define and pursue justice on their own terms.

This is not easy work. It demands that we examine our own positionalities, engage with discomfort, and challenge the systems that shape our fields and practices. It asks us to balance critique with compassion, honoring the resilience and agency of those navigating systems of oppression while working to dismantle those very systems.

Yet within this challenge lies profound hope. By interrogating harmful structures, honoring cultural wisdom, and actively applying justice principles to therapy, we co-create a world where reproductive justice is not a privilege but a universal right. In this vision, families thrive on their own terms, free from colonial constraints and empowered by relationality, sovereignty, and care.

As systemic therapists, we are responsible for moving beyond passive awareness to emboldened action. Let this be our shared commitment—to listen deeply, engage courageously, and build a future in which justice is the foundation of family healing.

References

Attree, P. (2005). Parenting support in the context of poverty: A meta-synthesis of the qualitative evidence. *Health & Social Care in The Community, 13*(4), 330–37. https://doi.org/10.1111/j.1365-2524.2005.00562.x

Bidmead, E., Hayes, L., Mazzoli-Smith, L., Wildman, J., Rankin, J., Leggott, E., Todd, L., & Bramhall, L. (2024). Poverty proofing healthcare: A qualitative study of barriers to accessing healthcare for low-income families with children in northern England. *PLoS One, 19*(4). https://doi.org/10.1371/journal.pone.0292983

Cleall, E. (2022). *Colonising disability: Impairment and otherness across Britain and its empire, c. 1800–1914*. Cambridge University Press. https://doi.org/10.1017/9781108983266

Djelid, A. (2024). "The master whished to reproduce": Slavery, forced intimacy, and enslavers' interference in sexual relationships in the antebellum South, 1808–1861. *American Nineteenth Century History, 25*(1), 21–43. https://doi.org/10.1080/14664658.2024.2317499

Ferreira, L. Z., Wehrmeister, F. C., Dirksen, J., Vidaletti, L. P., Pinilla-Roncancio, M., Kirkby, K., Ricardo, L. I., Barros, A. J., & Hosseinpoor, A. R. (2024). A composite index; socioeconomic deprivation and coverage of reproductive and maternal health interventions. *Bulletin of the World Health Organization, 102*(2), 105–16. https://doi.org/10.2471/BLT.23.290866

Griffin, F. (2022). Forced sterilization. *Voices in Bioethics, 8*. https://doi.org/10.52214/vib.v8i.9501

Hayward, A., & Cidro, J. (2021). Indigenous birth as ceremony and a human right. *Health and Human Rights, 23*(1), 213–24.

Hong, T., Case, V., Farcas, A. M., Whitfield, D., Muller, G., Schlesinger, S. A., Haamid, A. S., Middleton, M. T., Breyre, A., Buaprasert, P., Whitten-Chung, K., Lichtenbelt, K. J. C., Joiner, A. P., Pereira, C., & Brown, J. (2024). Caring for transgender and gender diverse prehospital patients: A NAEMSP position statement and resource document. *Prehospital Emergency Care*, 1–13. Advance online publication. https://doi.org/10.1080/10903127.2024.2411723

Hutnik, L.A., Zimmermann, A., Naliboff, L., & Brandi, K.M. (2022). Hyde and seek: Searching for solutions to the Hyde amendment's financial barriers to abortion. *The Journal of Science Policy & Governance, 21*(1). https://doi.org/10.38126/JSPG210105

Klinker, M. J., Kluver, R., Jordan, T., & Kearns, B. (2024). Confronting reproductive injustices: A discussion on decolonial, queer, anti-racist organizing. *Radical Teacher, 129*. https://doi.org/10.5195/rt.2024.1198

Laylor, A. (2024). Knowledge production and colonial myths: Centring Indigenous knowledges through decolonization. In Wane, N.N. (Ed.), *Education, colonial sickness: A decolonial African Indigenous project* (pp. 131–50). Palgrave Macmillan. https://doi.org/10.1007/978-3-031-40262-3_7

Levitt, H., Horne, S., Puckett, J., Sweeney, K., & Hampton, M. (2014). Gay families: Challenging racial and sexual/gender minority stressors through social support. *Journal of GLBT Family Studies, 11*(2), 173–202. https://doi.org/10.1080/1550428X.2014.958266

Lienjeh, L. N-P., Ngwa, C., & Lang, M. (2024). Transmutation of the reproductive life of women in Southern/West Cameroon(S) 1922–1972: A colonial manipulation. *Social Science and Humanities Journal, 8*(7), 4225–38. https://doi.org/10.18535/sshj.v8i07.1182

McCormick, T. (2022). *Human empire: Mobility and demographic thought in the British Atlantic world, 1500–1800*. Cambridge University Press.

McGoldrick, M., Carter, B., & Garcia-Preto, N. (Eds.). (2011a). *The expanded family life cycle: Individual, family, and social perspectives* (4th ed.). The Guilford Press.

McGoldrick, M., & Shibusawa, T. (2012). The family life cycle. In Walsh, F. (Ed.), *Normal family processes: Growing diversity and complexity* (pp. 375–98). The Guilford Press.

Mothoagae, I.D. (2022). Setswana medicinal practices and tensions with Western healthcare perspectives. In Smith, R.D., Boddie, S.C. & English, B.D. (Eds.), *Racialized health, COVID-19, and religious responses: Black Atlantic contexts and perspectives* (pp. 67–74). https://doi.org/10.4324/9781003214281-9

Neugebauer, J. (2024, August 7). *Economic barriers as a large part of the problem with access to healthcare* [Conference presentation]. The Open Scientific Conference, Athens, Greece. https://doi.org/10.52950/4osc-athens.2024.8.004

O'Sullivan, S. (2021). The colonial project of gender (and everything else). *Genealogy, 5*(3), 67. https://doi.org/10.3390/genealogy5030067

Pacheco, L., Mercerat, C., Aunos, M., Cousineau, M-M., Goulden, A., Swab, M., Brenton, B., & Moyo, S. (2024). Uncovering reproductive injustice toward women with disabilities: A scoping review. *International Perspectives in Psychology: Research, Practice, Consultation, 13*(3), 164–74. https://doi.org/10.1027/2157-3891/a000103

Price, K. (2010). What is reproductive justice? How women of color activists are redefining the pro-choice paradigm. *Meridians: Feminism, Race, Transnationalism, 10*(2), 42–65. https://doi.org/10.2979/meridians.2010.10.2.42

Roll, S. & East, J. (2014). Financially vulnerable families and the child care cliff effect. *Journal of Poverty, 18*(2), 169–87. https://doi.org/10.1080/10875549.2014.896307

Ross, L. & Solinger, R. (2017). *Reproductive justice: An introduction (Vol. 1).* University of California Press.

Sanders, K., Venkataraman, V., & Whelihan, K. (2024, May 2). *Addressing the black maternal mortality rate.* [Conference presentation]. Stratford Campus Research Day, Glassboro, New Jersey, USA. https://doi.org/10.31986/issn.2689-0690_rdw.stratford_research_day.172_2024

Sarmiento, I., Paredes-Solís, S., De Jesús-García, A., Maciel-Paulino, N., Meneses-Rentería, A., Amaya, C., Cockcroft, A., & Andersson, N. (2024). Traditional midwifery contribution to
safe birth in cultural safety: Narrative evaluation of an intervention in Guerrero, Mexico. *Community Health Equity Research & Policy, 44*(4), 377–89. https://doi.org/10.1177/0272684X221120481

Schoen, J. (2009). *Choice and coercion : Birth control, sterilization, and abortion in public health and welfare.* University of North Carolina Press.

Serrato Calero, M.D., Delgado-Vázquez, Á.M., & Díaz Jiménez, R.M. (2020). Systematized review and meta-synthesis of the sterilization of women with disabilities in the field of social science: From macroeugenics to microeugenics. *Sexuality Research and Social Policy, 18*, 653–71. https://doi.org/10.1007/S13178-020-00488-0

Stern, A.M. (2016). Eugenics, sterilization, and historical memory in the United States. *História, Ciências, Saúde-Manguinhos, 23*(1), 195–212. https://doi.org/10.1590/S0104-59702016000500011

Stote, K. (2022). From eugenics to family planning: The coerced sterilization of indigenous women in post-1970 Saskatchewan. *Native American and Indigenous Studies, 9*(1), 102–32. http://doi.org/10.1353/nai.2022.0013

VandeVusse, A., Hussain, R., Stillman M., Beavin, C., Kirstein, M., & Kavanaugh, M.L. (2023). Cost-related barriers to sexual and reproductive health care: Results from a longitudinal qualitative study in Arizona. *SSM: Qualitative Research in Health, 4*. https://doi.org/10.1016/j.ssmqr.2023.100360

Yearby, R., Clark, B., & Figueroa, J. F. (2022). Structural racism in historical and Modern US health care policy. *Health Affairs, 41*(2), 187–94. https://doi.org/10.1377/hlthaff.2021.01466

Zisman, L. H. (2024). Building our families: Navigating barriers in 2SLGBTQ+ family building through doula supports. *New Area Studies, 4*(2). https://doi.org/10.37975/NAS.67

Chapter 6

Rethinking Childhood

Neurovariance, Cultural Strengths, and Decolonialized Development Perspectives

Jessica Leith Claus

Introduction

As you reflect on the content of this chapter, it's important to recognize that my social location—shaped by a combination of privilege and mainstream identities—inevitably influences both my worldview and the approach I take in this work. I am a white, cisgender female, which places me within the dominant racial group in the United States and in many Westernized countries. Additionally, as someone from the middle class, I have had access to resources and opportunities that are often out of reach for individuals from marginalized economic backgrounds. I am acutely aware of how this privilege has shaped my own development. It is also significant to note that I am able-bodied and considered neurotypical, or, as my neurodivergent loved ones affectionately refer to me, a "normie."

This topic holds deep personal significance for me. I have seen loved ones spend much of their life slipping through the cracks, burdened by the experience shared by many—misdiagnosis or the absence of diagnosis—constantly measuring themselves against neurotypical standards and internalizing the belief that they were the problem. As I raise my two children, I am particularly sensitive to how my partner and I celebrate milestones, draw comparisons, and set benchmarks. It is vital that we foster a world in which all forms of neurovariance are recognized, valued, and included rather than marginalized or dismissed. Most importantly, we must challenge the prevailing notion that cognitive and developmental classifications are binary, a perspective that excludes the many who exist somewhere in between.

When I refer to "we," I am specifically referencing most child developmental models that reflect Western and linear perspectives on development. While prevalent, these models have overshadowed the way a number of other cultures think about development and offer opportunities for examining these distinctions. For instance, many Indigenous groups view neurodivergence through a holistic and spiritual lens, rather than a strictly medical one (Cajete, 2000; Gone, 2013; Kirmayer et al., 2000). In some tribes, neurodivergent individuals are seen not as having a disorder but as possessing special gifts or heightened spiritual connections (Battiste, 2002; Bruno et al, 2025; Nahwegiizhic, 2024). Among some Plains tribes, for example, individuals who exhibit deep focus or alternative ways of thinking are respected as visionaries, healers, or wisdom keepers, rather than being seen as deficient (Marker, 2006; Simpson, 2014).

Professionally, this chapter is the result of years of practice, research, and teaching in the field of child and family therapy. As a Marriage and Family therapist, my primary focus has been on evaluating treatment models and determining their ability to account for an

DOI: 10.4324/9781032679082-9

individual's or family's broader context. A natural extension of this work has been a critical examination of these models' adaptability in meeting the needs of diverse populations. One of the fundamental challenges in intervention design is securing sufficient funding to develop distinct models tailored to each population (Alizadeh & Chavan, 2016). Thus, a more sustainable approach has been to build upon existing frameworks, ensuring that interventions align with the cultural, social, and developmental contexts of the individuals they aim to support (Lilienfeld, 2014). This requires care providers to actively engage in critically analyzing their practices to avoid reinforcing oppressive pathologization and instead promote inclusive, context-sensitive therapeutic approaches (Brown & Gilligan, 1992).

My most comprehensive effort to address this issue was collaborating with colleagues at the University of Washington to develop a family therapy model that not only supported youth through challenges but also engaged the entire family to enhance the effectiveness of evidence-based strategies. We integrated insights from practice-based literature to differentiate between the content of the intervention and the mechanisms of its application, mirroring the distinction between content and process when working with families. Consistent with most family therapy models, we train providers to conceptualize clients within their broader context and to intervene accordingly, incorporating adolescent development psychoeducation rooted in brain science (Siegel, 2014) and neurovariance (Baird et al., 2023; Cherowick & Matergia, 2024).

The field of Marriage and Family Therapy (MFT) holds a distinct advantage over purely developmental models by emphasizing the assessment of an individual's context and meeting clients where they are—a foundational element of effective intervention. Theories such as the Satir Human Growth odel model (Banmen et al., 2006) and Solution-Focused therapy (de Shazer & Berg, 1997) honor individual differences, foster self-acceptance, and reinforce client strengths. Similarly, person-of-the-therapist models promote self-reflection and serve as essential frameworks for ensuring culturally responsive approaches to defining "normal" and "abnormal" behaviors and interactions Aponte et al., 2009). However, suppose our training programs—and, therefore, our students—are grounded in developmental models embedded within curricula that are flawed at their inception. How can we ensure a decolonized approach to this work? This chapter aims to explore this question and propose practical strategies for knowledge integration and clinical application within a culturally responsive developmental framework.

Background of Child Development

The concept of child development has been central to educational psychology, parenting, and societal structures for centuries. However, the early developmental models did not come to fruition until the late nineteenth to early twentieth centuries as folks began to become more interested in understanding human growth and behavior as well as to fully appreciate the cognitive, emotional, physical, social, and educational growth that children go through from birth and into early adulthood (Damon & Lerner, 2006; Henrich, Heine, & Norenzayan, 2010).

However, the frameworks used to understand and support child development have largely been shaped by Western ideologies rooted in colonial histories and cultural biases, which have led to years of pathologization and misinterpretation in populations who were not considered when developing these ideals (Rabello de Castro, 2021). They also form the basis for much of our understanding of parenting interventions and general human development classes (Jeong et al., 2021). Our goal in writing this chapter is to offer a deeper examination of how linear models of childhood development do not capture the variance and fluidity of childhood experiences and how this has limited the possibilities of neurovariant children and the professionals with whom they interact.

By challenging these dominant models and recognizing how they show up in our work, we can create more holistic and relevant approaches that respect the varying experiences and values of Indigenous, global, and marginalized communities (Rogoff, 2003). Additionally, it is essential to incorporate an understanding of neurovariance across populations, recognizing that neurological differences—including those associated with conditions like autism, ADHD, and other developmental variations—are not deficits but part of the natural spectrum of human diversity (Silberman, 2015; Pellicano et al., 2014). A decolonized approach to childhood development not only embraces this neurodiversity but also ensures that all children, regardless of their background or neurological profile, have the opportunity to thrive in environments that honor their unique needs and provide therapists with the tools to incorporate these variances into their own understanding of child and family development.

Origins of The Western Framework of Child Development

The Western models of child development are largely based on theories that emerged in the late nineteenth and early twentieth centuries, a period marked by colonial expansion, scientific rationalism, and the belief in a universal, linear trajectory for human development. Colonization during this time reinforced a "normal" way of viewing child development and often did not consider those non-Western populations who were victims of colonization (Barrett, 2021; Nsamenang, 1992). For example, Indigenous groups held specific milestones that were aligned with cultural beliefs and traditions and taught within their communities. When Europeans settled in the New World, they effectively dismantled this by forced integration into Western educational systems and forced removal from their families (Castagno & Brayboy, 2008).

Key figures such as Jean Piaget, Erik Erikson, and John Bowlby laid the foundation for the modern understanding of child development and notably were White men of European origin. Their work emphasized stages of cognitive, emotional, and social development that were thought to be universally applicable across cultures (Berk, 2013). However, these theories were often developed in highly specific cultural contexts and often do not reflect the lived experiences of children from non-Western backgrounds. An exception to this was the Russian sociologist Lev Vygostsky's Sociocultural Development model (Vygotsky, 1978), which differentiated from the others by reinforcing the importance of the cultural context *in addition to* biological factors that influenced a child's development. While this additional aspect of a child's environment was a useful advancement when it came to considering a typical developmental trajectory, it still did not account for the neurovariance that occurs during this critical period in childhood (Lerner, 2018).

The Stages of Development

Jean Piaget's theory of cognitive development, for example, delineated four stages of intellectual growth that were based on observations of European children. Piaget suggested that all children, regardless of cultural background, pass through these stages—sensorimotor, preoperational, concrete operational, and formal operational—at roughly the same age and in the same sequence (Damon & Lerner, 2006). Piaget's model assumes that cognitive growth is driven by interaction with the environment in a manner that aligns with Western educational practices, which may not be universally relevant. Additionally, we know that children on the spectrum have cognitive processes that are not linear but advance significantly in some areas and not in others (Kapp, 2020).

Like Piaget, Erikson's psychosocial stages outlined the emotional and social development of individuals across eight life stages, where successful navigation of each stage was thought to lead to healthy psychological outcomes. Although broader in scope than Piaget's, Erikson's model also assumes that social development progresses in a fixed, linear manner that does not consider varying cultural, neurological, and familial norms (Damon & Lerner, 2006; Rogoff, 2003).

Most adolescent developmental perspectives heighten the importance of peer relationships as a necessary component of social development (Brown & Larson, 2009; Siegel, 2014). However, my 16-year-old male client on the autism spectrum would disagree. When asked about his desire for social relationships, he reports that he has always found interactions with adults more fulfilling, and while he does not avoid social interactions among peers, he also does not seek them out and does not report any detrimental feelings of loneliness or isolation. What works for him is to engage with them on a more indirect level, such as through gaming or martial arts classes. Assuming all children place peer relationships at the top of their list of priorities would infer that there is something wrong with my client for not doing the same and thus creating a problem that doesn't necessarily exist.

On the other hand, I have many adult clients who struggle to connect in their interpersonal relationships and do describe a feeling of loneliness, but the important component here is that *it is not universal*. Often, loneliness is the result of believing that they cannot be themselves in relationships because of how they may be compared to others with different neurological profiles, and therefore, they are left to inhabit a world that reinforces "masking," which can create its own problems with depression and anxiety (Baron-Cohen, 2008; Silberman, 2015). The decolonized perspective would examine this as conformity to a system that was designed to heighten certain traits as beneficial or ideal (e.g., extroversion) rather than allowing for a collaborative method of engagement that considers all capacities for participation.

Western Conceptualizations of Neurovariance

In the context of neurovariance—terms like autism, ADHD, and dyslexia—Western models have historically categorized such conditions as deviations from a "norm," framing them as disorders or disabilities rather than natural variations of human neurodiversity. The DSM (Diagnostic and Statistical Manual of Mental Disorders) and the ICD (International Classification of Diseases) are key texts in our field that have pathologized these neurodivergences, particularly in the twentieth century. The term "neurotypical" is often used to refer to individuals who do not display these variations, further marginalizing those who exhibit different cognitive, emotional, and social processing patterns (APA, 2022; WHO, 2022).

For example, children diagnosed with ADHD are often expected to conform to standardized educational practices that demand attention, focus, and impulse control—behaviors that are culturally valued in Western educational systems. However, these systems fail to consider alternative ways of thinking, learning, and behaving that might be celebrated in different cultures or are a better fit for the way their brain operates (Grummt, 2024). When children do not adhere to these "neurotypical standards," they are stigmatized with additional disorders, such as disruptive behavior and/or oppositional defiant disorder. This often sets them up for failure in the school system and beyond (Haughton & McKenna, 2018).

School systems throughout the world have served as examples of how to provide accommodating educational systems for their students. Finland's education system prioritizes individualized learning plans and multitiered support in mainstream classrooms. Instead of labeling students as "special needs," the system provides early intervention and flexible instruction for all students (Sahlburg, 2011). In Japan, their educational philosophy emphasizes the whole child's development, integrating emotional, social, and cognitive growth within the learning process. A cultural commitment to group cohesion and collective responsibility ensures that neurodivergent students are supported within their peer groups rather than being isolated in specialized settings (Furuta & Osugi, 2016; Oka et al., 2021).

Themes Across Western Models of Child Development

Several recurring themes across Western models of child development contribute to their narrow scope and limited cultural responsiveness. These include universalism, individualism, the medicalization of neurodivergence, and an emphasis on normative pathways as a mechanism for optimal functioning and development. Each of these is discussed in more depth in the subsequent sections.

Universalism

Many Western developmental theories operate under the assumption of universality—namely, that all children, regardless of culture or context, develop linear and stage-based (Piaget, 1952). While certain attributes can be traced across populations, this assumption of universal developmental stages erases the role of culture, history, and context in shaping individual growth and development (Greenfield, 2000). For example, Piaget's stages of development assume that the acquisition of abstract reasoning is universal, but this is contested by indigenous knowledge systems where abstract thought might not be prioritized over relational, experiential, or oral forms of learning (Briggs, 1993).

In contrast, some models emphasize a universal way of understanding functioning, yet they do not prioritize this as part of a singular, systematic process. Namely, they consider a client's context and instead wrap the universal understandings into this to attribute it correctly (Satir, 1988). For example, Virginia Satir's Human Growth Model assumes we all possess eight universal human resources; however, each of these will look different across populations (Satir, 1988). It adds strength and value to an individual and their relationships rather than accounting for a deficit. The domains include a spiritual dimension, along with interactional, physical, sensual, and nutritional, to name a few. Within each client's context, they will determine what resources they harness in these areas, as typically, they all fall within these topics. An example of this in the therapy room would be someone who comes from a more collectivist culture in which the interactional domain would be a higher resource for them rather than the intellectual or spiritual (Satir, 1988). For neurodiverse folks, this could be considering areas of strength and resources that others have seen as a deficit.

Universalism can also be attributed to the way we understand brain functioning. Neurodevelopmental pathways are assumed to develop in particular stages throughout a child's development and can manifest in a number of ways when it comes to behavior and understanding (Shonkoff & Phillips, 2000). However, we know that folks on the spectrum can experience a divergence here in terms of information processing, communication, and emotion regulation (Baron-Cohen, 2002). There also tend to be sensory processing challenges. Hyperfocusing on these areas of difficulty can take away from leaning more into their strengths, such as creativity, attention to detail, and innovation in dormant processes (Grandin, 2006).

The Focus on Individualism

Western child development theories often emphasize individualism, personal autonomy, and independence as key markers of successful development (Sheehan & Wilkinson, 2022). This reflects broader societal values in the West that prioritize individual rights, personal achievement, and self-actualization (Kim & Sasaki, 2014). In many non-Western cultures, however, interdependence, collectivism, and communal values are more central to the child's role in society (Maynard & Chaudhary, 2021). These values challenge the individualistic orientation of Western developmental models and neglect important collectivist strengths that populations rely on (Hwang et al., 2020).

For example, in many African, Indigenous, and Asian cultures, the development of the child is seen not just as a process of personal maturation but as an unfolding of responsibilities within a family and community. The focus is on relationship-building and the intergenerational transmission of knowledge and values, often in a more fluid, collaborative manner than the rigid stages of Western developmental models allow for (Berk, 2013; Bruno et al., 2025; Nahwegiizhic, 2024; Casanova et al., 2021).

When I worked in Cambodia over a decade ago, I had the opportunity to experience this. I was part of a mobile mental health team that would travel to rural provinces throughout the country to promote mental health understanding to folks who are living with legacies of intergenerational trauma from the Khmer Rouge genocide of the 1970s (Van Schaack et al, 2011). When I first arrived, one of my initial surprises was that all or most of the children were on their own during the day - and not in school. In the US, this would be considered neglect. But here, everyone had a role to play, including the young children. Similar to how the US evolved over time, children are an integral part of the survival structure and are often responsible for themselves at a young age. One of my favorite memories was of a small boy fishing for his own dinner and the look of pride when he caught one and plopped it in his bowl to be cooked. I'm trying to imagine the look on my eight-year-old's face if I were to tell her to catch her own fish for dinner.

The Medicalization of Neurodivergence

In Western frameworks, neurodivergence—such as ADHD, autism, and dyslexia—is often medicalized. The assumption is that these conditions are pathologies that must be treated or corrected through medical interventions, behavior modification, or educational accommodations. This medicalization stems from a long history of viewing children who deviate from expected norms as "disordered" rather than different or simply neurodivergent (Kapp, 2020).

These diagnostic systems, deeply entrenched in Western biomedical discourse, tend to ignore cultural variations in the manifestation of these neurodivergences. For example, behaviors associated with ADHD, such as fidgeting or difficulty sitting still, might be normalized or even valued in specific cultures that have different educational structures or social norms than those in the West. In contrast, Zapotec and Maya cultures are two examples of Indigenous learning environments that emphasize learning by doing, observation, and participation in daily communal activities rather than formal schooling that requires long periods of stillness. Children are encouraged to learn practical tasks such as weaving, cooking, and farming through hands-on engagement (Delgado-Gaitan, 2001; Rogoff et al., 2003).

Emphasis on Normative Pathways

The Western approach often assumes that there are "normative" developmental pathways and any deviation from these is considered a problem (Acevedo & Nusbaum, 2020). This is particularly relevant in the context of neurodevelopmental disorders, where there is an underlying expectation that children will meet certain milestones at specific ages (LeBlanc & Gillis, 2012). For children who don't follow these trajectories, there is often a systemic failure to provide support or accommodations that align with their needs or potential (Mazumder & Thompson-Hodgetts, 2019). MFTs are often in the unique position of being able to perpetuate this harmful approach or normalize the fact that all children are on different spectrums of neurovariance (Daley & Birchwood, 2010).

The dominance of these early child development models has led to numerous issues for non-Western cultures, as well as a large population of children who experience neurodivergence (Daley & Birchwood, 2010; LeBlanc & Gillis, 2012). The assumption that all children develop in the same way not only disregards the rich diversity of cultures and parenting practices around the world but also fails to recognize the inherent strengths that children with neurodivergence possess and that many other cultures recognize. (Grinker, 2020; Delgado-Gaitan, 2001).

Cultural practices that prioritize communal child-rearing, extended family involvement, and oral traditions may be misunderstood or undervalued in Western-centric developmental models, and the skills learned from these practices may be disregarded (Greenfield, 2017). For instance, children in collectivist societies might be encouraged to learn through group activities, communal responsibilities, and observation rather than through the individualized academic tasks common in Western classrooms (Furuta & Osugi, 2016; Oka et al., 2021; Casanova et al., 2021).

Systems therapists are ingrained in this model of interaction with the world as we see individuals not just as an autonomous silo but as a person who is a product of multiple systems interacting with one another (e.g., communities, schools, institutions, policies). We have a pivotal choice to embrace and fully join these systems and their unilateral practices or be agents of change and advocate for a social justice-oriented approach (Pope et al., 2019).

Harmful Educational Practices

When Western developmental models are applied to non-Western children, educational systems may fail to accommodate different learning styles, communication patterns, or ways of expressing intelligence. For instance, many Indigenous communities emphasize learning through storytelling and experiential knowledge rather than through formal schooling (Bruno et al., 2025; Nahwegiizhic, 2024). When these practices are ignored or devalued in favor of standardized curricula, children may struggle in educational settings, leading to misdiagnosis, underachievement, and cultural dislocation (Castagno & Brayboy, 2008; Daley & Birchwood, 2010). This is most understood in such extreme cases as the school-to-prison pipeline, which is a system of policies and practices that push students out of schools and into justice systems. This has more significant implications when considering the demographics of folks in these correction systems (Mallet, 2016).

Colonial Legacies and Knowledge Suppression

Western models of child development are rooted in colonial ideologies that sought to "civilize" indigenous populations by imposing foreign educational systems, child-rearing practices, and belief structures. These models often discounted or invalidated indigenous knowledge, healing practices, and child-rearing methods (Harkness & Super, 2020). Consequently, there is a legacy of epistemic violence, where the wisdom of indigenous and non-Western cultures is sidelined or erased in favor of Western scientific approaches (Maynard & Chaudhary, 2021). This exclusion undermines valuable cultural insights and limits a more holistic understanding of child development that embraces relational, spiritual, and experiential ways of knowing (Sheehan & Wilkinson, 2022).

The forced assimilation of Indigenous children in the United States through boarding schools, such as the Truxton Canyon Training School in Arizona, reflects the damaging consequences of imposing a singular, Western-centric model of child development and education. These schools operated under the assumption that Indigenous cultural practices and worldviews were inferior, requiring children to abandon their native languages, traditions, and identities in favor of Western norms (Brave Heart, 1998). This approach reflects the broader belief that there is a "correct" or "universal" pathway to development, disregarding the cultural diversity of learning and growth.

A Decolonized Perspective When Working with Families

As a parent, I have often encountered situations many others have experienced, such as comparing my child's development to others. If another child uses more words than mine, do I need to get them into speech therapy? Do I need to explore occupational therapy if they struggle with basic motor tasks? If they struggle with emotional dysregulation, should I place them in child therapy? At various stages, I am probing for deficits and agonizing over how I will correct these "misalignments" to better fit into an immediate context that has defined development as a linear and universal path.

Leaning on a framework can help manage parental anxiety, and it can be helpful to have a template to refer to and capture signs of significant delays that may be time-sensitive (Sanders et al., 2002). For example, most early intervention services exist for children between the ages of 0–3, and identifying deficits early on can help improve long-term outcomes for speech and motor skills (*Guardian*, 2024). The risk is that families who do not align with these particular milestone goals are often either dismissed or pathologized for not accommodating one specific way of viewing development. Creating a person-centered rather than a theory-centered system would help prevent mistrust within these systems for many folks (Shim et al., 2018).

Systems therapists work among systems that fall into the threshold of mistrust with many historically marginalized groups. These same systems therapists rely on curricula developed within MFT graduate school programs that support this learning. This can include lifespan development, assessment, diagnosis, and treatment, and attachment models. They use this knowledge to shape their clinical training. They are at a pivotal point in their clinical development where they rely on frameworks to support their further understanding of child and family functioning (COAMFTE, 2025).

Decolonizing Child Development Perspectives

Decolonizing child development requires a radical shift in how we view children, learning, and neurodiversity. A decolonized perspective does not simply seek to critique Western models but to create inclusive, culturally responsive frameworks that honor the diversity of human experience and ensure that our MFTs are comprehensively trained in their programs to incorporate this into their work.

Acknowledging the Role of Culture and Context

A decolonized approach to child development must center culture as a foundational component of growth and learning. This means recognizing that developmental processes are not universal but are deeply shaped by culture, history, and geography (Sheehan & Wilkinson, 2022; Rogoff et al., 2003). Practitioners must consider the cultural context of children's lives, including family structures, community practices, language, and values.

For Marriage and Family Therapists (MFTs), integrating a cultural genogram into the practice of family genogram development is essential to capturing the unique cultural influences that shape family dynamics and individual behaviors (Chege et al., 2023). When working with new family clients, I first explore their cultural context and background. I ask questions that guide the creation of a family genogram, allowing me to map out family roles, legacies, and, in particular, parenting practices. During this process, we discuss their cultural values, beliefs, and preferences in depth. My focus is on addressing the issues they identify as problematic rather than imposing external judgments. By using a cultural genogram, I ensure that the family's cultural framework is central to understanding and addressing their concerns.

Valuing Neurodiversity

Neurodivergence should be reframed not as a pathology but as part of the natural diversity of human development. This shift challenges the biomedical model that views children with ADHD, autism, or dyslexia as needing to be "fixed" or "treated." Instead, children should be supported in ways that celebrate their unique ways of being, thinking, and engaging with the world.

A common symptom that often appears in my therapeutic space with my clients who have ADHD is a consistent sense of failure. At home, at school, and with peers. Impacts on executive functioning can mean that they are often late, disorganized, and impulsive, which can impact their academic performance and peer relationships (Kapp, 2020; Glenn, 2022). They are often seen as the problem, with expectations from family and schools to develop skills that accommodate them rather than the other way around.

Systems models have the potential to enhance self-worth, externalize shame, and adopt a solution-focused approach to challenges rather than reinforcing problem-saturated narratives. These strategies are well established within models throughout the marriage and family therapy (MFT) profession (Gehart, 2010). However, it is essential for clinicians to apply these approaches through a decolonized lens, ensuring that interventions are culturally attuned and grounded in an accurate understanding of the client's capacity to engage both intrapersonally and interpersonally. Aligning therapeutic goals with this framework promotes the recognition of outcomes that are both culturally appropriate and realistically attainable (Castagno & Brayboy, 2008; Heiphetz & Oishi, 2021).

Embracing Holistic, Relational Approaches

A decolonized perspective also calls for a holistic, relational view of child development. This means understanding that children's growth is not simply about acquiring individual skills or achieving milestones but involves a dynamic process of learning in relation to others—family members, peers, elders, and the natural world. Development is seen as a community process, where the child's identity and capacity are shaped by their relationships with others.

As we navigate an increasingly technology-centered childhood, it is more crucial than ever to shift the focus from an outcome-based intensive parenting approach to fostering more meaningful interactions with and among children in the real world (Haidt, 2024). Relationship enhancement, a widely used tool in clinical treatment for addressing family conflict, provides a valuable framework that Marriage and Family Therapists (MFTs) can leverage to promote positive interaction (Gardner et al., 2016). By encouraging parental modeling, fostering a sense of responsibility, and creating opportunities for children to build skills beyond the constraints of academics, MFTs can help children develop essential life skills and deepen family connections from a more culturally universal learning-by-doing perspective (Maynard & Chaudhary, 2021; Delgado-Gaitan, 2001).

Integrating Indigenous Knowledge and Practices

Decolonizing child development involves reviving and integrating indigenous knowledge systems and practices. This includes exploring alternative educational paradigms prioritizing experiential learning, storytelling, communal responsibility, and connection to land and spirituality. Indigenous models of child-rearing, which often focus on mentorship, group activities, and multigenerational interaction, offer valuable lessons on supporting children in ways deeply rooted in their cultural contexts (Rogoff, 2003).

Many adaptations have been made to various evidence-based models to treat trauma and/or behavioral challenges for youth and families that center this into the primary principles within the interventions. For example, "honoring children, mending the circle" is a trauma-based intervention that adapts trauma-focused CBT to, in this circumstance, an Indigenous community in Colorado (Bigfoot & Schmidt, 2010). Narrative therapy is a systemic approach that uses storytelling and use of language to understand challenges and engage in healing (Parry & Doan, 1994).

Promoting Cultural Humility and Reflexivity

Professionals working with children must adopt a stance of cultural humility—acknowledging that they do not have all the answers and being open to learning from the families and communities they work with. Reflexivity, or the practice of examining one's own cultural biases and assumptions, is key to ensuring that interventions and support systems are culturally sensitive and effective.

In my work as a trainer, consultant, supervisor, and practitioner, I consistently emphasize the importance of therapists and providers taking the lead in this process and meeting families where they are rather than imposing an external agenda. Approaching families with a narrow focus on problematic behaviors and interactions often exacerbates the marginalization of groups that already harbor distrust toward systems that are supposed to offer support. The child welfare system, for instance, has long been criticized for its tendency to separate families rather than support them. However, Washington State has recently shifted its approach to investigating child neglect and maltreatment by implementing the Family Assessment Response (FAR), a model that prioritizes keeping families intact and offering support within their communities instead of removing children based on Western-centric views of parenting. This approach reflects a more holistic, culturally sensitive response to family needs (Koti, 2024).

Using literature that supports cross-cultural healing and understanding through texts that provide a broadened perspective on child development and neurovariance can offer families alternative perspectives and strategies for managing challenging behaviors that may show up as a result. MFTs can refrain from colluding in the idea that there is a problem to be solved rather than a problem to be understood in context, allowing them to be responsive yet sensitive and thorough. If we are to be trusted members of their care teams, we must ensure that we are using resources that do not further stigmatize (Kirmayer & Jarvis, 2019).

Conclusion

The dominant Western models of child development have long failed to adequately account for the diverse ways children grow, learn, and interact with the world. By decolonizing child development perspectives, we can create inclusive, culturally responsive frameworks that are attuned to the neurodiversity inherent in all human beings. Such a decolonized approach validates the rich diversity of cultural practices and belief systems and provides more effective and compassionate support for all children, particularly those from non-Western backgrounds.

Marriage and Family Therapists (MFTs) are inherently embedded within many of these systems and have an ethical responsibility to promote child development through a holistic and culturally competent framework, responding in a manner that is both respectful and appropriate to the unique needs of each family. Through cultural humility, recognition of neurodiversity, and the integration of indigenous wisdom, we can begin to craft a more just and equitable future for child development across the globe. More importantly, we are not required to reinvent the wheel. Many populations, both locally and globally, are already engaging with this knowledge and wisdom. Our role is to ensure that we are not dismissing these ideals or values and to take a deconstructive lens to our theories and practices.

References

Acevedo, S. M., & Nusbaum, E. A. (2020). Autism, neurodiversity, and inclusive education. In *Oxford Research Encyclopedia of Education*. Oxford University Press. https://doi.org/10.1093/acrefore/9780190264093.013.1260

Alizadeh, S., & Chavan, M. (2016). Cultural competence dimensions and outcomes: a systematic review of the literature. *Health & social care in the community*, 24(6), e117–e130. https://doi.org/10.1111/hsc.12293

American Psychiatric Association. (2022). *Diagnostic and statistical manual of mental disorders* (5th ed., text rev.). American Psychiatric Publishing.

Aponte, H. J., Powell, F. D., Brooks, S., Watson, M. F., Litzke, C., Lawless, J., & Johnson, E. (2009). Training the person of the therapist in an academic setting. *Journal of marital and family therapy*, *35*(4), 381–94. https://doi.org/10.1111/j.1752-0606.2009.00123.x

Armstrong, T. (2010). *The power of neurodiversity: Unleashing the advantages of your differently wired brain*. Balance.

Baird, A., Candy, B., Flouri, E., Tyler, N., & Hassiotis, A. (2023). The association between physical environment and externalising problems in typically developing and neurodiverse children and young people: A narrative review. *International Journal of Environmental Research and Public Health*, *20*(3), Article 2549. https://doi.org/10.3390/ijerph20032549

Banmen, J., Gomori, M., & Satir, V. (1991). *The Satir model: Family therapy & beyond*. Science and Behavior Books.

Baron-Cohen, S. (2008). *The essential difference: Male and female brains and the truth about Autism*. Basic Books.

Berk, L. E. (2013). *Child development* (9th ed.). Pearson Education.

Bigfoot, D. S., & Schmidt, S. R. (2010). Honoring children, mending the circle: Cultural adaptation of trauma-focused cognitive-behavioral therapy for American Indian and Alaska Native children. *Journal of clinical psychology*, *66*(8), 847–56. https://doi.org/10.1002/jclp.20707

Brown, B. B., & Larson, J. (2009). Peer relationships in adolescence. In R. M. Lerner & L. Steinberg (Eds.), *Handbook of adolescent psychology: Contextual influences on adolescent development* (3rd ed., pp. 74–103). John Wiley & Sons, Inc. https://doi.org/10.1002/9780470479193.adlpsy002004

Bruno, G., Lindblom, A., Masternes, J.-A., Tupou, J., Waisman, T., Toby, S., Vining, C., & Magiati, I. (2025). Global Indigenous perspectives on autism and autism research: Colonialism, cultural insights and ways forward. *Autism*, *29*(2), 275–83. https://doi.org/10.1177/13623613251318399

Castagno, A. E., & Brayboy, B. M. J. (2008). Culturally responsive schooling for Indigenous youth: A review of the literature. *Review of Educational Research*, *78*(4), 941–93. https://doi.org/10.3102/00346543083230

Chege, C. N., Fu, M., Bustrum, J. M., & Jenks, E. H. (2023). The worldview genogram: A process model for enhancing diversity responsiveness and competence in education, training, and clinical supervision. *Psychological Services*, *20*(2), 219. https://doi.org/10.1037/ser0000719

Cherewick, M., Matergia, M. (2024). Neurodiversity in practice: A conceptual model of autistic strengths and potential mechanisms of change to support positive mental health and wellbeing in autistic children and adolescents. *Advances in Neurodevelopmental Disorders*, *8*, 408–22. https://doi.org/10.1007/s41252-023-00348-z

Commission on Accreditation for Marriage and Family Therapy Education (COAMFTE). (2025). *Accreditation standards and procedures manual (Version 12.5)*. American Association for Marriage and Family Therapy (AAMFT). Retrieved from https://www.aamft.org

Cooper-Haber, K., & Haber, R. (2015). Training family therapists for working in the schools. *Contemporary Family Therapy*, *37*, 341–50. https://doi.org/10.1007/s10591-015-9361-7

Daley, D. and Birchwood, J. (2010), ADHD and academic performance: Why does ADHD impact on academic performance and what can be done to support ADHD children in the classroom?. *Child: Care, Health and Development*, *36*: 455–64. https://doi.org/10.1111/j.1365-2214.2009.01046.x

Damon, W., & Lerner, R. M. (Eds.). (2006). *Handbook of child psychology, theoretical models of human development*. John Wiley & Sons.

De Shazer, S., & Berg, I. K. (1997). 'What works?' Remarks on research aspects of solution-focused brief therapy. *Journal of Family therapy*, *19*(2), 121–24. https://doi.org/10.1111/1467-6427.00043

Delgado-Gaitan, C. (2001). *The power of community: Mobilizing for family and schooling*. Rowman & Littlefield.

Furuta, H., & Osugi, N. (2016). Developing an inclusive education system in Japan: The case of Yamaga City, Kumamoto. *Bull of the Faculty of Education* (65), 139–144. https://ci.nii.ac.jp/naid/110010061346/en/

Gardner, F., Montgomery, P., & Knerr, W. (2016). Transporting evidence-based parenting programs for child problem behavior (age 3–10) between countries: Systematic review and meta-analysis. *Journal of Clinical Child & Adolescent Psychology, 45*(6), 749–62. https://doi.org/10.1080/1537 4416.2015.1015134

Gehart, D. R. (2010). *Mastering competencies in family therapy: A practical approach to theories and clinical case documentation.* Brooks/Cole.

Grummt, M. (2024). Sociocultural perspectives on neurodiversity—An analysis, interpretation and synthesis of the basic terms, discourses and theoretical positions. *Sociology Compass, 18*(8), Article e13249. https://doi.org/10.1111/soc4.13249

The Guardian. (2024, September 1). *'They're about two years behind': Fears for children born during lockdown as they start at school.* The Guardian. Retrieved March 11, 2025, from https://www.theguardian.com/society/article/2024/sep/01/fears-children-born-lockdown-start-school-covid

Haidt, J. (2024). *The anxious generation: How the great rewiring of childhood is causing an epidemic of mental illness.* Penguin.

Haley, J. (1976). *Problem-solving therapy: New strategies for effective family therapy.* Jossey-Bass.

Harkness, S., & Super, C. M. (2020). Culture and human development: Where did it go? And where is it going? *New Directions for Child and Adolescent Development, 2020,* 101–119. https://doi.org/10.1002/cad.20378

Heiphetz, L., & Oishi, S. (2021). Viewing development through the lens of culture: Integrating developmental and cultural psychology to better understand cognition and behavior. *Perspectives on Psychological Science, 17*(1), 62–77. https://doi.org/10.1177/1745691620980725

Henrich, J., Heine, S. J., & Norenzayan, A. (2010). The weirdest people in the world? *Behavioral and Brain Sciences, 33*(2–3), 61–83. https://doi.org/10.1017/S0140525X0999152X

Jeong, J., Franchett, E. E., Ramos de Oliveira, C. V., Rehmani, K., & Yousafzai, A. K. (2021). Parenting interventions to promote early child development in the first three years of life: A global systematic review and meta-analysis. *PLoS Medicine, 18*(5), Article e1003602. https://doi.org/10.1371/journal.pmed.1003602

Kapp, S. K. (Ed.). (2020). *Autistic community and the neurodiversity movement: Stories from the frontline.* Palgrave Macmillan.

Kim, H. S., & Sasaki, J. Y. (2014). Cultural neuroscience: Biology of the mind in cultural contexts. *Annual Review of Psychology, 65*(1), 487–514. https://doi.org/10.1146/annurev-psych-010213-115040

Kirmayer, L. J., & Jarvis, G. E. (2019). Culturally responsive services as a path to equity in mental healthcare. *HealthcarePapers, 18*(2), 11–23. https://doi.org/10.12927/hcpap.2019.25925

Koti, A. S. (2024). *Alternative response in Washington State: An exploratory analysis of re-reporting by child race and ethnicity* (Master's thesis, University of Washington).

LeBlanc, L. A., & Gillis, J. M. (2012). Behavioral interventions for children with autism spectrum disorders. *Pediatric Clinics, 59*(1), 147–64. https://doi.org/10.1016/j.pcl.2011.10.006

Lerner, R. M. (2018). *Concepts and theories of human development.* Routledge.

Mallett, C. A. (2016). The school-to-prison pipeline: A critical review of the punitive paradigm shift. *Child and Adolescent Social Work Journal, 33,* 15–24. https://doi.org/10.1007/s10560-015-0397-1

Maynard, A. E., & Chaudhary, N. (2021). Human development at the intersection of culture and globalization: Towards a more inclusive future. *Human Development, 64*(4–6), 250–57. https://doi.org/10.1159/000513046

Mazumder, R., & Thompson-Hodgetts, S. (2019). Stigmatization of children and adolescents with autism spectrum disorders and their families: A scoping study. *Review Journal of Autism and Developmental Disorders, 6,* 96–107. https://doi.org/10.1007/s40489-018-00156-5

Nahwegiizhic, L. G. (2024). Neurodiversity from an Indigenous perspective: Honouring the seven grandfather's teachings. In *Indigenous disability studies* (pp. 94–103). Routledge.

Nsamenang, A. B. (2006). Cultures in early childhood care and education. *Encyclopedia on Early Childhood Development,* 1–6.

Oka, T., Ishikawa, S. I., Saito, A., Maruo, K., Stickley, A., Watanabe, N.,... & Kamio, Y. (2021). Changes in self-efficacy in Japanese school-age children with and without high autistic traits after the Universal Unified Prevention Program: a single-group pilot study. *Child and Adolescent Psychiatry and Mental Health, 15*(1), 42. https://doi.org/10.1186/s13034-021-00398-y

Parry, A., & Doan, R. E. (1994). *Story re-visions: Narrative therapy in the postmodern world*. Guilford Press.

Pellicano, E., et al. (2014). A future made together: New directions in the ethics of autism research. *Journal of Autism and Developmental Disorders, 14*(3), 200–04. https://doi.org/10.1111/1471-3802.12070_5

Pope, M., Gonzalez, M., Cemeron, E. R. N., & Pangelinan, J. S. (2019). *Social justice and advocacy in counseling*. Taylor & Francis.

Rabello de Castro, L. (2021). Decolonising child studies: development and globalism as orientalist perspectives. *Third World Quarterly, 42*(11), 2487–504. https://doi.org/10.1080/01436597.2020.1788934

Rogoff, B. (2003). *The cultural nature of human development*. Oxford University Press.

Rogoff, B., Paradise, R., Mejía-Arauz, R., Correa-Chávez, M., & Angelillo, C. (2003). Firsthand learning through intent participation. *Annual Review of Psychology, 54*(1), 175–203. https://doi.org/10.1146/annurev.psych.54.101601.145118

Sahlberg, P. (2011). *Finnish lessons: What can the world learn from educational change in Finland?* Teachers College Press.

Sanders, M. R., Turner, K. M. T., & Markie-Dadds, C. (2002). Theoretical, scientific and clinical foundations of the Triple P-Positive Parenting Program: A population approach to the promotion of parenting competence. *Child and Family Behavior Therapy, 24*(3), 1–19. https://doi.org/10.1300/J019v24n03_01

Saskias Casanova, Melissa Mesinas & Sarait Martinez-Ortega (2021): Cultural knowledge as opportunities for empowerment: Learning and development for Mexican Indigenous youth. *Diaspora, Indigenous, and Minority Education, 15*(3), 193–207. https://doi.org/10.1080/15595692.2021.1910940

Satir, V. (2022). *The Satir model: Family therapy and beyond* (3rd ed.). Science and Behavior Books.

Sheehan, D., & Wilkinson, T. J. (2022). Widening how we see the impact of culture on learning, practice and identity development in clinical environments. *Medical Education, 56*(1). 110–16. https://doi.org/10.1111/medu.14630

Shim, R. S., Kho, C. E., & Murray-García, J. (2018). Inequities in mental health and mental health care: A review and future directions. *Psychiatric Annals, 48*(3), 140–146. https://doi.org/10.3928/00485713-20180213-01

Siegel, D. J. (2014). *Brainstorm: The power and purpose of the teenage brain*. TarcherPerigee.

Silberman, S. (2015). *NeuroTribes: The legacy of autism and the future of neurodiversity*. Avery.

Van Schaack, B. Reicherter, D., Chhang, Y., & Talbott, A. (2011) *Cambodia's hidden scars: trauma psychology in the wake of the Khmer Rouge: an edited volume on Cambodia's mental health*. Documentation Center of Cambodia.

Vygotsky, L. S. (1978). *Mind in society: The development of higher psychological processes*. Harvard University Press.

Walker, N. (2021). *Neuroqueer heresies: Notes on the neurodiversity paradigm, autistic empowerment, and postnormal possibilities*. Autonomous Press, 2021.

World Health Organization. (2022). *International classification of diseases* (11th rev.). World Health Organization.

Chapter 7

Grieving in the Wake of Colonialism

Using Creative Arts to Explore, Process, and Integrate Bio-Psycho-Social-Cultural Perspectives of Loss and Grief Across the Lifespan

Dani Baker and Alyssa Griskiewicz

A Note from the Authors: This chapter examines the significance of loss and grief experiences across the lifespan. Acknowledging and integrating all losses, not just death or traumatic loss, is tender, critical healing work and impacts every human being in profound ways. We, Dani, and Alyssa propose that the acknowledgment of loss, large and small, can help dismantle emotion-phobia and grief illiteracy prevalent in death-denying colonized societies. We believe that fostering creative engagement with natural losses and healthy grief at each developmental life stage contributes to individual and collective human thriving.

As mental health professionals and art therapists who hold multiple powerful and marginalized intersectional and positional identities, we work with the metaphors, symbology, and transformational potential of creative modalities and established frameworks. It is within this multifaceted and expansive container of nonverbal, creative modalities that we ethically and compassionately hold aspects of loss exploration, integration, and adaptation.

It is in this same spirit of holding that we offer a bio-psycho-social-cultural (BPSC) framework to explore a myriad of common losses and natural grief responses across the lifespan. It is intended to provide a comprehensive understanding of human experiences while acknowledging that utilizing any specific framework can be experienced as an oppressive perspective. In truth, no aspects of lived experience can fit neatly within specific categories, separate and contained by their labels.

As a matter of fact, we, the authors, rarely fit easily within specific categories. As creative arts therapists and dynamic humans honoring intersectional identities and agent and target identities, we feel more comfortable creating and redefining the spaces that we exist within. We also recognize that using a categorical approach to substantiate perspectives on loss and grief across the lifespan is incredibly useful. That said, we believe it is essential to critically evaluate how these categories are incomplete in their framing of human development and well-being. We understand that, though helpful in providing a frame, they will never fully encompass the lived realities of any human being, and certainly not those with marginalized identities (Mezzich et al., 2013).

As a result, we believe that therapists must ensure that the categories outlined in the BPSC model do not reinforce dominant narratives at the expense of diverse epistemologies and lived realities (Mezzich et al., 2013), nor do they squeeze the creative, complex, and vital wholeness from the developmental story. *We invite the reader to create and redefine the*

DOI: 10.4324/9781032679082-10

offerings here in ways that best move the needle toward collective liberation, creativity, and compassionate care.

Finally, for ease of use regarding the information provided throughout this chapter, below is a suggested approach to exploring loss and grief across your lifetime. You may use it within the context of your development as a therapist-in-training, as an experienced mental health professional in the field, or as a creative, complex intersectional human being with losses to explore, process, and integrate:

- With curiosity and kindness, consider where you may have experienced any bio-psycho-social-cultural losses across your lifespan. Easing into this experience, choose a lower-stakes loss and explore any unacknowledged grief associated with those losses that may have consciously or unconsciously impacted you and your well-being.
- Using your imagination, how could you acknowledge losses and gains across your lifetime? Notice with curiosity where you are compelled to downplay or minimize any type of loss experience or the associated experience of grief. Lean into your intuitive knowledge, asking who or what informs the need to lessen or curtail your reaction to the experience or outcome.
- How does this knowledge inform or influence your growing edges as a practitioner or therapist-in-training? How might it influence countertransference, case conceptualization, or your own attitudes toward clinical content or approaches to therapy?

An Overview of Loss and Grief in Western Societies

Evidence indicates that grief associated with nondeath-related loss is frequently avoided or suppressed within modern societies. One of the more subtle ways this is perpetuated is in language. In common usage, the term "grief" frequently precedes "loss," reflecting an emphasis on the emotional response rather than the loss itself. Essentially, this turn of phrase subtly bypasses the loss event, which must occur so the emotion of grief can then be experienced. This phenomenon of grief preceding loss can be explained by a strong desire to avoid the emotional details of a loss and is maintained by dismissal, distortion, or devaluation of natural grief, thereby compromising the legitimacy of loss and support of the grieving process (Devine, 2017). The authors are purposeful in using the terms "loss" and "grief" throughout this chapter and encourage the reader to deepen their awareness of how we perpetuate grief illiteracy (Devine, 2017) or collude with emotional phobia (Greenspan, 2004).

Loss, Grief, Mourning, and Pathology

All too often, acceptable grief is relegated to the death of a loved one. This socially sanctioned form of grieving is accepted for only a short period of time. After that, this natural response to significant loss becomes pathologized and diagnosable as prolonged grief disorder in the DSM-TR (APA, 2022). The DSM-TR (APA, 2022) and associations have long pathologized aspects of human experience, creating profound fear, mistrust, and medicalized oppression in Indigenous populations (Linklater, 2014) and stigmatized loss and grief for countless others.

This pathology exists in stark contrast to many loss and grief rituals and perceptions around the globe. In Indigenous Dagara culture, grief is perceived as so profoundly important to the human psyche that it is considered an emotion necessary for the human psyche to "maintain its healthy balance" (Somé, 1993, p.73). To do so, the Dagara perspective requires engaging with mystery, or *yielbongura* in their language, requiring both humility and wonder, as wonder offers refuge from the relentless pursuit of certainty and challenges assumed entitlement to definitive knowledge, encouraging engagement with the unknown (Jenkinson, 2015). Consciously and directly experiencing and processing the mystery of loss and grief is not an aberration; it is a necessity.

Moreover, the inability to tolerate natural, healthy grief responses to common, nondeath-related loss across the lifespan is particularly exacerbated within dominant Western societies. In these cultural frameworks, norms are greatly influenced by oppressive, colonizing, capitalist, and hegemonic forces that promote emotional fortitude and a limited capacity for engaging with the universal intricacies of sorrow within the mourning process (Baker-Cole, 2022). As a result, many individuals, families, and communities struggle with the overwhelming complexities of processing profound sorrow and genuine engagement with the natural grieving process. As a result, healthy grievers are often left without adequate support or understanding of a familiar yet emotionally complex process (McKee, 2015; Weller, 2015) related to all losses experienced across their lifetime.

Thus, within these oppressive cultural constructs, prevailing narratives suggest that grief and its big emotions should be evaded rather than welcomed with curiosity, authenticity, compassion, and empathy. This perspective hinders the natural grieving process, limiting opportunities for meaningful emotional expression and adaptation through supportive healing practices (Baker-Cole, 2022). Moreover, in societies shaped by capitalist structures and cis-hetero-patriarchal hierarchies, there exists an implicit belief that productivity and economic value take precedence over significant loss events, leaving those compromised by grief with limited time and space to navigate sorrow in healthy ways (Harris, 2010: Reynolds, 2002; Williamson, 2003). As a result, without adequate resources to externalize pain and support sorrow, healthy grievers may struggle to find ways to cope with unexpected change, hindering natural bio-psycho-social-cultural (BPSC) adaptation and healthy loss integration (Neimeyer et al., 2010).

In the last decade, as contemporary and decolonized perspectives on grief have evolved, Western mourning ideologies have increasingly adopted a bio-psycho-social-cultural framework to support the complex processes involved in validating and integrating common grief experiences across the lifespan. This shift from pathologizing natural grief responses toward a greater emphasis on adaptive coping mechanisms, adjustment strategies, and integrative practices has been tailored to meet the emotional, mental, physical, cultural, and communal needs of individuals and families (Neimeyer et al., 2010). By acknowledging healthy, decolonized approaches to navigating loss, these evolving perspectives contribute to a more compassionate, supportive, and liberated framework for *all* communities experiencing *all* aspects of natural loss and healthy grief across the lifespan (Baker-Cole, 2022; Goldenberg et al., 2010)

The experience of healing from loss is profound and transformative, often unfolding within the interconnected realms of personal sorrow and communal mourning (Baker-Cole, 2022). This process requires sustained perseverance, emotional resilience, and a supportive environment that acknowledges the depth and complexity of loss. (Chavez-Dueñas et al., 2019; French et al., 2020; Ginwright, 2011, 2015). Beyond the intrapersonal work of the griever, nature, land, animals, music, art, friends, family, community, trusted helpers, spiritual leaders, and blood and community-based ancestors can all provide witness and allyship along the way.

Embracing Decolonized Practices within a Liberatory Consciousness Framework

Decolonizing therapy is a transformative process that seeks to heal the psychological and systemic effects of colonization, imperialism, state-sanctioned violence, and structural oppression (Mullan, 2023). In therapy, this process begins by acknowledging the Indigenous land on which practice takes place, fostering a deeper understanding of the "soul wound" of internalized oppression within Indigenous communities (Duran et al., 2008). The lands a family has left behind may also be a source of recent or long past loss experiences that require tending. As a result, therapy standards, especially those that explore gains and losses across the lifespan, may require adaptation to include more holistic, community-centered approaches that acknowledge change and transformation (Singh et al., 2020). This shift then overtly positions therapists as social justice advocates and change agents, emphasizing the need for decolonized competencies to support systemic change (Ratts, 2009; Smith et al., 2009; Singh et al., 2020) within the context of common losses and natural grief across the lifespan.

Decolonization requires critically examining power, opportunity, and systemic inequities (Hernández-Wolfe, 2011). To enact genuine change, it is necessary to center Indigenous voices rather than reducing decolonization to a symbolic gesture (Tuck and Yang, 2012). Specifically, coloniality refers to the systemic suppression of marginalized cultures and knowledge systems by the dominant Eurocentric paradigm of modernity while also encompassing the knowledge and practices that emerge in response to this historical and ongoing oppression (Hernandez-Wolfe, 2011; Mignolo, 2005; Singh et al., 2020). Colonization enforces assimilation into dominant norms, perpetuating Indigenous oppression across societal domains and sustaining hegemonic power and privilege under the guise of societal normalcy (Mulan, 2023; Singh et al., 2020). Furthermore, traditional individual and family therapy theories, lacking a multicultural, intersectional, and anti-oppressive framework, were not intended to address systemic oppression and may inadvertently reinforce colonial power structures and marginalization. (Duran et al., 2008; Singh et al., 2020; Watkins & Shulman, 2008).

Intersectionality theory examines how multiple systems of oppression, such as identity and social location, shape daily experiences and reinforce systemic inequities (Singh et al., 2020). Therapists applying intersectionality theory to loss and grief must acknowledge that Crenshaw (1989, 1991) examined not only intersecting identities but also overlapping systems of power and control. These inequities compounded by power-over systems also contribute to unprocessed loss experiences across past and current lifetimes, shaping daily experiences and reinforcing systemic inequities (Singh et al., 2020). Thus, an intersectional framework highlights the relationship between identity and power, enhancing the understanding of sociopolitical forces, colonization, and how they can inform therapeutic relationships (Crenshaw, 2015, Hays 2001, 2024; Neito & Boyer, 2014; Singh et al., 2020) within individual, family and communal therapy.

In family therapy, intersectionality offers a lens to analyze clients' oppression within power structures (Carastathis, 2013) instead of a single-axis approach to minoritized communities, which overlooks intersecting identities such as age, development, (dis)abilities, dialect and language, gender identity, race, ethnicity, indigenous heritage, national origin, sexual orientation, size, and socioeconomic status, neurodiversity, further marginalizing and disempowering individuals (Collins,1989, 2022; hooks, 2015; Lorde,1984; Singh et al., 2020).

Equally relevant, the incorporation of Liberation psychology amplifies marginalized perspectives, enabling individuals to reclaim their histories, challenge oppressive structures, and restore cultural traditions through ancestral knowledge and practices (Chavez et al., 2016; Chavez-Dueñas et al., 2019; Singh et al., 2020). Rooted in Freire's (1970) framework, Liberation psychology also promotes the empowerment of individuals and communities in addressing oppression while simultaneously fostering reflexivity and enhancing a therapist's self-awareness of their own attitudes and beliefs (Norsworthy, 2017; Singh et al., 2020).

Love et al. (2000) expanded Freire's work by developing the Liberatory Consciousness framework to foster broader awareness of systemic oppression.

This work explores power dynamics and sustained structural inequities affecting marginalized groups, promoting a shift from individualism to collectivism, uncovering strategies for dismantling oppression and advancing social equity through awareness, analysis, action, and allyship/accountability (Goldblatt Hyatt & Sawyerr, 2024; Love & Jiggetts, 2019). Liberation in therapeutic practice involves rejecting Westernized "power-over" models in favor of collaborative, authentic relationships that embrace difference and cultivate meaningful connections, sometimes referred to as "power-with" models (Singh et al., 2020).

By integrating intersectionality theory with established therapeutic models and the multicultural and social justice counseling competencies (MSJCC), therapists actively challenge systemic power structures in mental health through these "power-with" approaches (Ratts et al., 2016; Walker, 2008; Singh et al., 2020). This process enables family therapists to critically engage in dismantling the coloniality of power and harm that persists within both society and therapeutic practice (Quijano & Ennis, 2000; Singh et al., 2020). In this way, healing work is more compassionate, comprehensive, and impactful for individuals, families, communities, and lineages.

Individual and Collective Loss and Sorrow; Bereavement in the Twenty-First Century

Bereavement is often understood as a period of mourning. Yet, it eludes confinement to any strict timeframe and often unfolds over a lifetime as individuals revisit memories and reflect on past events, gradually weaving the experience of loss into the broader tapestry of their lived reality (Baker-Cole, 2022; Lister et al., 2008).

Grief, the emotion that emerges from the experience of bereavement, is a natural response to the loss or absence of a cherished person or entity (Prechtel, 2015). Grief is often described as a profoundly intense or complex affective experience, encompassing responses such as shock, anger, guilt, confusion, longing, sadness, fatigue, relief, or despair (Baker-Cole, 2022; Klasen et al., 2017; Stroebe et al., 2001, Walsh-Burke, 2006; Weiss, 2008). Grief or mourning represents a period of sorrow, which can manifest in profound bio-psycho-social-cultural outward expressions of mourning (Baker-Cole, 2022; Humphrey, 2009).

In response to the powerful and complicated impact of loss and grief, research regarding significant loss and its effects has increased over the last three decades, supporting the reality that adjusting to life after profound loss holds a similar weight to navigating the effects of trauma and should be recognized as such (Baker-Cole, 2022; Bonanno, 2001; Stroebe et al., 2007a; Stroebe et al., 2007b; Weiss, 2008). As such, Weller (2015) posits that loss and grief have historically been closely linked to the loss of a loved one, with cultural rituals serving to navigate the emotional and practical complexities of death and mourning. Conversely, in modern societies, loss encompasses a spectrum of personal and collective experiences across the lifespan, reflecting an increasingly universal and interconnected social system of grief. Thus, acknowledgment and integration of multifaceted losses and gains are part of a lifelong process of adaptation and acceptance.

Furthermore, Western societies' fixation on happiness or productivity often requires the suppression of sorrow and vulnerability, hindering the natural externalization of common BPSC emotional responses necessary for authentic well-being. However, rather than a source of despair or dysfunction, grief serves as a transformative force, offering an opportunity to uncover hidden value at the intersection of loss and revelation (Weller, 2015). Ultimately, grief fosters deeper interpersonal understanding and communal resilience and advances the liberatory consciousness of marginalized grievers. It entails acknowledging systemic oppression and reshaping dominant loss narratives through intersectional frameworks that inclusively support the everyday but most often pathologized grief experiences (Rosenblatt & Wallace, 2021).

Indigenous Approaches to Grief

Indigenous approaches to processing loss and supporting healthy grief encourage clinicians to embrace uncertainty, challenging the tendency to pathologize and simplify the grieving process into a fixed framework (Gray & Hetherington, 2016; Goldblatt Hyatt & Sawyerr, 2024). Grief interventions should emphasize culturally rooted and contextually informed methodologies that connect individuals with ancestral knowledge, moving beyond conventional scales and colonial paradigms (Absolon, 2011; Goldblatt Hyatt & Sawyerr, 2024). Therapists can enhance culturally grounded grief work by incorporating traditional teachings, observation, and intuitive practices such as creative expression, dreams, and spiritual or collective ways of knowing to honor diverse epistemologies (Goldblatt Hyatt & Sawyerr, 2024; Lavallee, 2009). Subsequently, ancestral or spiritual contemplation provides a decolonizing framework for grief by prioritizing marginalized narratives and affirming anti-oppressive approaches that are fundamental to ethical therapeutic practice (Bordere, 2016; Goldblatt Hyatt & Sawyerr, 2024; Harris, 2010; Wade, 2021) across the lifespan.

Preserving cultural heritage remains essential for Indigenous communities in response to historical and perpetual discrimination and colonization (Brave Heart, 2007). A fully decolonized and anti-oppressive approach requires continually dismantling and restructuring systems to center marginalized populations' lived experiences, knowledge traditions, and worldviews (BlackDeer, 2023, 2024; Goldblatt Hyatt & Sawyerr, 2024). Any integration of Indigenous healing approaches into loss and grief support must be done with cultural respect, authenticity, accountability, recognition, and gratitude for the present influence, as it is vital to avoid appropriative practices in all aspects of grief work (BlackDeer, 2023, 2024; Goldblatt Hyatt & Sawyerr, 2024).

Oppression of the Griever

Grief is a deeply personal experience that influences self-identity and interpersonal relationships (Neimeyer et al., 2001). It necessitates that an attuned, supportive therapist advance equity in their approach and confront and deny oppressive bereavement practices and narratives (Harris, 2010). Examining the intersection of oppression and grief within cultural contexts is essential, particularly regarding norms that emphasize emotional avoidance, rapid return to productivity, self-reliance, and the expectation to "move on." Dominant grief narratives often marginalize individuals whose expressions of grief diverge from societal norms, particularly by excluding the lived experiences of vulnerable groups from prevailing discourse (Doka, 2002; Harris, 2010).

Instead, the intentional exploration of all loss and subsequent grief across the lifespan serves as an essential tool for developing feelings of interconnectedness with all life forms, establishing unity between the inner and external worlds, and fostering a holistic healing process that transcends a singular emotional experience (Weller, 2015).

Within decolonized cultural frameworks, grief is then acknowledged as an inherent part of the human experience across the lifespan, making accepting natural loss and cultivating healthy grieving practices both a collective responsibility and a spiritual imperative (Weller, 2015). Liberatory consciousness critically examines these narratives and attitudes, advocating for practices that validate diverse grief experiences and promote equity in bereavement care (Harris, 2016; Sawyerr, 2023). Understanding the perspectives of these subjugated groups reveals marginalized losses and common grief experiences while also exposing how bias and oppression operate within colonized loss and grief practices (Harris, 2016). Thus, all grievers must have time, space, support, and community to allow the natural integration of loss to occur.

A Deeper Look at Social Location within Therapy

There is a myriad of useful frameworks that a BPSC-attuned therapist might use to comprehensively consider a client's social location. Hays (2022, 2001) ADDRESSING Model and paradigms for cultural and critical genogram development (Hardy & Laszloffy, 1995; Kosutic et al., 2009) offer therapists useful frameworks for considering the multiple layers of a client's intersectional identity and their often-complex relationship to it. These approaches will consider a range of factors, including but hardly limited to gender, race, immigration status, migration experiences, indigeneity, spoken language(s) and literacy, sexual orientation, ability, and disability, body weight, shape and size, historical and intergenerational influences, and community dynamics (Hardy & Laszloffy, 1995; Hays, 2024, 2001; Kosutic et al., 2009).

Nieto and Boyer (2014) developed a comprehensive developmental strategy to support liberation, self-awareness, and social justice for individuals and communities. This model is helpful for BPSC-attuned family therapists, as it provides a framework for understanding the elements of social location outlined above and how society marginalizes and exalts these identities. It is complementary to Hays's (2001) ADDRESSING Model, which highlights aspects of personal identity across multiple domains. Some of these identity categories are fixed- such as race, indigeneity, and national origin, while others, such as age, disability, religion, gender, sexual orientation, body size, appearance, relationship status, and economic status may change over time (Hays, 2001; Nieto & Boyer, 2014). Supporting a client's awareness of their simultaneous Agent and Target identities allows them to more clearly see themselves as members of an oppressive colonial system that makes sense of their unique intersectional identity. By exploring these societally ascribed identities and consciously undoing them, liberatory work is increasingly possible within the individual and their family system.

In the 25 years since Hay's (2001) work was first published, additional categories have been added to create a more comprehensive model for assessing identity across multiple personal, interpersonal, and cultural domains. Specifically, an intersectional perspective underscores the importance of attending to both personal identity factors and systemic inequities like policy-driven or institutional frameworks that shape social determinants of health—such as adverse childhood experiences, food/housing insecurity, inadequate access to clean water, income inequality, and unemployment (Adames et al., 2018; Hays, 2022, 2024; Metzl & Hansen, 2018; Shim & Compton, 2018). By acknowledging these factors, the expanded ADDRESSING model offers a nuanced framework for the complex struggles and losses that impact overall health outcomes.

Nieto's (2014) seminal work further explores the concepts of status, rank, and power. She defines status as an observable set of behaviors related to social interactions. Status shifts rapidly, purposefully, and in service to the intentional navigation of social situations. Unlike status, rank categories are "socially ascribed" and relate to the tally of Agent and Target identities we carry and how our communities and ourselves experience them. Finally, Nieto (2014) conceptualizes power as a person's connection to the deepest and most authentic experience of Self. This part transcends social constructs and internalized oppression, and may be understood as psychological or spiritual, and is ultimately responsible for creating change and breaking cycles of oppression for Self and Other.

These factors, and many more, are all experienced by the individual, family, and community through the lenses of systemic oppression, heroic personal and community-based resilience, and within the arenas of earned and unearned privilege. By embracing a multiperspective lens for identifying social location, developing case conceptualization, and navigating loss, systemically minded therapists can support clients to recognize and respond to the impacts of institutionalized systems of privilege and oppression and their intersection with personal and interpersonal dynamics (McDowell et al., 2022). In this way, the work of the equity-based family therapist extends far beyond the walls of the clinic and into the fabric of a more liberated society.

Bio-Psycho-Social-Cultural Attunement in Therapy

Clients and families approach therapy in hopes of creating change, which, in and of itself, requires navigation of loss and grief. Any transformative process requires the loss of one way of being, even one that a client seeks relief from, before moving into growth and change. A bio-psycho-social-cultural (BPSC) approach to decolonized therapy considers the interconnectedness of these various factors of loss and how grief can influence individual, familial, and communal dynamics and well-being. This approach acknowledges that biological aspects, such as genetics and health, psychological factors like emotional regulation and mental health (Engel, 1977), social influences, such as relationships and socioeconomic status (Bronfenbrenner, 1979), and cultural elements like traditions, values, and beliefs (Sue & Sue, 2016) all shape how family members interact and cope with loss, change, and transformation across the lifespan.

Specifically, BPSC-attuned therapy attends to the interaction between a person's intersectional identity and clinical and therapeutic perceptions and treatment of dynamic, multifaceted identities. The BPSC-attuned therapist will use their knowledge of complex social systems, power, and privilege to support clients navigating these realities, reframe internalized narratives of oppression, and move toward resilience, growth, and change (McDowell et al., 2022).

The BPSC therapist will integrate awareness of societal structures, a client's unique social location, cultural awareness, and specific interventions to develop a therapeutic alliance and treatment plan that supports transformation. This also plays a role in determining aspects of a client's overall health (Hays, 2001; McDowell et al., 2022). Therapeutic work in this context occurs in spaces where individuals and families can safely explore relational dynamics within and across multiple influential systems and intersectional identity markers (McDowell et al., 2022). The unique relational experiences of each client must be understood within the context of not only their individual lived identities and experiences but also through the broader systemic influences that inform healthy verbal and nonverbal expression, destigmatized perceptions, and unbiased opportunities for themselves, their families and their communities (McDowell et al., 2022).

In addition to supporting the individual or those experiencing the impacts of systemic oppression and oppressive policies, the BPSC-attuned therapist may also play a critical role in advocacy work, influencing policy changes that address systemic issues and prevention efforts on a larger scale (Algeria et al., 2018). Through these efforts, the therapist may effect change and support the well-being of many more people than the ones that they serve in a family therapy session. Equally relevant is the consideration of power, privilege, and marginalization as critical to effective and lasting therapeutic treatment. The BPSC-attuned therapist is conscious and aware of these dynamics within Western societies and in themselves, seeking regular consultation and continuing education while simultaneously providing culturally responsive, liberation-based care to those exploring equitable and inclusive growth, change, and healing.

Finally, within the context and complexities of common BPSC gains and losses as humans navigate the lifespan, attuned therapists must cocreate with their clients a comprehensive and holistic treatment plan that fosters healthier individual and family engagement regarding common changes or transitions across the lifespan. This all-encompassing perspective ensures that interventions are tailored to the unique BPSC needs of individuals and families as they traverse the landscape of common yet transformative changes across the lifespan, leading to more sustainable outcomes and decolonized cultural frameworks of health and wellness (McGoldrick & Hardy, 2008).

Bio-Psycho-Social-Cultural Approach to Family Therapy

A bio-psycho-social-cultural approach to family therapy is essential as it considers the interconnectedness of various factors that influence family dynamics and individual well-being. This approach acknowledges that biological aspects, such as genetics and health, psychological factors like emotional regulation and mental health, social influences such as relationships and socioeconomic status, and cultural elements like traditions, values, language and beliefs all shape how family members interact and cope with challenges. By addressing these multiple layers, therapists can create a more holistic and personalized treatment plan, fostering healthier family relationships and more effective problem-solving in ways that are culturally competent and clinically sound.

Furthermore, a systemic family therapist's work is to support clients, their families, and their communities to move through the lifespan toward increased bio-psycho-social-cultural (BPSC) wellness via relational harmony and supportive, vibrant communities. This includes the profoundly important and often overlooked attention to experiences of loss and grief across the lifespan. An equity-based approach within any therapy model emphasizes the importance of understanding these losses within comprehensive contextual frameworks, integrating both broad systemic influences of individual and familial expression (McDowell et al., 2022). Moreover, recognizing loss, honoring it through a BPSC systemic lens, and integrating it through intentional, creative art therapy interventions is a powerful way to support families as they reach increased measures of health and well-being.

The work of equity-based and decolonial BPSC family therapy extends beyond significant losses, such as death, divorce, trauma, or tragedy, and into the subtler but consistent losses that show up in daily life across the lifespan. Even the most joyful experiences within the life cycle, such as partnership, births, a bat-mitzvah or quinceañera celebration, learning to drive, a new job, or pet parenting, all come with gains and losses for individuals, families, and their communities. Within the change of newness and celebration of these developmental milestones, it is critically important that the attuned therapist invites space for navigating the tender wisps of loss associated with each growth-related transition. This intricate work of progressive change and letting go of what is no longer needed is critical to a client's effective movement through each development stage while simultaneously entering the next stage of growth and development.

Bio-Psycho-Social-Cultural Gains and Losses Across the Lifespan

The following section explores gains and losses across the lifespan within a Bio-Psycho-Social-Cultural (BPSC) framework. To support this BPSC developmental structure, it is important to highlight Piaget's theory of cognitive development, which delineates how human beings acquire, process, and apply knowledge of their lived experiences (Hooyman et al.,2021). This expanded BPSC perspective makes room for inclusive coping strategies while also integrating cognitive and emotional growth into the broader understanding of developmental advances and deficits across the lifespan. (Hooyman et al., 2021).

The lifespan perspective explores human development from birth to death, emphasizing biological, cognitive, social, and cultural changes (Coker et al., 2022). Each time a human being transitions from one stage of the lifespan to the next, they must inevitably grieve what they are leaving behind in service of integrating change, as every developmental shift involves both gains and losses (Erikson, 1963; Baltes & Smith, 2003). In other words, individuals and families experience loss, grief, and adaptation in response to developmental transitions across the lifespan (McCoyd & Walter, 2021). For example, in childhood, moving from infancy to middle childhood means losing the complete dependence on caregivers and the simplicity of early play. Similarly, adolescence involves grieving the loss of childhood innocence and parental protection (Steinberg, 2014). The transition from emerging to young adulthood brings the loss of adolescent freedoms and the need to take on greater responsibilities, while middle adulthood often involves grieving unmet aspirations, the physical signs of aging, and shifting family roles (Levinson, 1986). Finally, in late adulthood, individuals may grieve the loss of career identity, independence, and eventually, physical abilities and social connections (Baltes & Smith, 2003).

Furthermore, McDowell et al. (2022) stress and oppression related to sociocultural factors, including race, gender, and socioeconomic status, shape how individuals and families experience these lifespan transitions, while Coker et al. (2022) highlight that development must be understood within cultural and contextual frameworks to truly process what is gained and what must be left behind in the spirit of growth or change.

Within the context of universal equity, Nieto & Boyer (2014) argue that social power structures and systemic inequities impact how individuals and families navigate pain and sorrow across the lifespan, particularly for marginalized groups. Hays (2024, 2022, 2001) further emphasizes the importance of cultural competence in clinical practice, recognizing that interventions that address change across the lifespan must be adapted to the unique cultural and contextual realities of each individual, family, and community navigating loss. Goldblatt, Hyatt & Sawyerr (2024) extend these discussions by introducing the concept of "liberating grief", which applies an anti-oppressive framework to understanding significant or multiple losses, advocating for acknowledging structural injustices and systemic disparities in how people experience and process grief across the lifespan. Thus, each stage of development across the lifespan, while often offering new opportunities, requires space for individuals, families, and communities to mourn all aspects of BPSC changes while simultaneously adapting to and integrating new realities at each stage of life.

Research and the lived experience of many healthy grievers show that a bio-psycho-social-cultural framework enables practitioners to support personalized meaning-making and adaptive grief processing by addressing responses shaped by the mind, body, prior attachments, and the individual's social and environmental context. (McCoyd et. al, 2021). As such, cognitive and emotional development, together with an individual's attachment style, significantly influence how grief is processed and understood, as each loss is shaped by the griever's developmental stage (McCoyd et al., 2021). Moreover, loss and separation often generate psychic distress by disrupting future expectations, activating emotional responses such as sadness, irritability, and rumination, and increasing vulnerability, anxiety, and stress (Hirsh et al., 2012; McCoyd et al., 2021). Finally, Western approaches to grief often emphasize the bio-psychological effects of cumulative losses, yet unresolved sociocultural loss histories can hinder adaptation to new loss events, as the emotional weight of previously unprocessed sorrow may contribute to social withdrawal precisely when communal support is most critical. (Brave Heart, 1998, McCoyd, et al., 2021).

Using Bio-Psycho-Social-Cultural Containers to Explore Loss and Hold Grief

This section is intended to discuss how to substantiate the use of categorical approaches in grief work; professionals must integrate intersectional and culturally responsive frameworks, ensuring that each category is applied to honor diverse ways of grieving and adapting to change. For example, within the biological container, Western models of grief often emphasize physiological responses such as stress and immune system changes (Stroebe et al., 2007). However, these biological markers may not fully capture the embodied grief experiences of Indigenous communities, who may view grief as deeply connected to land and ancestry rather than as an individual somatic response (Gone, 2013).

Similarly, within the psychological container, linear grief models often prioritize specific stages or goals based on productivity, which may not align with collectivist cultural understandings of mourning (Neimeyer, 2001). By expanding psychological frameworks to consider the valuable perspectives of Indigenous, African, and Eastern philosophical understandings of grief, therapists can move beyond Eurocentric models of bereavement. The social container often centers on nuclear family structures and community roles based on North American norms, which marginalize those from nontraditional family structures, LGBTQ+ communities, or cultures where extended kinship networks play a primary role in grieving (Silverman & Klass, 1996). Addressing these limitations requires acknowledging how social loss is experienced differently based on one's positionality within systems of power and privilege.

Lastly, the cultural container must recognize broad cultural differences and the dynamic, evolving ways marginalized groups resist and redefine dominant grief narratives. This requires moving beyond essentialized cultural interpretations of loss to embrace the fluid and intersectional nature of human identity (Crenshaw, 1991). While the categorical approach to loss and grief across the lifespan can offer a useful foundation, it must be applied in a way that decentralizes dominant perspectives and legitimizes diverse forms of grieving and post-loss transformation. By incorporating intersectionality, decolonial perspectives, and lived experiences into these categories, practitioners can mitigate the risks of systemic inequities and ensure that all grief experiences are recognized as valid and essential to understanding human well-being.

Bio-Psycho-Social-Cultural Therapy and Creative Arts

Creative arts therapies, such as art, music, drama, and dance and movement, can be particularly beneficial in supporting bio-psycho-social-cultural common factors in family therapy across the lifespan. These therapeutic modalities provide a nonverbal outlet for emotional expression, promote cognitive and emotional regulation, and help bridge cultural barriers by incorporating clients' cultural expressions and traditions into the therapeutic process (Malchiodi, 2012). Creative arts therapies also facilitate social bonding and communication among family members, especially in families dealing with trauma or mental health challenges, by allowing them to express themselves in ways that words alone may not achieve (Pancer, 2018).

By integrating creative arts into therapy, therapists can support individuals and families in navigating the complex interplay of biological, psychological, social, and cultural factors, leading to more effective and sustainable therapeutic outcomes. This comprehensive perspective ensures that interventions are not one-size-fits-all but instead tailored to the unique needs of the family, leading to more sustainable positive outcomes (McGoldrick & Hardy, 2008).

Creative, Non-Verbal Approaches to Exploring Loss Narratives

Just before the twenty-first century, it became commonplace within popular culture to refer to a person's story as their personal narrative. The understanding was that providing the opportunity to explore an individual's narrative brought to awareness the intricacies of their intersecting identities, positional viewpoints, and common BPSC lived experiences (Baker-Cole, 2022; Spector-Mersel & Ben-Asher, 2022).

Furthermore, recent BPSC studies have corroborated the value of personal narratives (Gergen, 2001; Immordino-Yang & Gotlieb, 2017; Veronese & Barola, 2018. Specifically, these studies offer neurological and psychological data supporting the theory that at each time across the lifespan, humans will externalize and re-story their narrative where any aspect of their story that is invalidating is diluted, and their authentic story is further reinforced (Baker-Cole, 2022; Chiao et al., 2010; Draper et al., 2022; Immordino-Yang & Gotlieb, 2017; Markus & Kitayama, 1991; White & Epston, 1990).

In therapy, it is common for clients to process and externalize the BPSC effects of gains and losses experienced across their lifetime. Thus, due to the unconscious fear of discomfort regarding loss, internal protective strategies may minimize the emotional significance tied to a loss. However, incorporating nonverbal interventions to explore a client's internal narrative can offer another way to gently explore emotions and determine appropriate bio-psycho therapeutic resourcing and social-cultural supports that affirm their natural grief responses (Baker-Cole, 2022; Gonzalez & Baker, 2019; Hammack, 2011; Lidchi et al., 2004; Neimeyer, 2000, 1998; Veronese & Barola, 2018). Moreover, revisiting personal narratives helps to maintain healthy connections or affection bonds to significant loss while simultaneously reconstructing the internal narrative to promote integration. BPSC resources inform this integration, which simultaneously supports healthy adaptation and a reconstructed narrative that affirms moving forward (Baker-Cole, 2022; Draper et al., 2022; Gonzalez & Baker, 2019; White, 1988).

Using Creative Arts to Integrate Grief by Re-storying the Narrative

Research indicates that art therapy interventions are helpful when exploring mental health issues (Donahue & Dykeman, 2021) and personal narratives of the bereaved, as they can be modified to explore the complexities of grief. Specifically, slowly exploring grief narratives with creative intention provides for a deeper look at social influences and internal messages, as these drive the griever's intimate realities of personal, familial, and communal insight, validation, and growth (Baker-Cole, 2022; Mate, 2020; Neimeyer, 2006, 2005; Neimeyer & Anderson, 2002; Veronese & Barola, 2018).

To illustrate this point, art therapist Shirley Riley (1997) built upon White and Epston's (1990) narrative therapy approach of externalizing an individual's narrative to facilitate expression through art making. Additionally, the projection of internal narratives of feelings and beliefs via the prompt "*What do you see*"(Betensky, 1995) onto images allows for aesthetic distancing (Landy, 1983) as the bereaved metaphorically step back, visually pan out and identify aspects of self, grief, and how two inform one another. Through this exercise of projecting into imagery, the griever begins to gain a clearer understanding of BPSC that supports that and will naturally facilitate the deconstruction of unsupportive messages, providing the impetus for constructing a new personal narrative that supports adapting to natural grief and healthy loss integration. (Baker-Cole, 2022; Gonzalez & Baker, 2020). Similarly, other nonverbal forms of expression, such as freewriting or journaling, can be used to explore the natural grief process. Pennebaker et al. (1997) found that free writing offers unique insight and awareness, promoting positive outcomes such as improved BPSC health (Lister et al., 2008).

Finally, because humans are natural storytellers, utilizing expressive arts to explore their "self-narrative" often inspires curiosity, finding personal meaning, and reevaluating emotional-spiritual-cultural aspects of their lived experiences (Baker-Cole, 2022; Neimeyer et al., 2009). Eventually, a reconstructed narrative via nonverbal and creative therapies can validate a griever's authentic reality of natural grief and healthy loss adaptation (Baker-Cole, 2022; Neimeyer, 2006; Neimeyer & Jordan, 2002) while protecting BPSC well-being and promoting collective liberation and growth (Baker-Cole, 2022; Veronese & Barola, 2018)

Art is not a Universal Language

When the impacts of loss and grief are further complicated by legacies of oppression and marginalization, talk therapy often is not a large enough container to hold the pain, grief, rage, and complex emotions a client or family system may bring to therapy. Art therapy, when provided by a social justice-informed practitioner, is a profoundly helpful tool for providing clinical care to grievers from all walks of life. According to the American Art Therapy Association (arttherapy.org, n.d.), art therapy "uses active artmaking, the creative process, and applied psychological theory—within a psychotherapeutic relationship—to enrich the lives of individuals, families, and communities." A decolonized approach to art therapy for grievers resists the pathologization of grief. Instead, it invites expression and ritual and nurtures healing through creative processes that align with the values, traditions, and worldviews of the people it serves.

Contrary to the popular trope, art is not, in fact, a "universal language." This idea overlooks the distinct cultural and intersectional perspectives that shape the expression, interpretation, and significance of color, imagery, and creativity in all forms (Moon, 2000). Any therapist integrating creative art making into their practice must make it their ethical responsibility to familiarize themselves with their own biases and assumptions about symbolism, imagery, and creativity (Baker-Cole, 2022), in addition to their attempts to decolonize their clinical and psychology-based praxis. The use of creative arts in loss and grief work must integrate a social justice-informed paradigm, acknowledging the griever's social location and how that impacts their lived experience and access to resources for healing and support (Talwar, et. al., 2019; Mullan, 2023).

At its essence, the practice of art therapy challenges the dominant, western-centric approach to therapy by centering creative expression and process-driven interventions. However, art therapy does not exist only as its essence; but as an arm of a colonizing and oppressive mental health system that has consciously and unconsciously perpetuated harm to anyone existing outside the narrow worldview of white supremacist, heteronormative, neurotypical culture. Since the 1960s, Cliff Joseph (2006), an artist and pioneering advocate for social justice in art therapy, has been raising awareness about the significant mental health impacts of hegemonic capitalism, unchecked imperial power, poverty, racism, sexism, and homophobia. His message and insistence on more racial sensitivity, cultural competency, and awareness of systemic oppression in the field of art therapy is as relevant today as it ever was (Joseph, 2006). Similarly, Estrella (2023) emphasizes these themes in her exploration of mestiza consciousness and the impacts of power structures, privilege, and oppression on expressive arts therapies, arriving at a clear call for more inclusivity and cultural self-awareness in all facets of art-based care.

Recognition that though art has been a powerful tool across all timelines and cultures, art therapy in mental health care is a "Western construct," and practitioners and those being trained in aspects of its use must be mindful of how this insight-oriented approach to healing is not held as valuable in all cultures, making the risk for a colonized practice of art therapy high (Kalmanowitz & Potash, 2010). Art therapists and practitioners using creativity in their approaches must actively dismantle white supremacy and the associated colonialist frames that exist within the field by challenging structural and systemic inequities in mental health care and education (Joseph, 2006; Mullan, 2022). This requires disrupting practices reinforcing white dominance across professional organizations, higher education, workplaces, research, and policy frameworks (Hamrick and Byna, 2017), fostering a more inclusive and equitable art therapy landscape. Without this necessary work, the decolonized essence of creativity in the service of healing cannot flourish. Intentional, social justice–informed practices must guide art therapy-based interventions for loss and grief support.

In a decolonized practice of art therapy, talking and verbal processing are adjunctive to the client's or family system's creative externalization and meaning-making process (Baker-Cole, 2022; Neimeyer et al., 2014). An attuned art therapist fosters a space for creative processes that invite, honor, and recognize each person's intersectional identities, values, traditions, and worldviews while actively acknowledging and engaging with the historical and intergenerational impacts of colonization, oppression, and harm that must be held in the creative container for meaningful healing to occur (Kalmanowitz & Potash, 2010; Talwar, 2019; Mullan, 2023).

An introduction to Creative Arts Interventions for Nonart Therapists

This chapter integrates the theoretical principles of creative arts therapies to a decolonized understanding of loss and grief from a BPSC-attuned perspective. By incorporating creative modalities into therapeutic work, clinicians can expand the possibilities for healing and connection while honoring the diverse ways individuals and communities experience and navigate loss. The creative interventions shared in this section are intentionally designed with beginners and nonart therapists in mind.

Ethical Engagement: A Note on Limited Scope and Creative Arts Directives

The creative feelings and emotions wheel (figure 7.1), the wellness wheel (figure 7.2), and the arts-based interventions (figures 7.3, 7.4, 7.5, 7.6) are designed to be safely used by non-art therapists for personal exploration and within a limited scope of practice for working with clients and families during their loss and grief journeys. Staying within the boundaries of size (8" x 10") and progressive directions, these interventions, as well as your clinical training, ensure that both the therapist and client are supported in a safe, ethical, and professional manner, preserving the integrity of the therapeutic process (Kalmanowitz & Potash 2010).

For readers interested in art therapy, further developing arts-based directives, or expanding on the interventions listed here, additional training is recommended to understand the underlying theoretical models and ethical guidelines that inform the art therapy interventions. Workshops, courses, training programs, and supervision from board-certified art therapists are approved sources that provide critical knowledge on how to safely and effectively incorporate artistic expression into therapy (AATA, n.d.).

Though loss and grief work is *not* trauma work, SAMHSA's (2022) trauma-informed approach provided excellent guiding principles for working with loss and grief and the expressive arts. Intentionally weaving safety, trustworthiness and transparency, peer support, collaboration and mutuality, empowerment and choice, and humility into the backdrop of these creative experiences will contribute to a more supportive environment to contain this tender and powerful work (SAMHSA, 2022).

Finally, it is important to note that engaging in the attached art interventions can bring up many profound emotions. When using the following interventions (figures 7.3, 7.4, 7.5, 7.6) for exploring your own loss journey or with clients under appropriate supervision, remember to plan in phases or titrate each intervention over several sessions to support ethical best practice. This includes taking breaks, checking in about feelings as they arise, and taking measures to ensure that there is a felt sense of containment and safety throughout the process. Leave ample time and space for processing big emotions and deep insight during and after the exercise.

BPSC-attuned practice reminds the therapist that the use of symbols, colors, and shapes may have some archetypal or universal meanings, but they are always unique to the individual (Abbenante, 2015; Moon, 2000). Remain curious about the images or artifacts that are created; do not place value or aesthetic judgments on the images, such as "beautiful," "scary," "amazing," "depressing," "perfect," etc. Abbenante (2015) reminds the therapist not to make assertions or interpretations about imagery's meaning. For example, assuming *a smile means happy, red means mad, a heart means love, black means scary, a tear means sadness, yellow means ease, a sun means a good day, etc.* Instead, use them as points of curiosity and evidence of an internal process that is ready to be witnessed (Fenner, 2015). The best and most supportive way to process creative and nonverbal expressions or artifacts is to ask yourself or your client what the symbolic or metaphorical meaning is and trust the intuitive knowing or external offering of yourself or others.

Creative Supports and Feelings Wheel

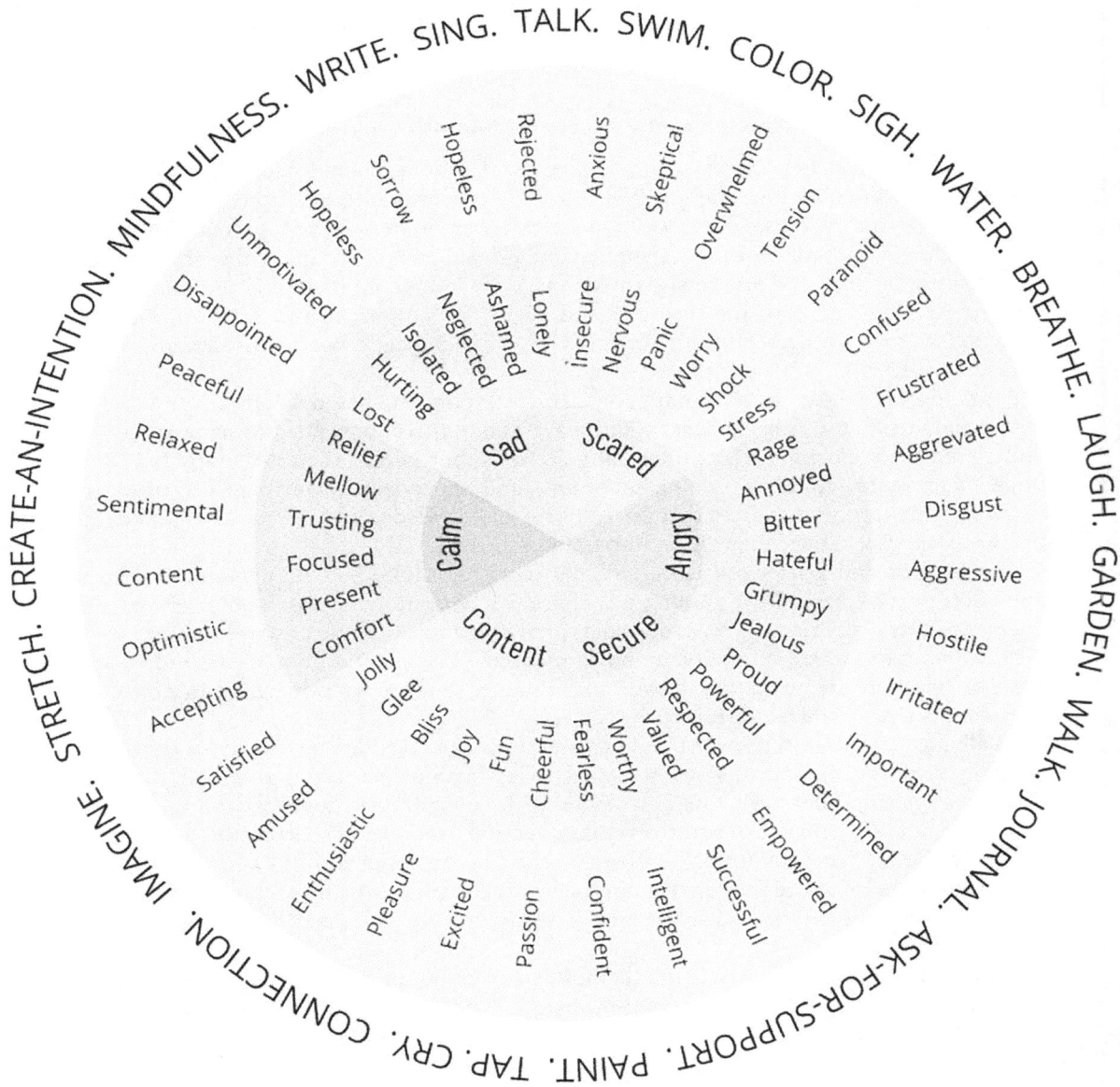

Figure 7.1 Creative Supports and Feelings Wheel.

Benefits of using a Creative Supports and Feelings Wheel

The feelings and supports wheel is a visual tool designed to help identify and support emotions. It consists of a circular diagram that categorizes emotions into core feelings at the center, which branch out to more nuanced emotions in surrounding layers.

The wheel also aids in recognizing the complexity of emotional experiences, enhances emotional literacy, and provides supportive ideas for creative resourcing while navigating significant and important feelings.

Creative Wellness Wheel

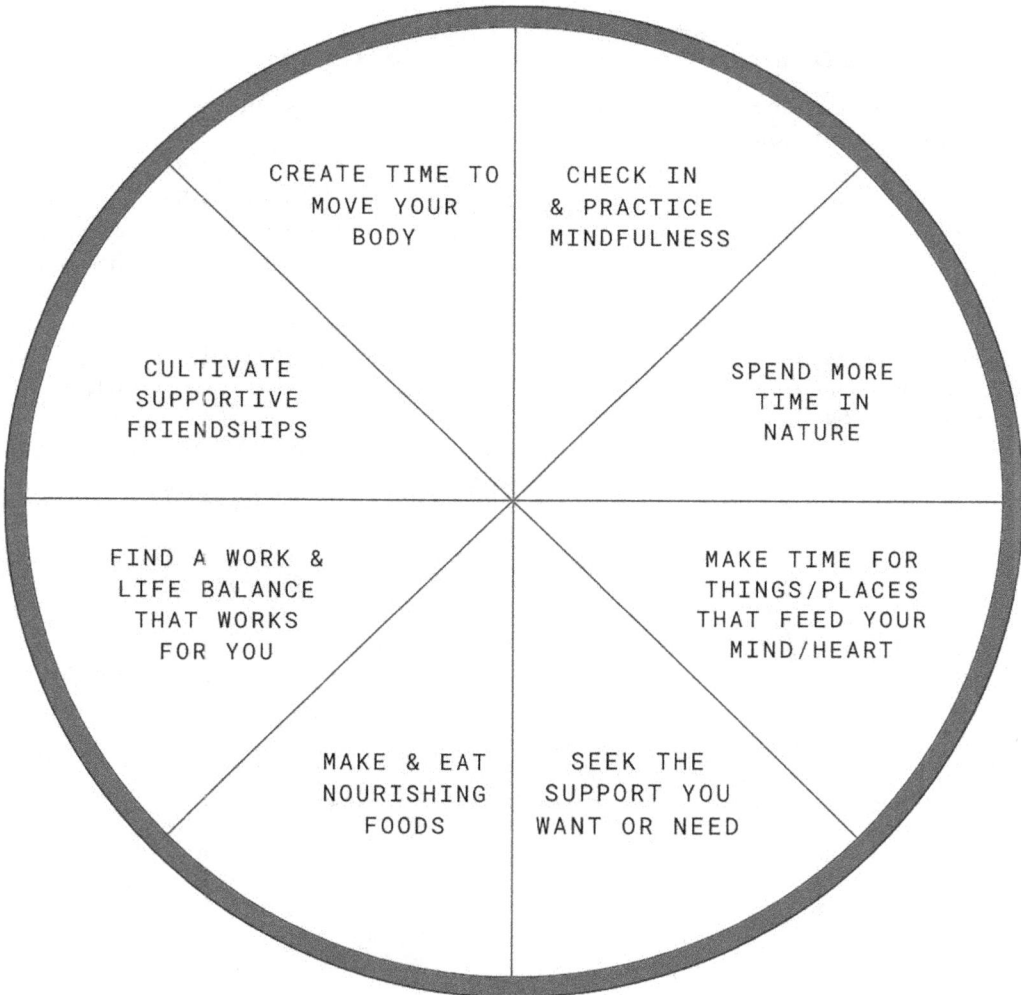

CREATE TIME TO MOVE YOUR BODY

CHECK IN & PRACTICE MINDFULNESS

CULTIVATE SUPPORTIVE FRIENDSHIPS

SPEND MORE TIME IN NATURE

FIND A WORK & LIFE BALANCE THAT WORKS FOR YOU

MAKE TIME FOR THINGS/PLACES THAT FEED YOUR MIND/HEART

MAKE & EAT NOURISHING FOODS

SEEK THE SUPPORT YOU WANT OR NEED

Figure 7.2 Creative Wellness Wheel.

Benefits of using a Creative Wellness Wheel

Using a wellness wheel offers numerous benefits for individuals seeking to enhance their overall well-being. This tool provides a holistic framework that encourages self-reflection and balance across various dimensions of life.

- Enhanced Emotional Awareness and Insight
- Improved Communication of Emotions and Needs
- Promotes Emotional Regulation and Grounding
- Supports Empathy Development and Wisdom
- Encourages Internal Resourcing and Supports
- Identifies External Resourcing and Supports

Creative Arts Directive Explore: Loss and Grief Collage

The purpose of this directive is to help grievers explore their loss and grief through visual expression. Consider the following:

- Creating a collage allows clients to externalize their feelings nonverbally through available images that take on new meaning as the griever arranges and organizes them on the page. Collage can be a potent method for exploring and communicating the complex emotions tied to loss.
- As such, it is important that the loss event a griever chooses to explore has a lower level of emotional weight or reactivity. In other words, choosing a lower stakes loss, such as a "3" on a scale from 1 to 10 for a first attempt, will ensure that there is a felt sense of emotional safety and support throughout the process.
- Finally, in subsequent sessions, the client can build up to loss events that may hold significant, yet natural, emotional weight or reactivity.

Materials include:

- Magazines, photocopies, or printed images
- Adhesive: school glue, glue stick or Mod Podge, and a brush
- Sheet of paper or canvas no larger than 5" x 7" or 8" x 10" (to manage overwhelm and/or emotional reactivity)
- Sharpies, markers, pens, or crayons for additional details
- Fabric scraps, textured papers, or personal items (optional)
- A small tray or surface to lay out materials for easy access
- Scissors

Directions:

- Prepare Materials: Begin by gathering a variety of materials. These can include magazines, newspapers, fabric, and any other items that include imagery or language that may reflect your feelings of grief associated with a low-stakes loss event.
- Reflect on your Grief: Take a few moments to reflect on your loss. What are you noticing regarding thoughts or feelings? What images, colors, textures, or words might represent your emotions?

Explore:

- Cut and Collect: Select and cut out images, words, or textures that resonate with your experience. These could represent emotions, memories, places, people, or symbols associated with your loss. Even if an image doesn't make sense to you now, but you feel called to use it, trust the process.
- Create and Collage: Begin arranging the pieces on your large sheet of paper. Let your intuition guide you as you place each piece down.
- Free Writing: After the creation process, hold or place your collage in front of you at arm's length. Looking at your collage of loss images, what do you see? Next, in response to the question, choose one to two of the following prompts to help you explore your answer by writing freely and without concern for grammar or structure. This exercise will help deepen your emotional connection to the process and allow for any insights to surface. Take approximately five-to-ten minutes to explore one of the following prompts:
  - Is there a particular image(s) or symbol(s) that stands out to you?
  - Which images are mysterious to you, or which make perfect sense?
  - Does oppression, intergenerational loss, or supremacy culture show up in your collage? If so, where and how has it impacted your experience?
  - How did creating your collage help you explore or express your grief?
  - What does the collage tell you about your grief journey?

Closing: Take time to reflect on the experience by engaging in free writing. Write freely and without concern for grammar or structure. This exercise will help deepen your emotional connection to the process and allow for any insights to surface.

Once you have finished the writing exercise, take time to consider what you would like to do with your collage. Will it be displayed in a prominent part of your home, or will you keep it in a private spot? Is there a community or family member you might share your insights with? You can come back to this exercise at any time to continue exploring your loss experience and how it evolves as you tend to it.

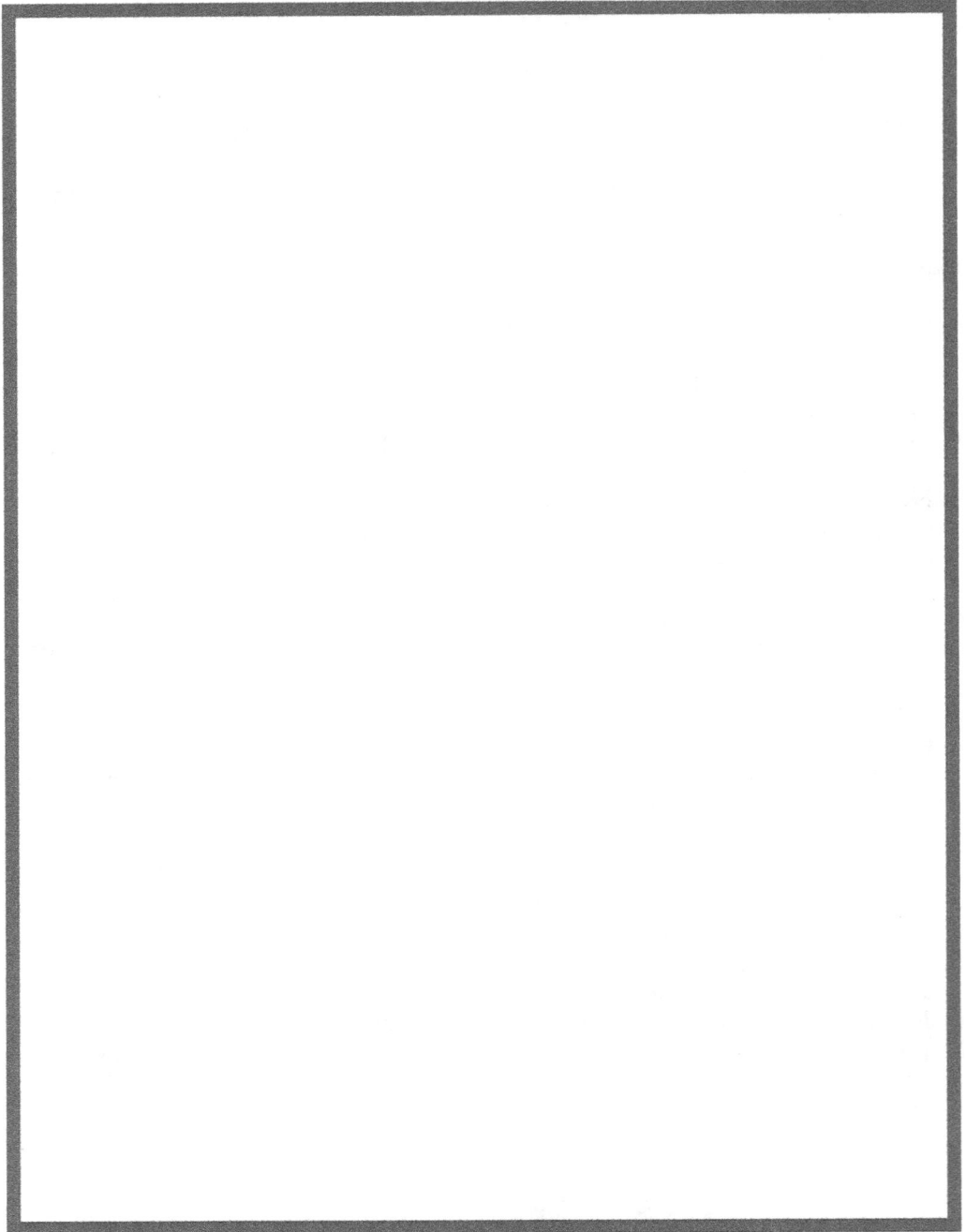

Figure 7.3 Collage Template.
Created by Dani Baker.

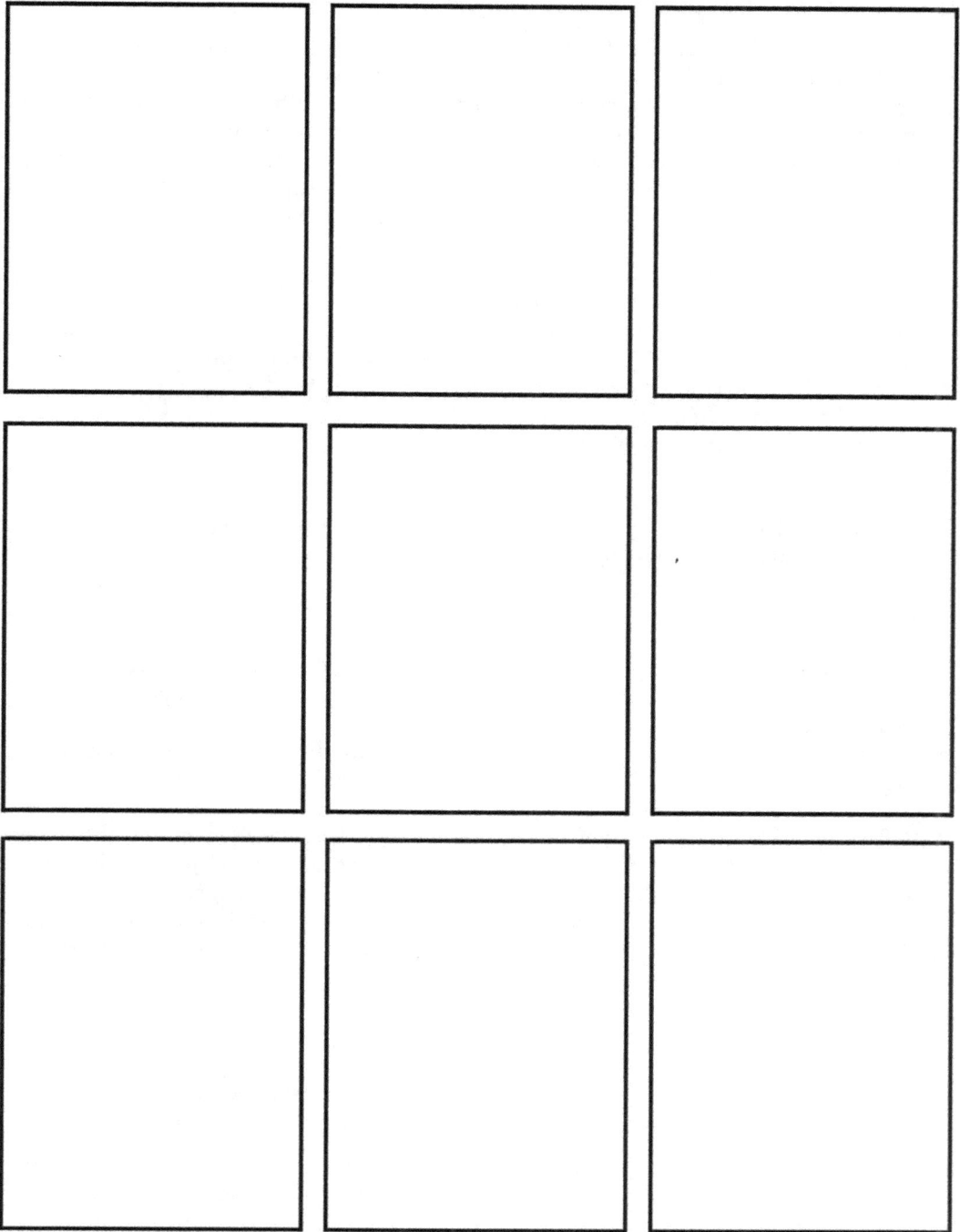

Figure 7.4 Collage Template.
Created by Dani Baker.

Creative Arts Directive Process: Body Mapping Grief

The purpose of this directive is for the griever to visually represent their loss experience, using the resource and container of the body. Grief and relief are experienced in the body, and attending to these sensations can support grievers in processing complex emotions, externalizing physical and emotional pain, and becoming more aware of their somatic experience. This body mapping exercise provides a way to process the impact of grief on the body, identify where complex emotions are held, and create a visual representation of the loss experiences that can be used to track the impact of the loss over time.

Materials include:

- Sheet of paper or canvas no larger than 5" x 7" or 8" x 10" (to manage overwhelm and/ or emotional reactivity) draw a full-body outline or use the outline provided in Figure 7.4
- Markers, sharpies, colored pencils, crayons, or oil pastels
- A pencil for sketching the body outline
- Adhesive: school glue or glue stick
- Scissors
- Bandages (template provided in Figure 7.5)
- Optional: Collage materials, fabric, or any textured materials to add to the body map or use the bandage template in Figure 7.5

Directions:

- Prepare Materials: Gather your materials, find a comfortable and quiet space to work in, and set up the paper on a flat surface. If desired, play some calming background music to create a peaceful environment.
- Sketch your Body Outline: Start by sketching or tracing the outline of your body on the paper. Start small. The outline should represent your body as a canvas to explore your grief.
- Reflect on Your Grief: Before you begin to map your grief, take a few moments to reflect on your grief and how it physically manifests. Where do you feel tension, heaviness, tightness, or pain in your body? Are there areas where you feel lighter, numb, or disconnected? Is there neutrality, strength, or pleasantness in the body? Grief and relief may be present in different body parts and in different ways, so allow yourself to work with whatever shows up.

Explore:

- Map the Landscape of Your Body: Begin by using colors, shapes, and symbols to map your emotional, mental, and physical experience onto your body outline.
  - Use different colors to represent emotions or physical sensations tied to your grief (for example, red for anger, blue for sadness, or crisscrossing lines to indicate tightness in the chest).

- Mark specific areas of your body where you feel grief most intensely. You might notice it in the heart, stomach, throat, head, or elsewhere.
- You may want to use symbols, works, or abstract shapes to represent different experiences or memories tied to your loss experience. Feel free to get creative with textures, layers, and marks that resonate with your emotions.

- Add Meaningful Details: As you continue working on your body map, think about adding additional details that represent aspects of your grief journey. This can include collage materials from the previous exercise. You might also include:

  - Symbols or imagery that connect with your emotional state.
  - Textures, lines, or patterns that evoke how grief feels in your body. Notice the difference between using crayons, markers, colored pencils, or pastels for this process.
  - Words, phrases, prayers, mantras, or names of people, places, communities, or animals that have helped or comforted you through your grieving process.
  - Personal objects, photographs, or cut-out images that represent your experience.

- Reflect on Your Body Map: once your body map is complete, take a moment to observe it. Notice the areas that feel heavy or intense and the areas that feel lighter or easier. Reflect on what the body outline is telling you about your grief and its impact on your body.
- Care for Your Body Map: Notice where areas of pain and tenderness within the body map. What do they need? What insights are you gaining about what needs healing or attention in your body outline? Cut out bandages from the bandage sheet. Write a personal or community resource that can serve as support for this area of pain or discomfort onto the bandage image and glue it to the body or next to it.
- Free Writing: After the creation process, take time to reflect on the experience by engaging in free writing. Write freely and without concern for grammar or structure. This exercise will help deepen your emotional connection to the process and allow for any insights to surface. Write for five-to-ten minutes, or as long as you need, about the following prompts:

  - How do the colors, shapes, or symbols on your body outline represent your loss experience?
  - Did you discover anything new about how you hold grief in your body?
  - Were there areas of relief, neutrality, or pleasantness in the body outline?
  - Does oppression, intergenerational loss, or supremacy culture show up in your body map? Where is it held? How may it have impacted your body's experience of your loss journey?
  - What was it like to add resources or supports to areas of pain or sorrow?
  - What might your body outline tell you about your healing process?

Closing: Once you've finished the writing exercise, take time to consider how your body map can serve as a tool for grounding or reflection as you process your loss experience. You may want to keep the body outline in a place where you can see it as a reminder of your grief journey, or you may choose to store it for private reflection. You can revisit this exercise at any time to track how your body is adapting to loss.

Figure 7.5 Body Mapping Support.
Created by Dani Baker and Alyssa Griskiewicz.

Figure 7.6 Resources Band-Aids.
Created by Dani Baker and Alyssa Griskiewicz

Creative Arts Directive Integration: Remembrance Vessel

The purpose of this directive is to support grievers as they contemplate loss integration through remembrance by creating a physical object to provide comfort, containment, or release, as common grief arises throughout life's journey. You might consider this vessel as a symbolic object of holding, such as a personal talisman or amulet, protecting, guiding, and affirming you as the waves of grief come and go. Using your imagination and trusting your internal knowledge, this small but mighty container may take the form of a metaphorical figure, animal, container, or creature. There are no rules. Let the process guide your hands as you create.

Materials include:

- Air dry clay
- Sculpting tools (optional but helpful for adding details—toothpicks and kitchen utensils will do)
- Water for smoothing and molding
- A surface to work on
- A cloth or paper towel for cleaning hands
- Optional: Acrylic paint, sharpie markers, or decorative notions to add to the vessel once it dries (Figure 7.6)

Directions:

- Prepare Materials: Begin by gathering your materials
- Reflect on Your Grief: Before you begin shaping your vessel, take a few moments to hold the clay in your hands and begin to gently bend and knead, while simultaneously reflecting on the loss events, big or small, that hold sorrow or grief.
- Processing: As you think about emotions you have experienced, what do you notice— maybe waves of emotion or an increase in your breathing?

  - You are encouraged to continue to notice, while also mindfully breathing and grounding to continue to notice while also mindfully breathing and grounding your body— elbows, sits-bones, legs, or feet—into the object you are sitting on or the ground underneath you.
  - As you mindfully bring support to your nervous system and body, what does remembering or revisiting your grief feel like in your body? Are there shapes, textures, or symbols that represent your loss? Again, pause here and notice it is time to take another deep and cleansing breath, to feel the ground solidly holding you?
  - Finally, the vessel you create can become the container that either embodies or holds any of these elements of feeling and emotion.

- Shape the Clay: Start molding the clay into a shape or form that resonates with your experience of grief. This could be an abstract shape, a symbol, an object, or perhaps even something that represents a part of your life that has been lost.
- Add Meaningful Details: As you shape your vessel, think about adding details or textures that are meaningful to you. Again, mindfully pause here and notice, is it time to

take another deep and cleansing breath, to feel the ground solidly holding you? Next, use your sculpting tools or your hands to press textures and patterns, carve symbols, or smooth areas of the clay. These details could represent specific emotions, memories, or aspects of your grief that need to be held or contained.

- Finish and Dry: Once your vessel feels complete, leave it to dry. When dry, you might add notions or other decorative elements to the finished piece.
- Free Writing: After the creation process, take time to reflect on the experience by engaging in free writing. Write freely and without concern for grammar or structure. This exercise will help deepen your emotional connection to the process and allow for any insights to surface. Before you begin, again, mindfully pause, take a deep and cleansing breath, feel the ground solidly holding you, and free write for 5–10 minutes about any of the following prompts:

  - What does your vessel represent to you?
  - How did the process of creating a vessel help you to connect to your loss and its grief?
  - What does your vessel know about your grief journey?
  - Which symbols or decorations stand out to you? Why?
  - How does this vessel hold or release experiences of oppression or ancestral harm?
  - How do you feel now that the vessel is created?
  - What will you do with your vessel? And whom might you like to share it with?

Closing: Once you've finished your writing exercise, take time to consider how your vessel can support reflection and integration of your loss experience. You may want to display the vessel in a place where you can see it, show it to family or friends, or use it to hold something as you honor and remember it's important to your life's journey. Finally, you are invited to revisit your vessel and notice how your relationship to the vessel changes over time.

Conclusion

BPSC-attuned therapy attends to the interaction between a person's intersectional identity and their society's perception and treatment of that dynamic, multifaceted identity. The work of equity-based BPSC therapy extends beyond significant losses, such as death, divorce, trauma, or tragedy, and into the subtler but significant losses that show up in daily life across the lifespan.

Furthermore, navigating and integrating the gains and losses of lifespan milestones offer valuable insights into human development within evolving family and communal contexts. Goldblatt Hyatt & Sawyerr (2024) advocate for an anti-oppressive approach to grief, challenging colonial-centric models of mourning and emphasizing the need for equitable, culturally responsive grief support. Recognizing these interactions allows for a more just, inclusive, and contextually informed understanding required to consciously navigate the complexities of development across the lifespan.

Finally, by incorporating intersectionality, liberatory perspectives, and lived experiences into BPSC-attuned family therapy, practitioners can mitigate the risks of systemic inequities and ensure that all grief experiences are recognized as valid and essential to supporting human well-being.

Figure 7.7 Remembrance Vessel Symbol/Metaphor Ideas.

Created by Dani Baker and Alyssa Griskiewicz.

References

Abbenante, J., & Wix, L. (2015). Archetypal art therapy. *The Wiley handbook of art therapy*, 37–46.

Absolon, K. (2011). *Kaandossiwin: How we come to know*. Fernwood.

Adames, H. Y., Chavez-Dueñas, N. Y., Sharma, S., & La Roche, M. J. (2018). Intersectionality in psychotherapy: The experiences of an AfroLatinx queer immigrant. *Psychotherapy 55*(1), 73–79. https://doi.org/10.1037/pst0000152

Alegría, M., NeMoyer, A., Falgàs Bagué, I., Wang, Y., & Alvarez, K. (2018). Social determinants of mental health: where we are and where we need to go. *Current Psychiatry Reports, 20*, 1–13.

American Psychiatric Association. (2022). *Diagnostic and statistical manual of mental disorders* (5th ed., text rev.). American Psychiatric Publishing.

Baker-Cole, D. (2022). *The impact of creative arts on meaning reconstruction and loss adaptation in widowed adults*. [Doctoral Dissertation, Antioch University]. https://aura.antioch.edu/etds/888

Baltes, P. B., & Smith J. (2003). "New frontiers in the future of aging: From successful aging of the young old to the dilemmas of the fourth age." *Gerontology 49*(2), 123–35. https://doi.org/10.1159/000067946

Betensky, M. G. (1995). *What do you see? Phenomenology of therapeutic art expression*. Jessica Kinsley Publishers.

BlackDeer, A. A. (2023). Unsettling feminism in social work: Towards an indigenous decolonial framework. *Affilia, 38*(4), 615–28. https://doi.org/10.1177/08861099231193617

BlackDeer, A. A. (2024). An indigenous scholar's journey toward decolonizing social work. *Qualitative Social Work, 24*(2–3). https://doi.org/10.1177/14733250241268730

Bonanno, G. A. (2001). Grief and emotion: A social–functional perspective. In M. S. Stroebe, R. O. Hansson, W. Stroebe, & H. Schut (Eds.), *Handbook of bereavement research: Consequences, coping, and care*, 493–515. American Psychological Association.

Bordere, T. C. (2016). *Social justice conceptualizations in grief and loss*. In. D. L. Harris & T. C. Bordere (Eds.), Handbook of social justice in loss and grief: Exploring diversity, equity, and inclusion (pp. 9–20). Routledge.

Brave Heart, M. Y. H. (2007). The impact of historical trauma: The example of the Native community. In M. Bussey & J. B. Wise (Eds.), *Trauma transformed: An empowerment response* (pp. 176–94). Columbia University Press.

Bronfenbrenner, U. (1979). *The ecology of human development: Experiments by nature and* Carastathis, A. (2013). Basements and intersections. *Hypatia*, 28, 698–715.

Chiao, J. Y., Hariri, A. R., Harada, T., Mano, Y., Sadato, N., Parrish, T. B., & Iidaka, T. (2010). Theory and methods in cultural neuroscience. *Social cognitive and affective neuroscience, 5*(2–3), 356–61. https://doi.org/10.1093/scan/nsq063

Chavez, T. A., Fernandez, I. T., Hipolito-Delgado, C. P., & Rivera, E. T. (2016). Unifying liberation psychology and humanistic values to promote social justice in counseling. *The Journal of Humanistic Counseling, 55*, 166–82. https://doi.org/10.1002/johc.12032

Chavez-Due.as, N. Y., Perez-Chavez, J. G., Adames, H. Y., & Salas, S. P. (2019). Healing ethno-racial trauma in Latinx immigrant communities: Cultivating hope, resistance, and action. *American Psychologist, 74*, 49–62. doi:10.1037/amp0000289

Crenshaw, K. (1991). Mapping the margins: Intersectionality, identity politics, and violence against women of color. *Stanford Law Review, 43*(6), 1241–99.

Coker, J. K., N., Cannon, K. B., Dixon-Saxon, S. V., & Roller, K. M. (2022). *Lifespan development: Cultural and contextual applications for the helping professions*. Springer Publishing.

Collins, P. H. (1989, 2022). *Black feminist thought: Knowledge, consciousness, and the politics of empowerment*. Routledge.

Crenshaw, K. W. (1989). Demarginalizing the intersection of race and sex: A Black feminist critique of antidiscrimination doctrine, feminist theory and antiracist politics. *University of Chicago Legal Forum*, 1989, 138–67.

Crenshaw, K. (1991). Mapping the margins: Intersectionality, identity politics, and violence against women of color. *Stanford Law Review, 43*, 1241–99.

Crenshaw, K. (2015, September 24). *Why intersectionality can't wait. Washington Post*. https://www.washingtonpost.com/news/in-theory/wp/2015/09/24/why-intersectionality-cant-wait/

Devine, M. (2017). *It's ok that you're not ok: Meeting grief and loss in a culture that doesn't understand*. Sounds True.

Doherty, W. J. (2009). The cultural context of family therapy: A framework for practice. *Journal of Marital and Family Therapy, 35*(4), 443–53.

Donahue, E., & Dykeman, C. (2021). *The Impact of a Switch from Conventional Media to Digital Media in the Treatment of Vicarious Trauma During Art Therapy*. https://doi.org/10.31234/osf.io/ja9q4

Draper, A., Marcellino, E., & Ogbonnaya, C. (2022). Narrative therapy and continuing bonds enquiry with refugees and asylum seekers: Bridging the past and the future. *Journal of Family Therapy, 44*(4), 520–34. https://doi.org/10.1111/1467-6427.12401

Duran, E., Firehammer, J., & Gonzalez, J. (2008). Liberation psychology as the path toward healing cultural soul wounds. *Journal of Counseling & Development, 86*, 288–95.

Engel, G. L. (1977). The need for a new medical model: A challenge for biomedicine. *Science, 196*(4286), 129–36. https://doi.org/10.1126/science.847460

Erikson, E. H. (1963). *Childhood and society* (Vol. 2). Norton.

Estrella, K. (2023). Expressive arts therapy: A profession in a "wild zone." *The Arts in Psychotherapy, 82*, Article 101992.

Fenner, L. B. (2015). Constructing the Self: Three-Dimensional Form. *The Wiley handbook of art therapy* (pp. 154–62). Wiley.

French, B. H., Lewis, J. A., Mosley, D. V., Adames, H. Y., Chavez-Dueñas, N. Y., Chen, G. A., & Neville, H. A. (2020). Toward a psychological framework of radical healing in communities of color. *The Counseling Psychologist, 48*(1), 14–46. https://doi.org/10.1177/0011000019843506

Freire, P. (1970). Pedagogy of the oppressed. New York, NY: Continuum International.

Gergen, K. J. (2001). Psychological science in a postmodern context. *American Psychologist, 56*, 803–13.

Ginwright, S. (2011). Hope, healing, and care. *Liberal Education, 97*(2), 34–39.

Ginwright, S. (2015). *Hope and healing in urban education: How urban activists and teachers are reclaiming matters of the heart*. Routledge.

Goldblatt Hyatt, E., & Tangela S. (2024). "Liberating grief:" applying an anti-oppressive framework to the field. *Studies in Clinical Social Work: Transforming Practice, Education and Research*, 1–20. https://doi.org/10.1080/28376811.2024.2430571

Goldenberg, M., Biggs, Q., Flynn, B., & McCarroll, J. (2010). The other side of sadness: What the new science of bereavement tells us about life after loss. *Psychiatry: Interpersonal and Biological Processes, 73*(4), 387–92. https://doi.org/10.1521/psyc.2010.73.4.387

Greenspan, M. (2004). *Healing through the dark emotions: The wisdom of grief, fear, and despair*. Shambhala Publications.

Gone, J. P. (2013). A community-based treatment for Native American historical trauma: Prospects for evidence-based practice. *Spirituality in Clinical Practice, 1*(2), 78–94. https://doi.org/10.1037/a0015390

Gonzalez, M., & Baker, D. (2019). *Using Creativity to Explore Socially Constructed Narratives as a Way to Promote Personal Liberation and Agency* (pp. 123–26). Routledge.

Gray, M., & Hetherington, T. (2016). Indigenization, indigenous social work and decolonization: Mapping the theoretical terrain. In *Decolonizing social work* (pp. 25–41). Routledge.

Hammack, P. L. (2011). Narrative and the politics of meaning. *Narrative Inquiry, 21*, 311–18. https://doi.org/10.1075/ni.21.2.09ham

Hamrick, C., & Byma, C. (2017). Know history, know self: Art therapists' responsibility to dismantle white supremacy. *Art Therapy, 34*(3), 106–11.

Hardy, K. V., & Laszloffy, T. A. (1995). The cultural genogram: Key to training culturally competent family therapists. *Journal of marital and family therapy*, 21(3), 227–37. https://doi.org/10.1111/j.1752-0606.1995.tb00158.x

Harris, D. (2010). Oppression of the bereaved: A critical analysis of grief in western society. *OMEGA-Journal of death and dying*, 60(3), 241–53.

Harris, D. L. (2016). Social expectations of the bereaved. In *Handbook of social justice in loss and grief* (pp. 165–75). Routledge.

Hays, P. A. (2001). *Addressing cultural complexities in practice: A framework for clinicians and counselors.* American Psychological Association. https://doi.org/10.1037/10411-000

Hays, P. A. (2022). *Addressing cultural complexities in psychotherapy and clinical practice: An intersectional approach* (4th ed.). American Psychological Association. https://doi.org/10.1037/11650-000

Hays, P. A. (2024). Four steps toward intersectionality in psychotherapy using the ADDRESSING framework. *Professional Psychology: Research and Practice.* https://doi.org/10.1037/pro0000577

Hernández-Wolfe, P. (2011) Decolonization and "mental" health: A mestiza's journey in the borderlands. *Women & Therapy, 34*, 293–306. doi:10.1080/02703149.2011.580687

Hirsch, J. K., Webb, J. R., & Jeglic, E. L. (2012). Forgiveness as a moderator of the association between anger expression and suicidal behaviour. *Mental health, religion & culture*, 15(3), 279–300.

hooks, b. (2015). Ain't I a woman: Black women and feminism. Boston, MA: South End Press.

Hooyman, N. R., Kramer B. J., & Sanders S. (2021). *Living through loss: Interventions across the life span.* Columbia University Press.

Humphrey, K. M. (2009). *Counseling strategies for loss and grief.* American Counseling Association.

Immordino-Yang, M. H., & Gotlieb, R. (2017). Embodied brains, social minds, cultural meaning: Integrating neuroscientific and educational research on social-affective development. *American Educational Research Journal, 54(1_suppl)*, 344S–367S. https://journals.sagepub.com/doi/10.3102/0002831216669780

Jenkinson, S. (2015). *Die wise: A manifesto for sanity and soul.* North Atlantic Books.

Joseph, C. (2006). Creative alliance: The healing power of art therapy. *Art Therapy*, 23(1), 30–33.

Kalmanowitz, D., & Potash, J. S. (2010). Ethical considerations in the global teaching and promotion of art therapy to non-art therapists. *The Arts in Psychotherapy*, 37(1), 20–26.

Klasen, M., Bhar, S. S., Ugalde, A., & Hall C. (2017) Clients' perspectives on outcomes and mechanisms of bereavement counseling: A qualitative study. *Australian Psychologist 52* (5), 363–71. https://doi.org/10.1111/ap.12280

Klass, D., Silverman, P. R., & Nickman, S. (Eds.). (1996). *Continuing bonds: New understandings of grief.* Taylor & Francis.

Kosutic, I., Garcia, M., Graves, T., Barnett, F., Hall, J., Haley, E., Rock, J., Bathon, A., & Kaiser, B. (2009). The critical genogram: A tool for promoting critical consciousness. *Journal of Feminist Family Therapy* 21.3 (2009): 151–76. https://doi.org/10.1080/08952830903079037

Landy, R. J. (1983). The use of distancing in drama therapy. *The Arts in Psychotherapy, 10*(3), 175–85. https://doi.org/10.1016/0197-4556(83)90006-0

Lavallee, L. F. (2009). Practical application of an indigenous research framework and two qualitative indigenous research methods: Sharing circles and anishnaabe symbol-based reflection. International Journal of Qualitative Methods, 8(1), 21–40. https://doi.org/10. 1177/160940690900800103

Levinson, D. J. (1986). A conception of adult development. *American psychologist*, 41(1), 3.

Lidchi, V., Tombs, N., Magalhaes, T., & Lopez, J. (2004). Hidden voices: The family biogram for working with families forcibly displaced in Colombia. *Australian and New Zealand Journal of Family Therapy, 25*, 212–21. https://doi.org/10.1002/j.1467-8438.2004.tb00621.x

Linklater, R. (2014). *Decolonizing trauma work: Indigenous stories and strategies.* Fernwood Publishing.

Lister, S., Pushkar, D., & Connolly, K. (2008). Current bereavement theory: Implications for art therapy practice. *The Arts in Psychotherapy*, 35(4), 245–50. https://doi.org/10.1016/j.aip.2008.06.006

Lorde, A. (1984). *Sister outsider: Essays and speeches.* Crossing Press.

Love, B. J. (2000). Developing a liberatory consciousness. In Adams, M. A., Blumenfeld, W. J., Catalano, C. J., DeJong, K. S., Hackman, H. W., Hopkins, L. E., Love, B. J., Peters, M. L., Shlasko, D., X. Zuniga (Ed.), Readings for diversity and social justice (pp. 470–74). Routledge.

Love, B. J., & Jiggetts, V. D. (2019). Black women rising: Jumping double-dutch with a liberatory consciousness. In S. Y. Evans, A. D. Domingue, & T. D. Mithcell (Eds.), *Black women and social justice education: Legacies and lessons* (pp. xi–xx). SUNY Press.

Malchiodi, C. A. (2012). Expressive arts therapy and multimodal approaches. In C. A. Malchiodi (Ed.), *Handbook of art therapy* (2nd ed., pp. 130–40). Guilford Press.

Malchiodi, C. A. (2012). *The art therapy sourcebook*. McGraw-Hill Education.

Markus, H. R. (1991). Cultural variation in the self-concept. *The Self: Interdisplinary approaches*. Springer.

Mate, G. (2020, April 29). The way to get through these terrible times is to let them make you sad. *Toronto Star*.

McCoyd, J. L., Koller, J., & Walter, C. A. (2021). Grief and loss: theories and context. *Grief and loss across the lifespan: A biopsychosocial perspective*, 29–58.

McDowell, T., Knudson-Martin C., & Bermudez J. (2022). *Socioculturally attuned family therapy: Guidelines for equitable theory and practice*. Routledge.

McGoldrick, M., & Carter, B. (2005). Remarried families. *The expanded family life cycle: Individual, family, and social perspectives*. Pearson Allyn & Bacon.

McGoldrick, M., & Hardy, K. V., eds. (2008). *Re-visioning family therapy: Race, culture, and gender in clinical practice*. Guilford Press.

McKee, T. (2015). The geography of sorrow: Francis Weller on navigating our losses. *The Sun*, 478(11).

Metzl, J. M., & Hansen, H. (2018). Structural competency and psychiatry. *JAMA Psychiatry 75.2:* 115–16. https://doi.og/10.1001/jamapsychiatry.2017.3891

Mezzich, J. E. (2013). Culturally informing diagnostic systems. *Cultural Variations in Psychopathology: From Research to Practice*, 137–53.

Mignolo, W. (2005). The idea of Latin America. Blackwell.

Moon, C. (2000). Art therapy, profession or idea? A feminist aesthetic perspective. *Art Therapy*, 17(1), 7–10.

Mullan, J. (2023). *Decolonizing therapy: Oppression, historical trauma, and politicizing your practice*. W. W. Norton.

Nieto, L., & Boyer, M. F. (2014). *Beyond inclusion, beyond empowerment: A developmental strategy to liberate everyone*. Cuetzpalin.

Neimeyer, R. A. (1998). Social constructionism in the counselling context. *Counselling Psychology Quarterly, 11*(2), 135–49 https://doi.org/10.1080/09515079808254050

Neimeyer, R. A. (2000). Narrative disruptions in the construction of the self. In R. A. Neimeyer & J. D. Raskin (Eds.), *Constructions of disorder: Meaning-making frameworks for psychotherapy* (pp. 207–42). American Psychological Association. https://doi.org/10.1037/10368-009

Neimeyer, R. A. (2001). *Meaning reconstruction & the experience of loss*. American Psychological Association.

Neimeyer, R. A., & Anderson, A. (2002). Meaning reconstruction theory. In N. Thompson (Ed.), *Loss and grief*. Red Globe Press.

Neimeyer, R. A. (2006). Narrating the dialogical self: Toward an expanded toolbox for the counseling psychologist. *Counselling Psychology Quarterly, 19*, 105–20. https://doi.org/10.1080/09515070600655205

Neimeyer, R. A., & Jordan, J. R. (2002). Disenfranchisement as empathic failure. In K. Doka (Ed.), *Disenfranchised grief* (pp. 97–17). Research Press. https://doi.org/10.4324/9781315229829-21

Norsworthy, K. L. (2017). Mindful activism: Embracing the complexities of international border crossing. *American Psychologist, 72*, 1035–43.

Pancer, E., Chandler, V., Poole, M., & Noseworthy, T. J. (2018). How readability shapes social media engagement. *Journal of consumer psychology, 29*(2), 262–70.

Pennebaker, J. W., Mayne, T. J., & Francis, M. E. (1997). Linguistic predictors of adaptive bereavement. *Journal of Personality and Social Psychology, 72*(4), 863–71.

Prechtel, M. (2015). *The smell of rain on dust: Grief and praise.* North Atlantic Books.

Ratts, M. J. (2009). Social justice counseling: Toward the development of a fifth force among counseling paradigms. *The Journal of Humanistic Counseling, Education and Development, 48,* 160–72.

Ratts, M. J., Singh, A. A., Nassar-McMillan, S., Butler, S. K., & McCullough, J. R. (2015). *Multicultural and social justice counseling competencies.* http://www.counseling.org/docs/default-source/competencies/multicultural-and-socialjustice-counseling-competencies.pdf?sfvrsn=20

Reynolds, J. J. (2002). Disenfranchised grief and the politics of helping: Social policy and its clinical implications. In K. J. Doka (Ed.), *Disenfranchised grief: New directions, challenges, and strategies for practice* (pp. 351–88). Research Press.

Riley, S. (1997). Social constructionism: The narrative approach and clinical art therapy. *Art Therapy, 14*(4), 282–84. https://doi.org/10.1080/07421656.1987.10759299

Rosenblatt, P. C., & Wallace, B. R. (2021). *African American grief.* Routledge

Talwar, S., Dhir, A., Kaur, P., Zafar, N., & Alrasheedy, M. (2019). Why do people share fake news? Associations between the dark side of social media use and fake news sharing behavior. *Journal of retailing and consumer services, 51,* 72–82.

Sawyerr, T. C. (2023). Invisibility matters: Adult sibling loss and the complicated grief experience. Reflections: *Narratives of Professional Helping, 29*(3), 32–44.

SAMHSA, Initiative, J. S. (2022). SAMHSA's concept of trauma and guidance for a trauma-informed approach.

Shim, R. S., & Compton, M. T. (2018). Addressing the social determinants of mental health: if not now, when? If not us, who?. *Psychiatric services, 69*(8), 844–46.

Singh, A. A. (2016). Moving from affirmation to liberation in psychological practice with transgender and gender nonconforming clients. *American Psychologist, 71,* 755–62.

Singh, A. A., Parker, B., Aqil, A., & Thacker, F. (2020). Liberation psychology and LGBTQ+ communities: Naming colonization, uplifting resilience, and reclaiming ancient his-stories, herstories, and t-stories. In L. Comas-Dias & E. Torres-Rivera (Eds.), *Liberation psychology: Theory, method, practice, and social justice.* American Psychological Association.

Smith, S. D., Reynolds, C. A., & Rovnak, A. (2009). A critical analysis of the social advocacy movement in counseling. *Journal of Counseling & Development, 87,* 483–91 doi:10.1002/j.1556–6678.2009.tb00133.x

Some, M. P. (1993). *Ritual: power.* Healing and Community, Swan Raven & Company.

Spector-Mersel, G., & Ben-Asher, S. (2022). Styles of narrative selection in crafting life stories. *Qualitative Research in Psychology, 19*(1), 43–64. https://doi.org/10.1080/14780887.2018.1545064

Steinberg, L. D. (2014). *Age of opportunity: Lessons from the new science of adolescence.* Houghton Mifflin Harcourt.

Stroebe, M. S., Hansson, R. O., Stroebe, W., & Schut, H. (2001). Introduction: Concepts and issues in contemporary research on bereavement. In M. S. Stroebe, R. O. Hansson, W. Stroebe, & H. Schut (Eds.), *Handbook of bereavement research: Consequences, coping, and care* (pp. 3–22). American Psychological Association. https://doi.org/10.1037/10436-031

Stroebe, M. S., Schut, H. A. W., & Stroebe, W. (2007a). Health consequences of bereavement: A review. *The Lancet Infectious Diseases, 370*(9603), 1960–73. https://doi.org/10.1016/s0140-6736(07)61816-9

Sue, D., & Sue, D. (2016). *Counseling the culturally diverse: Theory and practice* (7th Ed.). John Wiley & Sons.

Tuck, E., & Yang, K. W. (2012). Decolonization is not a metaphor. Decolonization: *Indigeneity, Education & Society, 1,* 1–40.

Veronese, G., & Barola, G. (2018). Healing stories: An expressive-narrative intervention for strengthening resilience and survival skills in school-aged child victims of war and political violence in the Gaza Strip. *Clinical Child Psychology and Psychiatry*, 23(2), 311–32. https://doi.org/10.1177/1359104518755220

Wade, B. (2021). Grieving while Black: An antiracist take on oppression and sorrow. North Atlantic Books.

Walker, M. (2008). Power and effectiveness: Envisioning an alternate paradigm. *Women & Therapy*, *31*, 129–44. doi:10.1080/02703140802146266

Walsh-Burke, K. (2006). Join the Allyn & Bacon First Editions Club.

Watkins, M., & Shulman, H. (2008). *Toward psychologies of liberation* (Vol. 74). Palgrave Macmillan.

Weiss, R. S. (2008). The nature and causes of grief. In M. S. Stroebe, R. O. Hansson, H. Schut, & W. Stroebe (Eds.), *Handbook of bereavement research and practice: Advances in theory and intervention* (pp. 29–44). American Psychological Association. https://doi.org/10.1037/14498-002

Weller, F. (2015). *The wild edge of sorrow: Rituals of renewal and the sacred work of grief*. North Atlantic Books.

White, M. (1988). Saying hullo again: the incorporation of the lost relationship in the resolution of grief. *Dulwich Centre Newsletter*, *3*, 29–36.

White, M., & Epston, D. (1990). *Narrative means to therapeutic ends*. W. W. Norton. Williams, H. (Ed.). (2003). *Archaeologies of remembrance. Death and memory in past societies*. Springer.

Part III

Beyond Therapy

Collective Healing, Advocacy, and Alternative Knowledge Systems

Jennifer M. Sampson and Fiona E. O'Farrell

Liberating Healing from the Confines of Traditional Therapy

What if healing wasn't something we bought in 50-minute increments? What if the work of therapy wasn't confined to private practice, insurance panels, and progress notes but instead lived in the streets, in community centers, in kitchens and gardens, in the quiet, steady rhythms of collective care?

For too long, the field of family therapy has operated under the assumption that healing is an individual or relational endeavor—something that happens in a room with a licensed expert, a treatment plan, and the right therapeutic modality. But therapy does not exist in a vacuum. Mental health is deeply entangled with capitalism, colonialism, and structural oppression. The systems that cause harm cannot also be the ones that save us. And yet, mainstream therapy continues to define healing through Western paradigms of individual progress, professional gatekeeping, and clinical detachment, reinforcing the very conditions that produce suffering in the first place.

This section invites us to look beyond the therapy room, beyond the marketplace of mental health services, and into the possibilities that emerge when we decolonize healing itself. What if therapy wasn't the default response to distress? What if the wisdom needed for healing was already held within communities—within ancestors, within relational and spiritual traditions, long erased by colonial modernity? What does it mean to reclaim those traditions and practice relational healing outside capitalist and institutional constraints?

In "Liberating Love," we dismantle the myth of the all-or-nothing relationship, critically examining how colonial, patriarchal, and heteronormative scripts have shaped romantic partnerships. This chapter challenges therapists to move beyond rigid relationship norms and embrace models of intimacy and differentiation that honor collectivist values, fluidity, and cultural multiplicity.

In "Agency-Centered Relational Therapy," we move further into decolonized relational work by introducing a therapeutic approach that prioritizes the restoration of agency—recognizing that systemic oppression does not just harm individuals but actively strips them of relational and bodily autonomy. Agency-Centered Relational Therapy (ACRT) offers an intervention model that not only names power but actively works to redistribute it, ensuring that healing is rooted in justice rather than assimilation.

The final chapter, "How Family Therapy Knowledge is Made and the World It Makes," takes aim at one of the most insidious forces shaping the mental health profession: capitalism.

DOI: 10.4324/9781032679082-11

This chapter is not merely a critique of profit-driven therapy models; it is a reckoning with the way capitalism dictates the very legitimacy of healing—what is fundable, who is served, and what counts as evidence-based care. This chapter dares to imagine alternative economies of healing that exist beyond institutional approval and state-sanctioned interventions.

If decolonizing family therapy is truly our goal, we cannot stop at reimagining what happens in the therapy room—we must imagine further. Critically examine how family and mental health therapists maintain the systems we claim to resist. We must examine our complicity in the nonprofit industrial complex, our role in state-funded gatekeeping, and the professionalization of care. Most importantly, we must remember that the knowledge we seek—the models of care that truly sustain and liberate—have already existed long before therapy was a profession.

Healing has always belonged to the people, and therapists can play a significant role in returning it to them.

Let's continue.

Chapter 8

Liberating Love

Rewriting the Fairytale and Expanding Relationship Norms

Fiona E. O'Farrell

Welcome to the Society of Happily Ever After

After a long and tireless day at work, you come home to find a thick, cream-colored envelope in your mailbox. The embossed gold lettering on the front reads: "You Have Been Chosen." Your hands tremble as you tear it open, revealing an invitation you have been waiting for your whole life but gave up on ever receiving. Inside, the card declares: "Congratulations! You have been deemed legitimate, valid, and worthy of membership to the exclusive Society of Happily Ever After." You exhale and immediately question whether the card is real—maybe they made a mistake. You carefully peel the thick wallet-sized card from the paper and flip it over. You scratch off the PIN and call the toll-free number to activate your membership. You give your name and date of birth, and they confirm that you have indeed been granted access to this exclusive Society. Still shocked, you review the other materials in the envelope and pull the benefits brochure from the pile.

The Benefits of Membership

Your eyes scan the endless list of membership perks this brochure has trademarked as "The Benefits of Eternal Bliss." You feel a sense of relief and settle into a deep sense that membership to the Society of Happily Ever After, aka *The Society,* will be truly life-changing.

Social Validation

- "We" Eligible: Gone are the days of sharing your autonomous experiences; as a member of the club, you are now eligible to live and share your life stories from a "we" stance.
- Milestone Recognition: Major life events are validated by others and celebrated.
- Societal Approval: You are now recognized and accepted from complete strangers to family and friends.
- Family Narrative Adjustment: Family members show interest in your new life and pride in your accomplishments. They also don't worry about you now that you are a member of the "Society."
- Social Media Approval: Likes, comments, and congratulations on posts about your life experiences and humble brags.
- Cultural Currency.

Everyday Convenience and Recognition

- "Plus One" Inclusivity: Invitations to events when you use your membership.

DOI: 10.4324/9781032679082-12

- Monogamy: No need to feel anxious or jealous; monogamy is included with your membership.
- Feeling "Complete": Gaining access to membership has been your life goal.
- Automatic Boundary: Why practice your "no" when you can flash your membership card and make it clear to others that you are not interested in them?
- Travel Perks: Members-only vacation deals and companion fares.

Legal and Financial Privileges

- Tax Benefits: Filing as a member of the Society provides tax advantages.
- Health Insurance: With your membership, you have health insurance. Lower Cost of Living: 30%–50% discount on life's expenses.
- Housing Preferences: Easier approval and more affordable rent or mortgage rates.
- Retirement: Access to membership retirement plans and matching.
- Immigration Sponsorship: Easier pathways for visas and residency.
- Shared Property Ownership: Favorable ownership rights for homes and other assets.
- Debt Consolidation: Easier access to shared credit or loans based on membership status.

Healthcare and End-of-Life Benefits

- Sick Care: When you are unwell enough to go yourself, someone will be available to go to the store, draw you a bath, or take you to a doctor's visit.
- Medical Decision-Making Rights: Automatic status as a healthcare proxy or next of kin.
- Hospital Visitation: Guaranteed access to see a partner in medical settings.
- Bereavement Leave: Workplace leave for the death of a spouse.
- Survivor Benefits: Rights to financial or legal benefits after the death of a spouse.

Parental Privileges

- Legal Parenthood: Automatic recognition of parentage in heterosexual relationships.
- Adoption Benefits: Easier pathways for adoption as a couple.
- Cultural Validation of Parenting: The "nuclear family" model is often seen as ideal for raising children.
- Educational Privileges: Preferential treatment for children of married, heterosexual couples in some schools or community programs.

Workplace and Professional Benefits

- Relocation Assistance: Spousal support during job relocations.
- Workplace Perks: Often better understood and accommodated in workplace policies (e.g., spousal benefits, PTO for family emergencies).
- Networking Benefits: Heterosexual, monogamous couples often gain social capital by participating in family-oriented or couple-based networking events.

Religious and Cultural Benefits

- Religious Sanction: Many religions actively celebrate monogamous, heterosexual unions, granting them moral legitimacy.
- Cultural Prestige: Seen as fulfilling societal expectations of adulthood and success.

Media and Representation

- Ubiquitous Representation: Almost all media—from movies to TV shows—reinforces monogamy and heterosexuality as the gold standard.
- Romantic Idealization: Love stories in mainstream culture overwhelmingly center on monogamous heterosexual couples.

Emotional and Psychological Validation

- Assumption of Stability: Society often views monogamous, heterosexual couples as inherently stable and responsible.
- Reduced Scrutiny: Less judgment or questioning of their choices compared to nontraditional relationships.
- Safety from Stigma: Avoidance of societal marginalization associated with being single, divorced, polyamorous, or queer.

Legal Protections

- Structured Divorce Rights: Legal frameworks are designed to help navigate divorce for married couples, including division of property and alimony.

As a member of "The Society," popular song lyrics, most movie plots, and retail holidays will now feel custom-designed for you. Membership life is featured in most media forms, and you will celebrate every anniversary of this day – the day you were chosen. You sigh as you take in this new feeling—security, acceptance, and feeling enough. It feels magical. Special. *Ordained*. You're part of the club now. You've made it.

But there's a catch, printed in small, elegant type at the bottom of the card:

Membership is exclusive. Terms and conditions apply. Any membership is automatically null and void for those who fail to maintain complete monogamy, heterosexuality, romantic attraction, White/dominant norms, prioritize nuclear family, or fail to maintain the appearance of success and satisfaction.

The weight of the fine print feels immense and confusing. You wonder what shadows lie outside the shimmering glow of your new privileges. What about those who never received their invitation—or worse, had theirs revoked? You tuck the card back in its envelope, your mind full of competing thoughts. What does it mean to be part of this club? What is the cost? And more importantly, what lengths will you go to maintain it?

Decentralizing Romantic Love

What comes up when you read through the description above? Consider the emotions, the body sensations, and thoughts that go through your mind. These feelings mirror the societal messaging that achieving a romantic partnership, particularly one that conforms to the norms of our society, centering on one kind of love, is a marker of personal success and legitimacy. The promise of privileges—social validation, financial benefits, and unspoken respect—reflects the tangible advantages afforded to those whose relationships meet these cultural standards.

However, the exclusivity of "The Society" invites a more profound critique. Who is left outside the velvet rope? The metaphor highlights how societal narratives prioritize romantic partnerships at the expense of relational diversity, often marginalizing those whose relationships deviate from the norm. By focusing so heavily on romantic relationships, we limit our love and diminish the value of friendships, chosen family, and community connections, narrowing social circles and increasing isolation.

This prioritization of romantic primacy also upholds broader systems of oppression, such as patriarchy, heteronormativity, and capitalism, by reinforcing a narrow ideal of "success" in relationships. As you reflect on this metaphor, consider the emotional and relational costs of maintaining membership in this exclusive club.

In my work as a relational sex therapist, I encounter this dilemma with my clients often—their stories are crosscuts of the more significant phenomenon of romantic primacy and all its drawbacks. My relational clients often present either in total distress, wholly disenchanted with their partners and their lives, or on the other end of the spectrum, completely disengaged, moving through the motion of a relationship without any dimension or intrigue.

I primarily work with people who identify as queer and/or gender expansive who arrive at therapy in a variety of relationship structures. Many of my clients have already gone through the difficult task of breaking free from cis heteronormativity to better embrace their own identity and live in alignment with themselves. Despite this, they, too, suffer from the untenable expectations we put on romantic partnerships. They are caught between their own self-knowledge and the desire to subscribe to the promise of happily ever after – believing that a relationship will provide them with the acceptance and security they have been seeking their whole lives. They still operate under the assumption that partnership is the anecdote to their internalized self-hatred and deep-seated anxiety of never being chosen.

Clients come to therapy seeking support in gaining access to the *promise* of what they thought their romantic partnerships would give them. On their own, it does not take long for reality to replace the ideals of expectation. One person cannot heal, repair, and fulfill every hurt a person has experienced. Finding "the one" will not make you feel complete and whole. Investing entirely in your partnership and, for some, their children is more likely to result in feeling limited rather than liberated. And the more disappointment we experience in this reality, the more we convince ourselves that if we invest in our romantic partnerships more, we will finally be rewarded with what we were promised.

Chained to an Empty Promise: The Limitations of Romantic Primacy

Among many other things, Dr. Ayesha Kahn (2023), a social justice scientist, writes:

> No wonder the family often becomes a cage that breeds resentment among members who paradoxically feel more alone than ever despite being chained to a few relationships. Chained is the key word. Any dynamic where people feel like they will be totally alone without it is one that will be a source of pain.

Unfortunately, relational therapists can directly affect our clients' commitment to romantic primacy. When our clients come seeking support in their relationships, they are often under the impression that therapy will assist them in achieving the ultimate goal of partnered bliss, correcting their disenchantment, and working toward a return to infatuation with one another. Rarely is this the solution.

Leblow & Snyder (2022) identified that many approaches to couple therapy provide temporary relief but fall short when addressing problems over the long term. As a professional standard, it is vital that we examine how the field of systemic therapy has contributed to maintaining and upholding the "all or nothing" relationship prescription where treatment is focused on immediate relief of relationship distress as opposed to actively exploring how to dismantle practices that prioritize romantic partnership in ways that better serve our communities more broadly. Our work can have a profound impact on combating patriarchal and capitalist systems and begin to cure the immense pain and isolation that our clients experience. Through decolonization and decentralization, we can support our clients in creating a diverse ecosystem of relationships, enhancing the well-being of more than one to two people.

The Way to Liberated Love

I have dedicated my professional journey and scholarship to helping relational clients and the relational therapists they resource to unburden themselves from the empty promises "The Society of Happily Ever After" has to offer. This begins with a critical examination of how we ended up in this paradigm in the first place, mapping the impact of colonization on relationship structures, assessing how the field of systemic family therapy and theories of human development have endorsed a cis heteronormative and exclusionary definition of partnership, and how these societal norms uphold and maintain systems of oppression. Next, we must explore how our own social locations and personal narratives intersect with the dominant relationship value system. Finally, we will explore the possibilities for building a more expansive understanding of relational satisfaction. We will propose how a growth-oriented view of partnership may promote diverse relationship structures, where any bond is interconnected and strengthened by multiple bonds from self to other.

Through this process, we can help our clients overcome their relationship distress and establish more agency. I often work with my clients to embrace complexity and invite them to "take the elevator down one more floor." How can we move away from problem-solving romantic relationship dissatisfaction and toward the examination of self and self within the community? Post-modern approaches to therapy have begun to grasp this process. How do we help our clients see that underneath the hurt, hate, resentment, fear, disappointment, and trauma they experience in their relationship is something deeper? Often, the loneliness, confusion, and utter disappointment are rooted in how hollow the promise of romantic primacy is.

As relational helpers, we can center our role to assist relational clients to be inspired to engage in meaningful relationships while holding onto a sense of self. We have the unique position of seeing more than our clients can see from their chained and distressed viewpoints. As relational therapists, we hold a unique position in shifting the enmeshed and problem-saturated view of relationship distress to an invitation for growth, wonder, and curiosity toward balancing self and other. We can support our clients in embracing relationships as abundant and vast rather than scarce and limited. Consider what your work would be like if our relational clients came to therapy seeking a pathway to multiplicity in relationships rather than clinging to the singular story they have been sold. What if our role as couple and relational therapists were to go from a *relationship mechanic* to a *relationship horticulturist*—fostering growth in our client's relationship capabilities? What an honor it is to help our clients build a sense of who they are, what they are available for, and where their limits lie. This approach to relational therapy is an active resistance to the crushing weight of dominant relationship norms and romantic expectations.

Now, I invite you to return to our opening anecdote. What do you think of The Society of Happily Ever After? *What comes up for you now? What do you notice?*

This is the dilemma I offer you to sit with throughout this chapter:

- On the one hand, how do we, as humans, as partners, as family members, as friends, as community members, and as therapists, unknowingly promote The Society of Happily Ever After?
- And on the other, how do we use our relational systems to promote third-order thinking and systemic change?

What might we gain if we challenge romantic primacy and create space for relational fluidity and liberated love? Dr. Kahn (2023) writes that our collective well-being and liberation depend on us being enmeshed in a diverse ecosystem of equally important relationships—*aka* a community. Join me in exploring how a broader, more inclusive framework allows for richer and more interconnected lives.

Person of the Author

Like many of my colleagues in this field, my work is deeply personal. I am the third-born child of cisgender parents who married under the same false promises I now critique in my scholarship—the belief that love alone is enough to sustain a lifetime of partnership. My parents came from vastly different cultural backgrounds, parts of the world, and value systems. Like so many, they fell in love quickly and believed in the fairytale. Growing up within the tension of their union, I witnessed firsthand how dominant relational narratives can collapse under the weight of real life. I entered the field of family therapy to work with adolescents—young people carrying heavy emotional burdens and struggling to find hope and belonging. Over time, that work led me to examine the systems that create those burdens in the first place and how expectations of love, partnership, caregiving, gender roles, and lifelong commitment have intergenerational impacts passed down from parents to their children. I fundamentally believe that by supporting couples in their relationships and assisting them in expanding their expectations of one another, we can have an immense impact on the family and community members that surround them.

How to Engage with this Chapter

I invite you to engage with this chapter in the same manner I suggest to my clients. In order to practice a new way of experiencing relationships, you will (a) bring both critical inquiry and curiosity, (b) be open to discovery, (c) suspend agreement or disagreement with any of the ideas offered, and (d) ask yourselves what you are learning about yourself as you move through this work? This practice will allow you to be present with what's in front of you instead of getting carried away with the urgent desire to solve, judge, or decide what you will do with the information. For now, take it in and see. This chapter will move you through these four steps:

1. Critically examine how the colonial agenda of privileging monogamous and heterosexual romantic relationships has impacted individuals, relationships, and the broader

community and how the normalization of romantic relationship primacy is central in therapeutic models for couple and family therapy.

2. Be open to uncovering the vast array of relationship structures available on this planet and how these models' scope, diversity, and availability shape cultural expectations.

3. I am disinterested in convincing you of anything. Replacing one dominant practice with another will return us to the same place. Instead, let's journey together and leave conclusions out of this chapter.

4. Be open to self-discovery. Does the information presented to you in this chapter allow you to learn something about yourself? What do you notice? What you notice may not be novel, it may be quite familiar. You may notice a seismic shift or a firm planting in your own perspective. No matter the experience, it is worthwhile to befriend.

This process will get you much further than a clinical application process. Moving through these four steps is a radical process of differentiation.

Disclaimer: This Chapter is NOT . . .

One of my professional heroes, Dr. Douglas Braun-Harvey (2020), said plainly: "We are walking, talking, breathing, judgment machines." To be human is to judge. We are very good at judging ourselves first and then equally good at judging others immediately afterward. It would be naive of me to think I could write a chapter critiquing the current practice of romantic love without your preconceived notions and judgments coming along for the ride. So, I'd like to clear a few things up and discuss what this chapter is not. This chapter is not an attempt to validate relationship structures beyond monogamy. This has already been done and done very well by others far more versed in the matter. Due to the decent volume of well-written texts and resources to help anyone understand multiple relationship structures already in existence, I am not going to spend precious word count on attempting to reiterate what has already been well-documented and validated.

This chapter is also not an attempt at abolishing romantic or loving relationships altogether. I'm Love's biggest fan. I believe that love, although difficult to quantify, is a life force within us. Fred Rogers (another professional hero) stated, "I think that everyone longs to be loved, and longs to know that he or she is loveable, and consequently the greatest thing that we can do is to help somebody know that they are loved and capable of loving" (2005). I endorse love so much that this entire chapter is predicated on the philosophy that love is abundant and available, especially when we expand the places where we seek it.

Finally, this chapter is not a "how-to" manual for therapists to suddenly relieve their clients of the real-life challenges of genuinely loving and being loved. It is the first in a journey to professional expansion. Moving through the four steps outlined above will require you to shift your focus, unlearn familiar patterns, and take a closer look at your own professional and personal blocks. First is the opportunity to examine your own notions, boundaries, signature themes, and beliefs—not only in your personal relationships but also in your clinical practice. Embracing this discomfort and ambiguity is not easy, but it's an essential part of becoming a more effective relational therapist. Ultimately, this chapter is an open dialogue for us to see the limitations of our existing relationship frameworks as a society and professional community.

Romantic Love, Partnership Expectations, and the Nuclear Family: A Critical Inquiry

One Relationship to Rule Them All: How did we get here?

Romantic love as the central focus of partnerships is a relatively new phenomenon in the broader arc of human history. For centuries, relationships were primarily utilitarian, designed to support collective survival and strengthen social, economic, or political ties. Marriages were frequently arranged, serving as contracts between families or communities to consolidate resources, establish alliances, or ensure lineage continuity. Emotional compatibility or personal desires were often secondary to these larger objectives. Love, if it developed at all, was considered a fortunate byproduct rather than a prerequisite for partnership.

The shift toward romantic love as the foundation of relationships began to take root in the late eighteenth and nineteenth centuries, influenced not only by cultural, social, and economic changes but also by the impact of colonization and Christianity. Colonial expansion imposed Western ideals onto diverse cultures, erasing or marginalizing relational structures that did not align with European norms. European colonial powers imposed their cultural norms on colonized societies, often undermining indigenous practices and emphasizing relational interdependence and community-wide care rather than centering relationships around marital pairings. Meanwhile, Christian missionaries played a significant role in this process by promoting monogamous, heterosexual marriage as the moral standard, aligning with Christian doctrines that emphasized the sanctity of such unions (Comaroff & Comaroff, 1991). This not only facilitated cultural assimilation but also reinforced patriarchal structures and control over colonized populations by dictating acceptable forms of relationships and family units. Christian teachings positioned marriage as a moral obligation tied to reproduction and the perpetuation of societal order. This framework was not only patriarchal but also heteronormative, setting the stage for marriage to evolve into a privatized, romanticized institution under Western cultural hegemony.

By the mid-twentieth century, with the rise of consumer culture and media-driven narratives, romantic love had been elevated to a societal ideal reinforced by the promise of "happily ever after." With the globalization of the internet, this centers straight, married, and monogamous romantic love as the ideal, while other forms of meeting and finding long-term relationships are delegitimized or viewed as outliers.

This ideal gave rise to "all-or-nothing" narratives, where relationships were no longer practical collaborations but all-encompassing partnerships expected to fulfill emotional, intellectual, and even spiritual needs. As psychologist Eli Finkel (2017) describes, this phenomenon of the "self-expressive marriage" shifted the focus inward, placing immense pressure on romantic partners to become the primary—and often sole—source of connection and fulfillment. This shift, however, has come at a great cost at every level of our societal system: individuals who do not experience this kind of sanctioned relationship are socialized to view themselves as unworthy, broken, or unloveable; partnerships are under extreme pressure to conform to a narrow definition of what constitutes relationship satisfaction; even those who break from cis heteronormative expectations of love often still struggle to understand where they fit, and finally we collectively suffer the more we insulate ourselves within our nuclear families, giving primacy to our romantic partnership and less significance to other forms of relationship. This is the ultimate threat to our broader social structures.

Historically, human survival and thriving depended on expansive social networks. Extended families, close-knit communities, and interdependent relationships provided diverse sources of support and connection. People relied on a web of relationships to meet their emotional, practical, and communal needs, distributing the weight of these expectations across many connections. In contrast, the prioritization of romantic love has diminished the size and significance of these social circles. As romantic partnerships have taken center stage, connections to extended family, friends, and community have become secondary, often neglected in favor of focusing on one's partner.

This narrowing of relationships has contributed to widespread social isolation, even among those in committed partnerships. By placing such immense emotional and logistical demands on a single relationship, Society has effectively limited the opportunities for deeper, meaningful connections with others. Friends and family, once central figures in a person's support system, are often relegated to the periphery, contacted sporadically, or maintained superficially. Furthermore, this prioritization leaves individuals vulnerable to significant loneliness and disconnection should the romantic relationship falter.

The consequences of this narrowing are not only individual but societal. The erosion of robust community networks diminishes collective well-being, leaving fewer safety nets for those who are single, divorced, widowed, or navigating nontraditional relationship structures. It also isolates couples themselves, as they face challenges without the communal support systems that historically sustained families, partnerships, and communities. In cultures where interdependence and community care remain central, relationships are understood as part of a larger relational web, highlighting the stark contrast to the insular model of modern Western relationships.

In systemic therapy, this historical and cultural context is essential for helping clients broaden their understanding of connection. By challenging the "all-or-nothing" narrative of romantic love, therapists can help clients rediscover the importance of relational diversity. Clients can be encouraged to nurture and invest in a variety of relationships—including friendships, chosen family, and community ties—reclaiming the interconnectedness that has sustained human communities for millennia. Recognizing that no single relationship can meet all needs, this expanded framework offers both liberation and resilience, allowing clients to build a richer, more connected relational life.

Systemic Family Therapy or Preservation of Normative Family Structures?

Systemic family therapy, celebrated for countering the individualism of mid-twentieth-century therapeutic paradigms, carries a complex legacy. Emerging in the 1970s and 1980s, it prioritized the family as the unit of intervention, challenging psychoanalytic and humanistic approaches that focused on the individual. On a societal level, the women's rights movement had emerged, and in turn, divorce rates in Western cultures were on the rise. Family therapy gained in popularity as an attempt to preserve marriage and nuclear families. Despite its innovation in working with relational units, systemic therapy, in an attempt to heal family fractures, ultimately reinforced the nuclear family model—aligned with Western, white, middle-class ideals—rather than embracing a more inclusive understanding of family systems.

Early systemic models, influenced by figures like Salvador Minuchin, Murray Bowen, and Virginia Satir, framed the nuclear family as the locus of relational health (Gehart, 2017).

Despite these pioneers' efforts to be the counterculture in the field of psychology, these frameworks unintentionally marginalized nontraditional structures. At the time these models were developed, queer partnerships, blended families, and chosen families were often treated as deviations from a typical structure. While systemic therapy sought to address family dysfunction and how familial health, function, and dysfunction were defined at the time, it prioritized the dominant Western narrative of "traditional" family preservation, neglecting cultural and relational diversity.

By positioning the nuclear family as central to societal stability, systemic family therapists validated economic and social hierarchies, excluding communities with relational structures that did not align with this paradigm. Cultural norms that prioritize interdependence and communal caregiving, such as those in Indigenous, African, and Asian contexts, were often pathologized as "enmeshment." Additionally, systemic forces such as racism, colonialism, and gender inequality were overlooked and treated as external rather than integral to family dynamics.

For marginalized communities, romantic love primacy has been particularly harmful. This model places unrealistic expectations on couples to fulfill a broad range of needs, often leading to relational strain. Alternative structures, including non-monogamous, platonic, or queer partnerships, were historically viewed as deviations from health or absent from the research and case studies. Interventions aimed to restore families to presumed White Western ideals rather than exploring diverse or fluid relational dynamics. The roots of systemic therapy undermined non-nuclear family practices. For example, immigrant families often prioritize transnational caregiving networks over localized nuclear units, reflecting migration realities. Queer individuals frequently rely on chosen families, and nonmonogamous relationships challenge the primacy of singular partnerships. Various cultures engage in intergenerational households and care networks rather than segregating by life stage and relationship status. Systemic therapy's historical failure to validate these configurations has limited its ability to serve a pluralistic society.

To transcend these limitations, systemic therapy must critically examine its historical alignment with Western ideals and embrace relational pluralism. This involves expanding theoretical frameworks to validate diverse relational structures, including chosen families, non-monogamous arrangements, and multigenerational households. It also requires confronting how systemic models have perpetuated white supremacist and patriarchal norms through their focus on the nuclear family. Amplifying the contributions of Black, Indigenous, and other marginalized scholars is essential for reimagining the field to reflect relational diversity.

Integrating an intersectional lens is vital to this process. Systemic therapy must explore how intersecting identities and oppressions—including race, class, gender, sexuality, and ability—shape family dynamics. Rather than "fixing" families to conform to predefined norms, therapists should support families' unique contexts and challenges. By reframing relational health to encompass community bonds, platonic partnerships, and chosen families, systemic family therapy can evolve into a discipline that champions diversity, cultural humility, and liberation.

Critically addressing its origins and deconstructing its alignment with dominant ideologies allows systemic family therapy to fulfill its transformative potential. By embracing pluralistic and decolonized approaches, the field can better serve a globally interconnected world and address the needs of those it has historically marginalized.

The Myth of Normality Revisited: How Relationship Therapy Reinforces Oppressive Relationship Norms

Theories of Development

Contemporary couple therapy has evolved into a prominent intervention modality with strong empirical support for reducing relationship distress and enhancing relationship quality. Despite this progress, many therapeutic models remain rooted in Western paradigms or coupledom that may not fully address the diverse relational dynamics present in global cultures (Teixeira de Melo & Alarcão, 2014). For instance, the Family Life Cycle theory, while acknowledging diverse family forms, often assumes milestones tied to Western, middle-class experiences, lacking full integration of intersectional factors such as racism, sexism, or ableism (Carter & McGoldrick, 1980). Evidence-based treatment approaches to couples therapy rely on data samples that meet cisheteronormative ideals, limiting the reach of application to couples beyond married, white, middle-class straight couples. Similarly, Attachment Theory and its therapeutic extensions posit secure attachment to your adult partner as universally optimal, overlooking culturally specific caregiving practices such as communal parenting and privileging monogamous, nuclear family norms. These models overemphasize couple achievement and seclusion, conflicting with collectivist cultures prioritizing community and relational interdependence.

Upholding Power and Control

Elevating romantic relationships above all other relational forms reinforces societal norms that can inadvertently foster unhealthy dynamics. Societal messages that prioritize romantic bonds at the expense of other supportive relationships often reinforce codependency, emotional enmeshment, and intimate-partner violence. The intense cultural pressure to derive one's identity, worth, and emotional fulfillment from a singular romantic bond often fuels conditions like emotional intensity. Moreover, the societal emphasis on romantic partnership primacy amplifies relational hierarchies that reinforce male privilege, rigid gender roles, and economic dependency—common elements of power and control (Knudsen-Martin et al., 2015). The romantic ideal often normalizes coercive behaviors under the guise of love or passion, disguising controlling behaviors such as minimizing, denying, and blaming as "typical" relational struggles rather than acknowledging them as mechanisms of harm. When romantic relationships are culturally positioned as the pinnacle of personal fulfillment, individuals may endure threats, intimidation, or even physical and sexual violence due to fears of social stigma associated with relational "failure." Decolonizing relational practices requires therapists and communities to critically interrogate these norms, expanding support networks beyond romantic relationships to foster healthier, interconnected, and safer relational ecosystems.

Contributes to the Loneliness Epidemic

Romantic relationship primacy contributes to social isolation by promoting the idea that fulfillment must be found within a singular, exclusive bond, often at the expense of broader social connections. Drawing from Robert Putnam's research (2020) on social capital, it becomes evident that prioritizing romantic relationships can lead to a decline in community engagement and broader social participation. Putnam's work suggests that strong social networks, including friendships, community involvement, and familial bonds, are critical for overall well-being and resilience. When romantic relationships are prioritized above these connections, individuals may experience increased loneliness, reduced access to social support, and a diminished sense of belonging within their communities. I have seen real-world examples of this in my office. Couples who spend all day at their jobs, spend their evenings shuttling their kids from event to event, and finally, their nights are preoccupied with the endless list of to-dos or unwinding from the busy day. Anything that is for their personal benefit (exercise, time with friends, hobbies) is considered to be extra, a bonus luxury, or worse, requires negotiation with the other partner. Living this way is far from the promise of eternal bliss with your beloved. Yet so many of us spend our time working tirelessly for the promise of something better. I hear my clients identify that although their lives are full and that they have each other, they still feel lonely, disconnected, or lacking the time or resources to actually enjoy their partnership.

Linneman (2023) speaks to this phenomenon by citing Marc Dunkelman's research (2014) on how certain bonds are strengthening and weakened through technological advances:

> Americans' closest relationships, the "inner-ring" connections of marriage, children, and parents, have not significantly changed over the past half-century. And we still have many "outer-ring" ties, those neighbors, coworkers, and drive-thru employees with whom we interact only in small, nonmeaningful pieces. But the frequency and quality of these middle-ring relationships—with friends, church members, close neighbors, coworkers, and fellow students—have been drastically reduced. Without these middle-ring ties, our social fabric begins to disintegrate. (p. xvii)

The "all-or-nothing" relationship enforces this process. The "inner-ring" takes primacy, even promoting over-connection (although at what quality?), whereas the "middle-ring" of our society, the one we rely on to thrive and survive, is disappearing. In 2023, the surgeon general of the United States issued a report declaring America's loneliness and isolation at epidemic proportions. When Eurocentric, patriarchal, and capitalist ideals become the standard definition of partnership, then upholding romantic relationship primacy becomes an accomplice to upholding systems of oppression, and the consequences are clear—the fibers that hold our society together fray and dissolve, and we face epidemic levels of loneliness and isolation.

By expanding our understanding of relational fulfillment to include diverse social connections, individuals can cultivate richer, more supportive relational ecosystems. When I work with my clients, teach emerging clinicians, or train practicing therapists on the consideration of supporting couples and relationships, it is vital that we consider the third-order thinking (McDowell et al., 2019) and the change that is available when supporting couples who come seeking therapy. It's far beyond relieving relational distress—when we expand our couples' networks and support the balance between autonomy and interdependence, we can repair the vanishing fabric of the middle-rings. We can encourage growth in a way that relieves our clients in partnership of the immense pressure and "all-or-nothing" stakes they feel daily. We can support their development by enhancing both the relationships within and between them, as well as the relationships that extend beyond their inner circle. This applies to both traditional and expansive relationship structures and identities. No matter who we are working with, they have suffered from the hierarchical constructs that promote isolation. Some may be further in their critical analysis and rejection of normative expectations, and at the same time, most of them still want support in moving that critique from theoretical to embodied.

Prioritizing romantic relationships often leads to the devaluation of other meaningful connections, such as friendships, family bonds, and community relationships (Cohen, 2024; Gupta et al., 2024; Hardy & Easton, 2017). Consider the other ways the "fairytale" dismisses other relationship experiences:

- Undermining youth relationships: Romantic primacy must be earned and fails to recognize the significance of young love in shaping identity and relational stories.
- Denying noncommittal relationships: Westernized culture often categorizes relationships into rigid categories, such as "serious" versus "casual" or "romantic" versus "platonic." These distinctions can obscure the complexity and value of different relational experiences.
- Dismissing arranged marriage/partnerships: When "love" is considered the most valid source for romantic partnership, then they dismiss cultural matching practices that are often grounded in shared values, compatibility between families, long-term stability, and collective well-being.
- Overlooking the benefits of multi-generational and community-based relationships. By critically examining these constructs, this section advocates for a broader, more inclusive perspective on relational fulfillment.

The current dominant narrative, which leads most couples to seek relationship therapy, undermines all of the relationships we encounter throughout our days, allowing members to become swallowed up or consumed by their partners. Validating diverse relational experiences across the lifespan challenges the notion that romantic relationships hold exclusive significance in human development.

A decolonizing perspective urges relational therapists to critically examine and transcend these limitations by embracing relational diversity, cultural specificity, and systemic justice. This includes valuing communal, chosen family, and kinship structures, recognizing multiple forms of secure attachment, and integrating collective healing, interdependence, and expansive community-based support systems. By broadening the scope of therapeutic models to incorporate these diverse perspectives, therapists can better address the unique needs of clients from various cultural backgrounds, fostering more inclusive and effective therapeutic practices.

Discovering Infinite Relationships

The term "Ubuntu," more common across the Global South, is an approach to relational ethics. Ewuoso & Hall, 2019 describe Ubuntu as a concept that "prizes relationships of interdependence, fellowship, reconciliation, relationality, community friendliness, harmonious relationships, and other-regarding actions such as compassion and actions that are likely to be good for others." Commonly translated to "I am because you are," Ubuntu is a principle that teaches people to respond to shared challenges together and encourages people to build mutually beneficial partnerships between many social spheres. Imagine how differently we would experience our relationships and partnerships if operated under a similar relational ethic. Intrinsically linking self and other, not by merging one into the other, but instead, we are an extension of one another. Under this premise, our relationships are reliant on treating ourselves as precious and important while, in turn, respecting the preciousness of all others. It would mean that our relationships would not rank in order of importance but promote mutually balanced relationships, ones that honor closeness and distance, giving and receiving as equally significant.

A Different Kind of Society

Let's return to our opening example. Now imagine a different kind of invitation. It doesn't arrive in a gilded envelope, nor is it marked with gold foil or terms and conditions. Instead, it is offered through a warm greeting, an open door, a shared meal, and a knowing nod. There is no velvet rope, no eligibility criteria, and no single definition of belonging. This is not the Society of Happily Ever After—it is a living, breathing relational web rooted in interlocking rings. An infinite Venn diagram. In this space, membership is not earned through conformity to rigid norms but through one's willingness to show up with curiosity, humility, and community care.

Here, love and connection are not scarce commodities, hoarded by the romantically coupled and monogamously committed. They are abundant, exchanged freely and reciprocally in friendships, chosen families, kinship systems, queer intimacies, spiritual alliances, and community care networks. Relationships are not ranked but revered for their unique contributions. Differentiation—the ability to be deeply connected while also fully oneself—is supported and celebrated. In this community, one's autonomy and authenticity are not threats to intimacy but the very conditions that make meaningful connection possible. *Compersion,* or "the feeling of taking joy in the joy that others you love share among themselves" (Ritchie & Barker, 2006, p. 595), is not reserved for open relationships but is experienced and practiced in friendship, partnership, parenting, and community relationships. This practice is not new; it has been acknowledged and centered in non-Westernized societies and religions. Sympathetic joy, or in Buddhism, *mudita,* refers to the human capability to participate in the joy of others and to feel happy when others feel happy. Although with different emphases, such an understanding can also be found in the contemplative teachings of many other religious traditions such as the Kabbalah, Christianity, or Sufism (Ferrer, 2019).

This decolonized collective space decenters ownership, control, and competition and instead promotes emotional generosity, interdependence, and relational fluidity. It refuses the binary of success versus failure, the myth of "the one," and the social scarcity model that says love must be exclusive to be real. Instead, it draws from Indigenous, Black, queer, and collectivist traditions that have long honored the relational self—one that is shaped through reciprocity, fluidity, and ongoing dialogue. Conflict is not a sign of failure; it is a doorway to deeper knowing. Intimacy is not reserved for couples; it thrives in communities, across generations, and between people who choose to hold each other with intention.

The benefits of this kind of "membership" are profound. Individuals are no longer isolated by the pressure to find one perfect partner or to preserve a single relationship at all costs. Relational nourishment comes from many sources. Agreements are made from a state of abundance rather than scarcity. Loneliness is softened by a constellation of care. Emotional labor is fluid, not centralized. And perhaps most importantly, people are free to define connection on their own terms—unburdened by the colonized scripts that tell them what love should look like. This vision does not erase romantic partnership, it embraces relationship diversity and, along with it, a variety of relationship agreements that are mutually generative.

As you envision this alternative, consider: What might it look like to live in a relational world where *everyone* is already enough, already in, already seen? What would it take to build therapeutic practices, family systems, and communities that hold this truth at their center? What would your role as a systemic therapist look like if you were promoting interconnectedness and growth?

Differentiation for Interrelationship Development

A more inclusive understanding of relational development necessitates moving beyond the romantic ideal and embracing differentiation as a key component of relational health. Differentiation—the process of balancing individuality and connection—provides a useful framework for exploring relational diversity.

Relational differentiation, introduced by Murray Bowen (1978), involves balancing emotional and intellectual functioning within relationships, enabling individuals to maintain their sense of self while maintaining an emotional connection to others. Bowen normalized that we each need both companionship and a degree of independence, that our experiences of family and culture remain with us throughout our lifetimes, and that patterns of differentiation can be passed through generations. David Schnarch (1997) expanded upon this by emphasizing differentiation's role in balancing two fundamental human drives: a) our desire for attachment and b) our desire for autonomy. Jessica Fern, author of Polysecure (2020), identifies differentiation as an important step in a relationship where partners learn to clearly define themselves and their boundaries as individuals while maintaining closeness and intimacy.

Ellyn Bader and Peter Pearson expand differentiation within relational developmental contexts, focusing on self- and other-differentiation as essential for navigating relational stages and intersectional cultural contexts (Bader & Pearson, 1988). Differentiation of self, according to Bader and Pearson, is the ongoing ability to articulate one's own desires and experiences while genuinely appreciating differences in a partner, fostering interdependent relationships characterized by mutual respect and clear self-definition.

Self and other differentiation are adaptations of a Westernized concept of relational development that can promote expansive growth and dismantle rigid independence or co-dependence in relationships. The practice of differentiation is the systemic therapist's *Ubuntu*, a therapy concept that, when reimagined, can support relational fluidity, self-agency, and awareness of the balance between both. Through differentiation, individuals articulate unique identities and boundaries without relational disconnection, resisting dominant narratives that enforce relational conformity (Hooks, 2000). Other differentiation facilitates the appreciation and understanding of a partner's or other person's distinct cultural and experiential realities, promoting relational spaces where cultural and relational diversity is actively affirmed and valued (Crenshaw, 1991). When we experience our relationships from a differentiated perspective, we lead our interactions with curiosity, intrigue, interest, and a fundamental respect for the other person's unique inner world and experiences. Differentiation promotes capacity growth in both the emotional and the intellectual planes. The capacities that develop in the relational practice of differentiation include a) the ability to self-reflect and self-soothe, b) an increase in self-accountability, c) an increase in the ability to tolerate ambiguity, d) an expanded experience of empathy, and e) the acceptance of others as separate and different from self. This level of acceptance allows for a greater ability to choose and want relationships with others rather than cling to relationships because we were falsely sold a fairytale with exclusive benefits.

Suspend Judgements

As we navigate the ideas presented in this chapter, dismantling narratives of the "all or nothing" relationships and examining relationship frameworks, you might notice emerging reactions within yourself—affirmations, resistance, curiosity, skepticism, or perhaps discomfort. This is expected and valuable. Before settling into conclusions about the ideas presented so far, we invite you to practice your own differentiation by suspending judgment, allowing space to explore and reflect through the lens of curiosity. Consider engaging with the following reflective prompts:

1. Noticing Reactions:

   - What initial reactions or feelings emerged for you while reading about decolonizing relational narratives?
   - How might your personal, professional, or cultural experiences influence these reactions?

2. Examining Beliefs:

   - Which aspects of the "fairytale" relational narrative resonate strongly with you, and why?
   - Which ideas presented challenge your previously held beliefs about relational success and normative milestones?

3. Exploring Curiosity:

   - What possibilities might open up if you temporarily suspend your need to agree or disagree?
   - What new insights might emerge if you approached these ideas with curiosity instead of evaluation?

4. Considering Impact:

   - How have your relational or therapeutic practices been influenced by dominant cultural narratives?
   - What might change in your interactions with clients if you openly engaged with more diverse relational frameworks?

5. Practicing Differentiation:

   - How does practicing differentiation—holding space for multiple truths without immediate judgment—feel in your mind and body?
   - What steps could you take to remain open, curious, and connected while continuing to engage critically with the content of this chapter?

By intentionally creating space for reflection and curiosity, you can foster deeper understanding and meaningful engagement, allowing insights to unfold naturally and thoughtfully.

Case Application

The following case examples demonstrate how relational therapy can actively dismantle limiting assumptions of relationships as either "all or nothing" while promoting differentiation and expanding the relationship to include community care. By doing so, therapists can support clients in cultivating relational fluidity and cultural specificity and embracing expansive relational dynamics.

Case 1: Chris and Kelly have been dating for five years. They reunited after both of their first marriages ended. Both have experienced relational strain due to differing relationship expectations. Chris seeks more traditional intimacy and partnership; he wants to move in together and have his kids spend time with her. Meanwhile, Kelly wants to continue living separately and keep the relationship more casual, spending time together 1–2 days per week. They have broken up and gotten back together a few times, reflecting struggles with insecurity, unmet expectations, and emotional management.

Assessment of Limiting Expectations:

- Chris' expectation of a singular partner fulfilling most emotional needs amplifies feelings of abandonment and inadequacy.
- Kelly's insistence on relational autonomy is often perceived by Chris as rejection, reinforcing his childhood abandonment trauma.
- Both individuals are preoccupied with defending their needs and struggle to better learn their partner's experiences.
- Both individuals default to binary thinking (together or apart), limiting potential relational structures and community support.

Facilitating Differentiation and Expanded Community:

- Encourage Chris to actively engage with diverse support systems beyond Kelly, reducing relational pressure and enhancing his self-regulation capacities.
- Support both members in clearly communicating their desires and support them in inquiring about the other person's experiences with curiosity and compassion.
- Remind the partners that they don't have to reach a consensus but should instead practice tolerating and embracing their differences.
- Foster dialogue around creative solutions, validating Kelly's significant external friendships and normalizing Chris's feelings while assisting him in challenging narratives of exclusivity and relational success.

Case 2: Gabriel and Eric, who have been married for 7 years, face tensions as they anticipate having to return to work in person. Issues of task-sharing, unresolved trust from past dalliances, and declining intimacy pose significant stress to the members. Eric struggles with anxiety around expectations of monogamy and sexual intimacy, while Gabriel feels limited in his ability to express his desires and is overwhelmed with tending to Eric's emotions and over-functioning in an attempt to offer care to his partner.

Assessment of Limiting Expectations:

- Eric's desire for blanket monogamy is a protective measure to ensure the trust is maintained. However, it restricts their relational dialogue, potentially exacerbating underlying tensions.
- Gabriel's assumption that Eric should anticipate his needs without explicit communication reinforces patterns of misunderstanding and resentment.
- Both individuals implicitly endorse a fairytale-like relational structure—expecting seamless collaboration, unwavering monogamy, and intuitive intimacy—which limits adaptive strategies for handling upcoming transitions.

Facilitating Differentiation and Expanded Community:

- Guide Gabriel toward identifying his own thoughts and experiences and practicing explicitly articulating expectations, encouraging ownership of his emotional responses, and fostering dialogue about roles.
- Encourage Eric to explore his anxieties around relational fidelity and explore the narratives from past relationship hurts and infidelity. Help him differentiate between his current relational context and past relationship patterns and express those to his partner.
- Facilitate conversations about engaging in low-stakes community activities and hobbies, household responsibilities, and emotional intimacy, reducing pressure on their dyadic relationship and promoting a more expansive view of relational health and intimacy.

These examples illustrate some ways in which therapists can challenge and expand traditional relational narratives, fostering environments where differentiation is valued, and communities play essential roles in relational health. By dismantling oppressive expectations and creating spaces for relational fluidity and collective support, individuals and couples can move beyond restrictive binaries to cultivate diverse, resilient, and culturally responsive relationships.

Summary

This chapter critically examines the dominant relational frameworks that privilege monogamous, heterosexual partnerships, and nuclear family structures as normative ideals. Through an intersectional feminist, queer, and decolonial lens, the chapter challenges the fairytale narrative of romantic love, highlighting how it marginalizes relational diversity and reinforces oppressive systems such as patriarchy, heteronormativity, ableism, capitalism, and white supremacy. The tangible and intangible privileges afforded to those who conform to these relational norms, as illustrated through the metaphor of membership in the "Society of Happily Ever After," reveal both the allure and the steep emotional and relational costs involved.

This chapter critically investigates how romantic primacy perpetuates unrealistic expectations, resulting in increased relational distress and contributing significantly to societal loneliness and disconnection. Systemic family therapy's historical alignment with Western ideals and nuclear family preservation perpetuates the very reasons clients seek therapy in the first place, exposing its implicit favor of exclusionary and hierarchical relational norms.

The chapter advocates for decentralizing romantic love, proposing other cultural practices and adapted differentiation—a balance of individuality and relational connection—as a transformative framework. It promotes relational fluidity, recognizing and affirming the value of non-monogamous arrangements, platonic partnerships, kinship networks, and community interdependence. Case examples provide practical strategies for therapists to foster relational fluidity and differentiation, supporting clients in navigating relationships beyond restrictive societal expectations.

Conclusion

Reframing relational development through a lens of relational diversity and systemic justice offers a profound opportunity to move beyond restrictive societal norms toward expansive and interconnected relational ecosystems. As a starting point, readers are invited to engage in personal reflection, examining their own internalized relationship narratives and assumptions. Returning to the reflective exercises and prompts provided earlier in the chapter can support readers in critically and compassionately exploring these narratives, fostering greater self-awareness and relational insight. By dismantling oppressive frameworks and embracing differentiation and relational pluralism, systemic therapists and individuals alike can help build richer, culturally responsive, and community-oriented relational networks, ultimately enhancing individual and collective well-being.

References

Bader, E., & Pearson, P. (1988). *In quest of the mythical mate: A developmental approach to diagnosis and treatment in couples therapy.* Routledge.

Braun-Harvey, D. (2020, February 1). The Six Principles of Sexual Health: Confident Conversations, Antioch University, Seattle, WA. https://www.theharveyinstitute.com/events/confident-conversations-with-doug-braun-harvey

Bowen, M. (1978). *Family therapy in clinical practice.* Jason Aronson.

Carter, E. A., & McGoldrick, M. (1980). *The Family life cycle : a framework for family therapy.* Gardner Press.

Cohen, R. (2024). *The other significant others: reimagining life with friendship at the center.* First edition. St. Martin's Press.

Comaroff, J., & Comaroff, J. (1991). *Of Revelation and Revolution, Volume 1: Christianity, Colonialism, and Consciousness in South Africa.* University of Chicago Press.

Crenshaw, K. (1991). Mapping the margins: Intersectionality, identity politics, and violence against women of color. *Stanford Law Review, 43*(6), 1241–99.

Dunkelman, M. J. (2014). *The Vanishing Neighbor: The Transformation of American Community.* Norton.

Fern, J. (2020). *Polysecure: Attachment, trauma and consensual nonmonogamy.* Thorntree Press.

Ferrer, J. N. (2019). From romantic jealousy to sympathetic joy: Monogamy, polyamory, and beyond. *International Journal of Transpersonal Studies, 38*(1), Advance online publication.

Finkel, E. (2017). *The All-or-Nothing Marriage: How the Best Marriages Work.* Dutton.

Ewuoso, C., & Hall, S. (2019). Core aspects of ubuntu: A systematic review. *South African Journal of Bioethics and Law, 12*(2), 93–103.

Gahran, A. (2017). *Stepping Off the Relationship Escalator: Uncommon Love and Life.* Off the Escalator Enterprises LLC.

Gehart, D. (2017). *Mastering competencies in family therapy* (3rd ed.). CENGAGE Learning Custom.

Gupta, S., Tarantino, M., & Sanner, C. (2024). A scoping review of research on polyamory and consensual non-monogamy: Implications for a more inclusive family science. *Journal of Family Theory & Review, 16*(2), 151–90. https://doi.org/10.1111/jftr.12546

Hardy, J.W., & Easton, D. (2017). *The Ethical Slut: A Practical Guide to Polyamory, Open Relationships, and Other Freedoms in Sex and Love.* (3rd ed.). Ten Speed Press.

hooks, b. (2000). *All about love: New visions.* William Morrow. Lebow J., & Snyder, D. K. (2022). Couple therapy in the 2020s: Current status and emerging developments. *Family Process*, 1–27. https://doi.org/10.1111/famp.12824

Linneman, J. (2023, October 3). *Feeling Alone in a Crowded Congregation.* Crossway. https://www.crossway.org/articles/feeling-alone-in-a-crowded-congregation/

Khan, A. (2023, July 11). Focusing on friendships helps us move beyond the confines of the nuclear family. Cosmic Anarchy (blog). https://wokescientist.substack.com/p/focusing-on-friendships-helps-us

Knudson-Martin, C., Huenergardt, D., Lafontant, K., Bishop, L., Schaepper, J., & Wells, M. (2015). Competencies for addressing gender and power in couple therapy: a socio-emotional approach. *Journal of Marital and Family Therapy, 41*(2), 205–20. https://doi.org/10.1111/jmft.12068

McDowell, T., Knudson-Martin, C., & Bermudez, J. M. (2019). Third-order thinking in family therapy: addressing social justice across family therapy practice. Family Process, *58*(1), 9–22. https://doi.org/10.1111/famp.12383

Office of the Surgeon General (OSG). (2023). *Our Epidemic of Loneliness and Isolation: The U.S. Surgeon General's Advisory on the Healing Effects of Social Connection and Community*. US Department of Health and Human Services.

Putnam, R. D. (2000). *Bowling Alone: The Collapse and Revival of American Community*. Simon & Schuster.

Ritchie, A., & Barker, M. (2006). 'There aren't words for what we do or how we feel, so we have to make them up': Constructing polyamorous languages in a culture of compulsory monogamy. *Sexualities, 9*(5), 584–601. https://doi.org/10.1177/1363460706069987

Rogers, F. (2005). You are special: Neighborly wit and wisdom from Mister Rogers. Random House.

Schnarch, D. (1997). *Passionate marriage: Keeping love and intimacy alive in committed relationships*. W. W. Norton & Company.

Strutzenberg, C. (2016). Love-Bombing: A Narcissistic Approach to Relationship Formation. *Human Development and Family Sciences Undergraduate Honors Theses*. https://scholarworks.uark.edu/hdfsrsuht/1

Teixeira de Melo, A., & Alarcão, M. (2014). Beyond the family life cycle: Understanding family development in the twenty-first century through complexity theories. *Family Science, 5*(1), 52–59. https://doi.org/10.1080/19424620.2014.933743

Agency-Centered Relational Therapy

Decolonizing Healing and Relationship Work

Tai Lee

Author's Note: All the textbooks that I read when I was in school did not have the author speaking to the reader. They were written in a third-person point of view and with a dispassionate tone. That is not a natural way for me to communicate with people, especially not about decolonization, social justice, and being a clinician. I would like to communicate with you, the reader, as a colleague, a storyteller, and an advocate.

Hi. I'm Tai Lee (they/them/their pronouns). It is a bit surprising to be invited to write this chapter. I only graduated from Antioch University Seattle with my MA in Couple and Family therapy less than two years ago. I completed the Sex Therapy Certificate program while I was there, as well. Some of the other contributors to this book are my former professors, whom I hold in the highest regard, and I am honored to be writing alongside them.

Prior to becoming a relationship and sex therapist, I spent many years providing peer and relational support in Seattle's Relationship Anarchy (RA) community. Most of the members of this community practice alternative lifestyles, such as having multiple partners and kinky relationships. Many identify as queer, BIPOC, neurodivergent, disabled, and having other marginalized identity factors. The aspects of my social location that are relevant to disclose are: I am an immigrant and a person of color. I identify as being under the gender-expansive umbrella of identities. I am a partner to a couple of amazing humans and a parent to a couple more.

Being in the RA community imparted to me that distress is fundamentally due to some degree of threat to one's sense of agency. Resolution of distress is then a matter of reclaiming and/or restoring agency. This planted the seeds for the therapy model that I would eventually write while I was in graduate school, agency-centered relational therapy (ACRT). It uses a novel approach to conceptualizing agency to help clients navigate away from distress and toward joy. ACRT advocates for the restoration of agency at all social-ecological (Bronfenbrenner, 1977) levels, including the loss of lives, lands, identities, and traditional ways of life that are legacies of colonialism. The normalized violation of agency that exists at the societal level is repeated at community, interpersonal, and intrapersonal levels. Our clinical work is not limited to resolving distress in our individual, relational, and family system clients. We are a part of building a groundswell of agency that has community- and societal-level impacts.

Centering Agency as a Decolonized Approach to Reducing Distress

I approach the topic of decolonization by reframing it as the restoration of agency for all. The term decolonization references the oppression that extends to time immemorial and

DOI: 10.4324/9781032679082-13

implicitly asks people to examine whether they are closer to the identity of the perpetrator or victim of that harm. This type of framing can foster solidarity among those who experience systemic oppression, but it can also foster solidarity at the other end of the social hierarchy. As I am writing this in the summer of 2024, the cultural climates in the United States and many other parts of the world are highly polarized. The accumulative effect of such strong solidarity centered on people's differences makes it harder and harder for meaningful dialogue.

The concept of agency may make it easier to have meaningful dialogue. *Agency* is tied to a fundamental need to exist, thrive, and evolve that goes beyond the human experience. To illustrate this point, I observe that most people are able to have joyful relationships that honor the agency of others regardless of spirituality, race, gender, socioeconomic status, nationality, and many other factors that are culturally divisive. This is evident in human relationships with domestic animals. Let's use my own furry friend as an example. I adopted a dog named Bruce about six years ago. Bruce and I do not share many identity factors. It would be unreasonable for me to expect that he shares my spiritual practices. Since we do not share the same language, I have not been able to ask him how "he" feels about his gender. We aren't the same race, much less the same species. I spend a lot of my hard-earned money on his care, yet there is no sense of scarcity that would cause me to call him a freeloader, ask him to pay his fair share, or ask him to leave. He protects my kids from aggressive dogs at the off-leash park and offers a caring *boop* when someone is having a bad day. Despite all our differences, we are brought together by our reciprocating care for each other's sense of agency.

If agency is such a fundamental part of understanding how beings relate to each other, how is it possible that it is so overlooked in our work as clinicians? I was taught many different therapy modalities during my ten quarters in graduate school. None of them conceptualized relational distress as the result of a violation of agency or proposed that the distress could be resolved by the reclamation and/or restoration of agency. I started looking for other models that at least talked about agency and came across Socio-Emotional Relationship Therapy (SERT; Knudson-Martin, 2010). I watched a video (FamilyProcess1, 2013) where Dr. Knudson-Martin talks about how important it is to look at power imbalances in relationships. She believes that clinicians should promote a sense of equality between partners. I absolutely agree with the concept of interrogating the power dynamics. I question if it actually helps clients develop a full sense of agency when the clinician is determining the power dynamic, especially when the clinician holds equality as the ideal power dynamic for most partnerships. Kink lifestyles are a great example of how people who negotiate their relational power dynamics with a full sense of agency may arrive at a power dynamic that is not equal. This begs the question: *Is the clinician's role to prescribe the power dynamic or to help the clients develop a full sense of agency to negotiate their own power dynamic?*

How to Use Agency with Our Clients

It comes as a surprise to my colleagues that an agency-centered approach to therapy uses the same process with clients regardless of their identity factors, their presenting issues, or how many people are in the session. The most frequently asked question I get is, "How do you work with their cultural background if you use the same process?" My answer often seems shocking to them. I don't specifically address their cultural background. I help my clients develop a full sense of agency to navigate their own cultural issues. Each person's culture is a part of their narrative. My position is that I cannot possibly understand the lived experiences that inform each person's narrative, even if I share many identity factors with them. Culture constantly evolves, so even people of different ages from the same identity group will have different narratives. Relationships in our modern world are becoming increasingly intercultural, creating new combinations of race, gender, spirituality, disability, neurotypes, etc.

Agency is a common factor that is multidimensional. A fluent understanding of each will help a person understand how their body is responding to distress (somatic), what is happening that creates distress (structural), and each person's conditioning that contributes to a normalized violation of agency (narrative). Agency-centered relational therapy works with clients to develop this fluency so that they can self-navigate away from distress and toward joy.

Somatic Attunement: Agency in the Body

Agency-centered relational therapy's first and most critical way of looking at client agency is through a somatic lens. Polyvagal theory (Porges, 1995) effectively observes the coordinated response between the vagus nerve and limbic system to the violation of agency. Identifying and honoring somatic knowledge was further validated by Van der Kolk (2014) in his seminal work, *The Body Keeps the Score*. This was one of the most useful things I learned in school, but it is also strikingly familiar to concepts I had been exposed to by my friends and partners who practice kink lifestyles. They negotiate their relational dynamics using green, yellow, and red labels for consent. I have noticed that my kids are also taught at school to use green, yellow, and red to understand their emotional regulation. I use the green, yellow, and red labels because they are accessible to a wide range of clients. I developed a "Verbal Litmus Test" to help clients identify their somatic response to a situation.

ACRT postulates that a healthy and sustainable relationship contains as many mutual "I would love to be" as possible, minimizes the "I should," and attempts to eliminate "I have to or else."

Table 9.1 Verbal Litmus Test

Polyvagal Label	ACRT Label	ACRT's Verbal Litmus Test
Ventral Vagal	Green	"I would love to..."
Sympathetic	Yellow	"I should..."
Dorsal Vagal	Red	"I have to _____ or else..." or "I'm afraid to..."

Structural Analysis: Studying the Violation of Agency

Agency-Centered Relational Therapy's second and most novel way of looking at agency is structural. Structural Family Therapy already exists (Minuchin, 1974), and I take a different approach to the concept of "boundaries." One of my colleagues described me as a "Bowenian anarchist" when they heard my approach because my conceptualization reframes the understanding of differentiation (Bowen, 1985). In comparison to these two fundamental concepts in systemic therapy, I break things down into smaller and more concise variables to facilitate communication. These variables are then held together by the structural framework I created called the Relationship Equalizer, which I shorten to RE. Consider the following scales:

- *Mutually Identified Relationship Status* (MIRS or just S): A scalable measure of relational importance and how a person individually ascribes this to the relationship. Colloquially referred to as "relational importance."
- *Voluntary Accountability* (VA or just A): A scalable measure of a person's behavioral input to a relationship. The ability to control this is a function of bodily autonomy. Colloquially referred to as how a person "shows up."
- *Granted Threshold of Influence* (GTOI or just I): A scalable measure of a person's emotional input to a relationship. The ability to control this is a function of emotional autonomy. Colloquially referred to as "emotional access."
- *Plane of Agency* (POA): The energetic plane that separates each person from other members of a relationship.

Agency-Centered Relational Therapy proposes that each person interfaces a relationship with their own set of sliders controlling MIRS, VA, and GTOI. The POA separates them from other individuals. This can be illustrated in the RE worksheet that I ask clients to print out on a piece of cardstock, which is then folded along the dotted line and placed between two individuals.

Distress arises in relationships when one person crosses the POA without consent in order to adjust a slider that is someone else's MIRS, VA, and/or GTOI. I use the common term "overreach" to describe a more generic way of breaking the POA. Specific ways of breaking the POA are described as "leveraging mechanisms." Each variable can be used actively or passively in an attempt to leverage another person:

Table 9.2 Leveraging Mechanisms.

Specific Leveraging Mechanism	What it sounds like...
Active leveraging of relational importance (MIRS)	"You should/have to meet my expectations because you are my [insert important relationship label] (partner, child, parent, sibling, etc.)"
Passive leveraging of relational importance (MIRS)	"I am withholding the affirmation of our [insert important relationship label] until you meet my expectations."
Active leveraging of showing up (VA)	"I do all these things for you; therefore, you should/have to meet my expectations."
Passive leveraging of showing up (VA)	"I won't show up until you meet my expectations" or "I will use abusive (lack of accountability) behavior to coerce you into compliance with my expectations."
Active leveraging of emotional access (GTOI)	"I will give you a lot of emotional access, so you should/have to meet my expectations."
Passive leveraging of emotional access (GTOI)	"I am withholding care/affection/attention until you meet my expectations" or "I will be angry/frustrated with you until you meet my expectations."

Concept by Tai Lee.

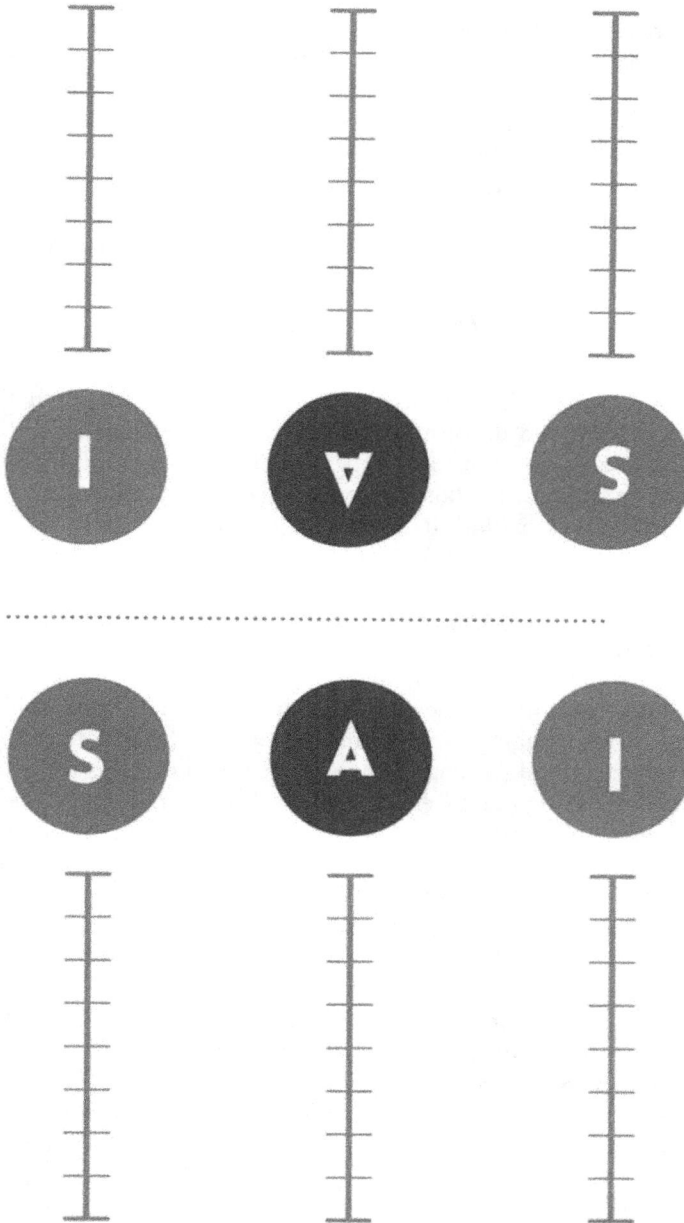

Figure 9.1 RE Boundaries Worksheet 2.

Concept by Tai Lee. Image by Jess McKinley.

Similar to Gottman's characterization of the Four Horsemen as toxic behaviors that can be predictors of relationship dissolution (Gottman, 1993), ACRT looks at interactions (leveraging mechanisms) that cross the POA in nonconsensual ways as the source of distress in a relationship. High-conflict relationships are often full of mutual overreach, with each person using leveraging mechanisms to obligate/coerce others into compliance with their expectations. We can apply the verbal litmus test by having a client say, "I would love to meet that expectation. I should meet that expectation. I have to meet that expectation or else." One of these statements will feel most accurate to the client, indicating the level of somatic response they are experiencing in this situation. Conversely, a person could recognize an external expectation they are not eager to meet and look for a somatic response that has become so normalized that it is ignored.

Narrative Interrogation and Deconstruction: Dislodging the Normalized Violation of Agency

Agency-Centered Relational Therapy's third and final way of conceptualizing agency is to help clients interrogate and deconstruct the narratives that normalize the violation of agency. For example, a person who has experienced a lot of emotional and/or physical violence as a child from an adult family member has experienced passive leveraging of GTOI and/or VA from a person with high MIRS. The repetitive violation of agency at this originating source is normalized, and this person is far more likely to tolerate the same leveraging mechanisms and use the same leveraging mechanisms on others in future important relationships. For many, this is simply what "love" feels like.

Various cultures have narratives that compel obligatory and/or resigned compliance. For example, my own culture-of-origin suggests that an individual would be much less important to the family and community if they did not behave in certain ways, which manifests as both active and passive leveraging of relational importance (MIRS) to generate an obligatory and/or coerced behavioral (A) compliance across the POA. This is not a narrative that is unique to my culture of origin. I have heard many clients across a wide variety of identity factors describe their own banishment from families- and cultures- of-origin due to a lack of compliance with sociocultural norms. Even before their banishment, they describe their efforts to comply as being "I have to or else" levels of engagement.

Most of this narrative approach to agency should be familiar to clinicians. It can be corroborated in our understanding of intergenerational trauma and studied with things like the Adverse Child Experiences Study (ACES; Felitti et al., 1998). Attachment Theory studies the lasting effects and coping mechanisms an individual could develop if that sense of importance is under constant threat during early developmental phases (Ainsworth & Bowlby, 1991). What ACRT adds to a clinician's work with the client is to interrogate the narrative by asking, *Did you consent to compliance with that expectation and the leveraging mechanisms used to enforce it?* When clients say, "No... I did not consent to these things", they begin reclaiming their sense of agency.

Clients can continue their work in the restoration of agency. This involves parties acknowledging the ways they have overreached in the past and making repairs for the effects of specific leveraging mechanisms. Relational clients who do this work with each other can bring new life to a relationship that seemed destined for dissolution. That said, I see quite frequently that relational clients end their relationship within the first few sessions. One or more members of the relationship begin to see how normalized the violation of agency is, how it exists in the relationship, and how narratives are unlikely to be dislodged. Restoration of agency is not always possible, particularly when working with individuals processing childhood trauma. The person at the originating source of trauma may not be willing, or is no longer available, to make the necessary repairs. Oftentimes, the most I get to do with clients is the reclamation of agency so that they can move forward with their lives with the ability to set healthy boundaries in future relationships.

Multidimensional Fluency of Agency: Somatic, Structural, and Narrative

An agency-centered approach tackles the client's cultural background without the clinician needing to have an encyclopedic level of knowledge of cultural norms across the globe. The clinician facilitates the client's multidimensional fluency with agency so that the client can pursue the best somatic outcome for all parties involved, minimize nonconsensual over-reach, and navigate their own cultural narratives. My take on a decolonized approach to therapy is to focus on the fundamental ways that we are similar, not the ways that we are supposedly different from each other.

Intersections of Identity

The concept of intersectionality (Crenshaw, 1989) looks at how different identity factors can compound to locate one's place in the social hierarchy. The Hays ADDRESSING model (Hays, 2007) takes a similar approach of looking at different identity factors to determine whether a person is *agentic* or *targeted*. When I advocate for a focus on how people are similar rather than how they are different, I want to clarify that I am not advocating that we ignore the accumulated harms that people live with because of their identity factors. Clients arrive at the beginning of therapy with very different experiences based on their race, assigned sex at birth, gender, disability, size, religion, age, neurotype, and so forth. At the heart of each of these categories is some aspect of the client's identity development that was shaped by obligation and resignation. There is an "I did not consent to..." statement that can be separately explored for each category, but the whole of a person's sense of resignation is often greater than the sum of the parts.

Coerced Identity Development

One of the terms that I developed with ACRT is "Coerced Identity Development," which I use as a replacement term for trauma. My anecdote about trauma is that society did not take it seriously when Freud identified abuse as the likely cause of hysteria in women (Breuer & Freud, 1893). We started looking at trauma more seriously when soldiers came back from the Vietnam War in the 1970s with what would eventually be diagnosed as Post-Traumatic Stress Disorder. Fast-forward to the present day, where there is now an emerging diagnosis of Complex Post-Traumatic Stress Disorder (CPTSD). If society continues to not take trauma seriously, we'll probably have Super-Duper Complex Post-Traumatic Stress Disorder (SDCPTSD?) as a diagnosis in another fifty years. How many more superlatives do we need to place in front of the word "trauma" before we take it seriously?

I often hear my clients not taking their own trauma seriously. It sounds like "my parents never hit me" or "I had it really good, relatively speaking." They will say that they experienced little, if any, trauma when they were young. Coerced identity development reframes trauma by asking, *"How was your identity shaped by* "I had to _____ or else..."? Said differently, *"How were you shoved into a box of someone else's expectations?"* This question generally makes it easier for clients to confront how normalized the violation of their agency was across many or all identity factors. A person who dismisses the violation of their own agency is far more likely to cause harm to others. This statement can be made anecdotally based on the clients that I see experiencing sexual or any other type of abuse. It is actively being discussed by people like Dr. Yamonte Cooper in his latest book "Black Men and Racial Trauma: Impacts, Disparities, and Interventions" (2024), which looks at the stigmatization of Black men as being sexually coercive while their lived experiences of being sexually coerced go unrecognized.

Visualizing the River of Harm

Harm flows like a river through our society, and intersectionality helps people socially locate themselves as being further upstream or downstream. A person who is upstream in the flow could be called a "perpetrator," and someone downstream could be called a "victim," but that is just the perspective of one fixed point on the river of harm. Clinicians who work with relational systems can disrupt the flow of harm by working with all parties to explore their narratives of coerced identity development, name the structural leveraging they did not consent to, and validate the somatic response of resignation that was installed in their bodies. In families, this may look like working with the parent to dislodge the normalized violations of agency they experienced as a child, which they are now passing through to their own children. With intimate partners, there is a good chance that the ways they were taught to love include some nonconsensual overreach.

Connecting to Practice

Now that I have described the framework of an agency-centered approach to therapy, it may be helpful to bridge the theoretical orientation with a composite case study and applied intervention. My areas of clinical focus are working with queer, multi-partnered, and neurodivergent clients. I really enjoy working with clients who would conventionally be labeled as "high conflict" by clinicians. In other words, I work with people who are currently or have in the past spent a lot of time in a red somatic state.

Composite Case Study

The case study that I am using is a composite of similar cases. These were relational cases with two individuals who had been in a long-term relationship. I will refer to them as Person A and Person B (I usually assign A to the person who reached out to me first). They present at therapy with a high degree of relational conflict and want to find a way to stabilize the relationship. Other compounding factors in these cases were that they both have multiple partners. Person C was an intimate partner with A and close friends with B. Person B, and Person C had a major falling out, which caused distress to all parties involved. Person A and Person B come to therapy looking for ways to de-escalate their conflict so that they can preserve their high level of relational importance. Person C also comes to therapy in one of these cases.

I first introduced somatic attunement to the clients, and they started paying attention to how much green, yellow, and red they were experiencing. They were, at best, interacting with each other in "I should" ways. Their conflicts regularly became yelling matches during our sessions, which happened via telehealth. They lived together and were in the same house but logged into the sessions from their separate rooms. The way they fought offered a clear view of the mutual overreach. They were both using their expressed anger with each other to get the other person to comply with their expectations. Person A expected that B would allow C to return to the house so that A and C could spend time together. Person B had set a boundary that they would not consent to C into their home space due to unresolved conflicts. Person B did not have any expectations of Person A other than they did not want to continue being pressured into letting Person C back into the home. They felt like there was not going to be any repair with Person C after previous attempts, so they also no longer had any expectations of Person C to do anything else.

Person A and Person B spent most of the first two sessions airing their grievances. I got a chance to do somatic work with them in session three. I introduced the RE structural framework in session four, and this was a major turning point. Person B, who had initially been a bit standoffish because they were pressured to come to therapy, started actively engaging because they could see that I was not taking any sides. We were able to help the clients identify the leveraging mechanisms that were being used, namely a passive leveraging of their emotional access (withholding of care and use of anger) to control each other's behavior. The narrative work during sessions five through eight explored why each of them normalized using anger to compel each other's behavioral compliance and how they both came from families where this type of leveraging was commonplace. They both could name that they did not consent to the withholding of care and use of anger to compel their behavior in their early developmental years.

Starting around session six, clients started seeing a decrease in their conflict intensity. The leveraging mechanisms were pointed out, and they were both doing their best to avoid overreaching. They held off on addressing some of the issues they had regarding Person C and refocused their attention on each other. I helped them work on decreasing the baseline of somatic responses from yellow to something closer to green by interacting with each other in ways that could be characterized as mutual "I would love to." This brought the bulk of their interactions back to things that felt green (joyful) instead of yellow (obligatory) or red (coerced).

Outcomes

As aforementioned, this case conceptualization is a composite of different cases. There were different outcomes across the cases:

Case 1

Persons A and B dissolve their relationship. Person A had stopped leveraging the emotional access (anger) but demanded that Person B resume a relationship with Person C because Person A could not tolerate their two partners (MIRS) not providing emotional access (GTOI) to each other. Person B had already been able to say that they did not consent to the leveraging with anger and were now able to say they did not consent to Person A's leveraging of relational importance to generate their compliance. Person B initiates the dissolution because they can now clearly see that Person A will continue to overreach with different leveraging mechanisms.

Case 2

Persons A, B, and C were able to continue cohabitating because they focused their attention on the RE sliders they could control instead of trying to leverage each other. Person C also started coming to sessions. Persons B and C took ownership of their own contributions (VA) to their conflict, resulting in a restored sense of agency for both. All three of them made commitments to each other to find the greenest somatic outcome. Having shared language about what was overreach helped them address conflicts before things got to red.

Case 3

Persons A and B transitioned out of partnership while continuing to cohabitate. This lowered their relational importance (MIRS) to something that was more appropriate for how they were showing up (VA) and providing emotional access (GTOI) to each other. Persons A and C continued their relationship outside of the home shared by Persons A and B. Persons B and C did not pursue further repair of their relationship.

Case 4

Persons A and C dissolve their relationship (MIRS), while Persons A and B continue with their partnership. Persons A and B were able to decrease their baseline levels of activation to something that increased their receptivity to each other's concerns (GTOI). Person B's description of Person C's leveraging mechanism is something that Person A also experienced from Person C. Person A had experienced so much of that type of overreach in their previous important relationships that they had learned to ignore and placate it.

Multicultural Factors of this Case Study

The cases involved individuals with a variety of identity factors:

- Race: Black, East Asian, Southeast Asian, white
- Gender: Transgender male, transgender female, gender nonbinary, gender nonconforming, male, female
- Religion: Jewish, Atheist, Christian, Muslim, nonpracticing
- Sexuality: Bisexual, pansexual, homosexual, and heterosexual
- Disability: No disability, chronic illness, chronic pain
- Neurotype: Autistic, ADHD, allistic
- Age: Ranging from late 20s to mid 50s
- Other identities: Kinky, queer, immigrant, and polyamorous

Each client's ability to interrogate their own narratives contributed to whether the outcome resulted in their relationship surviving or dissolving. One person's gender may normalize the use of anger to leverage another person's compliance with expectations. Another person's gender might normalize fearful compliance to external expectations. One person's religion may normalize the withholding of relational importance to leverage another person's compliance. Another person's religion might explain why they anxiously chase that relational importance. One person's race may normalize their control of another person's behavioral or emotional inputs into the relationship. Another person's race may normalize a fearful compliance to external expectations. One person's neurotype may have contributed to being invalidated and disempowered. Another person's neurotype may have normalized a very high level of caretaking that feels obligatory.

The method for the resolution of distress remains the same. When all parties in the relationship become fluent with the multidimensional aspects of agency, they will be better able to navigate their way toward the greenest somatic outcome together. This will likely include the least amount of nonconsensual overreach. Sustainable change comes from interrogating and deconstructing the narratives that normalized reaching across the plane of agency in ways that are nonconsensual.

ACRT Specific Intervention: Understanding Sequential Leveraging

I have found that clients' internalized narratives can be very hard to interrogate and deconstruct. The narratives become affixed to the client's coerced identity development. Some clients identify their ability to cope with the violation of agency as a strength or resilience, making it hard for them to want to validate the undesirable somatic response. I started observing patterns in clients who had persistent narratives that were difficult to dislodge, such as being a perfectionist or a people-pleaser. They experienced a sequence of leveraging mechanisms in early relationships that were designed to enforce their compliance with external expectations. The sequences of leveraging mechanisms took on two distinct forms.

Serial Leveraging

Serial Leveraging is when a person has experienced the same leveraging mechanism in a repetitive manner. For example, a child might be directed multiple times in a plain-spoken tone by a parent to take out their garbage or clean their room. If we were to use the verbal litmus test with the child, they would probably say, "I should finish my chores because my parent told me to," when first presented with the parent's expectation. When the child does not comply with the expectation after the first direction, the parent may issue the same direction with the same tone repeatedly until the child ultimately complies. The verbal litmus test for the child then becomes, "I should finish my chores because I'll be repeatedly directed until I do so." The somatically compelling reason now to finish the chores becomes avoiding the repetitive direction rather than avoiding the chore. The sequence of leveraging then looks like this:

1. Parent names the expectation and actively leverages their behavior (VA) in the form of providing direction across the POA to generate behavioral compliance (VA) of the child to finish the task.
2. Repeat active leveraging of VA from parent across POA to affect VA of child. The child resists by not complying.
3. Repeat active leveraging of VA from parent across POA to affect VA of child. The child complies with expectation and this incident is resolved.

A yellow or "I should" level of compliance now becomes part of the narrative of the parent-child relationship because the child ultimately completed the task to avoid repeatedly being asked by the parent. The missed opportunity in this situation is for the child to understand why completing the task will lead to a better somatic outcome for themselves and others, creating a verbal litmus test statement that sounds more like "I would love to clean my room because it will feel better for me" or "I would love to take out the garbage because our household runs smoother when everyone chips in to help."

Escalated Leveraging

Escalated Leveraging is when a person has experienced different leveraging mechanisms, with each subsequent one becoming more somatically compelling. Using the same example as above, the parent would first name the expectation and provide direction to the child in a plain tone. When the child doesn't comply, the parent may then resort to a different mechanism, such as changing their tone and yelling angrily at the child. The verbal litmus test for the child might now be, "I should finish my chores so that my parent will stop yelling at me." Let's say the child still does not comply with this second leveraging attempt. The flustered parent might then attempt to use yet another leveraging mechanism that is even more somatically compelling by saying, "You're the laziest of your three siblings because you didn't do your chores." The parent's use of the term "laziest," relevant to two other important members of the family, now assigns a lower level of importance to the child due to their noncompliance. Now, the child's somatic response phrased in the verbal litmus test is, "I have to comply with my parent's expectation, or I will be less important than two other known points of importance." The sequence of leveraging then looks like this:

- The parent names the expectation and actively leverages their behavior (VA) by providing direction across the POA to generate behavioral compliance (VA) from the child to finish the task.
- Passive leveraging of emotional access (GTOI) in the form of yelling from the parent across the POA to affect VA of the child. The child resists by not complying.
- Passive leveraging of relational importance (MIRS) in the form of implicitly stating the child is less important than siblings affects how the child shows up (A). The child complies with the expectation, and this incident is resolved.

The child has now been conditioned to complete tasks in a red ("I have to or else") range of somatic activation. The incident is over, but now the parent-child relationship has normalized a resigned level of compliance. The parent is a person with high relational importance (MIRS). Their predictable pattern of sequential leveraging will form the narrative for the child that important relationships normalize yellow and red levels of compliance to external expectations. That child may grow into an adult who cannot receive someone else's expectations without already experiencing the fearful or resigned somatic response that comes with subsequent leveraging mechanisms to enforce the expectation. The common label that clinicians use for this is "hypervigilance," which can be described as one person's compulsive need to serve the leveraging mechanisms they are accustomed to receiving from the other side of the POA.

How Internalized Narratives Develop

The mechanism for how a person internalizes a narrative is tied to their experience of sequential leveraging. A narrative becomes much harder to dislodge when it has been conditioned to be enforced with red interactions. A person can be compelled to self-enforce the initial expectation because they are trying to avoid the anticipated subsequent leveraging mechanisms. The verbal litmus test statement now becomes "I should perform to a level of perfection to avoid people being upset with me" or "I have to be perfect, or people will not treat me as being important to them."

A somatically compelling way of leveraging does not need to be characterized as abusive or red. For example, I had a client who was rewarded with praise when he did things like win a shooting competition and test up for his next belt in karate. These were not things that he particularly enjoyed, but the praise conveyed both emotional access and relational importance from his parent that he did not receive otherwise. The verbal litmus test statement was, "I should keep doing these things because my parent is happier, and I am more important to them." This forms an internalized narrative that he is only valuable to the important people in his life if he does things that make them happy.

Dislodging the internalized narrative for these perfectionist and people-pleaser clients is then a matter of helping them use consent statements to reclaim their sense of agency, with each of the identified sequential leveraging steps correlating with a separate consent statement. I could ask the client, "Did you consent to meeting other people's expectations that you will do things perfectly? Did you consent to being yelled at if you didn't do things perfectly? Did you consent to your sense of relational importance being threatened if you didn't do things perfectly?" or "Did you consent to only receiving emotional access and validation of your relational importance if you did what other people wanted you to do?" which is essentially the same question as "Did you consent to the withholding of emotional access and relational importance until you did what other people wanted you to do?" It can be an awkward question for them to hear because they've never been asked about their consent. They frequently respond with a very resigned no. I ask them to try responding with a statement that begins with "I did not consent to..." The shift in somatic response is immediately noticeable because "I did not consent to..." is said with more defiance. This subtle move away from resignation is the reclamation of agency that dislodges the narrative.

Subsequent work with clients will continue to move toward helping them visualize what would have been green. For example, I asked the people-pleaser client, "Instead of receiving care and relational importance for martial arts and shooting, what would you have loved to be validated for instead?" His response was, "I would have loved to have been seen as a kind and caring person without the need to take down an opponent or shoot something." His ability to form an "I would love to" statement helped him name what his authentic identity development would have looked like instead of the more performative ways he was conditioned to behave as a child.

Sequential Leveraging and Systemic Oppression

The previously described pattern that generates a person's compliance to external expectations at interpersonal levels can also be seen at community and societal levels. A great example of this is a conversation I had with a student around a topic that they were very passionate about: fat liberation. The society in which this person exists has an expectation around size, which can explicitly be named as "Being skinny is better and being fat is worse." Running that expectation through the verbal litmus test produces an accurate response somewhere in the range of "I should comply with the external expectation to be skinny" to "I have to be skinny, and I'm afraid to be fat." The leveraging mechanisms that this person has experienced, and continues to experience, when they did not comply with this societal expectation is passive leveraging of all the variables (MIRS, VA, and GTOI). The more common and immediate leveraging mechanism was passive leveraging of how people showed up (VA) and provided emotional access (GTOI) because of their size. They have experienced a lifetime of people not wanting to be around them or show them care. Running these through the verbal litmus test produces an accurate response of "I am afraid of people withholding care and how they show up for me because of my size, including receiving their emotional and physical violence toward me." If they fail to respond with compliance to the passive leveraging of VA and GTOI, they ultimately experience the with-holding of relational importance (MIRS). This person has experienced a lifetime of feeling less valued by their family, partner, and society because of their size. There are even attacks on their identity that their size means they shouldn't even feel valuable to themselves. The shame they've lived with their entire life and the years frantically spent trying to lose weight are the ways that we can conceptualize how they have attempted to self-enforce their com-pliance to the expectation to avoid the subsequent leveraging mechanisms.

"I have to or else" is synonymous with "I did not consent to." Helping a client name that they did not consent to compliance with the expectation, receiving emotional and physical violence, and loss of relational importance to coerce their compliance begins to dislodge the resignation. This is the shift away from red to yellow, which often shows up as anger. Over time, clinicians can facilitate their ability to express, "I would love to be the happiest and most authentic version of myself, whatever size that is." Reclaiming this agency is how they learn to joyfully validate relational importance, show up, and provide emotional access to others so they are no longer being coerced into compliance.

Restoration of agency in the face of systemic oppression is a daunting thought and may feel like an impossibility in the current moment. For the student mentioned above, the res-toration of their own sense of safety and joy would likely need to be an acknowledgment of the harms that were caused to them by those who coerced them into compliance with sociocultural norms around size, a meaningful repair for those harms, and some safeguards put in place to make sure they won't have to face the sequence of leveraging again. As clini-cians, we won't have the opportunity to facilitate this with all our individual and relational clients. Any opportunity that we get to do so helps to normalize that the restoration of agency is critical in order to find sustainable safety and joy in our relationships. While our work is largely happening at an interpersonal level, we can be part of a larger movement that advocates for the restoration of agency at all social-ecological levels. Making repara-tions to the descendants of chattel slavery and repatriating stolen lands to Indigenous com-munities would likely have a far greater chance of moving forward if and when more people have experienced and would advocate for the restoration of agency.

Multicultural Influences of Agency-Centered Relational Therapy

The agency-centered perspective that led to creating ACRT was largely inspired by how kinky people negotiate their scenes and relationships. That level of clarity in how each per-son's agency was to be handled proactively dealt with relational distress. The kink commu-nities I was exposed to included people of various genders, races, nationalities, disabilities, and neurotypes. I could see how people with many different identity factors collectively created a common relational language. I later learned in graduate school that this was the language of the mammalian body as described by Polyvagal theory.

Acknowledging the Lived Experiences of Indigenous People and the Enslaved

Another source of inspiration was the work of Kim TallBear, aka "The Critical Polyamor-ist." She hails from the Dakota Nation and is a Professor in the Faculty of Native Studies at the University of Alberta. I was first exposed to her concepts of decolonizing love and sex in 2016 and have attended two conferences where she was the keynote speaker. She has "spoken widely on the role of compulsory marriage, monogamy, and heterosexuality in relation to private property in settler-colonialism in the US and Canada" (TallBear, n.d.). Her perspective opened my eyes to how the violation of agency at a societal level also normalized it elsewhere. In much of the colonized world, the land that people live on is stolen, and economies were built by stolen bodies with stolen labor. This normalized violation of agency at the societal level casts a dark shadow that prevents the joyful development of individual identities, consensual partnerships, and vibrant communities. When the people at the bottom of contrived social hierarchies are casually disposed of in unmarked graves and bred like domesticated farm animals, it informs everyone else that they have to comply with sociocultural norms... or else.

Addressing Systemic Harm in the Mental Health Field

I rhetorically pondered earlier how it is possible that agency, arguably the most critical common factor to our work as mental health providers, could be so overlooked. This is not for a lack of our field being put on notice. Freud's Studies on Hysteria in 1895 pointed to trauma as the source of symptoms but were met with scorn by his colleagues, who did not believe it was possible that women's sense of agency had been so systemically ignored. Dr. Martin Luther King, Jr.'s speech at the 1967 American Psychological Association annual conference implored clinicians not to help clients become well-adjusted to systemic oppression (King Jr., 1967). I am not convinced that our fields took Dr. King's advice. When I started graduate school in January 2020, one of my textbooks suggested that couples who were fighting a lot should "get beyond the blame and keep doing it" (Brown, 2017). I was shocked that one of the first things I learned as a relational therapist was to treat sex as a performative and compulsory interaction between partners. I wondered if anyone else was alarmed and would address this when we discussed it in class. No one did, so I raised my hand and asked, "What about consent?" Here was a glaring example of clinicians being instructed to ignore agency, and there were plenty more in my next two years in graduate school.

Clinicians need to engage critically with, and even push back against, these harmful perspectives taught in the classroom because we cannot rely on institutions to do so. When I teach ACRT, I remind students that their first and most important client is themselves. We need to interrogate and deconstruct our own narratives so that we won't casually ignore the normalized violations of Agency that present as relational distress in our clients. Even more critical in the clinical setting is the impact this therapeutic work has on our own minds and bodies. I could spend six hours a day either helping people develop sufficient coping mechanisms to deal with the oppression they are experiencing or I can work with them to take incremental steps toward a greater sense of agency. While both can make for a long clinical day, the latter is the one that I would love to do again when I wake up the next morning.

Conclusion: Envisioning Equitable Futures

What is our role as clinicians in the restoration of agency at all social-ecological levels? I was invited back to my alma mater to teach ACRT less than two years after I graduated. The class contained 20 licensed or intern clinicians, along with myself and one of my colleagues assisting me with teaching the class. Let's assume that each clinician has an average of 25 clients. That means there will be about 550 clients working with clinicians who do not ignore the agency in the near future. My hope is these clinicians can foster a groundswell of agency that makes a meaningful societal-level impact. This would align our work with current social movements like #LandBack, #BlackLivesMatter, and #MeToo. Eventually, it would create an ever-growing contrast to the status quo upheld by our institutions and accrediting bodies that have prevented a meaningful change to how clinicians are educated.

Some takeaways from this chapter:

- Agency is a common factor of human and mammalian distress.
- When agency is reclaimed and restored, distress will be diminished. This formula works across cultures, even species.
- The focus on agency as a common factor demands the acknowledgment and repair of past violations of agency to marginalize individuals and communities.
- Agency can be used as a multidimensional mechanism for moving away from fear and toward joy. It is held in our bodies (somatic), visible in our interactions (structural), and informed by our conditioning (narrative).
- Healthy and sustainable relationships contain as many mutual "I would love to" as possible, minimize the "I should," and attempt to eliminate "I have to or else."
- The societal backdrop of colonialism normalizes the violation of agency at all social-ecological levels.
- Clinicians can push back on the normalized violations of agency being taught by our institutions.
- We can align our work with social movements by facilitating the reclamation and restoration of agency in our individual and relational clients.

ACRT Terms for Reference

Agency: A fundamental capacity to exist, thrive, and evolve, often diminished by systemic, relational, or internalized forces.

Agency-Centered Relational Therapy (ACRT): A decolonized systemic therapy framework that focuses on the restoration of agency to reduce distress and build relational health.

Coerced Identity Development: A framework for understanding trauma as the result of being forced to conform to others' expectations, especially during formative experiences.

Dorsal Vagal / Red: A state of collapse or shutdown; somatically expressed as helplessness or resignation (e.g., "I have to... or else...").

Escalated Leveraging: A pattern of applying progressively more intense or coercive strategies to gain compliance.

Granted Threshold of Influence (GTOI or I): A scalable measure of how much emotional input a person grants others, representing emotional access and autonomy.

Leveraging Mechanism: Strategies—both active and passive—used to coerce or obligate another into meeting expectations by crossing the POA.

Mutually Identified Relationship Status (MIRS or S): NA measure of how individuals value a relationship and how this value is expressed and negotiated mutually.

Narrative Interrogation and Deconstruction: The therapeutic process of unpacking and challenging narratives that normalize violations of agency.

Plane of Agency (POA): The conceptual and energetic boundary between individuals that protects personal autonomy.

Polyvagal Theory: A theory describing how the nervous system responds to threat and safety, used in ACRT to assess somatic cues.

Relationship Equalizer (RE): A conceptual framework and visual tool that maps the structural components of a relationship (MIRS, VA, GTOI, POA).

Restoration of agency: The process of repairing past violations of agency to reclaim autonomy and reduce distress.

Serial Leveraging: Repeated use of the same type of leveraging to produce compliance (e.g., persistent nagging).

Somatic Attunement / Green-Yellow-Red Framework: A framework within ACRT using Polyvagal theory language to label client responses (Green—safe, Yellow—hypervigilant, Red—shutdown).

Structural Analysis: The assessment of power imbalances and boundary violations through mapping relational input/output dynamics.

Sympathetic/Yellow: A heightened state of activation; often somatically felt as pressure or tension (e.g., "I should...").

Ventral Vagal/Green: A state of safety and engagement; somatically experienced as joy, comfort, or excitement (e.g., "I would love to...").

Voluntary Accountability (VA or A): A measure of how a person shows up behaviorally in a relationship, grounded in bodily autonomy.

References

Ainsworth, M. S., & Bowlby, J. (1991). An ethological approach to personality development. *American Psychologist, 46*(4), 333–41. https://doi.org/10.1037/0003-066X.46.4.333

Bowen, M. (1985). *Family therapy in clinical practice*. Jason Aronson.

Freud, S., & Breuer, J. (1893). On the physical mechanisms of hysterical phenomena. In Freud, S. (Ed.), *Collected papers* (pp. 225–305). International Psychoanalytic Press.

Bronfenbrenner, U. (1977). Toward an experimental ecology of human development. *American Psychologist, 32*(7), 513–31. https://doi.org/10.1037/0003-066X.32.7.513

Brown, J. (2017). *Growing yourself up: How to bring your best to all of life's relationships*. Exisle Publishing.

Center for Disease Control and Prevention (n.d.). *The Social-Ecological model: A framework for prevention*. https://www.cdc.gov/violenceprevention/about/social-ecologicalmodel.html

Cooper, Y. (2024). *Black men and racial trauma: Impacts, disparities, and interventions*. Routledge.

Crenshaw, K. (1993). Demarginalizing the intersection of race and sex: A Black feminist critique of antidiscrimination doctrine, feminist theory and antiracist politics. In Weisberg, D. K. (Ed.), *Feminist legal theory: Foundations* (pp. 383–95). Temple University Press.

FamilyProcess1. (2013, January 24). Why power matters: Creating a foundation of mutual support in couple relationships [Video]. YouTube. https://www.youtube.com/watch?v=eDCFB-f2fgE

Felitti, V. J., Anda, R. F., Nordenberg, D., Williamson, D. F., Spitz, A. M., Edwards, V., & Marks, J. S. (1998). Relationship of childhood abuse and household dysfunction to many of the leading causes of death in adults: The Adverse Childhood Experiences (ACE) Study. *American Journal of Preventive Medicine, 14*(4), 245–58. https://doi.org/10.1016/s0749-3797(98)00017-8

Gottman, J. M. (1993). A theory of marital dissolution and stability. *Journal of Family Psychology, 7*(1), 57–75. https://doi.org/10.1037/0893-3200.7.1.57

Hayes, A. M., Laurenceau, J. P., Feldman, G., Strauss, J. L., & Cardaciotto, L. (2007). Change is not always linear: the study of nonlinear and discontinuous patterns of change in psychotherapy. *Clinical Psychology Review, 27*(6), 715–23. https://doi.org/10.1016/j.cpr.2007.01.008

King Jr, M. L. (1967). King's challenge to the nation's social scientists. American Psychological Association.

Knudson-Martin, C. & Huenergardt, D. (2010). A socio-emotional approach to couple therapy: Linking social context and couple interaction. *Family Process, 49*(3), 369–84. https://doi.org/10.1111/j.1545-5300.2010.01328.x

Minuchin, S. (1974). *Families and family therapy*. Harvard University Press.

Porges, S. W. (1995). Orienting in a defensive world: Mammalian modifications of our evolutionary heritage. A polyvagal theory. *Psychophysiology, 32*(4), 301–18. https://doi.org/10.1111/j.1469-8986.1995.tb01213.x

TallBear, K. (n.d.). https://kimtallbear.com/

Van der Kolk, B. A. (2014). *The body keeps the score*. Penguin.

Chapter 10

How Family Therapy Knowledge is Made and The World It Makes

Nonprofit Practice, Capitalism, and the Politics of Knowledge

marcela polanco

When I first meet people in therapy, I am keenly interested to learn how they chose therapy to address the enduring circumstances that brought them in: "Why therapy?" I ask this question in my role as a licensed family therapist. I am a *Colombiana inmigrante*, practicing under the institutionalized regulations of the Eurocentric marriage and family therapy (MFT) licensure in the United States. I have practiced under the monetized *parámetros* of four different southern states from the East to the West Coast.

Currently, I practice in the state of California with another 30,889 employed licensed family therapists, according to the United States Bureau of Labor Statistics (2023). The next state with the largest number of employed MFTs is Minnesota with 4,230 therapists (U.S. Bureau of Labor Statistics, 2023). *En mi English de inmigrante, mi Español Colombiano*, and *fronterizo* Spanglish, I have worked with people and their partners, *comadres*, children, grandparents, *concuñes*, caretakers, case workers, teachers, siblings, classmates, roommates, living mates, animal companions, or *otres comuneres*. Most folxs I meet are also immigrants, mostly but not exclusively from Abya Yala (América Latina) y el Caribe. Some folxs come to therapy *voluntariamente*.

My interest in asking people why they chose therapy is a bit different from what I learned during my training in family therapy. I am not inquiring about people's prior therapy experiences, their hope and expectancy for problem resolution, or what worked or not for them with previous therapists, if applicable. Nor am I seeking to assess the problem or what they want to get out of therapy to begin working toward a goal definition. I want to learn about the circumstances that made therapy a therapeutic option for them, possibly among others—or maybe just the only option. Interestingly, for many folxs my question often generates surprise, especially in the communities with whom I have shared life for the past five years, in San Diego, the Kumeyaay land that 'Ilipai-Tiipai peoples first inhabited for at least 12,000 years. I say this as an immigrant, having lived across five different states and living simultaneously in two languages, thus gaining a life skill to discern communally negotiated differences in everyday life across different contexts. Thus, shortly after my arrival to the state, I quickly learned that in California, not only folxs with economic access to put down thousands of dollars a year for weekly ongoing therapy sessions are more open to publicly discussing not only that they go to therapy, but what transpires in their therapy sessions with any of the 30,890 MFTs in the state.

Thus, seeing people's raised eyebrows in response to my question tells me that they hear me as if I were a cook and would have asked them: "What are you doing going to the kitchen to make dinner?" People's surprise by my question is, however, not at all surprising. I understand it to be a material expression of modernity's success. Therapy has become,

DOI: 10.4324/9781032679082-14

more prominently in some places than others, what modernity has made it to be, given its world-making colonial system of power and epistemic control. It is the legitimized option for the resolution of mental health problems, also configured by modernity.

I have spent the past few years understanding the ethics and politics of the decolonial option (Espinosa Miñoso, Lugones, & Maldonado-Torres, 2022; Quijano, 2000; Lugones & Crowley, 2025; Mignolo, 2021; Vázquez, 2020; Vallega, 2019; Walsh, 2023) how therapy knowledges, in particular, family therapy became legitimized and at what cost. As it is placed in the colonial system of power as the Westernized, hence single and monetized option, therapy thus has prevented therapists to do, sense, think, and feel other than what the Eurocentric canon of thought demands militantly. Decoloniality has offered me an understanding to reflect upon the ethics of why therapists do what we are doing so that we have the possibility to do differently. It has shifted my inquiry away from the logic of modernity that focuses on investigating clients' behaviors, emotions, or meanings in relation to therapy access or anything else. I am interested instead in the politics of knowledges in relation to therapists' actions—my actions—and structures of power that have made therapy what it has become, along with its epistemic and economic costs. This is so as to open other alternatives to reconfigure practices of healing and transformation more so within a universality (Escobar, 2020).

How Family Therapy Knowledge is Made and The World It Makes

Episteme or knowledges invents, shapes, and sustains worlds. Knowledge is world-making or worlding. The world in which many of us live today is founded on a specific perspective of knowledges—modernity's European and Anglo-North American-centric knowledges (Grosfoguel, 2013). For the decolonial option (Quijano, 2000; Mignolo, 2021), the dispute for the control and administration of the production and dissemination of world knowledges is at the forefront of its explorations. So, writing about the underlying modern logic of family therapy knowledges that has made family therapy what it is, from the decolonial option, requires addressing first the relationship between what is known or understood and the system in which the knowledges or understanding is being integrated, controlled, and managed. This is equivalent to the relationship between the family therapy practices and the system in which such practices are ultimately invented, integrated, controlled, and managed at times beyond what they intended in the first place. Or the stories that people bring to therapy and the structures within which those stories are embedded. This is the politics of knowledges. As the Jamaican philosopher Sylvia Wynter said in conversation with Canadian professor in Black Studies Katherine McKittrick:

> What I've been struggling with and working on, then, is to come up with a way of getting [my work] across, without falling into the traps laid down by our present system of knowledges, which means that I am often afraid that I will not be able to get it all across... (McKittrick, 2015, p. 18).

Having worked in more than one family therapy master's program in academia in the United States., Spain, and Colombia, I have had front-row seats to the system of knowledges Wynter may be alluding to. I also have had the experience of being an active player, a contributor to its sustainability, and becoming its benefactor. This is the system of knowledges that I believe family therapy fell into, and it is now trapped by modernity's design and its operating system of power–coloniality—whereby its intentioned practices may not be able to get across, as I am attempting to illustrate in this chapter.

Family Therapy's Economy of Knowledges: The Marketplace

Most of the family therapy programs I have been a part of, either as a student or as faculty, have been oriented by European and Anglo-American systemic, postmodern, poststructural, and social constructionist perspectives. It is not uncommon that tension comes by adopting such a philosophical stance to family therapy practice, specifically in the United States *Por ejemplo*, a common narrative I have heard throughout the years by folxs training in these programs is that these perspectives exist in some sort of a bubble because, in their experience, what is learned is not applicable, accepted, known, or even respected in the "real world."

From decoloniality, the particular reality such a world might be referring to is modernity, therefore coloniality. Decolonially, I understand modernity as a global 500-year-old Eurocentric, future-oriented, persuasive, and self-preserving story about how to world the world (Quijano, 2000). Now, it can be one hell of a story, but for a single story to world the world, something other than a story is needed. That is, an instrument or operating feature to put the story to work. Modernity's operating feature is coloniality (Quijano, 2000; Mignolo, 2021; Vázquez, 2020).

Coloniality is a decolonial term. It refers to modernity's behind-the-scenes system that ensures the sustainability of modernity's success, no matter what and at what human and nonhuman cost (Espinosa Miñoso, 2022). Decoloniality introduced me to a different way of understanding systems than the systemic epistemology of Eurocentric family therapy I was trained to consider other possibilities. At the same time, however, the Eurocentric understanding of systems I was trained in helped me better grasp the operation of the colonial system of power. I discuss this system of power throughout the chapter.

The world rendered otherworldly, bubble-wrapped, inapplicable, and not known where postmodern or social constructionist perspectives are situated by trainees and therapists could be understood to be in connection to the forming interdependable elements of coloniality—the control of knowledges and money. Coloniality has put together a kind of economy of knowledges—capitalism, whereby the administration and control of money are inseparable from the administration and control of knowledges as it is also inseparable from race and gender. They do not operate independently until they intersect. Rather, their existence is interdependent, therefore always operating simultaneously, like twisting fibers that create a thread of yarn; thus, it has configured a family therapy yarn out of twisted fibers of a capitalist economy of knowledges. Family therapists are entangled in these fibers, as I discuss next.

Untaxed Threads of Power

The real world of family therapy practice that trainees and therapists might refer to could be understood to be tied to the reality of the 501(c)(3) tax-exempted types of community social service organizations. Tax-exempt organizations are a model of modernity's design that imposes and, therefore, demands a specific kind of knowledges, directly shaping family therapy practice. Understanding the system within which they operate is an important departing place for decolonial explorations on knowledges in family therapy and what decoloniality might entail, possibly engaging practices within other kinds of economies than capitalism, about which I say more toward the end. Notwithstanding, perhaps the readers will find this discussion a bit dull because it does not pertain to the "how" of clinical practice, even though it is directly connected to it. I can only hope they bear with me while I get through information that might feel as dry as the Mojave Desert, located in between California, Nevada, Utah, and Arizona, known for its harsh conditions and haunting landscapes. Thus, hiking through the harsh and haunting discussion next on the 501(c)(3) system might require some hydration.

501(c)(3) is a Code Section by the US agency responsible for collecting federal taxes and enforcing tax law–the Internal Revenue Service (IRS). That Revenue Service Code not only gives qualified not-for-profit organizations a status that exempts them from having to pay federal taxes from their income. It also benefits multimillionaire donors who give money to 501(c)(3) organizations through their philanthropies, guided by their self-interests and legacies rather than a democratic vote, for example. It is not uncommon that universities, hospitals, schools, etc., receive large donations in exchange for buildings to be called in the donor's name. In addition, their donation is a tax write-off, meaning that it qualifies as a type of expense that will help reduce their taxable income, lowering the amount of taxes they have to pay that year, saving them money, and thus protecting their wealth. *Por ejemplo*, en el 2021, the not-for-profit online newsroom *ProPublica* (2021) reported on the paradox of tax laws in the U.S. They reported that the richest men in the US, like Jeff Bezos, Elon Musk, Michael Bloomberg, and George Soros, in various years managed to pay no federal income tax whatsoever, legally. In this capitalist disorder of things, with my income as a university professor and a family therapist, I pay more taxes than these multimillionaire white US men.

Tax-exempt organizations have a significant role in the country's economy and forge a militant model of practice. It demands epistemic obedience. In 2024, there were 1.8 million tax-exempt organizations in the United States (Tax Foundation, 2024); about 50% of these organizations were health related; they managed over $8 trillion in assets and represented 15% of the US economy. *Estas no son como la tiendita del barrio de Don Paco a la vuelta de la esquina*. The 501(c)(3) organizations intend to support behavioral therapy services nationwide, like the organizations I worked at for a few years during the beginning of my career as a family therapist, training in narrative therapy. I worked with families in the foster care system.

While working in these organizations, I was never made aware of the financial or administrative operating structure beyond learning who the supervisor I had to report to, who the clients I had to work with, and the documentation required from me to provide evidence of my home visits, which my salary depended on. Any activities in the agency beyond that were seemingly irrelevant to the clinical tasks I was responsible for, and quite frankly, I found it uninteresting, dry, dehydrating, and a bit dull by not being about clinical practice. I was not aware at the time that the administrative matters of the real world of the agency were actually critical in shaping the kinds of clinical work that was expected of me, which was not in line with the narrative practice framework I was learning.

I was not aware that many tax-exempt mental health organizations are dependent on federal or state funds. For example, at the beginning of 2024, the U.S. Department of Health and Human Services (HHS) (2024) announced that the Biden-Harris administration was giving $240 million in funding for behavioral health care services. From these funds, $36.9 million was allocated to increase capacity for behavioral health services, which included specifically mental health family therapy work. In May of the same year, $46.8 million was allocated to promote youth mental health, access to culturally competent services, and recovery support. In June, $31.4 million in funds aimed at improving behavioral health for racial and ethnic minorities. In July, $27.5 million in funds aimed at services that sought to improve women's behavioral health. The more than $142 million to address mental health, and many more millions I am not referencing here, was administered by the agency the U.S. Congress created in 1992 within the Department of HHS for that purpose. This agency is the Substance Abuse and Mental Health Service Administration (SAMHSA).

SAMHSA's (2023) purpose is to lead public health by supporting efforts that advance behavioral mental health, ensuring access to services, and supporting initiatives toward better outcomes. It is one of the highest authorities that administers the money that funds what is a rather significant portion of the mental health and behavioral services in the country. Although here I am focusing my discussion on SAMHSA as the authority that supports services, the National Institutes of Health (NIH) is the other authority agency within the U.S. Department of HHS dedicated to funding research, including mental health research, and functions within the same logic as SAMHSA and its control of knowledges. I have documented a decolonial analysis of the control of knowledges in relation to research elsewhere (polanco et al., 2020).

The amount of government funds allocated for SAMHSA to administer mental health services varies every year. It does so according to each administration—which means that the allocation of funds does not come from a neutral position, it is political, given modernity or coloniality's design of the Nation-State kind of governance. According to Mignolo, "Knowledge is not independent of the location of the bodies and institutions that embody and institutionalize it" (López-Calvo, 2016, p. 176). So, every fiscal year, SAMHSA administers whatever government funds are available depending on who we voted for by putting out a notice of funding opportunities as grants and requesting applications for grant-based organizations to get them. These funding opportunities have a material impact on what many family therapists' practices look like since the 501(c)(3) organizations where we practice are among the most frequent grant applicants. Their entire operation depends highly on donations and these kinds of grants that pay for family therapists' salaries as all employees, granting families access to services at a low cost or no cost. These organizations, where trainees in family therapy programs complete their practicums, internships, or traineeships, and graduates complete their licensing hour requirements, and some are later employed as licensed therapists, have to compete against each other for the money. This competitive setup is a crucial game changer in the development of a hierarchy of knowledges. It is also a 500-year-old operation of modernity's self-sustaining model of economy through coloniality: capitalism. I will discuss next how I have come to understand the complex term of capitalism that modernity depends on.

The Value Knowledge Adds to Valuing and Devaluing Knowledges

Capitalism is something more than the use of money. Thus, the fact that the government gives money to social service organizations to have an operating service is not necessarily what makes a capitalist economy. It is modernity's system of power put in place through coloniality, whereby money is used to generate an unequal and violent market for the dispute of the control and management of knowledges on mental health practices, in this case. It creates a hierarchy of knowledges. In the hierarchy, there are degrees of legitimized practices whereby the most legitimate are at the top and the destitute knowledges at the bottom, according to Eurocentric parameters. Such parameters, in turn, are based on which one can compete toward achieving higher degrees of fundable knowledges. 503(c)(3) organizations compete against each other for money, following the single parameters of SAMHSA inconspicuously determine which practices are more marketable or fundable, thus legitimate. Furthermore, if they are deemed legitimate in the U.S., they are consequently legitimate worldwide.

For the Argentinian-Mexican Philosopher Enrique Dussell (2013), capitalism is a kind of economy that creates a type of value that has the ability to generate/give/heighten or take/lessen value, *es el valor que da valor*. In this case, in a self-serving capitalist economy of knowledges, knowledge is a value that adds value, in turn devaluing other kinds of knowledges. *Por ejemplo*, in the capitalist economy of knowledges, in California, becoming a family therapist has more value than in other states where there are not as many family therapists, as I stated above. Or, Eurocentric practices have been given global value, making them not only more appealing but required in academic licensing curriculums, consequently devaluing and excluding any other knowledges and ways of knowing and understanding. Educational accreditation is also an example of the coloniality of knowledges or the dispute and control of knowledges in the capitalist market of training programs. Although, in some contexts, graduating or not from an accredited program is not a qualification required for employment, the market has the tendency to elevate the value of programs that are accredited.

Modernity gives money a social value that is equivalent to the value of labor or objects, treating them as if they were a measurement of a person's value or worthiness instead. *Por ejemplo*, my worth as a bilingual family therapist is equivalent to the amount of dollars of my salary. My salary is used to determine whether I am being valued or not. But there is a twist to it. When I compare myself to STEM professionals, even if we have the same number of years of experience or research in our respective professions and are hired by the same university, my salary would most likely be lower. Likely, therapy professions make less than STEM professions, and therefore, while I could argue for equity by highlighting similar efforts to STEM professionals to negotiate a higher salary, this argument would be irrelevant for the Dean of my colleague since my value as a professional is beyond merit when considering the capitalist market that have given more value to STEM profession over therapy professions. The return of STEM professions' investment is higher than for therapy, hence, STEM is higher in the hierarchy of professions.

The Parameters for the Hunger Games of Knowledges

In the words of the Health and Human Services (HHS) Secretary Xavier Becerra, as of 2024, SAMHSA's grants are to "directly impact the behavioral health of communities around the nation... enhancing accessibility of evidence-based, effective behavioral health care services." (SAMHSA, 2024, para 3). The highest authority that manages the control of money to fund knowledges and its applicability in practice is promoting evidence-based and behavioral services that can be proven to be effective. This is where NIH also comes in place by determining evidence-based research as the legitimate means for SAMHSA's criteria to place certain knowledges as the only ones at the top of the fundable and non-taxable list. Therefore, evidence-based research and effectiveness are modernity's kinds of knowledges higher in the hierarchy created by coloniality. The hierarchy materializes in the parameters found in the application guide to compete for SAMHSA's grants, in line with Becerra's perspective. Grant writers of 501(c)(3) organizations require the skill to articulate their organization's practices according to the application's demands to provide evidence of legitimacy and effectiveness for the services they are competing for. NIH, SAMHSA, and grant writers help shape the real world of therapy practice therapists and trainees refer to, and where frameworks that are lower in the hierarchy are rendered otherworldly and inapplicable to this evidence-based driven reality.

The government is not going to give millions and millions of taxpayer's dollars (with the exception of some of the rich white men who are legally not taxpayers) to organizations with a motivational hallmark card, a bouquet of flowers, and a box of chocolates, with good vibes, wishes, prayers, crossing fingers, *prendiendo velitas*, with lifting messages from the spirits if they show up in Becerra' dreams the night before, or hopes that the money will do some sort of service to whomever they trust will need it. The stakes are high, and so are the painstakingly thorough requirements to compete a la *Hunger Games* for that money, out of which there will be winners and losers. I have been on both ends of the harsh and haunting game of grants in my university job.

Thus, modernity/coloniality has created a system of dependency. Grants are required, and their requirements entail a way of thinking about knowledges—a Eurocentric way that family therapists are familiar with. Grant writers, among which are family therapists, are required to think knowledges in grant's criteria thus in monetized, evidence-based, and effective terms such as: *goals and outcomes, behavioral descriptions of change, concise and measurable results, assessment instruments, data collection mechanisms* and *strategies*, and *evidence of professional expertise*, and a clear definition of the *clinical population* 'targeted' in mental health terms. This is the knowledges that adds value. Any other knowledges might as well stay in a bubble outside of any capitalist hunger game competition because the results of how much taxpayer money they may get can be predicted right at the outset of the competition. Thinking knowledges Eurocentrically in outcome-oriented, concrete, measurable, assessable, collectable, data-able, professional-able, mass-produced, and expertise-able is absolutely imperative to be funded. This is the only language that mental health money speaks. Mental health is monolingual, no matter how many languages the services are delivered in—it is driven by "the monologic law of the marketplace" (Tichindeleanu, 2010, p. 1). Consequently, coloniality denotes a historical movement of erasure, of the negation of other worlds of meaning and the obstruction of plurality, systematically destructing worlds of meaning through the extinction of languages, practices, and therefore, the dignity of other worlds of sensing (Icaza & Vazquez, 2018; Vazquez, 2011).

Practicing under grant money, 501(c)(3) organizations are scrutinized and required to put the money to work as they said they were going to and with the knowledges indicated. They are required to operate in monolingual and monologic mental health money language since they are required to collect evidence for their operation. This means that family therapists who are hired into these organizations either are required to come with expertise in family therapy money language, or they must train in it and comply accordingly. Families who come to therapy must comply as well with the clinical definitions given to them, thus euro-phizing themselves, in order to receive services according to the grant.

To further illustrate, according to SAMHSA (2024), California is the state that spends the most on mental health, $6,762,808,997. During the 2024 fiscal year, it was the state that received the most funding from SAMHSA's funding opportunities for prevention, treatment, assistance, and advocacy to address mental health and substance use, $308,699,375.

While I am far from being any kind of statistician or a data analyst of any sort, I may not be too far off if I speculate that there is a connection between the billions of dollars invested in mental health access in California and the large number of family therapists in the state compared to other states; as well as to the openness of people speaking about their therapy sessions in public; and people's surprise when I ask them why they come to therapy if it has become a dominant taken for granted practice.

If my speculation is not too far off, I would say that modernity would claim this as another expression of its success. Once again, it has made a monetizable structure whereby knowledges becomes a culture shifter that adds or obstructs value depending on where they are placed in the hierarchy. This way of thinking has spread like a fucking virus–this kind of monetized therapy knowledges has gone beyond grant writing into education, private practice, for-profit services, and consumers'/clients' ideas about therapy and healing. This is where the tension comes for programs that take a philosophical stance that critiques modernity, like postmodernism, social constructionism, or post-structuralism, let alone decolonial alternatives. Faculty in these programs grapple with the binary tension of training students as fearless competitors in the hunger game marketplace or not. Coloniality sets up a self-sustaining binary system in favor or against it through an authority that monetizes knowledges in a way that motivates epistemic competition to elevate certain knowledges deemed as fundable and devaluing others as not legitimate or worthy of any kind of investment to serve communities.

Epistemic Persuasion and Translation

The critique of postmodern and social constructionist practices as otherworldly to the real 501(c)(3) world makes more than just a bit of sense. Most of the practices informed by these philosophies, like narrative therapy, although still European, did not emerge from or seek to sustain the mental health language and logic but are rather critical of it. They are a European critique of Eurocentric practices. In this economy of knowledges, they can very well be rendered unfundable or not monetizable, falling down the epistemic hierarchy as less competitive or worthy. If they want to be up for the epistemic hunger game against their colleagues from down the road with whom they share from time to time a cup of tea, *un tintico, o mate acompañado con bollos Argentinos, tal vez en la tiendinta de Don Paco en la esquina*, they must translate their bubbled wrap knowledges into mental or behavioral health money language if they have any ambition or aspirations of becoming fundable or legitimate in the mental health real modern world. They must discipline their professional disciplines.

The translation of unfundable philosophies and practices into fundable capitalist hunger game winners means that their knowledges ought to be rendered manualized, techni-fied, outcome-based presented, assessment-driven, evidence-based, and professional and expert looking when exhibited in professional settings via clinical case examples that demonstrate applicability into family therapy. This is very much the case. Hence, in other words, they have to stop being what they are to "expand the epistemic territory of modernity" (Vázquez, 2011, p. 27).

Por ejemplo, for years I have been in conversations with folxs with an interest in narrative therapy including its co-developer David Epston, about the ways in which the creative and adventurous spirit of narrative therapy that both David and Michael White, his counterpart developer, began engaging at the outset of their practices, is getting lost. Although they did not intend for narrative practices to become a therapy model, narrative therapy is very much a therapy model that more recently has *incursionado* in the evidence-based and Eurocentric research structures in the form of manuals, techniques, outcome-based forms, and *parámetros de efectividad*; all of which is fascinating, certainly appealing for many, and, of course, is highly respectable.

Understanding the colonial system of power that has formed an economy of knowledges for family therapy, it makes a lot of sense that narrative therapy has been translated into monological mental health language. It might not be a matter of scholars misunderstanding the origins or ethics of the practice or betraying epistemically its politics, to put it dramatically, but more so, they might be responding to the monetized culture shift that modernity and coloniality's capitalism demands for epistemic worthiness and survival. So, in fact, such efforts are not conceived as a departure from narrative therapy ethics and politics but a modern success of narrative therapy making it into the seemingly reputable, although violently set up marketplace. Therapists' added value is in the knowledges they produce and practice–practicing evidence-based narrative therapy versus unfundable narrative therapy adds value, employability, professional respect, etc.

Now, modernity would want to persuade us–with its progress, development, and inclusion rhetoric of a better future–into considering its good deeds and success—maybe similar to how the respectable and admirable narrative therapists' evidence-based researchers, grant writers, or scholars were persuaded as well. Modernity would want us to consider how our taxes are responsibly (depending on the political agenda we voted for[1]) being allocated by the Administration toward 503(c)(3) mental health organizations to operate nationwide in a way that they can protect their funds by not having to pay income taxes, investing their revenue instead in their operation, including the hire of family therapists. In turn, the family therapy profession continues to be relevant, and families are successfully persuaded against their former (rather rightful) biases against therapy to be helped at a lower cost, otherwise unable to access private practice fees–especially in California. So, modernity's rhetorical question would be: Is there anything wrong with this picture? Modernity's own answer is predictable. Decoloniality might not necessarily focus on answering the question but on unveiling its premises, as I attempted to address above.

Decoloniality and The Marketplace Temptation

Modernity's promotion of European knowledges through a very convincing 500-year-old story of development and prosperity that disseminates through capitalist colonial power and configurations of people (i.e., race, gender, laborers, therapists, consumers, clients) centers such knowledges as universal and legitimate. In doing so, it excludes not only other ways of knowing and understanding but knowers. Eurocentrism has been naturalized by modernity. In the face of epistemic exclusion, European perspectives that critique modernity, like the ones I have been positioning in my discussion–postmodernism, social constructionism, and poststructuralism–have opened a path motivated by the liberalized politics of inclusion. Also forged by Europe, this path has opened accessibility for the excluded to also show up in textbooks, curriculums, therapy training, etc.

Decolonial practices could very well follow this path to try to show up shoulder to shoulder with legitimate therapy practices and also to play an important role in the mental health or behavioral health system of services. In fact, it is already happening as decolonization begins to show up more frequently in the mental health rhetoric–providing evidence as an alternative. These are important steps. Now, going through the path that requires crossing the fundable border from exclusion to inclusion, like the crossing of any geopolitical border in this world, has its costs. This is something I am intimately familiar with as an immigrant. If decolonial practices have the intent to cross toward the center to be included, questions will be asked, and requirements to meet the parameters of what constitutes therapy practices will need to be met—thus leaving any decolonial intent behind. Therefore, any decolonial practices with ambition to cross or settle into curriculums, workshops, publications, etc., must speak the same language or translate itself to address questions like these:

- What practical examples or case studies (evidence) are there to demonstrate how therapists can implement decolonial practices in their work?
- How can Western structures linked to family therapy practices be dismantled?
- How can family therapists bring Indigenous communities' knowledges into their therapy practices?
- What decolonial interventions do therapists need to practice decolonial therapy?
- What are the practical applications of decolonial theory?
- What concrete successful initiatives within family therapy demonstrate decolonial principles?

As a Westernized therapist and faculty member, I have developed the skill to facilitate the inclusion of excluded knowledges into the center if I were to accept the premises of these questions. I could address them by conducting research, perhaps on my own Africana, Paijao, or Muisca ancestry. I would be searching for Muisca healing practices, conceptions of healing, or skills of the healers to translate Indigenous knowledges into English or Spanglish in my therapy conversations to constitute it as decolonization—bringing indigenous knowledges into the Westernized therapy structure. I would record, transcribe, analyze, and then publish as case examples on theory and practice, calling it decolonization work that I will not only bring to my practice but also my family therapy master's courses, following the coloniality of knowledges and production of knowledges in the marketplace. Graham et al., (2011) maps the data from the Web of Knowledges Journal Citation Reports (JCR) to identify the inequity of knowledges in published journals:

> The United States and the United Kingdom publish more indexed journals than the rest of the world combined; Western Europe, in particular Germany and the Netherlands, also scores relatively well; most of the rest of the world then scarcely shows up in these rankings; one of the starkest contrasts is that Switzerland is represented at more than three times the size of the entire continent of Africa; the non-Western world is not only under-represented in these rankings but also ranks poorly on average citation score measures; despite the large number and diversity of journals in the United States and United Kingdom, those countries manage to maintain higher average impact scores than almost all other countries. (p. 15)

So, investigations motivated by the questions above are not only certainly interesting, important, and, of course, worth considering, but they are also tempting for one's respectability and popularity for advancing decolonization in the marketplace. Yet, as tempting and important as it may sound, such initiatives still belong to modernity's logic of the capitalist marketplace of knowledges, not being the focus of decolonial explorations to delink from modernity.

Alternatively, the liberalized politics of dismantlement might propose something a bit different but with the same effect of further sustaining modernity and coloniality's binary logic of destruction. The proposal of dismantling modernity's structures means that new proposals, decolonial or any others, would have to still further advance a monologic premise to replace one with another (Tichindeleanu, 2010). Therefore, pursuing questions like the ones above not only sustains the universal design of modernity's Eurocentric knowledges. They do not resolve modernity's violent totalizing features and a monologic, monolingual, and mono-epistemic way of knowing and understanding.

The understanding of behavioral or mental health in terms of case examples, therapists, and therapy, all of which are modernity/coloniality's configurations of the capitalist mental health marketplace, remains intact in these questions. Learning remains centered on the consumption of evidence or case example illustrations of theory applied to practice to be disseminated widely. So, modernity asks about case examples as evidence of decolonial theory to qualify decoloniality as a practice for further dissemination–stopping it from being decoloniality, in turn, for some at least. This ratifies modernity's colonial power. Meanwhile, decoloniality asks about alternative ways of learning or pedagogies and knowledges and understandings as much as economies that delink from the colonial system of power. Furthermore, most importantly, it does so without requiring dependency toward decoloniality as the only way to do so, or even as a way at all.

Certainly, pursuing questions like the ones above might give us a sense of justice by claiming space in Eurocentric family therapy. But, as I see them, they would be instead another example of modernity's success, persuading us to believe that we have diversified our practices, while in fact, our way of knowing and understanding would remain dependent on the same technologies of capitalism and eurocentrism, promoting the consumption of evidence of applied theory into interventions, steps, or techniques as the single way to know how to do therapy.

Thus, to think and sense in decolonized ways would mean to ask different questions, engage other pedagogies, and know knowledges and understand understanding from a different relationality, shifting the inquiry more so toward unlearning modernity:

> the decolonial does not seek to open the canon of modernity to be inclusive of other 'modernities' in that way. Instead, it wants to overcome the notion of modernity that is inseparable from coloniality. The decolonial posture is about going beyond the modern, beyond the contemporary, and not about claiming a place in it or diversifying it. (Mignolo, 2021, para 10)

Therefore, unlearning modernity's logic of knowledges and understanding therapy via consumption of clinical knowledges, has to do with my intent to shift away from focusing on the analysis of clients as subjects of clinical interventions or illustrations for academic debate. I am not illustrating clinical case examples of mental health or family therapy practices here. But I do read and learn from clinical examples from colleagues with whom I share a cup of tea or not *en la tienda de Don Paco*–I am not suggesting that it is a practice that must be eradicated in any way.

Rather, in this chapter, I am positioning decoloniality to illustrate my understanding of the operation of mental health or family therapy colonial systems as a different point of entrance to unlearn and relearn knowledges on transformative practices or healing. *Por ejemplo*, during my classes at the university with folxs who are beginning their traineeship at a social service agency, many of which are 501(c)(3), I am not creating a movement in order for them to go and practice elsewhere or to go against the agency's practices. I actually encourage them to work there to learn about the system to better understand mental health monolanguage and monologic while serving families who cannot afford to go elsewhere. Therefore, our conversations include discussing their work within the context of the funding sources of their training sites and how it shapes the expectations the site has for them as therapists. In these conversations, I do not teach decoloniality. Instead, I am guided by decolonial ethics as in Mexican sociologist Rolando Vázquez (2022); kinds of decolonial questions such as with whose eyes are therapists looking and through whose funded untaxed institutional eyes are we being made to see?

Notwithstanding, other colleagues might certainly have different analyses on decoloniality and decolonization, informed by proposals from various geopolitics and body politics. My perspective of decoloniality comes from the geopolitics and body politics of Abya Yala, el Caribe, and Eastern Europe. My enfleshed experiences as an immigrant in the U.S. led me to read literature other than therapy—because therapy did not provide understandable frameworks. Within the last few years, among the existing fascinating wide literature on decolonization, I have been drawn to the work of the decolonial option that I have been referencing throughout this chapter. I have attended specific training on decoloniality outside academia (similar to how I continued to study narrative therapy after my professor Jim Hibel introduced it to me during my doctoral studies) that connected to the history of my body as a racialized Colombiana. I studied with the GLEFAS, a Latin American group of study, formation, and feminist action founded by Afro-Dominican feminist activist Yuderkys Espinoso Miñoso in 2007; the Maria Lugones Decolonial Summer School led by Walter Mignolo and Rolando Vázquez in The Netherlands, and the Decolonizing Knowledges and Power: Postcolonial studies, decolonial horizons program led by Ramón Grosfoguel in Barcelona.

Of the many activists across these programs who facilitated these trainings, none were therapists or taught therapy—but taught me a lot about therapy and how blinded I have become by the violent dispossession of knowledges throughout my entire education. From them, I learned, lived, sensed, imagined, received, and became inspired about transformative possibilities that are not dependent on modernity's approval, funds, inclusion, legitimization, or binary dismantlement. Agreeing with Maldonado-Torres, et al., (2023) work from the Martinique psychiatrist Frantz Fanon:

> [T]o the recognition of exclusion, the modern/colonial framework proposes inclusion as the cure. But inclusion often becomes just another word for assimilation within a process of minimal change. With inclusion as a goal, modernity continues to work toward an idea whose value is affirmed in a way that prevents recognition of the catastrophic character of exclusion in the first place.... [and lead us to] remaining ignorant of the catastrophic scale of violence, dispossession, and injustice in the making of modernity/coloniality. (p. 536–537).

Rendering Capitalism a Witness: Family Therapists Knowing Otherwise

I hope to have illustrated above the tremendous reach of capitalism and modernity's politics of knowledges in family therapy—it is after all a global power. For the Peruvian sociologist

Anibal Quijano (2000) and Romanian philosopher Ovidiu Tichindeleanu (2010), the implacable totality of capitalism cannot disappear completely to be replaced by *un equivalente*;

> the radical thinking of alternatives to capitalism depends upon the development of an epistemic space of alternatives that identifies *tactics of resistance in co-existence with capitalism as the basis of anti-capitalist politics*. (Tichindeleanu, 2010, p. 324. Emphasis in the original)

The alternatives to capitalism for family therapists mean alternatives to universal modernity's therapy and the logic of its economy of untaxed, taxed, or bubble-wrapped knowledges and practices that are solely driven by Eurocentric evidence-based and competitive hierarchical relationality. Decolonial alternatives are, therefore, not about developing new different family therapies but alternatives to institutionalized, universal, monetized, taken-for-granted, and dependency-driven family therapies (Escobar, 2020), even though we still have to work within those structures. These are alternatives whereby family therapists delink from binaries and toward the co-existence of capitalist and noncapitalist (Tichindeleanu, 2010) knowledges and practices. Tichindeleanu proposes:

> The non-capitalist alternative can only become real by acknowledging the actual historical experience as a valid point of departure [of the field and its practices]. Only then, capitalism stops being an incommensurable totality, size and materiality can finally be added to the equation, and the capitalist economy emerges as a finite form in the universe of daily economical transactions. (p.10)

Co-existence recognizes the existence of capitalism in family therapy but is reduced in scale, means, geography, and power (Tichindeleanu, 2010). In turn, it means to humble modernity (Vázquez, 2012) toward dialogues across epistemic differences and relationalities with voices from the outside of professionalism, academia, textbooks, journals, etc., whose knowledges and practices have been annihilated. Therefore, in addition to extensive grant-based practices of family therapy embedded in capitalism that therapy will continue to depend on in the foreseeable future, autonomous healing is possible (polanco, 2024). This is when we search for relational and contextual practices already happening across various cultures in places that professionalism and academia have dismissed. These are autonomous to the governance of the marketplace of therapy. In doing so, we render capitalism a witness to other economies based on relationality and solidarity.

The co-existence of autonomous healing and capitalist approaches would also mean for those of us in academia, to train therapists on the European foundations of family therapy to develop skills to search in the elite literature for capitalist best practices for Eurocentrically defined clinical problems. This, however, is done by locating European-based practice as one humble perspective to respond to suffering among many others. And also, it would mean engaging people studying in family therapy programs not from their capitalist social role as therapists but as community members forging transformative relationships with other community members, partners, *comadres*, children, grandparents, *concuñes*, caretakers, siblings, classmates, roommates, living mates, animal companions, or *otres comuneres*. That means to locate knowledges and practices learned as something not to be applied onto clients within the binary of separation therapist-client but as life-giving learnings to re-exist in a shared community.

An autonomous healing framework to practice also means that, as in my conversations with folxs who study in the family therapy program at the university at which I work, learning how to be in community with a person whose unsuffering not only depends on the therapist possessing the family therapy knowledges to be delivered but to accompany families to draw healing practices from their memories about their sensing, thinking, doing, caring, and storytelling. We would depart from the premise that people who come into family therapy programs to learn or to teach and people who come to therapy consultations are not knowledge-orphans who ought to depend on European, patriarchal white knowledges to know how to engage in solidarity and healing relationally. Our recognition as knowers seeks to undo coloniality's annihilation of memory via capitalist eurocentrism, hence "the task of remembering who we are in a system that makes us forget and captures us as being only one in the present" (Vázquez, 2020), as I attempted to do in this chapter, is critical. In the words of activist Maya Kaqchiquel from Guatemala Aura Cumes (2022), the annihilation of knowledges means the destruction of memory:

> Colonization ontologically reinvented the colonized when it provoked the destruction of memory via the annihilation of knowledges, and when it sought to impose identities of orphanhood and servitude. The ontological and epistemological colonization seeks to destroy those peoples of ancient pasts and leave 'masses' of 'miserable' 'Indians without past', 'demon worshipers', 'barbarians', who shouldn't rebel against the colonial servitude and looting, but rather be grateful for been rescued by 'those good Christians'. This way, the bodies whose memories have been erased would be more useful for forced labor, for those who do not remember that they were once free did not seek their freedom. For this reason, the annihilation of memory is crucial to the perpetuation of colonial domination (para 2).

Therefore, with people interested in healing and transformative actions, whom I have called here therapists or family therapists, either via therapy or otherwise, conversations that locate our racialized bodies, erased histories, and humiliated stories are the point of departure for unlearning modernity, not to dismantle it, but to find its cracks (polanco et al., 2024). This recognizes that all knowledges comes from places and bodies, and that the places and bodies from where we come are also knowledged, *sabedoras*, and have transformational force. This requires us, however, to reposition our listening:

> Under the sign of the task of listening modernity appears as a system that holds the monopoly of speaking, of broadcasting, the monopoly of non-listening. Modernity appears as a system that silences the other, or better that produces the other as silent, non-existent or as 'pure representation' (Vázquez, 2012, p. 244)

We have been educated by fundable knowledges rendering us deaf to our own histories in favor of the histories, bodies, languages, grammars, and storytellings of Europe and Anglo-America. Listening from an ethical orientation that conceives knowledges as a relationality and as something that not only Europe and the US has (polanco and Pham, 2024; Vázquez, 2012) is also critical. It means for us to listen to the silenced, including our own ancestries, many of whom are *comuneres*, or people we live in a community with who might not have doctoral degrees, licenses, or published texts.

Note

1 I began writing this chapter during the Biden-Harris administration. By the time I completed the final edits for its publication, Trump had just been reelected for his second tenure as the president of the United States. During his first 100 days, he signed a series of executive orders, including a freeze in federal funding, among other sectors, directly impacting nonprofit mental health programs and diversity and inclusion initiatives. This disrupted organizations. Their services faced reduced services or closing nationwide. This shift in administration underscored the influence of the coloniality of knowledges and capitalism, where therapy services are deeply embedded in the marketplace. It also highlighted the administrative control of mental health under the civilizatory promise of progress and democracy of modernity, which dictates what is deemed worthy of any investment, under what terms, by whom and for whom, and, most crucially, in whose interest.

References

Cumes, A. (2022). *Decolonizing politics and theories from the Abya Yala*. E-International Relations.

Dussel, E. (2013). *Ethics of liberation: In the age of globalization and exclusion*. Duke University Press

Escobar, A. (2020) *Pluriversal politics: The real and the possible*. Duke University Press

Espinosa Miñoso, Y. (2022). *De por qué es necesario un feminismo descolonial*. Icaria.

Espinosa Miñoso, Y., Lugones, M., & Maldonado-Torres, N. (Eds.). (2022). *Decolonial feminism in Abya Yala: Caribbean, Meso, and South American contributions and challenges*. Rowman & Littlefield

Esche, C. Vázquez, R., & Cos Rebollo, T. (2013). Decolonial aesthesis: Weaving each other, a conversation. *L'Internationale Online*. Retrieved from https://archive-20142024.internationaleonline.org/opinions/1106_decolonial_aesthesis_weaving_each_other_a_conversation/

Galeano, E. (2009). *Mirrors: Stories of almost everyone*. Nation Books.

Grosfoguel, R. (2013). The structure of knowledge in Westernized universities: Epistemic racism/sexism and the four genocides/epistemicides of the long 16th century. *Human Architecture: Journal of The Sociology of Self-Knowledge, 1*, 73–90.

Graham, M., Hale, S. A., & Stephens, M. (2011). *Geographies of the world's knowledge*. Convoco! Edition.

Icaza Garza, R., & Vázquez, R. (2018). Diversity or Decolonization? Researching Diversity at the University of Amsterdam. In G. K. Bhambra, D. Gebrial, & K. Nişancıoğlu (Eds.), *Decolonizing the University* (pp. 108–28). Pluto Press.

López-Calvo, I. (Interviewer). (2016, November 26). *Coloniality is not over, it is all over: Interview with Dr. Walter Mignolo* [Interview]. Ignacio López-Calvo's blog. https://ignaciolopezcalvo.blogspot.com/2017/01/coloniality-is-not-over-it-is-all-over.html

Lugones, M., & Crowley, P. M. (Eds.). (2025). *Decolonial thinking: Resistant meanings and communal other-sense*. Indiana University Press.

Maldonado-Torres, N., Bañales, X., Lee-Oliver, L., Niyogi, S., Ponce, A., & Radebe, Z. (2023). Decolonial pedagogy against the coloniality of justice. *Educational Theory, 73*(4), 530–50. https://doi.org/10.1111/edth.12596

McKittrick, K. (Ed.). (2015). *Sylvia Wynter: On being human as praxis*. Duke University Press.

Mignolo, W. D. (2021). *The politics of decolonial investigations*. Duke University Press.

polanco, m., Hanson, N. D., Hernández, C., Le Feber, T., Medina, S., Old Bucher, S., Rivera, E. I., Rodriguez, I., Vela, E., Velasco, B., & Le Feber, J. (2020). How to be unfaithful to Eurocentrism: A Spanglish decolonial critique to knowledge gentrification, captivity and storycide in qualitative research. *The Qualitative Report, 25*(1), 145–65. https://doi.org/10.46743/2160-3715/2020.4098

polanco, m., & Pham, A. (2024). Suicide and the Coloniality of the Senses, Time, and Being: The Aesthetics of Death Desires. *Social Sciences, 13*(11), 576. https://doi.org/10.3390/socsci13110576

polanco, m. (2024). Autonomous healing: Calling on the unfuckwithables, putamente radicales. In E. Segal, C. Hoff, & J. Cho (Eds.), *An encyclopedia of radical helping* (pp. 68–70). Thick Press.

polanco, m., Kumar, P., Olyad, F., & Enemark, C. H. (2024). Decolonially speaking, sensing, and thinking: Racialized tuition-based family therapists learning without teaching. *Family Process, 00*, 1–14. https://doi.org/10.1111/famp.13034

Eisinger J., Ernsthausen J., & Kiel P. (2021). *The secret IRS files: Trove of never-before-seen records reveal how the wealthiest avoid income tax*. ProPublica. https://www.propublica.org/article/the-secret-irs-files-trove-of-never-before-seen-records-reveal-how-the-wealthiest-avoid-income-tax

Quijano, A. (2000). Colonialidad y modernidad/racionalidad. *Perú Indígena 13*, 201–46. Substance Abuse and Mental Health Services Administration.

The Substance Abuse and Mental Health Services Administration (SAMHSA). (2024). *Biden-Harris administration announces $46.8 million in behavioral health funding opportunities to advance President Biden's unity agenda as part of May Mental Health Awareness Month*. (2024). https://www.samhsa.gov/newsroom/press-announcements/20240508/biden-harris-administration-announces-46-million-behavioral-health-funding-opportunities

The substance abuse and mental health services administration (SAMHSA). (2023). SAMHSA's 2023–2026 Strategic Plan. https://www.samhsa.gov/about-us/strategic-plan

Tichindeleanu, O. (2010). Non-capitalist economies and the post-communist transition. *Science & Society*, 74(3), 322–43.

Hodge S., (2024). Reining in America's $3.3 Trillion tax-exempt economy. *Tax Foundation*. https://taxfoundation.org/research/all/federal/501c3-nonprofit-organization-tax-exempt/

Vallega, A. A. (2019). *Tiempo y liberación: Exordio a pensamientos liberatorios, vivenciales y decoloniales*. Akal.

Vázquez, R. (2022). *Transforming institutions: Decolonial aesthesis and transition in art, design, and fashion*. Keynote presented at the Jan van Eyck Academie. https://www.janvaneyck.nl/videos/771696182

Vázquez, R. (2020). *Vistas of modernity: Decolonial aesthetics and the end of the contemporary*. Jap Sam Books.

Vázquez, R. (2012). Towards a decolonial critique of modernity: Buen vivir, relationality, and the task of listening. In R. Fornet-Betancourt (Ed.), *Capital, poverty, development* (pp. 241–52). Mainz.

Vázquez, R. (2011). Translation as erasure: Thoughts on modernity's epistemic violence. *Journal of Historical Sociology, 24*(1), 27–44. https://doi.org/10.1111/j.1467-6443.2011.01387.x

Walsh, C. E. (2023a). *Rising up, living on*. Duke University Press.

U.S. Department of Health and Human Services (2024). *Biden-Harris administration announces historic investment to integrate mental health and substace use disorder treatment into primary care*. https://www.hhs.gov/about/news/2024/09/19/biden-harris-administration-announces-historic-investment-integrate-mental-health-substance-disorder-treatment-primary-care.html

United States Bureau of Labor Statistics. (2023). *Employment projections: 2023–2033*. U.S. Department of Labor. https://www.bls.gov/emp/

Conclusion

A Vision Beyond The Jar: The Journey Toward Liberation

Jennifer M. Sampson and Fiona E. O'Farrell

We began this book with the story of a butterfly—one that went to sleep in a sunny, open field only to wake up in a jar. What was once vast and unbounded had become small and confined, leaving the butterfly disoriented, questioning, and searching for a way out. This metaphor has carried us through these pages because it mirrors the experience of awakening to systemic oppression. Whether through personal experiences, within our work as therapists, or in the lives of the clients we serve, there comes a moment when the structures we once took for granted—therapy, education, policy, and institutions—come into sharper focus. We begin to see the ways they have been built to control rather than liberate, to maintain power rather than to nurture collective well-being. Like the butterfly in the jar, we ask: *Where am I? How did I get here? And how do I break free?*

For therapists, "seeing the jar" means recognizing the colonial legacies, Eurocentric frameworks, and oppressive systems that have shaped our field. It means acknowledging the ways these structures have confined not only our clients but also our own training, our clinical models, and even our very imaginations about what healing and justice can look like. But awareness alone is not enough. Decolonization is not a passive observation—it is an act of resistance. It is the conscious, intentional work of dismantling harmful systems and cocreating pathways toward something better.

This is not easy work. It asks us to interrogate our own positionality—our identities, our privileges, our assumptions. It requires us to acknowledge where we have been complicit in upholding the very systems we seek to dismantle. And it demands that we look beyond individual healing to challenge the structures that produce harm in the first place. Yet, as difficult as this work is, it is also deeply freeing. Decolonization invites us into a new way of thinking—one that prioritizes relationship over hierarchy, collective care over individualism, and cultural knowledge over imposed norms. It calls us to move beyond the narrow confines of Western therapy and into a more expansive, interconnected, and justice-oriented way of being.

This book is just the beginning of that journey. Within these pages, you have been invited to see the jar—to critically examine the frameworks we use to understand families, relationships, and human development. You have explored the histories of colonialism, systemic inequities, and structural violence that continue to shape the world around us. And you have been given tools to imagine something different—something more liberatory, more just, and more attuned to the full complexity of human experience.

But knowing the jar exists isn't enough. We must act. Decolonization demands more than awareness—it requires us to disrupt oppressive structures in our work, challenge the status quo in our professions, and advocate for systemic change. It asks us to move from

DOI: 10.4324/9781032679082-15

simply "doing no harm" to actively building conditions where families, relationships, and communities can thrive. This is not a destination we will reach but an ongoing process that requires humility, courage, and a steadfast commitment to justice.

The butterfly cannot undo the fact that it woke up in the jar. But it can understand where it is, how it got there, and what it will take to return to the open world where it belongs. As practitioners, we, too, must grapple with the realities of the systems we work within while holding onto the possibility of something greater. We must stretch our wings, test the boundaries of what we thought was possible, and begin to imagine a world beyond these glass walls.

So, as you close this book and step back into your work, we hope you'll carry this metaphor with you—not as a simple story but as a framework for reflection and action. See the jar. Understand it. Challenge it. And most importantly, commit to breaking it.

Because beyond those walls, there is a vast and beautiful world waiting—one filled with possibilities for liberation, equity, and connection. Together, we can cocreate that world where the jar is a distant memory.

The Unraveling of Progress

For years, the field of mental health—and systemic therapy in particular—has been slowly moving toward greater awareness of oppression, equity, and justice. Concepts like cultural humility, intersectionality, and decolonization have entered graduate programs, supervision models, and therapeutic frameworks. Institutions have begun integrating anti-racist and decolonized approaches into training (Xin, 2023) and many practitioners have worked to center justice in their practice (Mullan & Jones, 2024). It has been far from perfect, but it was movement and expansion.

And now, we are watching it unravel.

As we are drafting this book for publication, efforts to dismantle systems of oppression are actively being met with systemic backlash. In the name of "neutrality," diversity, equity, and inclusion (DEI) initiatives are being stripped from workplaces and universities (Gretzinger et al., 2025). In the name of "parental rights," entire histories are being erased from school curricula (Standford, 2023). In the name of "protecting free speech," institutions are restricting discussions about systemic racism, colonialism, and intersectionality (McRae, 2024). The language of justice is being distorted and weaponized to reinforce the very systems it sought to challenge.

These are not abstract shifts. The families we serve are feeling the impact. Laws restricting access to reproductive healthcare disproportionately harm marginalized communities, particularly Black and Indigenous women (Suarez-Balcazar et al., 2023). Anti-LGBTQ+ policies target queer and trans youth, threatening their safety, mental health, and fundamental rights (Khonina & Salway, 2024). Immigration policies that separate families and strip protections from asylum seekers are fueling intergenerational trauma (Risely, 2023). The rollback of civil rights protections is not an academic discussion—it is a direct assault on the well-being of the very people therapists and human-service professionals are meant to support.

For many therapists, students, and mental health professionals, this moment feels deeply unsettling. We were trained to believe in a field that promotes healing, advocacy, and equity. And yet, we are now practicing in a system that is actively working to suppress conversations about oppression and restrict access to justice-oriented care.

This is not just a political moment; it is a professional crisis.

Join us in critically engaging with these shifts—if we are not actively resisting the erasure of systemic oppression from our field—then we are complicit in maintaining these systems. Therapy does not exist in a vacuum. The policies enacted today will shape our clients' families, relationships, and lives for generations to come.

The Field of Family Therapy is Interconnected

Therapy has never been separate from the broader social, political, and cultural landscape. Yet, as mental health professionals, we are often trained to think of our work as neutral—free from the influence of power, oppression, and systemic inequities. This illusion of neutrality is precisely what allows oppressive systems to thrive within our field. And now, as policies and institutional shifts actively work to suppress conversations about justice and equity, therapy is at risk of becoming a tool of compliance rather than liberation.

The rollback of DEI initiatives, restrictions on discussions of systemic oppression, and the increasing push for "political neutrality" in education and practice are not just inconveniences—they are direct attacks on the ability of therapists to provide ethical, effective, and affirming care.

- *Erasure of Systemic Oppression from Training & Education:* Graduate programs that once aimed to integrate anti-oppressive frameworks are now pressured to remove content related to racial justice, colonialism, and intersectionality (Brown, 2025). This means that a new generation of therapists is entering the field without a critical understanding of how systems of oppression shape mental health. Without this foundation, practitioners risk reinforcing harmful narratives that blame individuals for struggles that are rooted in systemic inequities.
- *Restrictions on Gender-Affirming and Culturally Responsive Care:* Laws targeting trans and nonbinary individuals have placed therapists in impossible positions—forced to choose between ethical, evidence-based care and legal restrictions that deny people the right to affirm their identities (Hope & Puckett, 2024). Similarly, efforts to erase discussions of race, migration, and family separation from professional practice mean that many therapists must navigate an ethical minefield: follow policies designed to maintain oppression or provide the care their clients actually need.
- *The Threat of Licensure and Professional Regulation:* As states introduce legislation to restrict discussions of systemic oppression, many mental health professionals are questioning whether their licenses will be threatened for practicing through an anti-oppressive lens. If talking about racism, structural violence, or colonialism becomes framed as "political indoctrination," therapists risk being reported, disciplined, or even disbarred for simply doing their jobs.

The impact of these shifts is not theoretical. It is real and immediate. We are witnessing a coordinated effort to push therapy back into a model that prioritizes compliance—one that strips the field of creativity, envisioning, and a unique position to address the root causes of client and family distress. This book has zoomed in on one aspect of the influence of colonized legacies on this field. But the jar can be viewed from many angles, and we invite the reader to find the lens that they might be best suited to challenge. Because therapy that does not challenge oppression is not therapy at all.

The Power of Community and Collaboration

Examining and exploring family development from a decolonized approach was not a solitary endeavor. The authors of these chapters embraced collaboration across disciplines, across communities, and across generations. When we engage in expansive collaboration, we create new possibilities that move us beyond critique and into action. This means:

- Centering marginalized voices in policy and decision-making spaces.
- Redefining expertise to honor community-based knowledge as equally valid to academic training.
- Building partnerships that are rooted in mutual accountability rather than top-down interventions.
- Advocating for structural change that extends beyond professional practice and into the social, legal, and economic systems that shape our lives.

A decolonized approach is not about making minor adjustments to existing systems—it is about fundamentally reimagining how we relate to one another.

Beyond Therapy: Expanding the Reach of a Decolonized Approach

While this book has focused on decolonizing family development in systemic therapy, its principles stretch far beyond the walls of the therapy room. The frameworks, tools, and perspectives explored here are not just for therapists—they are for anyone working within systems where human relationships, justice, and care intersect. Decolonization is not a task confined to mental health professionals; it is a universal call to action that challenges us to rethink how we engage with families, communities, and institutions.

At its core, a decolonized approach is about relationships—our relationship to each other, to the communities we serve, and to the structures we navigate. Whether you are a social worker, educator, healthcare provider, or community organizer, these relationships are central to your work. The same colonial legacies that shape therapy also permeate schools, hospitals, workplaces, and legal systems. By adopting a decolonized lens, professionals across disciplines can begin to dismantle oppressive structures and build more equitable spaces for those they serve.

Decolonizing our understanding of families and human development means moving beyond narrow, discipline-specific frameworks. It invites us to think more expansively about the systems we work within and the ways they either support or harm marginalized communities. Consider the following examples:

- **Education:** Teachers and school administrators can apply a decolonized approach by recognizing how colonial values influence curricula, disciplinary practices, and the marginalization of non-Western histories and knowledge. Educators can disrupt harmful systems and foster inclusive, empowering learning environments by centering relationality, cultural strengths, and student agency.
- **Healthcare:** Medical providers often operate within systems that devalue cultural practices and impose Western norms of health and wellness. By embracing a decolonized perspective, they can validate and integrate diverse healing practices, advocate for equitable access to care, and challenge the systemic biases that disproportionately harm marginalized communities.

- **Community Organizing and Advocacy:** Organizers and activists can use a decolonized framework to address systemic inequities at their roots. By centering the voices of those most impacted by oppression and building coalitions rooted in relationality and respect, they can advance systemic change in ways that honor the collective wisdom of communities.

In each of these examples, the decolonized approach encourages practitioners to ask: *Whose voices are missing? Whose experiences have been erased or devalued? And how can we disrupt systems of harm to cocreate spaces that honor the full complexity and diversity of human experiences?*

The Power of Partnership

For too long, the helping professions have centered the "expert"—the clinician, the educator, the policymaker—at the expense of the communities they serve. This hierarchy perpetuates the very power imbalances we seek to dismantle. A decolonized approach flips this dynamic, recognizing that true expertise resides within communities themselves. It invites practitioners to step back, listen deeply, and partner with communities as equals.

Collaboration isn't just about sharing resources or working together on projects; it's about building relationships grounded in respect and reciprocity. This means honoring the cultural knowledge, traditions, and values of the communities we serve and being accountable to their needs—not imposing our own agendas.

Consider these examples:

- Therapists Partnering with Cultural Leaders: Imagine a therapist working with a family from a Somali immigrant community. Instead of solely relying on Western therapeutic models, they collaborate with local community leaders, such as elders or religious figures, to better understand the family's cultural context. This partnership not only enriches the therapeutic process but also fosters trust and cultural alignment.
- Community-Led Reproductive Justice Advocacy: A group of community organizers launches a campaign to address disparities in maternal health outcomes for Black women. Health professionals join the effort not as leaders but as collaborators, providing data, resources, and advocacy while centering the voices and experiences of Black mothers themselves.
- Education as a Collaborative Process: In a rural Indigenous community, school counselors work alongside tribal leaders to design a curriculum that integrates traditional knowledge, language, and cultural practices. By grounding education in the community's values, they create a system that uplifts students' identities and strengthens intergenerational ties.

Each of these examples underscores the transformative potential of partnership. When we engage in true collaboration, we open the door to more equitable and effective practices.

Rebuilding Trust

Collaboration is impossible without trust—and for many marginalized communities, trust in institutions has been eroded by histories of harm. From the forced removal of Indigenous children to the systemic neglect of Black families, these legacies have left deep scars. Rebuilding trust requires more than good intentions; it is fully experienced and received in action, accountability, and a willingness to confront uncomfortable truths.

We continue to urge practitioners to ask themselves:

- *How has my profession contributed to systemic harm?*
- *What steps am I taking to repair that harm?*
- *How can I demonstrate my commitment to justice, not just in my words but in my actions?*

Rebuilding trust is a long-term process. It requires showing up consistently, honoring commitments, and centering the voices of those who have been historically excluded. Most importantly, it requires humility—a recognition that we don't have all the answers and that communities are the ultimate experts in their own lives.

Honoring the Community Behind This Book

The very creation of this book is a testament to the power of community and collaboration. It is not the work of a single voice but a chorus of perspectives, lived experiences, and cultural wisdom. The authors who contributed to this collection brought with them their own stories, expertise, and courage to challenge the status quo. Together, we have woven a tapestry of insights that could not exist in isolation.

This book reflects the diversity of systemic therapy itself. It includes voices from a wide range of social locations, cultural contexts, and professional backgrounds. Each chapter is a piece of the larger conversation, offering a unique perspective on how to decolonize family systems and relationships. Some authors share deeply personal reflections; others offer tools and frameworks drawn from their clinical practice. All of them contribute to the larger goal of dismantling oppressive systems and reimagining what is possible.

This collaborative process was not just about sharing ideas; it was about modeling the very principles this book advocates for. We aimed to hold space for each other's voices, challenged each other's assumptions, and leaned into the discomfort of growth. The result is not a single perspective, but a collection of works that reflect the complexity, richness, and beauty of decolonized thinking.

Community as a Source of Strength

Decolonization is not just about dismantling systems of oppression; it's about rediscovering and sharing the strength, wisdom, and resilience that have always existed within our communities. For centuries, these communities have resisted colonial domination through acts of relationality and solidarity. They have cared for one another, built networks of support, and preserved their cultural knowledge despite immense systemic pressures. In practice, centering community means shifting our focus from individual outcomes to collective well-being. It means recognizing that healing is not an isolated process but a relational one, rooted in connection to others. Whether it's fostering mutual aid networks, celebrating cultural traditions, or advocating for systemic change, communities have always been—and will continue to be—a wellspring of strength and transformation.

A Call to Collaborate

The work of decolonization cannot succeed without a shared commitment to collaboration. As practitioners, we must see ourselves as part of a broader movement—one that includes clients, communities, activists, educators, and countless others working toward justice. This book has provided tools and frameworks to guide your journey, but the real work begins when you take these ideas into your relationships, partnerships, and communities.

So, let's return to the metaphor of the butterfly and the jar. While the butterfly may feel alone in its struggle, it is not. There are others—therapists, community leaders, advocates—working to dismantle the glass walls and create spaces where everyone can thrive. Together, we can create a world that not only acknowledges the jar but works to shatter it, replacing it with something far more expansive and liberating.

The invitation is clear: engage deeply with the communities you serve. Build partnerships rooted in mutual respect and accountability. Amplify the voices of those whose stories have been ignored. And hold onto the power of collective action to transform systems and lives.

In the end, the butterfly's journey is not just about escaping the jar—it's about rediscovering the vast, open world where it was meant to thrive. Similarly, decolonization is not merely about dismantling oppressive systems; it is about imagining and building something better in its place.

This book does not claim to have all the answers, but it offers a place to begin. It is an invitation—to think critically, to act boldly, and to refuse to accept the limits of the systems we have inherited.

As you leave these pages behind, we encourage you to ask yourself:

- *What is my role in this work?*
- *What systems am I embedded in, and how can I disrupt them?*
- *How can I use my voice, my position, my influence to create change?*

There is a vast community of people—activists, educators, healers, and advocates—who are engaged in this same struggle. You are not alone in breaking the jar. And beyond it, there is a world waiting to be built. Let's build it together.

The Ethics of Decolonization: Responsibility and Accountability

Decolonizing family systems work is not just a technical exercise or theoretical framework; it is deeply ethical work that requires practitioners to confront their own complicity in systemic oppression. With great intention comes great responsibility. The process of decolonization demands humility, accountability, and an unwavering commitment to doing no further harm—qualities that, in many ways, align with the foundational ethics of therapy itself. For practitioners, this raises critical questions: *How do we ensure that our efforts to decolonize do not perpetuate the same harm we seek to dismantle? How can we navigate the complexities of this work with care, cultural humility, and a willingness to learn from mistakes?*

In this section, we explore the ethical challenges and opportunities inherent in adopting a decolonized approach to systemic therapy, offering guidance for walking this path with integrity and respect.

Navigating Ethical Dilemmas

The journey of decolonization and any endeavor that involves the real lives of human beings has fertile ground for ethical dilemmas. As practitioners strive to disrupt oppressive systems, they often find themselves navigating gray areas where answers are not clear-cut. For example:

- Cultural Appropriation vs. Cultural Integration: How do we honor and incorporate cultural knowledge, traditions, and practices without appropriating them or divorcing them from their original context? Practitioners must continuously ask themselves: Are we centering the voices and expertise of the communities these practices belong to? Are we seeking permission and building reciprocal relationships?
- Tokenization vs. Authentic Representation: In the quest to "diversify" therapeutic approaches, there is a risk of tokenizing marginalized voices or treating cultural practices as add-ons to existing models. True decolonization requires going beyond surface-level inclusion to fundamentally reimagine how therapy is conceptualized, taught, and practiced.
- Challenging Power Dynamics: Decolonization involves challenging entrenched hierarchies within therapeutic relationships, institutions, and broader systems. This can be uncomfortable for practitioners who have been socialized to see themselves as "experts." Ethical decolonization requires a willingness to let go of this control, share power, and prioritize the agency of clients and communities.

Commitment to Ethical Practice

To navigate these challenges, practitioners must ground themselves in a set of ethical commitments that reflect the principles of decolonization:

- Cultural Humility: Decolonization is not a destination but an ongoing process of learning, unlearning, and growth. Practitioners must remain humble, acknowledging what they do not know and being open to feedback from those they serve.
- Reciprocity and Accountability: Ethical decolonization is not about extracting knowledge or resources from communities—it is about building reciprocal relationships that honor their contributions and prioritize their needs. Practitioners must remain accountable to the communities they engage with, ensuring their actions align with the principles of justice and equity.
- Transparency and Reflexivity: Practitioners must regularly reflect on their own positionality, biases, and the potential impact of their work. This includes being transparent with clients and communities about their intentions, limitations, and the steps they are taking to decolonize their practice.
- Centering Lived Experience: Ethical practice requires centering the voices, knowledge, and lived experiences of marginalized communities. This means actively listening, amplifying these voices, and cocreating solutions rather than imposing outside frameworks.

Our call to community engagement will be the most effective way to navigate these aspects of the practice. The more you surround yourself with those who can lovingly "call you in," the more you will embrace these grey areas with continued acknowledgment of your own positionality and journey.

The Courage to Be Imperfect

Decolonization is inherently messy, and practitioners will inevitably make mistakes along the way. The ethical imperative is not to avoid imperfection—it is to approach the process with humility, accountability, and a commitment to repair. When harm occurs, practitioners who are willing to acknowledge it, learn from it, and take steps to make amends will continue to grow and expand their practice. This work requires courage to confront uncomfortable truths, disrupt entrenched systems, and hold oneself accountable to the communities we serve. It also requires vulnerability and the willingness to admit when we are wrong, to seek guidance, and to continue learning even when the path is unclear.

Honoring the Authors' Ethical Contributions

The community of authors who contributed to this book exemplify these ethical commitments in their work. Their chapters are not just academic exercises—they are acts of care, accountability, and solidarity with the communities they serve. By sharing their knowledge, reflections, and lived experiences, these authors have modeled courage, vulnerability, and the risk of being imperfect. Their work invites us to think differently and to imagine new possibilities for viewing growth and development, systemic therapy, and family systems. It is a reminder that ethical practice is not a static set of rules—it is a dynamic, relational process that evolves in response to the needs of the people and communities we aim to support.

A Shared Responsibility

The ethical considerations outlined in this section are not just for individual practitioners—they are a call to action for the entire field. Decolonizing family systems requires collective accountability: from academic institutions that shape our training to professional organizations that set standards of practice, from community organizations to policymakers. Together, we can build structures that support ethical decolonization and hold one another accountable for commitment to reimagining and expansive practice.

A Shared Vision for Liberation

As we reach the conclusion of this book, it's time to turn our attention to the future: *What does an equitable, decolonized field of systemic therapy look like? How can we, as individuals and as a collective, take meaningful steps to disrupt harmful systems and cocreate liberatory spaces for families, relationships, and communities?* At its core, it is about imagining new possibilities—dreaming beyond the limitations of colonial frameworks and daring to believe in a world where everyone is free to thrive in relationships.

A Vision Beyond the Jar: An Invitation to Join the Movement

As we step away from this collective exploration, we want to leave you with this thought: the work of decolonization is both deeply personal and profoundly communal. It begins within ourselves—our assumptions, biases, and practices—and ripples outward to the systems and communities we touch. It is not easy work. It will ask much of you—courage, humility, and persistence. But it is also profoundly rewarding, offering the possibility of transformation not just for others but also for yourself.

This book is not the end of the journey—it is a beginning. It is a starting point for rethinking systemic therapy and imagining what justice and liberation can look like in our field. And it is a reminder that you are not alone in this work. You are part of a broader community of practitioners, educators, and advocates who share your commitment to creating a world where all families and individuals can thrive.

We invite you to take what you've learned here and carry it forward—to your clients, your classrooms, your colleagues, and your communities. We invite you to share your own stories, perspectives, and ideas, adding to the collective wisdom that will continue to shape this field. And we invite you to dream boldly, act courageously, and hold tightly to the vision of a more just and equitable future.

Ultimately, the butterfly's journey is not just about escaping the jar—it's about rediscovering the vast, open world where it was meant to thrive. Similarly, decolonization is not merely about dismantling oppressive systems; it is about imagining and building something better in its place.

This book does not claim to have all the answers. It is a beginning, not an endpoint. A foundation, not a final word. It is an invitation: to think critically, to act boldly, and to refuse to accept the limits of the systems we have inherited.

And the work is far from over. At this moment, under the weight of escalating political agendas, legislative attacks on marginalized communities, and the resurgence of authoritarianism, this work has never been more urgent. The current administration is actively rolling back protections, restricting bodily autonomy, and reinforcing colonial frameworks of control and punishment. What we are witnessing is not just policy—it is the deliberate tightening of the jar's lid.

As long as oppression persists, our resistance must persist alongside it. This book is part of that resistance—a small but necessary act of rupture against the systems that seek to confine us. And resistance takes many forms. Some protest in the streets. Some organize and advocate. Others, like us, write.

What an Equitable Future Looks Like

Imagine a world where families are not pathologized for their differences but celebrated for their unique strengths and contributions; communities have access to culturally rooted healing practices, free from the constraints of colonial power dynamics; identities such as race, age, profession, sexuality, and gender are elements of internal authenticity to be shared relationally rather than categorized and ranked; advances in technology such as AI are resources shared openly for the betterment of our communities and the relief of undue labor; knowledges are not competitive or hierarchical but freely exchanged for the purpose of expansion and collective wisdom, capitalism does not dictate mental health access and funding; therapists are not gatekeepers but collaborators, working alongside clients to dismantle systemic barriers and build relational equity, policies prioritize the well-being of families and communities, ensuring access to reproductive healthcare, paid family leave, and other essential supports; education systems honor the knowledge and histories of all cultures, preparing future practitioners to engage in justice-oriented, decolonized work. Anything is possible.

This vision may feel ambitious, even overwhelming but it is not the product of a single mind or voice—it is a collective effort shaped by the contributions of the authors, practitioners, and communities who made this book possible. Their chapters, case studies, and reflections are more than academic insights; they are acts of care, resistance, and imagination. Together, they demonstrate the power of collective knowledge and collaboration in envisioning a better future.

Gratitude and Acknowledgments

As we conclude this book, we want to take a moment to reflect on the journey that brought us here and to express deep gratitude to everyone who made this work possible. This collection would not exist without the diverse voices and perspectives that came together to challenge the status quo, to dream of a better future, and to reimagine the possibilities of systemic therapy.

To the contributors who poured their expertise, lived experiences, and hearts into these chapters: thank you for your courage and generosity. Your willingness to share your stories, your knowledge, and your unique visions has created a body of work that we hope will inspire generations of therapists, educators, and advocates. This book is not just ours—it is a collective effort, a testament to the power of collaboration and shared purpose.

To the families, clients, and communities who have inspired us with their stories, struggles, and triumphs, thank you for teaching us what it means to be resilient, relational, and rooted in justice. Your lives and experiences have been the foundation of this work, reminding us of the importance of humility, accountability, and care in the work of decolonization.

To the readers who have joined us on this journey: thank you for your openness, your curiosity, and your commitment to growth. By engaging with this book, you have become part of a broader movement toward equity, liberation, and healing. We are grateful to have you as part of this community.

The Legacy of This Work

This book is not just a collection of chapters; it is an invitation to rethink, reimagine, and rebuild. It challenges you to look beyond the familiar frameworks of systemic therapy and to see the ways in which colonial legacies continue to shape the families and systems we work with. It offers you tools and perspectives to dismantle these legacies and cocreate spaces of justice and care.

But more than that, this book is part of an ongoing conversation—one that will continue long after you turn the final page. Decolonization is not a static process; it is a living, evolving practice that demands ongoing engagement, reflection, and action. We hope this book serves as both a guide and a catalyst for your own journey in this work.

Writing as Resistance: An Invitation to Future Editions

If you are an academic, clinician, student, thinker, or storyteller, your words have power. Your voice matters in the ongoing work of decolonization. This book exists because its authors dared to challenge what had been handed down to them and offer something new. And we know that this conversation is far from finished.

This is an open invitation. If you feel the pull to contribute, reach out. Let us know if you have seen the jar in ways we have not yet named. We welcome ideas, strategies, or resistance practices that can move this conversation forward. Because this book, like the decolonization of family development itself, is not meant to be static. It will grow, shift, and evolve with the collective knowledge and voices of those who refuse to accept the world as it is.

Closing Words

In the metaphor that began this book, we spoke of the butterfly waking up to find itself in a jar. We spoke of the questions it must ask—Where am I? How did I get here? How do I get out?—and of the work it must do to break free and reclaim the open sky. But we have come to understand that this work is not the butterfly's alone. It is ours as well. The jar was not built by the butterfly—it was built by systems of power, control, and domination. Working together will increase the likelihood of dismantling it.

And so, as we close, we leave you with this: *May you always remember that the jar is not the whole world. May you see the vast sky that lies beyond it. And may you never stop working toward the day when every family, every community, and every individual is free to soar.*

References

Boykins, B., Samman, S.K. (2023). Decolonizing Higher Education Through Incorporating Antiracist Pedagogy in Doctoral Students' Academics, Mentorship, and Training. In: Nice, L.A., Eppler, C. (eds) *Social Justice and Systemic Family Therapy Training*. AFTA SpringerBriefs in Family Therapy. Springer, Cham. https://doi.org/10.1007/978-3-031-29930-8_8

Brown, S. (2024, January). *Trump singled out these 130 colleges as possible targets for investigation. is yours on the list?*. Trump Singled Out These 130 Colleges as Possible Targets for Investigation. Is Yours on the List? https://www.chronicle.com/article/trump-singled-out-these-130-colleges-as-possible-targets-for-investigation-is-yours-on-the-list

Hope, D. A., & Puckett, J. A. (2024). Bans on Evidence-Based Care for Transgender and Gender Diverse People Present Risks for Clients and Dilemmas for Mental Health Providers. *Cognitive and Behavioral Practice, 31*(1), 15–19. https://doi.org/10.1016/j.cbpra.2023.12.003

Gretzinger, E., Hicks, M., Dutton, C., & Smith, J. (2025, March 3). *Tracking higher Ed's dismantling of Dei*. Tracking Higher Ed's Dismantling of DEI. https://www.chronicle.com/article/tracking-higher-eds-dismantling-of-dei

Khonina, M., & Salway, T. (2025). The rise of anti-trans laws and the role of public health advocacy. *Canadian Public Health Journal, 116*, 97–99. https://doi.org/10.17269/s41997-024-00942-1

McRae, E. G. (2024, April 25). *Censored, erased, and whitewashed: Jim Crow Education in the twenty-first century*. Poverty and Race Research Action Council. https://www.prrac.org/censored-erased-and-whitewashed-jim-crow-education-in-the-twenty-first-century-january-april-2024-p-r-article/

Mullan, P., & Jones, C. J. (2024). *Decolonizing therapy: oppression, historical trauma, and politicizing your practice*. Tantor Media.

Risley, A. (2023). 'Doing Harm Was the Point': Family Separations at the Border. *The International Journal of Children's Rights, 31*(4), 890–915. https://doi.org/10.1163/15718182-31040007

Stanford, L. (2023, September 12). *Parents' rights groups have mobilized. what does it mean for students?* Education Week. https://www.edweek.org/leadership/parents-rights-groups-have-mobilized-what-does-it-mean-for-students/2023/08

Suarez-Balcazar, Y., Buckingham, S., Rusch, D. B., Charvonia, A., Young, R. I., Lewis, R., Ford-Paz, R., Mehta, T. G., & Perez, C. M. (2024). Reproductive justice for Black, Indigenous, Women of Color: Uprooting race and colonialism. *American Journal of Community Psychology, 73*, 159–169. https://doi.org/10.1002/ajcp.12650

Index

Note: **Bold** page numbers refer to tables; *italic* page numbers refer to figures and page numbers followed by "n" denote endnotes.

ableism 91, 93, 95, 111
abortion 88, 90, 94, 103
"absent father" narratives 9–10
abstract reasoning 121
accountability: collective 228; systemic 104, 105, 112; *see also* self-accountability
acculturation 22, 23, 36; and family life cycle development 40–41; in refugee families 41–42
ACRT *see* agency-centered relational therapy
activism 21, 69
ADDRESSING model 22, 23, 50, 137–38, 193
ADHD 119, 120, 122–23, 125
adolescence 18, 23, 120, 140
adoption 88, 89, 111
adulthood 18, 23, 140
Adverse Child Experiences Study (ACES) 192
advocacy: in ethical AI development 76–77; as an intervention 27, 42, 69; reproductive justice 95, 103–04, 224; through storytelling 105; *see also* self-advocacy
affinity groups 37
Afghani refugee families 41–42
African cultures 28
African people 72
agency 187–89; in the body 189; and change 62; and connectedness 40; multidimensional fluency of 193–94; narrative approach to 192–93; restoration of 192–93, 199; violation of 189–94
agency-centered relational therapy (ACRT) 187–203; case studies 194–97; multicultural influences of 200–01; sequential leveraging 197–200
algorithms 73–74
All About Love: New Visions 33
ambivalence 108
analytic software 66, 67
ancestral knowledge 20, 135, 136

anti-immigrant policies 27
anxiety 55, 120
Aponte, Harry 49
arranged marriages 28, 29, 179
artificial intelligence (AI) 8, 66–77; biases 73; and colonialism 66, 70, 72, 74–76; facial recognition 74; implications for therapists 75–77; and mental health care 66–68, 70–73, 75–77; potential harm 72–75; and racism 73, 74
art therapy 142–57; body mapping grief 152–53, *154*, *155*; decolonized approach 143–44; loss and grief collage 148–49; processing images and artifacts 145; remembrance vessel 156–57, *158*
Asian cultures 28
assimilation 22, 27, 124, 134
attachment style 141
Attachment Theory 177, 192
attunement: sociocultural 31, 37–38, 42; somatic 189, 194
authenticity: as the goal 63–64; reclaiming 48, 49
autism 72, 119, 120, 122
autonomy: emotional 190; individual 20, 99; personal 122; relational 92, 183; reproductive 89, 91, 93–95, 103; and sense of self 40
awareness 3, 56–57; *see also* self-awareness
Ayurvedic tradition 29

Bader, Ellyn 181
Beginner's Mind 57
behavioral disorders 68
behavioral health care services 207–08, 212
bereavement 135, 136, 141
biases: in AI technologies 73–74; in health care 40, 72; of the therapist 25–26, 57, 58
binary concepts 54–55

bio-psycho-social-cultural (BPSC) framework 131, 133, 138–42, 144–45, 157
BIPOC *see* Black, Indigenous, and People of Color
Birhane, Abeba 74
birthing practices 95–96
Black families 8
Black feminists 38, 95, 96
Black in AI (group) 77
Black, Indigenous, and People of Color (BIPOC) 40, 187
Black men 74, 194
Black Men and Racial Trauma: Impacts, Disparities, and Interventions 194
Black mothers 10
Black people: forced sterilization 91, 93; systemic barriers to fertility treatment 109; *see also* Black families; Black men; Black mothers; Black women
Black women 93, 94
Body Keeps the Score, The 189
boundaries 189–90, *191*
Bowen, Murray 175, 181
Bowlby, John 119
BPSC *see* bio-psycho-social-cultural (BPSC) framework
brain functioning 122
Braun-Harvey, Douglas 173
Bronfenbrenner, U. 39
Buddhism 180

Cambodia 122
Canada 94, 201
capitalism 52, 53, 54, 91, 94, 206–09, 211, 215–17
CBPR *see* community-based participatory research
CBT *see* cognitive behavioral therapy
ceremonies 108, 110
CFT *see* Couple and Family Therapy
change: and agency 62; embracing 58–59; social 69; systemic 4, 98, 101, 103, 134, 172
ChatGPT 71
Chekroud, Adam 67
childcare 91, 105
child development 85, 117–27; background of 118–19; colonial legacies 124; decolonized perspective 124–27; harmful educational practices 123–24; holistic view 126; individualism 122; medicalization of neurodivergence 122–23; normative pathways 123; role of culture and context 125; stages of 119–20; universality 121–22; Western models of 119–24
childhood 18, 140; trauma 193; *see also* adolescence; children; infancy
child neglect 122, 127
child-rearing 10, 21, 95, 123, 124, 126

children: affected by war 42; of color 68; forced removal from parents 10, 110; immigrant 42–43; refugee 42; *see also* child development; childhood; child neglect; child welfare system
child welfare system 127
chosen families 9, 10, 26, 92, 95, 99–101, 176
Christianity 174, 180
chronic diseases 40
cissexism 59
classism 53
Claude 71
client-centered collaboration 69
clinical documentation platforms 66
COAMFTE *see* Commission on Accreditation for Marriage and Family Therapy Education
codependence 36, 177
coerced identity development 193
cognitive behavioral therapy (CBT) 54, 126; and marginalized groups 69–70
cognitive development 119–21, 140, 141
cognitive processing psychology 49
collaboration 104, 224–26
collages 148–49
collective accountability 228
collective caregiving 3, 8
collective engagement 42
collective gatherings 36–37
collective healing 36
collective identity 20–21, 28
collective knowledge 99–101
collective meaning 20
collective storytelling 40
collective well-being 20, 40, 175
collectivism 40, 122
collectivist cultures 36, 123
colleges 24, 28
colonialism: and AI 66, 70, 72, 74–76; "digital" 74; effects of 3, 68; and family systems 91; and models of child development 124; and reproductive injustice 93–95
"coloniality" 68, 134, 135, 206, 208–15, 217
colonization: and assimilation 134; of the mind 54; and reproductive justice 87–88
Commission on Accreditation for Marriage and Family Therapy Education (COAMFTE) 33
communal activities 29, 123
communal caregiving 21
communal events 37
communal mourning 133
communal parenting 92, 97, 177
communal resilience 21, 136
communal values 122
communication role-play 54
community-based participatory research (CBPR) 41
community care 175, 180, 182
community engagement 104, 178, 227

community-led solutions 4
community networks 175
community support 3
compersion 180
complex post-traumatic stress disorder (CPTSD) 193
Confucianism 28
connectedness 40
conspiracy theories 73
consultation 114, 139
contraception 94
conversion therapies 54
COO *see* culture of origin
Cooper, Yamonte 194
corruption 35
Couple and Family Therapy (CFT) 33, 38–39
creative arts 142–57
creative supports and feelings wheel 145–47
creative wellness wheel 145, 147–48, *147*
Crenshaw, Kimberlé 31, 38, 134
crime prediction 74
critical race theory 22, 23
critical thinking 61
cross-dressing 56–57
cultural appropriation 227
cultural being 34
cultural competence 10, 26, 112, 140
cultural continuity 20, 26
cultural expressions 8
cultural fit 42
cultural genograms 34–35, 125
cultural heritage 23, 103, 136
cultural humility 22, 26, 36, 70, 126–27, 227
cultural identities 27, 52, 54, 57, 59, 102
cultural influences 27, 34, 125
cultural integration 227
cultural leaders 224
culturally responsive care: dismantling of 11–12, 222; reproductive 105, 107
cultural myths 60–61
cultural narratives 27
cultural preservation 21
cultural psychology 22
cultural reflexivity 38, 126–27
cultural sensitivity 29, 38, 109
cultural traditions 20, 29, 34, 36, 40, 96, 100, 110, 135
cultural transmission 20
cultural wisdom 29, 97
cultural worldviews 20
culture of origin (COO) 51, 53
cultures of domination 33
curiosity 61

Dagara people 132–33
data labeling 74
decision-making 28, 100
decolonized lens 3

dehumanization 33, 93
DEI initiatives 7, 221, 222
depression 120
development: ecological 21–22; lifespan perspective 140–41; nonlinear 20, 23; prenatal 18; spiritual 21–22; traditional milestones 20, 23, 28; *see also* child development; Human Development and Family Life Cycle Model
Diagnostic and Statistical Manual of Mental Disorders (DSM) 70, 120, 132
diagnostic tools 2, 70, 73, 120, 123
dietary recommendations 29
differentiation 180–84
"digital colonialism" 74
Disability Rights & Education Defense Fund (DREDF) 95
disabled people: forced sterilization 91, 94; and parenting 94, 95, 111
discomfort 59
discrimination: in AI technologies 74; in health care 40; and mental health 68
displacement 11, 17, 27
diversity: courses 70; of family structures 3, 6, 9, 40, 96, 97; of writing style 8
divorce 175
doom-scrolling 38
doula support 103, 107
DSM *see* Diagnostic and Statistical Manual of Mental Disorders
Dunkelman, Marc 178
Dussell, Enrique 209
dyslexia 120, 122

EAPs *see* employee assisted programs
Eastern philosophies 28
ecological balance 21
ecological conditions 34; *see also* human ecological framework
ecological development 21–22
economic barriers 27, 94
educational systems 123–24
egg donation 107, 108
elders' guidance 100
electronic health record (EHR) platforms 75
embryo freezing 107
emotional access 190
emotional autonomy 190
emotional development 120, 121, 141
emotional regulation 122
emotion-phobia 131, 132
employee assisted programs (EAPs) 67
empowerment 27, 135
"enmeshment" 27, 37, 39, 176, 177
environmental disasters 35
Epston, David 211
equity-based approach 139–40
Erikson, Erik 119, 120

escalated leveraging 198
ethical considerations 226–28
ethnicity 40–41; *see also* race
eugenics movement 93–94
Eurocentrism 7, 8, 10, 12, 28, 206, 212
exercises: reclaiming authenticity 48, **49**;
    reflections on biological sex **50**; reflections
    on family **53**; reflections on gender **51**;
    reflections on relationships **52**; reflections
    on sexuality **52**; sexual and romantic
    orientation **51**
externalizing 35, 41, 143, 152

facial recognition 74
familial interconnectedness 28
families: as biopsychosocial construct 52;
    Black 8; chosen 9, 10, 26, 92, 95, 99–101,
    176; in context 3, 6, 91; colonization of 52;
    decision-making process 28, 100; decolonized
    lens 3; development 26; diversity of forms
    3, 6, 9, 40, 96, 97; extended 26; "healthy"
    8; Indigenous 11, 100; LGBTQ+ 11, 95, 99;
    linear progression 9, 10; low-income 71, 94;
    multiethnic 40; nontraditional 10, 21, 92,
    99, 110, 113, 141; normative assumptions
    33, 92, 175–76; nuclear 8, 21, 26, 40, 92,
    176; queer 92, 95, 111; reflective exercise
    52, **53**; relationality 3, 6; transnational 26,
    40; "white picket fence" conceptualization
    59–60; *see also* family-building; family
    conflict; family gatherings; Family Life Cycle
    theory; family needs; family of origin (FOO);
    immigrant families; kinship systems
Family Assessment Response (FAR) 127
family-based legislation 37
family-building 89; and gender norms 94;
    non-linear 97; and relational autonomy 92
family conflict 126
family gatherings 36–37
Family Life Cycle theory 177; and acculturation
    40–41; critique of 97–98; expanding the
    view of 39–40; intersectional perspective
    38–39; limitations of 9–10; and reproductive
    justice 96–98
family needs 33, 34, 42–43
family of origin (FOO) 36, 51, 53, 61
family therapy knowledge 205–15
Fanon, Franz 216
fat liberation 199–200
feminists 38, 95, 96
Fern, Jessica 181
fertility preservation 94
fertility treatment 105–09; *see also* infertility
Finkel, Eli 174
Finland 121

first-order thinking 69
fluidity 3, 6
FOO *see* family of origin
forced sterilization 91, 93, 94, 105
free writing 143, 149, 153, 157
Freire, P. 135
Freud, Sigmund 193, 201
friendships 175, 178, 179

Gebru, Timnit 74
Gemini 71
gender: exploring identities 49–51; norms 94;
    reflective exercise **51**; roles 9, 10; and sex
    50–51
gender-affirming care 11, 222
gender-diverse people 94
genograms 26–27; cultural 34–35, 125
"ghost work" 74
Global South 74, 179
Google 74
Granted Threshold of Influence (GTOI) 190,
    192, 195, 196, 198–200
grants 209–10
grief 131–57; acceptable 132;
    bio-psycho-social-cultural (BPSC) perspective
    131, 133, 138–42, 157; creative arts therapy
    143–57; healthy approach to 133; impact
    of 135–36; Indigenous practices 132–33,
    136, 141; intersectionality theory 134, 138;
    "liberating" 140; Liberatory Consciousness
    framework 135, 137; and oppression
    136–37; pathologized 132, 133; *see also* grief
    illiteracy
grief illiteracy 131, 132
group therapy 69
growth 19–21
GTOI *see* Granted Threshold of Influence
guilt 35, 108

harm: in mental health field 201; "river" of 194;
    systemic 92, 104, 108, 113, 201
healing: bell hooks on 36; collective 36;
    culturally rooted practices 103; holistic
    approaches 29; Indigenous practices 29;
    land-based 21; from loss 133; as a marker of
    growth 21; through reproductive justice 92
health care 10, 11; bias in 40, 72; commodity 94
health disparities 35
"healthy" families 8
"healthy" relationships 12
here-and-now moments 40
heteronormativity 89, 93, 170
heterosexism 59
historical trauma 21, 110
holistic approaches 29, 70

Holliday, Maynard 75
homeostasis 58
homophobia 73, 111, 144
"honoring the children, mending the circle"
    intervention 126
hooks, bell 33, 36
Human Development and Family Life Cycle
    Model 17–18; decolonized approach 19–29;
    expanding the view of 22–25, 39–40; power
    imbalances 19–20
human ecological framework 34, 39, 42
Human Life Cycle 17–18
human resources 121–22
Hyde Amendment 94
hyper-individualism 36
hysteria 54, 193, 201

ICD see International Classification of Diseases
identities: agent 137, 138, 193; collective
    20–21, 28; cultural 27, 52, 54, 57, 59, 102;
    decolonizing 48; exploring 48–53; formation
    of 20–21, 27; interdependent 20–21;
    intersections of 22, 24–25, 193; relational 20;
    target 137, 138, 193
immigrant communities 22, 69
immigrant families 10, 17, 18, 22–25, 28–29,
    40, 99, 176; family therapy needs 42–43;
    reproductive justice 92
immigrant women 24–25
immune system 141
incarceration 8
India 29
Indigenous communities 134; and child
    development 119; ecological development 21;
    forced sterilization 91, 93; grief in 132–33,
    136, 141; healing practices 29; kinship
    systems 8, 95, 97; learning environments
    123, 124; and neurodivergence 117;
    pathologizing of 72; spiritual development
    21; traditional birthing practices 95–96; see
    also Black, Indigenous, and People of Color
    (BIPOC); Indigenous families; Indigenous
    knowledge; Indigenous land
Indigenous families 10, 100
Indigenous in AI (group) 77
Indigenous knowledge 94, 121, 124, 126, 213
Indigenous land 134
individual autonomy 20, 99
individualism 3, 10, 36, 122
infancy 18, 140
infertility 102, 104–05; see also fertility
    treatment
information processing 122
interdependence 3, , 9, 20, 25–26, 36, 122
interdisciplinary projects 69, 76

intergenerational conflict 26
intergenerational reciprocity 97
intergenerational trauma: effects of 68;
    Indigenous families 10, 91; and reproductive
    justice 91, 102, 105, 110
intergenerational wisdom 20, 26
internalized narratives 198–99
International Classification of Diseases (ICD) 120
intersectionality 22, 24–25, 33, 55, 193;
    applying to loss and grief 134, 138; and
    family life cycle needs 38–39; and systems
    theory 38
isomorphism 37–38
IVF 106

Japan 121–22
jar metaphor 1–2, 220–21, 226, 229, 231
Joseph, Cliff 144
journaling 48, 62, 143, 213
judgments 173, 182
justice-oriented approach 4, 7

Kabbalah 180
Kahn, Ayesha 170
Kaqchikel, Maya 217
King, Martin Luther, Jr. 201
kink lifestyles 188, 189, 200
kinship systems 3, 21, 39, 141; Indigenous 8,
    95, 97
knowledge: ancestral 20, 135, 136; collective
    99–101; coloniality of 209, 213, 218n1;
    experiential 124; family therapy 205–15;
    Indigenous 94, 121, 124, 126, 213;
    intergenerational transmission 122;
    land-based 21

language: misuse 35; pathological 35–36;
    power-conscious 113
large language models (LLMs) 71, 73
Latinx people 93
leveraging mechanisms 190–91, 197–200
LGBTQ+ communities 100–01, 107, 111
LGBTQ+ families 11, 95, 99
liberated life cycle approach 39–40
"liberating grief" 140
liberation 90, 114
liberation psychology 134–35
Liberatory Consciousness framework 135, 137
lifespan perspective 140–41
lifespan transitions 140
LLMs see large language models
loneliness 120, 175, 177–79
Lorde, Audre 2
loss 131–33; bio-psycho-social-cultural (BPSC)
    perspective 131, 138–42, 157; creative arts

therapy 143–57; experience of healing from 133; impact of 135–36; intersectionality theory 134, 138; personal narratives of 142–43
loss and grief collage 148–49, *150*, *151*
love 51; *see also* romantic relationships
low-income families 71, 94
lust 51

maladaptive patterns 59, 60
marriage 174; arranged 28, 29, 179; heterosexual 9; as a milestone 9; "self-expressive" 174; *see also* romantic relationships
"masking" 120
maternal mortality 10, 94
Maya culture 123
McGuire, Thomas G. 40
McKittrick, Katherine 205
meditation 29
men 94
mental health: and art therapy 143, 144; and BIPOC people 40; disparities 35, 40; funding for services 207–08; institutions 68; and oppression 68; parental 42; precision 67–68; refugee families 42; resources 36, 40; Western paradigms 36; *see also* mental health assessments; mental health care; mental health disorders; mental health services
mental health assessments 67, 71; *see also* diagnostic tools
mental health care 10, 11; access to 71; and AI 66–68, 70–73, 75–77
mental health disorders 40
mestiza consciousness 144
Mexican border 42
migration studies 22
mindfulness 29
Mingus, Mia 95
Minuchin, Salvador 36, 175
Miranda, Jeanne 40
MIRS *see* Mutually Identified Relationship Status
misogyny 61
mistakes 63
modernity 205, 206, 208–16
moral supremacy 53
mortality 40
mourning 133, 135, 141
mudita 180
Muisca healing practices 213
multicultural and social justice counseling competencies (MSJCC) 135
multiethnic families 40
multigenerational households 3, 10, 27, 91, 99, 176
multi-level approaches 42
Mutually Identified Relationship Status (MIRS) 190, 192, 195, 196, 198–200

narrative approaches 20; *see also* narrative therapy
narrative inquiry 26
narrative therapy 54, 102–03, 126, 211–12; externalizing the problem 35, 41; grief and loss 143–44; *see also* storytelling
National Black Midwives Alliance 95, 107
National Institutes of Health (NIH) 40, 208, 209, 210
Native Americans 110
neurodevelopmental disorders 123
neurodivergence: and Indigenous communities 117; medicalization of 122–23; and natural diversity 125
neurodiversity 119, 120, 125–26
"neurotypical standards" 120–21
neurovariance 119–21, 123
Noble, Safiya Umoja 73
nonbinary people 94
nonverbal expression 143
non-Western philosophies 28–29
"normal", a concept of 63–64
normalization 27, 108
nuclear family 8, 21, 26, 40, 92, 176

OpenAI 71, 76
oppression: and AI 73; cycle of 68; and grief 136–37; medicalization and pathologization of 11; and mental health 68; structures of 2; systemic 2–4, 27, 31, 89, 101–02, 104, 134, 199, 222
"over-involvement" 27

parental mental health 42
parent-child relationship 197–98
parenthood: biological 9; and disability 94, 94, 111; single 104, 105; *see also* parental mental health; parenting
parenting: communal 92, 97, 177; exploring identities 48; as a systemic challenge 92; *see also* parental mental health; parenthood
Partnership on AI 76
pathologizing frameworks 10, 11, 27, 35–36, 39, 70, 72, 91, 94, 105, 113, 118, 133
patriarchy 59, 61, 91, 93
Pearson, Peter 181
peer communities 107
peer relationships 120
people of color: access to mental health care 71; in AI sector 75; in mental health institutions and prisons 68; *see also* Black, Indigenous, and People of Color (BIPOC)
percentage scales 56
perfection 59
personal autonomy 122
personal narratives 142–43
personal practices 108

personhood 21
Person of the Therapist (POTT) model 22, 23, 33, 38, 118
perspective differentials 57
physical health 29
Piaget, Jean 119–21, 140
Place of Not Knowing 57
Plane of Agency (POA) 190–92, 197, 198
polyamorous relationships 59–60
polyvagal theory 189, 200
post-traumatic stress 42
post-traumatic stress disorder (PTSD) 193
poverty 91
power imbalances: and colonizing practices 68; identifying 70; interrogating 4; in models of human development 19–20; in relationships 188; in therapy 69; traditional 61
"power-over" models 135
"power-with" models 135
precision mental health 67–68
prenatal development 18
prisons 68
productivity 54, 133, 136
professional partnerships 224
psychic distress 141
psychological theories: adapting 61–62; creating new 62
public wellness 33
purity culture 59
pushback 62
Putnam, Robert 177

queer families 92, 95, 111
Queer in AI (group) 77
queer relationships 9, 176
Queer theory 22, 23, 51
questionnaires 42
questions: binary 56; open-ended 26, 41, 56, 57; scaling 56

race 40–41
racism: and AI 73, 74; and developmental trajectories 27; and family systems 91; and health care 10, 11, 40; internalization of 54; structural 33, 40, 69; systemic 8, 11, 94, 104, 105, 109
rank 138
RE see Relationship Equalizer
reciprocity 97, 227
reflexivity 4, 22, 33, 99, 227; cultural 38, 126–27
refugee families 11, 41–42
relational autonomy 92, 183
relational diversity 169, 175, 176, 178–81
relational importance 190
relationality 3, 6, 97
relationship enhancement (tool) 126
Relationship Equalizer (RE) 190, 195

relationships 167–85; "all or nothing" narratives 174–75, 178, 182; behavioral input to 190; case studies 182–84; colonization of 52; decolonized 180–81; differentiation 180–84; emotional input to 190; high-conflict 191; monogamous 59, 167–69, 174–75; noncommittal 179; non-monogamous 176; parent-child 197–98; platonic 176; polyamorous 59–60; power imbalances in 188; queer 176; reflective exercise 52; verbal litmus test 189, 191, 197, 198, 199; "white picket fence" conceptualization 59–60
remembrance vessel 156–57, 158
repetition 59
reproductive autonomy 89, 91, 93–95, 103
reproductive health 11, 91; access to 94, 106, 221; colonial legacies in 93–95; culturally responsive care 105, 107; and gender norms 94; Indigenous knowledge 94; navigating Western medical systems 106–09
reproductive justice 87–114; active engagement 113; advocacy 95, 103–04, 224; case examples 88–90, 109–12; and colonization 87–88; community engagement and collaboration 104; and cultural resistance 95–98; and Family Life Cycle 96–98; as a framework for therapy 98–106; healing through 92; initiatives 104; organizations 103, 104; origin of the movement 90; in practice 104–05; systemic justice approach 112–13; and traditional family therapy 90–92; tools and techniques aligned with 102–05
reproductive rights 90
resilience: challenges as 26; communal 21, 136; and intergenerational conflict 26; promoting 102; spiritual 22
resistance: collective gathering as 36–37; decolonization as 7
Riley, Shirley 143
rituals 108, 110, 135
Rogers, Fred 173
role-play 54, 110
romantic love 174
romantic orientation 51
romantic relationships: decentralizing 169–76; monogamous and heterosexual unions 167–69, 174–75; prioritization above other connections 169–72, 174–79; upholding power and control 177
Ross, Loretta 90

SAMHSA see Substance Abuse and Mental Health Service Administration
Satir, Virginia 175
Satir Human Growth Model 118, 121
Satir process 36

scaling questions 56
schema 56
Schnarch, David 181
schools 121, 124, 223
school-to-prison pipeline 124
second-order thinking 69
self: and autonomy 40; differentiation of 182; exploration of 49–53
self-accountability 181
self-actualization 20, 122
self-advocacy 106–07, 111
self-assessment 26
self-awareness 22, 25–26
self-determination 90, 103
self-narratives 143
self-reflection 4, 70, 118, 147, 181
self-reflexivity 33
self-reliance 136
self-worth 126
sensory processing 122
serial leveraging 197
SERT see socio-emotional relationship therapy
sex: act of 51–52; as a biopsychosocial construct 50; and gender 50–51; reflective exercise 50; see also sex positivity; sexuality
sex positivity 51
sexual behavior 51
sexual identities 54
sexuality 51–52; exploring identities 49–52; reflective exercise 52
sexual orientation 51
SFBT see solution-focused brief therapy
shame: externalization of 126; internalization of 35
single mothers 89
single parenthood 104, 105
SisterSong 95
skin cancer 74
slavery 93
social capital 177
social change 69
social constructionist perspective 69
social development 120, 121
social inequality 68
social isolation 175, 177, 178
social justice 69, 70
social location 137–38
social media 38, 73
social networks 175, 178
social support 178
"Society of Happily Ever After" 167–69, 171, 172, 184
sociocultural attunement 31, 37–38, 42
Sociocultural Development model 119
socio-emotional relationship therapy (SERT) 188

sociopolitical systems 68, 70, 76, 91
solution-focused brief therapy (SFBT) 54; see also solution-focused therapy
solution-focused therapy 118, 126; see also solution-focused brief therapy (SFBT)
somatic attunement 189, 194
sorrow 133, 135
spaces of service 33–34
spectrums 56
spiritual development 21–22
spiritual practices 29, 107–08
spiritual resilience 22
spiritual well-being 21
Spring Health 67
status 138
STEM professions 209
stereotypes 8, 74
storytelling 20, 26; advocacy through 105; collective 40; empowerment through 27; and expressive art 143; learning through 124; and reproductive justice 105
stress 141; post-traumatic 42
structural analysis 27, 189–92
structural barriers 27, 34, 92, 103, 105, 110
Structural Family Therapy 36, 189
structural racism 33, 40, 69
Substance Abuse and Mental Health Service Administration (SAMHSA) 145, 208–10
Sufism 180
suicide 71
supervision 114
survival strategies 27
sustainability 21
sympathetic joy 180
Syrian refugee families 42
systemic accountability 104, 105, 112
systemic awareness 57
systemic change 4, 98, 101, 103, 134, 172
systemic complexity 55
systemic family therapy 10, 87, 171, 175–76, 184
systemic harm 92, 104, 108, 113, 201
systemic oppression 2–4, 27, 31, 89, 101–02, 104, 134, 199, 222
systemic poverty 91
systemic racism 8, 11, 94, 104, 105, 109
systemic reforms 103, 105
systems theory 38

TallBear, Kim 200
tax laws 207
therapeutic practice: decolonizing 25–30, 68–75; ethical 136; integrating non-Western philosophies in 28–29; isomorphism in 37; liberation in 135

therapeutic techniques 26–27
therapists: and AI 75–77; burnout 9; challenging status quo 101–02; guidance and tips for 25–27, 60–63; and psychological theories 61–62; radical reflexivity 99; shortage of 71; staying open to client's experience 57; understanding own biases 25–26, 57, 58
Therapists in Tech 77
third-order change 38, 69, 178
Tichindeleanu, Ovidiu 216
tokenization 227
transgender people: access to reproductive health 94; reproductive justice 92, 110
trans men 94
transnational families 26, 40
transparency 227
trauma 193: childhood 193, 200; group therapy 69; historical 21, 110; war-related 42; *see also* coerced identity development; intergenerational trauma; trauma-focused CBT; trauma-informed approaches
trauma-focused CBT 126
trauma-informed approaches 21, 145
"truer", a concept of 63
trust 224–25
Truxton Canyon Training School 124

Ubuntu 179, 181
United States: funding for mental health care services 207–08; tax laws 207
United States Congress 208
United States Department of Health and Human Services (HHS) 207–08
United States/Mexico border 42

universal equity 140
universalism 121–22
"utopian syndrome" 120

VA *see* Voluntary Accountability
validation 27
values 41, 122
Van der Kolk, B. A. 189
Venezuela 74
verbal litmus test 189, 191, 197, 198, 199
Vietnam War 193
Voluntary Accountability (VA) 190, 192, 195–200
Vygostsky, Lev 119

war 42
well-being: collective 20, 40, 175; creative wellness wheel 147–48; holistic approaches to 29; indicators of 21; multiple pathways to 20; spiritual 21
"What do you see" prompt 143
White, Michael 211
"white picket fence" 59–60
White supremacy 53, 59, 93, 94, 144
women: agency of 201; autism in 72; immigrant 24–25
writing styles 8
Wynter, Sylvia 205

xenophobia 27

Yalom, Irving 49

Zapotec culture 123